ANCIENT AND MODERN BRITONS
Vol. 1

ANCIENT AND MODERN BRITONS

Vol. 1

BY DAVID MAC RITCHIE

Lushena Books, Inc.
www.lushenabks.com

ANCIENT AND MODERN BRITONS
Vol. 1

All rights reserved. No part of this book may be reproduced in any form without written permission from the publisher, except by a reviewer who may quote brief passages in a review to be printed in a newspaper or magazine.

First Printing: January, 2008

Published and Distributed by:

Lushena Books, Inc.
607 Country Club Drive, Unit E
Bensenvile, IL 60106

ISBN 978-1-930097-87-2

Printed in the United States of America

DEDICATION

TO NELSON MANDELA

SO LONG AS YOU ARE READY TO DIE FOR HUMANITY, THE LIFE OF YOUR COUNTRY IS IMMORTAL.

GIUSEPPE MAZZINI

CONTENTS.

BOOK I.

CHAPTER I.

Fair Whites and Dark Whites—The Australioids—Craniological Testimony—Ugrians and Iberians—A "Red Indian" Theory—Stone-Circles and their Makers—Distribution of the White Races—Early Migrations—British Types 3

CHAPTER II.

Orientals and Scythians—Scythian Characteristics—Manners of Pre-Roman Britons—The Pictish Marsh-Dwellers—The Ogres—"White" and "Black"—The Black Huns—Hypotheses . . . 22

CHAPTER III.

The Silurian Picts—The Oestrymnic Isles—British Iberians—The Painted Moors—The Word "Mor"—The Scottish "Moors' Country"—Colonization of North-Central Scotland—"Moors" of Heraldry and Tradition—Colour-Agnomens—Domnall Breac—The "Speckled" People . 39

CHAPTER IV.

Diarmaid and Grainne—A Hebridean Cave-Dweller—Queue-Wearers—Habits of the Marsh-Dwellers—The *Ciuthachs* of Ireland—The Manners of Fourteenth-Century Dublin—Nineteenth-Century "Survivals"—An Early War-Cry—"Native Men" and Immigrants—A Blending of Races 62

CHAPTER V.

Head-Hunting—Archaic Cries—British War-Whoops—Hints of Early Savagery 83

CHAPTER VI.

Mull Fashions Two Hundred Years Ago—Buckram Suits and Mantles—Coats of Arms—Human "Beasts"—"Shelly-Coat Cows"—"Adder-Beads"—North-British Cannibals—A Bloody Custom—Heathen Traits 92

CHAPTER VII.

Hungarian Invasions—The Cimbri or Danes—"Black Heathen"—Some Early Danes—Feuds and Inter-Marriages—Black Danes as Picts—Complexion of the Hebrideans—The Dutch Colonists . . 110

Contents.

CHAPTER XIV.

"The Sons of 'The Black'"—A Tribe of "Cats"—The People of Inchegall: Their Characteristics—Cave-Dwellings—"Turf-built Cots"—Gipsy Tents—Dress of the *Ciuthachs*—Primitive Manners—Deucaledonian Savages—The Fashions of Inchegall—The Dress of Gipsies—"Moorish" Attire—A Galway Tribe—Fossil Nationalities—Laws Against Nomadic "Oppressors"—The Malays of Inchegall—Primitive Cookery in Scotland—Minstrels and Minstrelsy—The Bagpipes; and the Pipers of England—The Sorners, Minstrels, *Magi*, and Jugglers of the West Highlands—"*Cærulei*" or "*Virides*"—Ian Gorm—Blue Donald and Green Colin—"The Blue Squadron"—Scottish "Gipsy"—Scottish "Tory"—Highland Gentry, "Tacksmen," and Commonalty—Black Tribute and Black Watches—Characteristics of the Highland Banditti—The Game of "Tables"—Its Association with Gipsies . 265

BOOK II.

CHAPTER I.

The Old School of Prize-Fighters—Gypsy Athletes and Gypsy Riders—The "Old-Fashioned English Gypsy"—Border Jockeys and Mumpers—Horse-Dealing Castes—Circus-Horsemanship—German Mountebanks—Archaic Customs and their Supporters—The Groundwork of Our Society—"English Traits"—"English People Like Ourselves"—Vanishing Customs and a Vanishing Type—Mohock Cudgel-Players—"The Black Guard"—Gypsies of Southwark, Moorfields, and Norwood . 335

CHAPTER II.

Recent British Nomads—Gypsies of Norfolk, Durham, and Northumberland—Moon-Men—"Beggar"—"Gypsy"—"Black Oppressors"—Adjectives of Colour—Tattooing and Painting—A Modern Druid—Blueskins and Green-Men—Unnoticed Characteristics . . . 366

CHAPTER III.

Old-Fashioned British Customs—Traditional Songs and Legends—The Ways of Our Forefathers—Itinerant "Moorish" Minstrels—Bagpipes—Gypsy Fighters 389

Contents.

CHAPTER VIII.

"Black" Topography—Examples — Miscellaneous "Black" Terms—Black-Tribute—"Ethiopian Minstrels"—The Gipsies—The Bataillard Theory—Egyptians and Pagans—Sorcerers, Jugglers, and Pugilists—Painted Buffoons—The Identity of "Druidess" with "Witch" . 126

CHAPTER IX.

Specimens of the Dubh Gennti—"The Tawny People"—Welsh Examples—Ethnological Deductions—Memories of the Blacks—A Teviotdale "Blackamoor"—The Value of Surnames 150

CHAPTER X.

Moorish Marauders—Black Conquests—Gipsy Warfare—Saracens, Moors, and Pagans—Christendom *versus* Heathennesse . . . 164

CHAPTER XI.

The Tinklers of Scotland—The Gipsies as Picts—Faws and Gillies—British "Indians"—The Picts of Galloway 174

CHAPTER XII.

Early British Populations—The Celtic Tongues—"English" or "Gaelic?"—The "Old Irish" Letter—Pictish Dialects—The Minstrels' Language 185

CHAPTER XIII.

The Early Scots—"Transmarine Nations"—Scots Regarded as Gipsies—North-British Races—The Black Douglases—A Struggle of Dynasties—Rebels and Patriots—The Moors of Galloway—"The Ancient Privilege of the Douglases"—A Clan of "Black Tinklers"—Moor *versus* Norman—Black Families in Early Scotland—Græmes or Grimes—Scotch Moss-Troopers—Scots-Proper and Scots-General—"Felons, commonly called Moss-Troopers"—Mounted Gipsies—Border Thieves—Moss-Troopers or Gipsies—Scottish "Moon Men"—Scots and Scotts—Border Tribes Expelled or Exterminated—Existing Black-Douglases—The "Black Art" of the Borderers—Authenticated Attributes of the "Mossers"—Border Minstrels—Their Songs and Traditions—Our Unreclaimed Borderers—The Religion of the Marsh-Dwellers—Religious and Social Persecution—Antagonism—"The Survival of the Fittest"—Colour Problems 198

BOOK I.

TO REGARD OURSELVES IN THE MASS AS 'WHITE PEOPLE', EXCEPT IN A COMPARATIVE DEGREE, IS QUITE A MISTAKE.

DAVID Mac RITCHIE

ANCIENT AND MODERN BRITONS.

CHAPTER I.

WHOEVER has gone into one of our Antiquarian Museums, and glanced with some curiosity, and perhaps with growing interest, at the withered fragments of canoes, preserved from total decay by the peat out of which they were dug,—at the stone heads of weapons whose handles have rotted long ago,—at the flint knives and arrow-heads,—at the sun-dried pottery,—at the gaudy beads of amber or of coloured glass,—at the combs and ornaments curiously carved out of bone,—and at all such other relics of a remote past,—has soon, in all likelihood, found himself speculating upon the nature of the people who made and used these things. The things themselves are plainly allied to the weapons and ornaments of existing savage races, and we know that the people vaguely spoken of as "Ancient Britons," to whom these articles are attributed, were themselves allied to such races by community of custom. They wore little or no clothing, they tattooed their bodies and faces, they painted themselves blue or green, and some tribes smeared themselves over with iron ore; some of them are stated to have been cannibals:—could all such resemblances have existed if the races themselves, however far separated now, had not all belonged to a common stock? Can there be community of custom, apparent in most minute details, without there being community of blood?

Surely not. Such a practice as cannibalism might easily exist among nations who had lived apart from each other since "the making of the world;" similarity of design in weapons, ornaments and pottery might, with less probability, belong to unconnected races; but there can be no reasonable explanation of the community of such an unnatural custom as tattooing the skin except this one—that the races amongst whom it was and is in use have derived it from a common original, however distant in time the point of union may be.

But to this it may be objected:—"The Ancient Britons were my ancestors, and the tattooed races of to-day are dark-complexioned men: I am a white man: how could my ancestors be anything but white men too?" The question suggests many counter-questions:—"Who are *you?*" "*Were* your ancestors 'Ancient Britons'?" "What are the physical qualifications belonging to 'a white man,' and are you fully entitled to be so described?" Such counter-questions, or some of them, are not so easily answered as may at first appear. The average Modern Briton would be somewhat nonplussed if he were required to give the names of all his progenitors of the reign of Queen Anne, and not one could produce a pedigree that would show, to the satisfaction of critical antiquaries, the name and race of every ancestor and ancestress living at the date of the Norman Conquest. (The limit might safely be placed some centuries nearer our own time, but the Norman Conquest will do.) And as for the question of complexion and physical traits, it is becoming more apparent every day that we are a "mixed race"; though most of us seldom realize the full force of the words, and many of us are unacquainted with the heterogeneous nature of the mixture. It will be well to ascertain the opinions on this subject arrived at by men of science.

Professor Huxley states, in his remarks relative to his "Map showing the Distribution of the Chief Modifications of Mankind" (published in the *Journal of the Ethnological Society of London*, Vol. II. No. 4), that the inhabitants of the British Islands are a blending of two great types,—the *Xanthochroi* and the *Melanochroi*. The first division is composed of the "*fair whites*," who are described as "of tall stature," having the skin "almost colourless, and so delicate that the blood really shows through it. The eyes are blue or grey; the hair light, ranging from straw-colour to red or chestnut; the beard and body-hair abundant. The skull presents all varieties of forms, from extreme dolichocephaly to extreme brachycephaly." (That is, that this class includes men with very long and very short heads.) The second type is that of the "*dark whites*," of which he says:—" Under its best form this type is exhibited by many Irishmen, Welshmen, and Bretons; by Spaniards, South Italians, Greeks, Armenians, Arabs, and high-caste Brahmins. A man of this group may, in point of physical beauty and intellectual energy, be the equal of the best of the Xanthochroi: but he presents a great contrast, in other respects, to the latter type; for the skin, though clear and transparent, is of a more or less brown hue, deepening to olive, the hair fine and wavy, is black, and the eyes are of a like hue. The average stature, however, is ordinarily lower than in the Xanthochroic type, and the make of the frame is usually lighter. . . . . I am much disposed to think that the Melanochroi are the result of an intermixture between the Xanthochroi and the Australioids."

When one learns that the people who are understood to represent the oldest known inhabitants of our islands are thus classified under a denomination which covers the descendants of a supposed blending of "fair whites" and "Australioids,"—one naturally enquires further as to the position and characteristics of these "Australioids." On looking at the map referred to, it is seen that they consist of the whole aboriginal population of Australia,—of the natives of Interior India (the Dekhan),—and of the inhabitants of Middle and Upper Egypt (the whole area, indeed, that is occupied by the descendants of the Ancient Egyptians). Mr. Huxley depicts the Australioids in the following words:—" The males of this type are commonly of fair stature, with well developed torso and arms, but relatively and absolutely slender legs. The colour of the skin is some shade of chocolate-brown; and the eyes are very dark brown or black. The hair is usually raven-black, fine and silky in texture; and it is never woolly, but usually wavy and tolerably long. The beard is sometimes well developed, as is the hair upon the body and the eyebrows. The Australians are invariably dolichocephalic, the cranial index rarely exceeding 75 or 76, and often not amounting to more than 71 or 72. The brow-ridges are strong and prominent, though the frontal sinuses are in general very small or absent. The *norma occipitalis** is usually sharply pentagonal. The nose is broad rather than flat; the jaws are heavy, and the lips remarkably coarse and flexible. There is usually strongly marked alveolar prognathism.† The teeth are large, and the fangs usually stronger and more distinctly marked than in any other forms of mankind." As regards those of this group to be found in India, he says:—" The only people out of Australia who present the chief characteristics of the Australians in a well-marked form are the so-called hill-tribes who inhabit the interior of the Dekhan, in Hindostan. An ordinary Coolie . . . . would pass muster very well for an Australian, though he is ordinarily less coarse in skull and jaw." As I have mentioned, he also includes the descendant of the Ancient Egyptian under this heading. "For although the Egyptian has been much modified by civilization and probably by admixture, he still retains the dark skin, the black, silky, wavy hair, the long skull, the fleshy lips, and broadish alæ of the nose which we know distinguished his remote ancestors, and which cause both him and them to approach the Australian and 'Dasyu' more clearly than they do any other form of mankind."

The same eminent authority states in another place ‡:—" I shall be inclined to look among the Papuan races of New Guinea and New Holland for the nearest allies of men to whom the Shell-Mounds [of Europe] once belonged." Of these people he speaks in the following terms:—" In the Andaman Islands, in the Peninsula of Malacca, in the Philippines, in the islands which stretch from Wallace's line eastward and southward, nearly parallel with the east coast of Australia, to New Caledonia, and, finally, in Tasmania, men with dark skins and woolly hair occur who constitute

---

* I find that the plain English for this scientific term is "the shape of the occipital outline—the skull being viewed from behind."

† "The projection of the upper jaw in front of the face."

‡ Quoted on p. 121 of Vol. II. No. 2, *Ethnological Society's Journal*.

a special modification of the Negroid type—the Negritos. Only the Andamans have presented skulls approaching or exceeding an index of 80; all the Negritos, the crania of which have been examined, are dolichocephalic. But the skulls of the eastern and southern Negritos present, as I have mentioned, a remarkable approximation to the Australioid type, and differ notably from the ordinary African Negroes in the great brow-ridges and the pentagonal *norma occipitalis*. The best known and the most typical of these eastern Negritos are the inhabitants of Tasmania and of New Caledonia, and those of the islands of Torres Straits and of New Guinea. In the outlying islands to the eastward, especially in the Feejees, the Negritos have certainly undergone considerable intermixture with the Polynesians; and it seems probable that a similar crossing with Malays may have occurred in New Guinea."*

The now-extinct Tasmanians, who belong to "the most typical" division of the eastern Negritos, have been particularly described by Mr. James Bonwick, F.R.G.S., in his "Last of the Tasmanians";—the contents of which book are thus summarized in the *Ethnological Society's Journal*:—"The Tasmanians are described as having been a people of moderate stature, and, compared with the Australians, stout and robust. The skin was of a dark brown colour, or nearly black, and was ornamented with cicatrices cut upon the chest, the shoulders and the thighs; while the entire body was bedaubed with a mixture of grease and red ochre, which was also liberally applied to the hair . . . . . It is notable that certain stone circles, and piles of stones evidently of human erection, have been found in the interior of the island."

The importance of studying this Tasmanian section of the Australioid division is very apparent. Not only does Mr. Huxley argue from the appearance of certain existing Britons that they represent, in a degree, a British race of Australioid type,—but there are visible and tangible proofs of the previous existence in our island of such a people. These proofs are craniological. "We know (says the writer of a small pamphlet on this subject)† . . . . that the first inhabi-

* "Remarks on the Distribution of Mankind"—before referred to.
† "The Early History of Scotland," &c. : J. C. Goodfellow, Hawick, 1881.

tants of Britain [let us say, certain tribes of ancient Britons], and more especially those of the northern parts, were craniologically of a type approaching to the Negro or to the Australian race. In the autumn of 1865, Mr. Samuel Laing discovered a quantity of human remains near Kiess, in the county of Caithness. They were submitted by him to Professor Huxley, whose notes on these remains point markedly to such a conclusion. The skulls found in chambered mounds in Great Britain, and which Dr. Daniel Wilson refers to as being those of the earliest race, are generally long and narrow shaped, and prove beyond doubt that the race to which they belonged was absolutely at that time—however much development might take place afterwards—of the very lowest type of humanity." The grounds for the assertion that the Australioid type belonged "more especially" to the northern parts of the island are not given in the pamphlet just quoted from, but the presence of that family in the Caithness district is shown most clearly by the Kiess skulls. Their era does not seem to be agreed upon, and indeed the length of the epochs of pre-historic incidents is somewhat bewildering, by reason of the conflicting conclusions arrived at by various *savants*—and their followers—some of whom manipulate their hundreds of thousands of years as calmly and as easily as an ordinary man does his centuries. But in dealing with those Stone-Folk and Troglodytes one must remember that both exist at the present day, side by side with higher races, and that consequently, their era in Britain may not be so very remote after all.

In his remarks upon the aborigines of Tasmania, Mr. Bonwick refers more than once to their kinship (structurally) with certain pre-historic Europeans. "Mr. Carter Blake, a competent judge, describes a skull from a cist in Uist Island of Scotland, as of an 'ovately dolichocephalic form,' and having a narrow forehead, with great projecting brow, like the Tasmanian." "Mr. Samuel Laing, in his interesting revelations of the Caithness cists, imagines 'the earliest inhabitants of North Britain were *Kumbocephalic* (boat-headed), approaching to a Negroid or Australian, rather than to a Mongol or Arctic type.' Again, he writes:—'This tribe of aboriginal Britons must have more closely resembled the Australian or Tasmanian, than the Laplander or Esquimaux." "Dr. Pruner Bey (to make a final extract from Mr. Bonwick's book) compares our Southern Blacks with the pre-historic cave-men."

All this craniological evidence, then, while it does not actually prove the correctness of Mr. Huxley's conjecture as to the Australioid origin of the *Melanochroi*, proves at any rate that, *structurally*, certain of the inhabitants of Britain in former times belonged to the Australioid family. Whether, their complexion was as swarthy as that of their Southern kindred remains yet to be proved. The Tasmanian customs of tattooing, of smearing the skin with iron ore, and of erecting cairns and circles of stones, were also at one time British customs. An Australioid people once inhabited Britain as well as the Antipodes. We *know* they were alike in their physique: it would be strange if they differed in complexion.

Another and most important race to be considered, when glancing at the people of Ancient Europe, is that of the Ugrians. "During the last 2,000 years," says Mr. Howorth, in a paper read before the Ethnological Society,* "we find that . . . . . there has been a constant move in one direction at least,—a gradual encroachment by the Celtic, Germanic, and Slavic races upon the humbler races on their frontiers, and these latter invariably of the Ugrian family. The Basques in Spain are now penned in a small corner of their ancient patrimony in the time of the Romans. The Fins and Laps have been pushed back in Scandinavia to a very small portion of their ancient holding. In Livonia, in Esthonia, and in three-fourths of European Russia the Ugrians were, even in the 11th century, the preponderating population. Proofs are now accumulating that before the Christian era this process of displacement was taking place even at a greater rate, the area to be occupied having been much more fertile and inviting. I have attempted to show, in a paper read before the British Association, that a very great element in the Celtic language is Ugrian, and I believe

---

* On 25th January, 1870.

the same to be true of the Latin and Greek.* The German-speaking race can, I believe, be shown to have occupied Central Europe since the 3rd century B.C., the Celts and the Slaves to have arrived since the 9th, and the Indo-European element of Italy and Greece since the 10th or 11th. If this be so, then we get a very recent date comparatively for the period when the Basques in Spain and the Fins in Sweden, now mere wrecks and waifs of the original population, were close neighbours; and one homogeneous people occupied, if not a ring round the world, at least one reaching from Britain to Kamskatka, when Europe was overrun by fishermen and hunters, such as we find in Siberia, where we ought to go if we are to study the religion, the manners, and government of the so-called stone-folk."

The Mongoloid families, one of the chief of which is the Ugrian, are thus spoken of by Professor Huxley† :—

"An enormous area, which lies mainly to the east of a line drawn from Lapland to Siam, is peopled, for the most part, by men who are short and squat, with the skin of a yellow-brown colour; the eyes and hair black, and the latter straight, coarse, and scanty on the body and face, but long on the scalp. They are strongly brachycephalic, the skull being usually devoid of prominent brow-ridges, while the nose is flat and small, and the eyes are oblique. The Malays proper, and, I suspect, the indigenous people of the Philippines who are not Negritos, fall under the same general definition."

The Voguls, a division of that race, are pictured by Dr. Latham in similar terms: "their hair is black or brown, seldom yellow or red; the beard scanty; the skin glabrous and pale; the cheek bones project; the face broad and flat." And Mr. Howorth makes the following remarks upon the ancient Hungarians, Ungari, or Ugrians‡. They are described,

* "Of the presence of a large Turanian admixture among the ancient Romans, which Dr. Hyde Clarke exerts himself to prove, I entertain not the slightest doubt," says Mr. Karl Blind, in the *Contemporary Review* of September, 1881.

† In his remarks on the Distribution of Mankind.

‡ "The Ungri and Ungari of the western writers, and the Ouiggroi of the Byzantines, are both derived from the Slavic Ugri." The *words*, that is to say. (Part V. of Mr. Howorth's article "On the Westerly Drifting of Nomades," *Ethnological Society's Journal*, Vol. II. No. 4; from which these extracts are taken.)

he says, "as living by fishing and hunting, and as fighting with bows and arrows." "The notary of Bela tells us they had no cities nor fixed houses, nor did they live upon the produce of agriculture, but on flesh and fish; their young men were continually hunting; and thus it happened that, even in his day, the Hungarians were the most renowned hunters. This tallies well with what we have said of the affinities of the Hungarians with the Voguls. Leo has furnished Gibbon with material for some sonorous phrases in his description of the Hungarians. 'Their tents were of leather, their garments of fur; they shaved their hair, and scarified their faces; in speech they were slow, in action prompt, in treaty perfidious.'"

The Spanish Basques, in the opinion of the writer on whom we have just relied, are among the purest representatives of this ancient Ugrian type. Now, this is a little confusing. For these Basques are also held to represent the Iberians. And while the Ugrians are described as a round-headed folk, the skulls of the people called Iberians are long or oval. Let us hear what is said about those Iberians.

"To the question, who are the Iberians? it is impossible to give a satisfactory answer in the form of a concise definition. . . . Historical, numismatical, linguistic, and anthropological evidences have been brought to bear on the problem of their affinity, and the result is, on the whole, not so much light as darkness visible." This is not encouraging to an inquirer. But one learns from the same source* that scientific men, on the whole, are pretty unanimous as to certain leading beliefs. Humboldt gave out his hypothesis in 1821, of which "the main arguments were these :—that the Iberians were one great people, speaking a distinct language of their own; that they were to be found in Sicily, Sardinia, and Corsica, in Southern France, and even in the British Isles; and that the Basques of the present day were the distinctly recognizable remnants of the race which had elsewhere been expelled or absorbed. . . . [It is stated that] the great current of ethnographical speculation still flows in the direction indicated by Humboldt, though it breaks up into a number of distinct channels. The anthropological researches of Broca,

* " Encylopædia Britannica "; ninth edition.

Thurnam and Davis, Huxley, Busk, Virchow, Tubino, and others have proved the existence in Europe of a Neolithic race, small of stature, with long or oval skulls, and accustomed to bury their dead in tombs. Their remains have been found in Belgium and France, in Britain, Germany, and Denmark, as well as in Spain; but they bear a closer resemblance to the Basques than to any other living people. This Neolithic race has consequently been identified with the Basques and the Iberians; and extreme exponents of the theory do not hesitate to speak of the Iberian ancestors of the people of England, recognizing the racial characteristics in the 'small swarthy Welshman,' the 'small dark Highlander,' and the 'Black Celts to the west of the Shannon,' as well as in the typical inhabitants of Aquitania and Brittany. . . . Some investigators go even further. M. D'Arbois de Jubainville, for example, regards the Iberians as the descendants of the Atlantes (*i.e.* the hypothetical inhabitants of Plato's great western isle the Atlantis), and maintains that in Europe they possessed Spain, Gaul, Italy, and the British Isles, penetrated into the Balkan peninsula, and occupied a part of Northern Africa, Corsica, and Sardinia."

Thus we see that the Basques, or Euskars, when looked at as Ugrians, are *brachycephalic*, or round-headed; and sallow, rather than tawny in complexion. As Iberians, they are *dolicho-* or *kumbo-cephalic*; and of swarthy hue. According to the one conjecture, they are nearer the Eskimo than the Tasmanian; according to the other, they are more Australioid than Mongoloid. The points which they share in common, viewed from either position, are their short stature and black hair and eyes.

The probability is that the Ugrians were a greatly-mixed people, and that they constituted a meeting-ground for those two great human families whose qualities they possess in varying degrees. Indeed—so far as nomenclature goes—there is evidence of their hybrid character. There were *Czernii Ugri*, or Black Ugri, as well as White,—Black Khazars and White Khazars, Black Bulgarians and White Bulgarians; all of whom belonged to this classification of Ungari, Ugri, or Ogors. But this evidence is so slight as to be little more than conjecture, since it is not clear whether the terms "white" and "black," as thus used, really bore reference to the complexions of those various races. And besides, if they did so, the fact would suggest many questions which it is convenient to shelve—questions reflecting upon the ancestry of the *Xanthochroi*, or "fair whites." At present—and chiefly—our purpose is to consider those peoples whose complexions have been pretty well ascertained to be "coloured."

In addition to the black, or brown, and yellow races already spoken of as pre-historic Europeans, there is a theory that a copper-coloured race, closely akin to some branches of American Indians, once inhabited Europe—or rather the southern parts of Europe, and North Africa. Proofs of this are said to be visible in the complexion of the modern Copts, which is "reddish," and of the Nubians, who are described as "of a deep red colour," "with nothing of the negro in their profile, and with oval faces." This theory has been started by an Italian archæologist, named Gennarelli, and may be seen at length in the "Journal of the Anthropological Institute."* Its leading points are thus summarized:—" In support of the hypothesis of kinship between the red races of Europe and America, Gennarelli adduces: (*a*) the existence of pyramids in Egypt, America, and Etruria; (*b*) of labyrinths in Egypt, America, and Etruria; (*c*) of the title 'Children of the Sun,' borne both by the Incas and the Pharaohs: (*d*) of mummies in Egypt and America, and images of mummies in Etruria; (*e*) of hieroglyphic languages in Egypt and America; (*f*) of languages having a similar structure in America, Iberia, and Etruria (Humboldt thought there were affinities between the Basque and Etruscan): (*g*) of the Nile in Egypt, and a Nile region in Guatemala, from the Cordillera of Sconusco to the Pacific; (*h*) of canopies and sacrificial vases in Egypt, Mexico, Yucatan, and Peru, with names similar to the deities they represent; (*i*) and of the root 'Atl,' which in its original signification he asserts to belong not to the European but to the American languages. Gennarelli further supports his theory by the assertion that animals of American origin,

* Vol. III. No. 2. Communicated by C. H. E. Carmichael, M.A., &c.

unknown to Africa, are to be found among the Egyptian hieroglyphics, and in the paintings or sculptures on the vases and monuments of Etruria." ... He also points to evidence of the existence in Italy of races "which were neither Aryan nor Semitic, under the various names of Aborigines, Siculi, Liguri, Umbri, etc." And he also suggests that the Phœnicians were of this copper-coloured hue.

It is perhaps scarcely correct to describe this as a *third* division of dark-skinned people, for Signor Gennarelli's "red" is not very different from Professor Huxley's "chocolate brown," the colours ascribed by each to the Ancient Egyptians.

The connection between this last theory and the consideration of "Ancient Britons" becomes apparent when one remembers that not only are these people allied to the Egyptians, as being both "Australioids," but there is also a legend that the Scots are of Egyptian descent;[*] while of the Phœnician intercourse with Britain there is no doubt. However, the red colour of the Phœnicians seems only a suggestion.[†]

As with the Iberians (according to M. D'Arbois de Jubainville), this red race of the Italian antiquary is assumed to have come into Europe out of the sunken island-continent of Atlantis, which our grandfathers spoke of as the "fabled" Atlantis, but which the voyage of the *Challenger* and the study of geology have both proved to be no fable. The point of difference between scientific men now seems to be rather the probable date of the subsidence of that continent; which, it is contended by some, must be so remote as to preclude the possibility of establishing a race-connection between the two continents, in this way.

But, at any rate, there are several reasons for believing that the un-identified builders of our stone-circles, cairns, and dolmens, were dark-skinned people; and the races with which they have most similarity are Professor Huxley's *Australioids* and *Negritos*. Not only is it asserted by him

---

[*] Skene's "Celtic Scotland," Vol. I. p. 176.

[†] Mr. Bonwick, however, quotes Julius Firmicus, to the effect that "in Ethiopia all are born black; in Germany, white; *and in Thrace, red*." ("The Daily Life of the Tasmanians," p. 104.)

that there is an actual blood-relationship between those two families and British people of this and past generations, plainly visible in many outward features,—but there is also the testimony of similar customs, some of which will be afterwards specified. One of these is the practice of tattooing the body, and another is the kindred practice of painting or smearing it with various colours. But the most telling evidence is that afforded by the stone monuments, which are found in all the countries which have been inhabited by those races. Tasmania, home of the Negritos, has its stone circles and cairns; and Scotland shows the presence of the same people and the same works. In the Australioid Deccan there are dolmens and stone-circles, as in the Australioid Britain and West Europe. And there is, within the jungle of one part of Borneo, a great area known to the Malays as *Jallan Batoe*, "The Field of Stones." It contains rocking-stones, standing-stones, and others;—and many of these are covered with marks resembling "the curious 'picture-writings' found on scattered stones and rocks in British Guiana and other parts of South America." The present inhabitants know nothing of their origin, and believe them to be haunted by spirits,—a memory, doubtless, of the time when their builders, a different race, lived among them.* These it may be reasonably presumed, were the Negritos now found in the islands to the south-east. (The Negritos, although not identical with the Australioids, are yet said to present "a remarkable approximation to the Australioid type," and the two divisions may logically be held to have been one in the days of the Ancient Britons, though since modified by intermixture with other races.)

Accepting, therefore, the existence of Australioids and Mongoloids within these islands as a fact which is likely to become more and more clearly established as time goes on, the object now set before us is to find out, if possible, whether there are any proofs of their presence, as distinct races, yet traceable in our own customs, language and traditions. There ought to be such, if those races were really the ancestors of many among us. It is unreasonable

---

* See Carl Bock's "Head-Hunters of Borneo," p. 155.

to assume that a mixed people can only inherit the history of one section of its ancestry.

The question of the origin of the white races which have now long held the supremacy in these islands, scarcely enters into the present enquiry, which has to do more with their coloured predecessors. But it may be as well to bear in mind that the now familiar theory of successive "Aryan" migrations is only a theory, founded upon an unquestionable speech-connection. Indeed, in a comparatively recent essay in the *Atlantic Monthly*,* a transatlantic writer has had the courage to question the "formidable array of olden credences and modern hypotheses" which are the mainstay of this belief. He asserts that, so far as we know, there is as much historical evidence in favour of migrations eastward from Central and Western Europe into Asia, as of movements from Asia westward; that "if civilized Europe has repelled civilized Asia, it is probable that barbaric Europe repelled barbaric Asia;" and, in short, that all one can say regarding the peopling of Europe is this, "that there came a period when it was found to be inhabited by races which yet abide there, and which in the main have kept their possession good against intruders from other continents."

The exact locality of "the cradle of the human race" is not likely to be ever unanimously agreed upon,—and, as the writer just spoken of signifies, all discussion regarding it is almost useless. One has placed it near the Euphrates,—another on the Asiatic table-lands, and a third in the southern portion of the hypothetical continent of Lemuria,† somewhere to the east of Madagascar; while a fourth, as we see, hints that the *home* (if not the *cradle*) of the white race was Europe. But there seems little probability of any of these theories ever becoming substantiated. We have just seen that many scientific men hold that there are some grounds for believing that portions, at least, of Europe have formerly been inhabited by black, tawny, and copper-coloured races. And we are also learning that the white race has not always been confined to the "Eastern Hemisphere." Mr.

---

* February, 1878. "The Cradle of the Human Race."
†· This theory has, however, been pronounced untenable.

Désiré Charnay has lately told us* that the Toltecs, whom he believes to be the builders of the monuments of Mexico and Central America, were white men.† "Physically," he says, "Veytia describes the Toltec as a man of tall stature, white, and bearded,"—and he himself adds confirmatory evidence. "I have in my possession a bas-relief, found at Tula, coinciding very well with this description; the man is full face, and has a large hooked nose, his beard being wide and fan-shaped." There are also apparent proofs of white blood among the American "Indians" of the present day,—quite distinct from any results of the European invasions of the last few centuries. "The eastern nations of Chili have but a slight tinge of the brown colour, and the Boroanes are still whiter. On the north-west coast, from latitude 43° to 60°, there are tribes who, though embrowned with soot and mud, were found, when their skins were washed, to have the brilliant white and red which is the characteristic of the Caucasian‡ race: . . . . . within the tropics, the Malapoques in Brazil, the Guaranis in Paraguay, the Guiacas of Guiana, the Scheries of La Plata, have tolerably fair complexions sometimes united with blue eyes and auburn hair; and, in the hot country washed by the Orinoco, Humboldt found tribes of a dark, and others of a light hue, living almost in juxtaposition."§ And the Shawnees, or Shawanoese, who formerly inhabited West Florida, of which country they did not believe their ancestors to be the aborigines, have, or used to have, a belief "that Florida had once been inhabited by white people, who had the use of iron tools. Black Hoof affirms [and this was in 1819, sixty-five years after he and his tribe had left Florida], that he has often heard it spoken of by old people, that stumps of trees covered with earth, were frequently found, which had been cut down by edged tools."‖ And Major Serpa Pinto has lately encountered

---

* October, 1881. *North American Review.*
† Thereby flatly contradicting Gennarelli's "copper-coloured" hypothesis.
‡ Professor Huxley protests against this term. "It is to the Xanthochroi and Melanochroi, taken together, that the absurd denomination of 'Caucasian' is usually applied."
§ "America:" *Encyc. Brit.* 9th edition.
‖ "Transactions, &c., of the American Antiquarian Society," Vol. I. p. 273: Worcester, Mass. 1820.

in Africa, "a race of *white* Hottentots, hideous beyond belief, like caricatured Mongolians, and evidently lower even than the Fuegians of South America in the scale of humanity."* And even in the South Seas there is the tradition of a white race, now remembered as supernatural beings. "Their appearance is that of human beings, *nearly resembling a European's; their hair being very fair, and so is their skin."†*

It must be remembered, however, that traditions are not always so old as they are often hastily assumed to be. The Polynesian "fairies" might be Europeans of only last century; and the whites of Florida were perhaps, and indeed probably, the Spaniards and French of the sixteenth century. So also may the various white "Indians" be descendants of the comrades of Drake and Raleigh. Or they may descend from immigrants who ante-date even Columbus by centuries. The date of the "discovery" of America (to non-Americans) is every now and then pushed farther back. The claim of Columbus has long ago yielded to that of the Norsemen, and they in turn have given place to some Buddhist priests from China, who reached Mexico in the fifth century. There is a theory that the Phœnicians colonised Florida at an earlier period still. But this has two readings. If the Phœnicians were white men, they may have been the traditional whites of the Shawnees. If they were, as Signor Gennarelli suggests, a copper-coloured race, then they were likely the progenitors of the Shawnees themselves; who assert that their forefathers were not indigenous, but came across the ocean—from whence they know not,—in memory of which event they continued to celebrate "a yearly sacrifice for their safe arrival" in America, up till the beginning of the present century.‡ Another such colonization is that of the Welsh under Prince Madoc, in the year 1170, of which there is the distinct tradition upon this side of the Atlantic, and some curious and corroborative facts upon the other side.§ Whether this was really *another* migra-

* Quoted from *Atlantic Monthly*, December, 1881.
† *Contemporary Review*, August, 1881; Karl Blind's "Water Tales."
‡ "American Antiquarian Society's Transactions," Vol. I. p. 273.
§ Which are summarized in the "Popular History of the United States" (William Cullen Bryant and Howard Gay), Vol. I. pp. 66 *et seq.*

tion than that of the Shawnees, may be doubted. For the age of the Shawnee tradition is quite uncertain, and their Eastern forefathers may either have been early Phœnicians or later Welsh. And the question of complexion need be no obstacle to this last hypothesis, until it is proved that Madoc and his followers were white men.

All of these facts and semi-facts point, with more or less distinctness, to remote "folk-wanderings" of various races. And they seem to suggest—what, indeed, Comparative Ethnology asserts—that movements almost or altogether as extensive as the modern branching-out of the British people over all the globe, have taken place in distant, unrecorded periods. Not wholly unrecorded, either. Until the places named in such ancient records as those of the Hebrews and the Chinese have been fairly identified and translated into modern speech, we cannot say that such remote colonizations have never been placed upon record.

Whatever be the origin of the *Xanthochroi*—whether they migrated westward in almost historic times, or whether they were gradually evolved from lower forms within the precincts of their present home—it seems agreed by men of learning that among the earliest inhabitants of these islands were the Troglodytes, or Cave-Dwellers, known later by such titles as Australioids, Mongoloids and (historically) Iberians or Euskarians. As separate types, these have, in successive epochs, ceased to exist. But from this stock—or one of these stocks—have come the modern *Melanochroi*. And in these *Melanochroi* most of us are bound to take an interest; for it has been decided by an eminent authority "that in modern Britain the dark type of humanity now distinctly preponderates over the light type." This fact, therefore, compels the majority of us to regard those depraved "Australioids" (whose skulls still bear witness to their depravity) as, in some measure, our lineal ancestors. That is, if the supposed derivation of the "dark white" from the "Australioid" be correct.

The two great divisions of Professor Huxley are so closely intermingled that it can scarcely be invidious to dwell upon the disagreeable features of this line of the "dark-white" ancestry. For the two types, in a vast number of cases, find representatives under one family roof; so that you shall see the rosy-cheeked, blue-eyed, golden-haired sister, and the dark-skinned, black-haired, dark-eyed brother playing amicably side by side. The types are not extinct, but they are represented by the one united people. Besides, although it is proposed, in these pages, to ascertain if haply there may be any good reasons for believing that the British Australioids were as swarthy as any other branches of that family, yet even to prove this would do nothing to prove that the clear-skinned "fair whites" had not an equally humble lineage. The abject and hideous race of Hottentots encountered by Serpa Pinto were white-skinned men, and he assigned them the very lowest place in the scale of humanity. And, at any rate, if the theory of evolution be a true one, it is evident that the origin of all the human families must unquestionably be humble—whether white or black. Further, the incidental feature of complexion is of little importance ethnologically, since it is the anatomical construction that determines the rank of the being, human, or otherwise.

Not only are the two types closely intermingled as to colour, but the irregular and less pleasing characteristics of the "Australioid" may be easily detected even in families whose complexion would, of itself, proclaim them to be pure Xanthochroi. We have all a pretty fair idea of the kind of face belonging to this latter division. A perfect specimen of it is such as the painters give to Adam or to the angels, and such a face is exquisitely handsome. But many who seem at first to belong exclusively to this division cannot undergo successfully a closer scrutiny. One has the "coarse and flexible" mouth of the Australioid, another shows his kinship to that race in the formation of his upper jaw, or in the shape and size of his teeth, while a third has the short, flat nose of the Mongoloid and the Australioid. The hair though light in colour, may be as crisp and curly as a negro's, and other race-signs (alien to the purest "fair white") may be visible in the natural growth of the beard, or in its scantiness, or its total absence. All of these marks may be detected among men who, at the first glance, appear to be Xanthochroi, and they proclaim a mixed lineage quite as indisputably as does a tawny complexion, or raven hair.

You may see faces of a distinctly Mongolian, and even of a Negroid cast, in families whose pedigree may be traced for many generations without disclosing the slightest hint of extra-British blood. It may be only in the structure of the head and jaw, the complexion being clear red-and-white, and the eyes blue; or it may be in structure and complexion both that this resemblance is visible.

Since, therefore, the least-handsome of the physical attributes of our heterogeneous nation are shared, in some degree, by the most of its members, there can be little fault in specifying particular localities, and their inhabitants, where it may be convenient to do so. Indeed, this has been done over and over again. Thackeray, for example, notices the "flat Tartar faces" and squat figures of the south-western Irish. A recent writer dwells upon the fact that in certain districts of England, "where the names of the towns and villages show that the Saxon and Danish conquerors occupied the country in overwhelming numbers," the descendants of a race "not unlike the modern Eskimo" are still found. The Hebrideans—who will be referred to more particularly—are described by another writer as being very Mongolian in feature. And indeed, the prominent cheek-bones that form a most striking feature of the Mongoloid are regarded by many as the attribute of every "Scotchman." But, as that word is often loosely used to designate any native of Scotland—of whatever lineage—this feature need only be the property of certain Scottish tribes. So far as complexion goes, there can be no doubt as to the presence of a vast infusion of "coloured" blood. There are, of course, no living Britons who are as black as negroes, but some are as dark as mulattoes, and many darker than Chinamen. To regard ourselves, in the mass, as "white people," except in a comparative degree, is quite a mistake.

This varied ancestry connects us, therefore, with almost every nation under the sun. And as we have inherited the blood that is akin to that of many savage races now alive, it is only logical to infer that any customs, or it may be words common to us and to them, have come down to each of us from the same original.

CHAPTER II.

THE Jews—the Phœnicians—the Chaldees—are all stated to have visited our islands at various periods, and perhaps to have colonized them. It is the delight of one school of Gaelic writers to discover many affinities between the Hebrew and Gaelic tongues; and assuredly, to a mere layman, these resemblances seem distinct and unmistakeable. The Irish name for the golden gorget of the Druids, the *Jodhan Morain*, is identical with the Chaldee name for Urim and Thummim. "In short (continues Governor Pownall, *Early Irish Antiquities, Archæologia*, Vol. VII.) my friend the Rabbi [Heideck] will have it, that none but Jews or Chaldees could have brought the name and the thing to Ireland." When Martin visited the island of St. Kilda last century, he made the statement that "the ancient [Hebrew] measure of omer and cubit continues to be used in this isle." And, whatever the fact may be worth, the emblem known as Solomon's Seal has been found by Scottish antiquaries upon many a "sculptured stone." There seems little doubt that the Phœnicians, at any rate, were here. They, indeed, appear to have been as great navigators as the British ever were. They are said to have crossed the Atlantic, and planted a settlement in Florida. They are believed to have sailed far into the Eastern seas, and to various parts of Africa, and they are admitted to have visited all the western coasts of Europe, and—in the time of Hiram, King of Tyre —to have voyaged far and wide in search of treasure, at the bidding of Solomon the Great. They are supposed to have traded, at this time, with the metal-workers of Cornwall, aad to have colonized some parts of Ireland, and, presumably, it was during this period that the Seal of Solomon was carved upon the Scottish stones. Some of this is conjecture —some fact—but it is interesting to think of our islands as at one time the possible dependencies of Solomon's vast empire. And it gives him a new and quite friendly character to reflect that, if this were the case, we should have some grounds for imagining that we, too, may be the posterity of one or other of his very numerous family.

But the claims of the Jew and the Phœnician to be regarded as Ancient Britons, are shadowy though not uncertain. The Scythians, however, have a clearer right to be so regarded, for most antiquaries agree in holding the Scythians as the ancestors of the Ancient Britons. The word "Scythian" is, however, delightfully vague, and is becoming or is already out of date. It was used to include all the nations to the north and east of the Black Sea and the Caspian Sea, and indeed all the unknown North-European races, and some of the philologers derive it from *Sceótan* to shoot, thereby giving it the meaning of "bow-man" or "archer," but even as to this there seems to be some difference of opinion. The late Lord Strangford (who is, indeed my authority for the derivation just given) says of them*:— "Some of the Scythian peoples may have been Anarian, Allophylic, Mongolian; some were demonstrably Aryan, and not only that, but Iranian as well, as is best shown in a memoir read before the Berlin Academy this last year; the evidence having been first indicated in the rough by Schaffarik the Slavonic antiquary. Coins, glosses, proper names, and inscriptions prove it." Another, writing on this subject, says :—" Ethnographers are not unanimous in respect to the ethnic position of the Scythians. Bockh, Niebuhr and many others set them down as Tatars. But Humboldt, Grimm, Donaldson and others maintain, both on physical and philological grounds, their ethnic affinity with the Aryans. Rawlinson, in his essay, 'On the Ethnic Affinities of the Nations of Western Asia' (*Herodotus*, Vol. I. p. 523, etc.) distinctly ranges the Scythians among Tatar nations. He even maintains that a Tatar element is manifest in the oldest records of the Armenians, Cappadocians, Susianians and Chaldæans of Babylon. In a later essay, 'On the Ethnography of the European Scyths' (*Herodotus*, Vol. III. p. 158), he argues as distinctly that this nation was Indo-European. F. Müller is

* "Letters and Papers," posthumously published, pp. 171-2.

of the opinion that some of the Scyths were Ural-Altaic and others Aryan (*Novara-Expedition*, Ethnographie, p. 145)."[*]
It is thus apparent that the term "Scythian" is too comprehensive to be of much use, and that it is "surely a negative rather than a positive term, much like our *Indian*, or the *Turanian* of modern ethnologists, used to comprehend nomads and barbarians of all sorts and races."

Nevertheless, since every one says that some, at any rate, of the original races of the British Islands were "Scythians," it behoves us to look a little closer into their history and characteristics. From Lempriere we learn this:—"The Scythians were divided into several nations or tribes; they had no cities, but continually changed their habitations. They inured themselves to bear labour and fatigue; they despised money, lived upon milk, and covered themselves with the skins of their cattle." He adds that "the virtues seemed to flourish among them," but, in opposition to this (or, more correctly, in support of the statement that "the Scythians" comprehended "several nations or tribes") he goes on to say :—"Some authors, however, represent them as a savage and barbarous people, who fed upon human flesh, drank the blood of their enemies, and used the skulls of travellers as vessels in their sacrifices to their gods. The Scythians made several irruptions upon the more southern provinces of Asia, especially B.C. 624, when they remained in possession of Asia Minor for 28 years; and we find them at different periods extending their conquests in Europe, and penetrating as far as Egypt . . . . . . In the first centuries after Christ, they invaded the Roman empire with the Sarmatians." Of these Sarmatians, evidently a kindred race, Lempriere says that they were "a savage uncivilized nation, often confounded with the Scythians, naturally warlike, and famous for painting their bodies to appear more terrible in the field of battle. They were well known for their lewdness, and passed among the Greeks and Latins by the name of barbarians; . . . . . . at last, increased by the savage hordes of Scythia, under the barbarous names of Huns, Vandals, Goths, Alans, etc., they successfully invaded and ruined the empire in the 3rd and 4th centuries of the Christian

[*] Dr. Winchell's "Preadamites," p. 47, note.

era. . . . . . . They lived upon plunder, and fed upon milk mixed with the blood of horses."

These Scythians, then, who, under various names and possessed of many different qualities of character and of nature, covered the whole north of Europe and a large portion of Asia in the days of the Romans, seem in the main to identify themselves with the Ugrians spoken of by Mr. Howorth, as quoted in the foregoing chapter. The area in which they dwelt, and also their era, agree. And the brief descriptions quoted also tally with each other. "The chronicler Rheginon describes the Hungarians as living by fishing and hunting, and as fighting with bows and arrows." (That is, according to Lord Strangford, they were *Scyths*.) The ancient Hungarians "scarified their faces," that is, tattooed themselves, and the Sarmatians are at least said to have "painted their bodies." But the connections between the two races, or the same race under different names, are too striking and too numerous to require to be detailed. One of these, the milk diet of Lempriere's Scythians, and the milk-and-blood of his Sarmatians, stands out clearly if we remember that, not so *very* long ago "the Basques in Spain and the Fins in Sweden, now mere wrecks and waifs of the original population, were close neighbours," and that about that period "Europe was overrun by fishermen and hunters, such as we find in Siberia, where we ought to go if we are to study the religion, the manners, and government of the so-called stone-folk." With this in mind, then, one is not surprised to find that the *Concani*, who once occupied the district now known as the Basque Provinces, are said to have "lived chiefly on milk mixed with horses' blood,"* or that the Nordenskiöld expedition ascertained that the Siberian tribe of Chukches are exceedingly fond of a soup of which the principal ingredient is seal's blood.

And since the "Voyage of the Vega" has thrown considerable light upon the customs of this people, it may not be out of place to quote further from the account thus obtained. "In summer the Chukches eat cloud-berries, red bilberies and other berries, which are said to be found in great abun-

---

* I quote this from a curious old Latin dictionary, the "Cambridge Dictionary," 1693. I daresay there are other authorities for the statement.

dance in the interior of the country . . . . . . The writers who quote the Chukches as an example of a race living exclusively on substances derived from the animal kingdom thus commit a complete mistake. On the contrary, they appear at certain seasons of the year to be more 'graminivorous' than any other people I know, and with respect to this their taste appears to me to give the anthropologist a hint of certain traits of the mode of life of the people of the Stone Age which have been completely overlooked. To judge from the Chukches our primitive ancestors by no means so much resembled beasts of prey as they are commonly imagined to have done, and it may, perhaps, have been the case that 'bellum omnium inter omnes' was first brought in with the higher culture of the Bronze or Iron Age."* The other descriptions given by the distinguished leader of the expedition, relative to the weapons, pottery, and general characteristics of this race, though necessarily meagre, are full of interest, and point in many ways to their ancient kinship with the primitive inhabitants of Britain. The custom of tattooing, for example, which they have inherited from their "Scythian" ancestors, has also been handed down to us from the same source and can scarcely be said to be yet extinct among us; while the unpleasant Chukch method of warding off or healing the effects of the frost upon the hands is still practised by the Scottish peasantry. And this reminds me that the milk-diet of the ancient Scythians, and the similar food of the old Basques and the modern Chukches found favour also with that branch of the same people which dwelt in certain parts of Britain at the coming of the Romans. Of the Hebrideans of the first century "it was reported that they knew nothing of the cultivation of the ground, but lived upon fish and milk, which latter (adds Mr. Skene) implies the possession of herds of cattle."† A race of "fishermen and hunters" and cattle-owners, like the Ugrians of Mr. Howorth and Lempriere's Scythians.

The sketch given by the learned author of "Celtic Scotland," of the ancient Britons is so much a picture of the Scyths and Ougres that it may be briefly quoted here. In addition

---

* "Voyage of the Vega," Vol. II. p. 111.
† "Celtic Scotland," Vol. I. pp. 40, 41.

to what has just been repeated of his account of the Hebrideans, Mr Skene says:—"They had, it was said, one king, who was not allowed to possess property, lest it should lead him to avarice and injustice, or a wife, lest a legitimate family should provoke ambition. In short, they [the Romans] learned that there existed among this new people a state of society similar to that which Cæsar reported to have found among the indigenous inhabitants of the interior o Britain." By "the interior of Britain" is meant the interior, more particularly, of what is now England,—but the account which Mr. Skene gives of the ancient Caledonii will suit the supposed aborigines of England as well as of the Hebrides. "The manners of the two nations [the 'Caledonii,' and 'Mæatæ,' two confederacies of all the kindred tribes living in central and north-central Scotland at the beginning of the third century, known later on as 'Picti,'] are described as the same, and they are viewed by the historians in these respects as if they were but one people. They are said to have neither walls nor cities, as the Romans regarded such, and to have neglected the cultivation of the ground. They lived by pasturage, the chase, and the natural fruits of the earth. The great characteristics of the tribes believed to be indigenous were found to exist among them. They fought in chariots, and to their arms of the sword and shield, as described by Tacitus, they had now added a short spear of peculiar construction, having a brazen knob at the end of the shaft, which they shook to terrify their enemies, and likewise a dagger. They are said to have had community of women, and the whole of their progeny were reared as the joint offspring of each small community. And the third great characteristic, the custom of painting the body, attracted particular notice. They are described as puncturing their bodies, so as, by a process of tattooing, to produce the representation of animals, and to have refrained from clothing, in order that what they considered an ornament should not be hidden."*

(It may be mentioned, also, that "the nation of the 'Mæatæ' consisted of those tribes which were situated next the wall between the Forth and Clyde on the north.

* "Celtic Scotland," Vol. I. pp. 83, 84.

The 'Caledonii,' lay beyond them." And Mr. Skene derives 'Mæatæ' from Gaelic 'Magh,' a plain, because this confederacy inhabited the "plains and marshes;" were, in short, "lake-dwellers." For, even although the Roman historian had not said so, it is a geological fact that the level stretch of "carse" land through which the River Forth winds, was a morass within comparatively recent times, and it may fairly be presumed that the tribes of the Mæatæ dwelt in those pile-buildings, known in Scotland and Ireland as *crannoges*, the remains of which are found in great numbers throughout these two countries, as well as in Norfolk, and in various other parts of Europe.)*

Although the British Scythians appear as painted or tattooed people from the beginning, they did not receive the general designation of *Picti* until the third century. So says Innes, in his Essay on the Ancient Inhabitants of Scotland,—and he adds that "the *Britains*, or *Welch*. . . call'd all these northern people, their ancient enemies, *Phychthead;*

---

* The existence of great tracts of marsh-lands is indicated in Pytheas' description of "Thule," quoted by Strabo :—"It was neither land, nor sea, nor air separately, but a certain concretion of them all, like *sea-blubber*, in which, he says, that land and sea and all things are suspended; and that this is as it were the bond (*i.e.*, boundary) of all things, being neither passable by travelling nor by sailing; that he had himself seen the resemblance of this *blubber*, but that the rest he described by hearsay." (Lysons' "Our British Ancestors," p. 2.) What part of the British Islands "Thule" was, if any, is, of course, uncertain; but if "Ultima Thule" was Orkney, Shetland, or the Hebrides, then Scotland seems the likeliest to be "Thule" itself. The marshes, enveloped in malarial mists, of which Pytheas speaks so quaintly, seem to have stretched over a great part of Scotland even in the sixth century; for Procopius, writing from Constantinople at that period, describes the districts north of the Forth and Clyde as "a region infested by wild beasts, and with an atmosphere so tainted that human life could not exist." And Mr. Skene (from whom I am quoting) adds that "Stephanus Byzantinus, writing from the same place half a century earlier, considered 'Albion'" to be actually a separate island; while "even Gildas, himself of British descent, and writing from the neighbouring shore of Armorica," and "taking his description of the size of Britain from the cosmogony of Ethicus, written two centuries earlier," "evidently considered the country north of the Firths of Forth and Clyde as a separate island from the rest of Britain." An island it could not have been, but the statements here cited seem clearly to argue that this portion of Scotland was narrowed into a mere isthmus about the time of the Roman occupation: and the wide expanse of now solid land that lies to the south and east of Aberfoil was then a fen district, with here and there islands of firm ground, on which were situated the villages of the Mæatæ, built upon pile-supported platforms, as in the Malayan Archipelago at the present day; or more solidly of stone, as in the orthodox British *crannoge*.

the Saxons named them *Pehts*, or *Pyhtas;* and the *Irish* and ancient *Scots*, expressed the same thing in equivalent terms of their language, calling them *Cruithneach*, from *Cruith*, which signifies forms or figures, such as they used to paint or mark on themselves."* The same writer (whose Essay is characterized by Mr. Skene as "admirable," and regarded by him as of real importance) decides that the various tribes of the Picti found the northern parts of the island " as yet uncultivated, and void of inhabitants when they came in." As to the place from whence they came there is some difference of opinion. Innes concludes that it was Gaul, and that the Picti and the Britons were of the same original stock. He also cites the conjectures of Tacitus and of Bede, the first bringing them from "Germany" and the second from "Scythia," but, as he pertinently observes, the same place is understood by both, for Tacitus called all Northern Europe *Germania Magna*, while Bede included among "Scythians" the ancient inhabitants of Norway, Sweden, and Denmark, the Daci, Getæ, and other nations. And he further states that the first Roman writers who speak of these northern nations mention their custom of painting and tattooing their bodies with particular emblems. Among these tribes are the Arii, the Agathyrsi, the Geloni, and the Getæ, described by Tacitus and also by Solinus in the same terms as the Cruithneach or Picti of Ireland and Scotland.† With these

---

* Innes's "Essay, &c.," 1729, p. 62.
† Buchanan states that "the Britons, the Arii in Germany, and the Agathyrsi, painted their bodies," but that the Picts (specially so called) "marked their skins with iron, and delineated the figures of different animals upon them." He also quotes Claudian to show that the tribes of the Geloni and the Getæ tattooed themselves in the same way. The first-named are described as—

" —— the Geloni, who delight
Their hardy limbs with iron to imprint."

And of the others it is said—

"The nobles of the long-haired Getæ sat
In council, skin-clad, and their bodies bore
The seamy ornament of many a scar."

These Getæ, then, resembled strongly the fur-clad, "scarified" Hungarians or Ugres of whom Mr. Howorth has written, and they were likely enough akin to each other. The Geloni, who, it is seen, were accustomed to tattoo their bodies, were also used to paint them. For they are one with the Agathyrsi. Mr. Skene

facts in view, one would naturally argue that these latter tribes arrived in this country from North Europe rather than from Gaul. But perhaps the real explanation of such apparent incongruities is to be found in the probable fact that this tattooed Ugrian race occupied at the date under discussion a great part of its old territories in Gaul and Hispania.

Whatever may be the antecedents of the yellow-haired, white-skinned *Xanthochroi*, it is clear that this totally-different Ugrian race is the chief one to be considered in dwelling upon the Europe of two thousand years ago, if it really did about that epoch occupy "if not a ring round the world, at least one reaching from Britain to Kamskatka." It must be remembered that "a very great element" in the Celtic, Latin, and Greek languages has been shown to be Ugrian, and that, apart from linguistic connection, more than one scholar has ascertained the existence of "a large Turanian admixture among the ancient Romans," as well as among the present Negro populations of Northern Africa. (Perhaps the word Mongoloid, "as expressing affinity with Mongolians, without implying identification,"* is the most comprehensive and therefore the most suitable term to use, when speaking of a period so remote.)

These Ugrians are all the more interesting to us, because they have been identified with the Ogres of our nursery tales, therein described as a race of cruel, anthropophagous tyrants, against whom our forefathers,—or at least the forefathers of some of us,—fought a stubborn and eventually a winning fight. The name "Hungarian" is another form of the word. "The Ungri and Ungari of the western writers, and the Ouiggroi of the Byzantines, are both derived from the Slavic Ugri. Ugri is the form in Nestor; Uhry, Wegry,

(in his "Celtic Scotland," Vol. I. p. 175) says that these Agathyrsi were, according to Irish tradition, the Cruithnigh or Picts who settled in Ireland; that they were the children of Gelonus [whence *Geloni*], son of Hercules; that they came from the land of Thrace, passed through France, where they built the city of *Pict*avis; and that they then crossed over to Ireland, where they received an offer of a district from the King of Leinster, on condition that they would drive out a people called the Tuatha Fidhbhe—which they did. From this tribe, then—assuming the truth of the tradition—might be derived the "flat, Tartar faces" observed by Thackeray.

* To borrow a phrase from the author of "Preadamites."

and Wengri in other authors." The same authority* states that "Constantine Porphyrogenitus tells us, the Hungarians (by him called Turks) formerly dwelt near the Chazars, in a place called Lebedias: then, he says, they were not called Turks but Sabartoiasphali. Zeuss ingeniously conjectures that the first syllables are equivalent to the German *swart*, *schwarz*, ' black ;' and that the whole word is a translation of the Slavic *Czernii Ugri*, Black Ugri, by which the Hungarians are known in later Russian writers . . . White and black, as is well known, means, with Eastern writers, little more than dominant and dependent ; thus the Black Kazars, or Hungarians, were the subjects of the White Kazars."

Now, before going further, it is necessary to look into this last statement pretty closely. For the origin of this nomenclature may be found to lie very deep. I find it stated elsewhere† that "the Tatarian tribes are very fond of expressing by certain colours the changes of political condition to which a nation may be subjected. *Black* or *Kara*‡ has the meaning of dependency and servitude, while *White* or *Ak* has that of sovereignty and freedom. . . . But these colours are employed only so long as they really describe the position of a tribe ; for if a dependent horde becomes independent and sovereign, the former *Kara* or *Black* will be changed into *Ak* or *White* ; the Tatars, to whom the mighty conqueror Tchingyz-khan belonged, were named before his time *Kara*-Tatars, while another tribe was called *Ak*-Tatars or White Tatars. This is also the reason why the Emperor of Russia is called the White Zar, and the divisions of Russia into White and Black express the same meaning." But this custom is not confined to Asia and the East of Europe. It obtains, or did obtain in Britain as well, and, like the word

---

* H. H. Howorth, "On the Westerly Drifting of Nomades"; *Ethnological Society's Journal*, January, 1871.

† By Dr. Gustav Oppert, in a paper read before the Ethnological Society of London, 11th January, 1870, "On the Kitai and Kara-Kitai." This word, as pointed out by Dr. Hyde Clarke, is the "Cathay" of the poets.

‡ This word is an example of the Ugrian element in Celtic speech. In Gaelic it is *Ciar*, which is spelled *Carr*, *Carre*, *Ker*, *Karr*, and *Kerr* in modern Scottish surnames, all of which are simply *Ciar*. The final "a" of the slower-speaking Mongoloids has dropped off, but the word is the same. It now means "swarthy" or "dark-brown" rather than "black," which signification attaches more distinctly to the word *dubh*.

Kara itself, has plainly an Ugrian origin. It still survives in the word "*black*-guard," which, though now applied very loosely, is more strictly defined by Halliwell as meaning "a nick-name given to the lowest drudges of the court, the carriers of coal and wood, the labourers in the scullery, &c." Its Scotch form, "*black*-ward," is given by Dr. Jamieson as "a state of servitude to a servant," in support of which he quotes Richie Moniplies :—" So that you see, sir, I hold in a sort of black ward tenure, as we call it in our country, being the servant of a servant." Jamieson also says that a "*black*" is "a vulgar designation for a low scoundrel, corresponding in sense to the English *blackguard ;*" while in Halliwell's *Dictionary* I find "*black-tan*" stated to be a term used in speaking of gipsies in Kent, and perhaps elsewhere. The same thing is seen in Scottish Gaelic. "A girl of the lowest rank of peasantry" is a "*dubh-chaile*" (black hussy), "a strolling female or gipsy" is a "*dubh-shiubhlach*" (black vagrant), and Armstrong also gives an obsolete word, "*duibhearach*," (in Irish Gaelic, "*duibheartha*") as signifying "the vernacular."

It is, perhaps, from a like custom that we ought to trace our word "sir." "Klaproth says that in the Vogul dialect and in Western Siberian, sar, sarni, sorni, and sairan mean 'white.' In many Samoyede compounds the same word is found, as syr, sirr, and siri."* This is Welsh *syr*, English *sir ;* and although *ak* does not exist in our language, this equivalent has taken its place, just as *Kara* or *Ciar* has been pushed aside by *Dubh*. But the result is the same. In this country, as in the East, a word meaning "white" is attached to the ruling class, and "black" is synonymous with "dependency and servitude."

The reason of this is not far to seek. Although now used without the slightest reference to the complexion of either caste, the words assert themselves, as distinctly as words can, to be "survivals" of a period of White Conquest, when a Black was a *serf ;* just as that word and *slave* may be, and

* Mr. Howorth, in "The Westerly Drifting of Nomades," Part IV. Thus the title which the Russian peasants, the "Black People," give to their Emperor —the great *white* Tsar—is tautological. (It may be remarked that this derivation of *sir* does not clash with the theory that that word comes from *sire*, father. It is quite opposed, however, to the belief that *sir* and *sire* are derived from *senior, sendra*, &c.)

are, derived from conquered Serbs and Slavs (Even at the present day, "white," in American slang, has the idea of high qualities attached to it; though in this case it is likely that the usage started afresh with the practice of Negro slavery in modern times.)

As the result of this digression, then, we have found that all over the north of Europe and of Asia, there are word-tokens of the presence of Professor Huxley's *Australioids*, at some unascertained date, and the presumption is that they were finally subjugated by the white race. Let us return to the Hungarians or Ugrians.

Speaking of "the Black and White Ughres of Nestor, the former of whom were the Hungarians or Magyars," Mr. Howorth states that "they correspond also, as I believe, to the Black and White Huns of other writers." This race, then, known to themselves as Magyars (Mogerii, according to "the notary of Bela," who "also gives the forms Deutumoger and Hetumoger,") and to others as Turks, Sabartoiasphali, Czernii Ugri or Black Ugri, Ughres, or Ogres, are to be identified with the Black Huns. Now this fact is important, because it brings us face to face with a large and important nation of "Scythians" who were not only *styled* " black," but who actually were so. And, therefore, knowing how numerous they were, and how they spread themselves like a flood over Europe, it is to them we must look if we want to learn something of the history and manners of what may be called the maternal ancestors of the *Melanochroi*. Not that they constitute the whole of this branch of the pedigree, but plainly they form a considerable part of it, if they left descendants as numerous, or half as numerous, as themselves.

They are called in Latin, *Hunni*, and in Greek, *Ounni* and *Chounoi*. Ptolemy speaks of a people of Sarmatia, named *Chuni*, who are, I fancy, the same. Lempriere's account of the Sarmatians was, it will be remembered, that they were "a savage uncivilized nation, often confounded with the Scythians, naturally warlike, and famous for painting their bodies to appear more terrible in the field of battle. They were well-known for their lewdness, and passed among the Greeks and Latins by the name of barbarians; ... at last, increased by the savage hordes of Scythia, under the barbarous names of Huns, Vandals, Goths, Alans, &c., they successfully invaded and ruined the empire in the third and fourth centuries of the Christian era. . . They lived upon plunder, and fed upon milk mixed with the blood of horses." As described by Rheginon, they also "lived by fishing and hunting," and fought with bows and arrows. And they tattooed their faces in addition to painting themselves. Such Scythians, it was also noticed, inhabited the Basque Provinces, the Western Islands, and the interior of Scotland, and apparently the interior of England also, at the date of the Roman invasion, and the ancestral habits are still, to some extent, kept up by that section of the race now inhabiting Northern Siberia. All these people were closely allied, by many characteristics, the most striking of which gave rise to the nick-name applied to the division who lived in Britain, but which might have as suitably attached itself to all the other branches of the race. For all were, in effect, *Picti*.

But it is that division known as Huns, and more especially as *Black* Huns, that we are at present to consider. Let me transcribe a brief history of this people:—

"The Huns were of Asiatic origin, and, in all probability, of the Mongolian or Tartar stock; therefore akin to, and perhaps to be identified with, the Scythians and Turks. According to De Guignes, whose theory has been accepted by Gibbon, the Huns who invaded the Roman empire were lineally descended from the Hiong-nou, whose ancient seat was an extensive but barren tract of country immediately to the north of the great wall of China. About the year 200 B.C. these people overran the Chinese empire, defeated the Chinese armies in numerous engagements, and even drove the Emperor Kao-ti himself to an ignominious capitulation and treaty. During the reign of Vou-ti (141-87 B.C.) the power of the Huns was very much broken. Eventually, they separated into two distinct camps, one of which, amounting to about 50,000 families, went southwards, while the other endeavoured to maintain itself in its original seat. This, however, it was very difficult for them to do; and eventually the most warlike and enterprising went west and north-west, in search of new homes. Of those that went north-west, a large number established themselves for a while on the banks of the Volga. Then crossing this river, they advanced into the territories of the Alani, a pastoral people dwelling between the Volga and the Don. At what period this took place is uncertain, but probably it was early in the 4th century. The Alani, who had long dwelt in these plains, resisted the incursions of the Huns with much bravery and some effect, until at length a bloody and decisive battle was fought on the banks of the Don, in which the Alan king was slain, and his army utterly routed; the vast majority of the survivors joined the invaders.

The Huns are described as being of a dark complexion, almost black; deformed in their appearance, of uncouth gesture, and shrill voice. 'They were distinguished,' says Gibbon, 'from the rest of the human species by their broad shoulders, flat noses, and small black eyes deeply buried in the head; and as they were almost destitute of beards, they never enjoyed either the manly graces of youth, or the venerable aspect of age. A fabulous origin was assigned worthy of their form and manners—that the witches of Scythia, who for their foul and deadly practices had been driven from society, had copulated in the desert with infernal spirits; and that the Huns were the offspring of this execrable conjunction. Such was the origin assigned to them by their enemies the Goths, whom the Huns now invaded with fire and sword. Hermanric, the aged sovereign of the Goths, whose dominions reached from the Baltic to the Euxine, roused himself to meet the invaders, but in vain. His successor, Withimir, encountered the Huns in a pitched battle, in which he himself was slain, and his countrymen utterly routed. These now threw themselves upon the protection of the Emperor Valens, who in 376 gave permission to a great number of them to cross the Danube and settle in the countries on the other side as auxiliaries to the Roman arms against further invasion. The Huns now occupied all the territories that had been abandoned by the Goths; and when these, not long afterwards, revolted against Valens, the Huns also crossed the Danube, and joined their arms to those of the Goths in hostilities against the Roman Empire. In the wars that followed, the Huns were not so conspicuous as the Goths their former enemies. Indeed, we now hear but little of the Huns during the remainder of the 4th century. It is supposed, however, that early in the following century they were joined by fresh hordes of their brethren, a circumstance which encouraged them to press onwards towards further conquests. In the reign of Theodosius the younger, they had increased so considerably in power, that their sovereign Rugilas, or Roas, was paid an annual tribute to secure the Roman empire from further injury.

Rugilas, dying in the year 434, was succeeded in the sovereignty of the Huns by his nephews Attila and Bleda. With Attila's death, however, in 454, the power of the Huns was broken in pieces. A few feeble sovereigns succeeded to him, but there was strife now everywhere among the several nations that had owned the firm sway of Attila, and the Huns especially never regained their power. Many of them took service in the armies of the Romans, and others again joined fresh hordes of invaders from the north and east, aiding them in their repeated attacks upon the moribund Roman empire."

Of Attila himself it is said that he,

"was the son of Mundzuk,

a Hun of the royal blood, and in 434 A.D. succeeded his uncle Roas as chief of countless hordes scattered over the north of Asia and Europe. His brother Bleda, or Blödel, who shared with him the supreme authority over all the Huns, was put to death by Attila in 444 or 445 A.D. The Huns regarded Attila with superstitious reverence, and Christendom with superstitious dread, as the 'Scourge of God.' It was believed that he was armed with a supernatural sword, which belonged to the Scythian god of war, which must win dominion over the whole world. It is not known when the name 'Scourge of God' was first applied to Attila. He is said to have received it from a hermit in Gaul. The whole race of Huns was regarded in the same light . . . . . . The Vandals, Ostrogoths, Gepidi, and many of the Franks, fought under his banner, and in a short time his dominion extended over the people of Germany and Scythia—*i.e.*, from the frontiers of Gaul to those of China . . . . . . In 451, Attila turned his course to the west, to invade Gaul, but was here boldly confronted by Aëtius, leader of the Romans, and Theodoric, king of the Visigoths, who compelled him to raise the siege of Orleans. [These two generals finally defeated him, with great slaughter] near the site now occupied by the city of Chalons-sur-Marne . . . . . . This, if old historians are to be trusted, must have been the most sanguinary battle ever fought in Europe; for it is stated by contemporaries of Attila, that not less than 252,000 or 300,000 slain were left on the field. Attila, having retired within his camp of waggons, collected all the wooden shields, saddles, and other baggage into a vast funeral pile, resolving to die in the flames rather than surrender; but by the advice of Aëtius, the Roman general, the Huns were allowed to retreat without much further loss, though they were pursued by the Franks as far as the Rhine . . . . . . [Two years later, he died suddenly, on the eve of another invasion of Italy.] His death spread consternation through the host of the Huns. His followers cut themselves with knives, shaved their heads, and prepared to celebrate the funeral rites of their king. It is said that his body was placed in three coffins—the first of gold; the second of silver; and the third of iron; that the caparison of his horses, with his arms and ornaments, were buried with him; and that all the captives who were employed to make his grave were put to death, so that none might betray the resting-place of the king of the Huns."

The name of this powerful monarch, who ruled over an empire as extensive as any on record, is said to be the same as the Hungarian *Ethelc*, which is understood to be a title of honour, and is apparently no other than Saxon *Ethel* and German *Adel*, noble.* Of his physical appearance, it is said

* Like *kara* (black), it may be taken as an example of an Ugrian word in a non-Ugrian, or partly Ugrian language; and in both cases the final "a" of the slow-speaking Mongoloid (a mere after-breathing or drawl) has been dropped by the borrowers.

that he possessed "the Mongolian characteristics—low stature, a large head, with small, brilliant deep-seated eyes, and broad shoulders."

From the sketch just quoted,* of Attila, or Ethele, and his race, and also from the preceding remarks, the following inferences may be drawn :—

1. That the *Picti* of the Hebrides and of other districts of Britain and Ireland have many points in common with the Mongoloid *Picti* who were their contemporaries, and who covered an immense area of Asia and Europe; and that although the British *Picti* have not been proved to be of similar complexion to the black-skinned Huns or Ogres who constituted a large section of the Asiatic *Picti*, yet there is word-evidence in our Islands, as elsewhere, of a time when a conquered race was of black colour.

2. That, assuming the historical sketch just quoted to be exact, the Hiong-nou, Huns, or Ogres, who separated into two bands about the beginning of the Christian era, the one going southward from their point of departure (the outskirts of China), and the other west and north-west, eventually branching also into the countries bordering the Mediterranean, coincide in almost every respect with the Mongoloids of Professor Huxley (marked 8B upon his map), who inhabit the vast territory "which lies mainly to the east of a line drawn from Lapland to Siam" and are figured as "men who are short and squat, with the skin of a yellow-brown colour; the eyes and hair black, and the latter straight, coarse, and scanty on the body and face, but long on the scalp." This general division of Mongoloids reaches as far south as the southmost islands of the Malayan Archipelago, and takes in "the Malays proper," and, I suspect, the indigenous people of the Philippines who are not Negritos; and this may be reasonably supposed to be the result of the southward movement of the 50,000 Hun families in or about the first century of our era. The position of the European branch of this Mongoloid race, according to Professor Huxley, agrees also, in the main, with that of those Huns who spread themselves over the greater part of Europe during the third, fourth, and fifth centuries.

* From "Chambers's Encyclopædia," under *Huns* and *Attila*.

3. And as that division which included the Black Ogres, Huns, or Chazars is described as "almost black" in complexion, it is evident we have in them an element more akin to the now extinct Tasmanians, who, it may be remembered, were "of a dark brown colour, or nearly black," were "of moderate stature" and robust frame (as the Black Huns were), and who also were *Picti*, both as regards painting and tattooing (as were the Huns also). These Tasmanians have, it has been noted, stone circles and cairns in the country which they inhabited, and in this particular (not the only one) strongly resemble the *Picti* of Britain. The Negrito race, to whom the Tasmanians belong, are marked on Professor Huxley's map as occupying New Caledonia, New Guinea, and some of the islands to the east of it, including part of Fiji, the interior of Lower Siam, the Andaman Islands, and, of course, Tasmania. They present "a remarkable approximation to the Australioid type," the most marked points of resemblance being apparently the heavy brow-ridges and sharply pentagonal skull, and the chief differences being that the Negrito's hair is woolly, while that of the Australioid is wavy and silky; and the skin of the latter is a shade of "chocolate-brown," and, therefore, not so dark as the Negrito's. Making allowance, then, for various crossings with different varieties of men, during a period of about two thousand years, it may be conjectured that among the southward-moving Huns, as among those who came into Europe, there was a considerable body of Black people, akin to the Australioids; that they were the authors of the stone circles and cairns of Tasmania and of Borneo, which island they may first have settled in; that they formed the bulk of the inhabitants of Australia and also of the "Negrito" islands (becoming fused with slightly different races); and that the stone circles and cairns of North-Western Europe were, like those of the Antipodes, the work of Negrito-Australioid people, such as those whose skulls were found in Caithness, and who were identical with, or ancestors of, the Black Huns of European history.

CHAPTER III.

"A DISTINGUISHED writer on ethnology lays down certain propositions which he terms fixed points in British ethnology. His first proposition is this: 'Eighteen hundred years ago the population of Britain comprised peoples of two types of complexion, the one fair, and the other dark. The dark people resembled the Aquitani and the Iberians; the fair people were like the Belgic Gauls.' His second proposition is, 'The people termed Gauls, and those called Germans, by the Romans, did not differ in any important physical character.' These two propositions we may accept as well-founded."*

A splendid example of this fair race is the "Barbarian Prisoner," supposed to be Caractacus, portrayed (from the marble in the British Museum) in the Dilettanti Society's publication of Antique Marbles and Bronzes. If this be truly an "Ancient Briton," then the marble fully corroborates the united opinion of the ethnologist and the historian, and shows that the kind of man who is regarded by some as "a regular Englishman," or "clearly of Norman descent," was a native of Britain centuries before either of those two races entered, or, at any rate, ruled over it. For the noble, manly features of this "Barbarian" are exactly those attributed to the "aristocrat" of the popular fancy. That he himself was a real aristocrat there can be no doubt, whatever the name of his race, for his countenance is charged with dignity and force. And if such a face was rightly regarded at one time as that of a member of the ruling class, then it would appear that one of the several nations of pre-Norman and pre-English Britons had re-asserted itself in the long run, though overborne for a time by "Saxon and Norman and Dane."

* "Celtic Scotland," Vol. I. p. 164.

This style of man was not peculiar to the South of England, if tradition may be credited. Some, at any rate, of the Ossianic heroes were of the same kindred. The central figure, for instance, Fingal or Fionn, — who is thus sketched :—

> " Marble his skin,
> The rose his cheek,
> Blue was his eye,
> His hair like gold."

And that he possessed the high, chivalric qualities expressed in the features of the other, is told by such lines as these :—

> " Generous, just,
> Despised a lie.
> Of vigorous deeds,
> First in song.
>
> A righteous judge,
> Firm his rule.
> Polished his mien,
> Who knew but victory.
> * * *
> All men's trust,
> Of noble mind.
> Of ready deeds,
> To women mild.
> * * *
> With miser's mind
> From none withheld.
> Anything false
> His lips ne'er spoke."

There is, of course, great uncertainty as to the lineage, era, and nationality of the second of these two figures; and legendary poetry is not so tangible as sculpture; but both men plainly belonged to this Gaulish or German people, known ethnologically by the formidable title of *Xanthochroi*. And of the first it may be said, with some degree of certainty, that he and his nation inhabited some part of Britain eighteen hundred years ago.

But our islands contained other races at that period. " When the war with the Silures, who occupied territories in the south-west, brought them [the Romans] in contact with that people, Tacitus records the result of their observation. Their complexion was different and of a darker hue. Their hair was curly, and they resembled the Iberians; ...."

"At an early period the Greek writers, in whom we find the earliest notices of Britain, seem to have had a persuasion that the portion of the inhabitants of Britain who were more particularly connected with the working of tin, possessed peculiarities which distinguished them from the rest. At first they knew only of islands called the Cassiterides, so called from a word signifying tin, as the quarter from whence tin was brought. They then became aware that tin was wrought in Britain as well, and they came to view the Cassiterides as islands lying between Spain and Britain. Diodorus tells us that 'they who dwell near the promontory of Britain which is called Belerion (Land's End) are singularly fond of strangers, and, from their intercourse with foreign merchants, civilized in their habits. These people obtain the tin by skilfully working the soil which produces it.' .... He also says, 'above the country of the Lusitanians, there are many mines of tin in the little islands called Cassiterides from this circumstance, lying off Iberia, in the ocean, and much of it also is carried across from the Bretannic Isle to the opposite coast of Gaul, and thence conveyed on horses by the merchants, through the intervening Celtic land, to the people of Massilia, and to the city called Narbonne.' ... By the Cassiterides, the Scilly Islands seem to be intended."

"Strabo reports of Posidonius that he says that tin is not found upon the surface, as authors commonly relate, but that it is dug up; and that it is produced both in places among the Barbarians who dwell beyond the Lusitanians, and in the islands Cassiterides; and that from the Bretannic Isles it is carried to Massilia; and he adds, 'The Cassiterides are ten in number, and lie near each other in the ocean, towards the north from the haven of the Artabri: one of them is desert, but the others are inhabited by men in black cloaks, clad in tunics reaching to the feet, and girt about the breast; walking with staves, and bearded like goats. They subsist by their cattle, leading for the most part a wandering life.

And having metals of tin and lead, these and skins they barter with the merchants for earthenware and salt, and brazen vessels.' . . . "

"Pomponius Mela and Pliny in the first century both allude to the Cassiterides, so called, say both, because they abound in tin, and so does Solinus in similar terms; but the latter also states that 'a stormy channel separates the coast which the Damnonii occupy from the island Silura, whose inhabitants preserve the ancient manners, reject money, barter merchandise, value what they require by exchange rather than by price, worship the gods, and both men and women profess a knowledge of the future.' His description resembles that of Diodorus, and he probably considered Cornwall as an island, and connects it by name with the Silures. In the following century we find that the name of Cassiterides has been dropped, and they are now called Hesperides, while their inhabitants were believed to have been Iberians. Dionysius Periegeta says, in the end of this century—'But near the sacred promontory, where they say is the end of Europe, the Hesperides Isles, whence tin proceeds, dwell the rich sons of the noble Iberians.'

"In the fourth century, Rufus Festus Avienus calls these islands the Oestrymnides. He says that the northern promontory of Spain was called Oestrymnis, and adds, 'Below the summit of this promontory the Oestrymnic bay spreads out before the inhabitants, in which the Oestrymnic Isles show themselves'—

> Lying far off, and rich in metals
> Of tin and lead. Great the strength of this nation,
> Proud their mind, powerful their skill,
> Trading the constant care of all,
> The broad boisterous channel with boats and southerly wind,
> They cut the gulf of the monster-filled ocean;
> They know not to fit with pine
> Their keels, nor with fir, as use is,
> They shape their boats; but, strange to say,
> They fit their vessels with united skins,
> And often traverse the deep in a hide.

Then, after mentioning the sacred island of the Hiberni and the island of the Albiones, he adds, 'It is customary for the people of Tartessus to trade in the bounds of the Oestrymnides;' and Priscianus Periegeta, who flourished in the beginning of the sixth century, calls them the Hesperides, and says that over against the sacred promontory which men call the end of Europe lie the Hesperides, full of tin, which the strong people of the Iberi occupy."

Dr. Skene, from whose chapter on the Ethnology of Britain I have made this rather long extract, adds, at this place,—

"If these notices show that a persuasion existed among many that the population of the Scilly Isles, Cornwall, and South Wales was Iberian, an examination of the ancient sepulchral remains in Britain gives us reason to suppose that a people possessing their physical characteristics had once spread over the whole of both of the British Isles." And he cites archæological evidence in proof of this.

Although the exact position of the Cassiterides is not a matter of much moment, it may be remarked, in passing, that their identification with the Scilly Isles does not seem to be very clearly proved. Most of the writers just quoted appear to have regarded them, whether as Hesperides, Oestrymnides, or Cassiterides, as islands of considerable size, in comparison with which the Scilly Isles form a mere handful of rocks. And their inhabitants are spoken of as an independent nation, though of Iberian blood. And also, the locality is, in most of the instances, indicated as near to *Spain* rather than to *England*. Even in the loosest kind of description, one could scarcely include the Scilly Isles as lying in the Bay of Biscay, or bring oneself to imagine that they were visible or nearly so, to a man standing on the northern coast of Spain, which would be equivalent to seeing (in fact or in fancy) the Norwegian coast from the cliffs at Scarborough. The Cassiterides are "above the country of the Lusitanians," or Portuguese, "lying off Iberia," or Spain, "towards the north from the haven of the Artabri," and their inhabitants are said to have worn black garments, like Lempriere's Lusitanians. Remembering that the adjective *Bretannic* belongs to both sides of the Channel, and that both countries also have a tradition of a submerged western territory, the Lyonnesse of romance, which was covered so recently that the ancestors of some existing Cornish families are said to have come out of it, and that geological reasoning fully supports the legend,—one has some excuse for supposing that the Cassiterides formed an archipelago stretching between the promontories of the Spanish and English coasts,—of which the Scilly Isles were an insignificant fraction.

But, at any rate, the people known as Iberians were spread all over the British Islands, whether indigenous or immigrants, and some of their tribes were known as Damnonii and Silures. This seems to be generally admitted. Physically, they were swarthy of colour, had curly hair, and were bearded like goats. They, or some clans of them, "worshipped the gods," and "both men and women professed a knowledge of the future." So then, the Druids and Druidesses " who had colleges in an island near the coasts of Brittany,"* who " professed a knowledge of the future," who (the men, at least,) were figured as " bearded like goats," and who "worshipped the gods," were dark-skinned, curly-haired Iberians, of the tribe of the Silures or Damnonii? This seems a fair inference.

The Druidesses of this island, or of one of these islands, are mentioned more than once, and eventually they suffered the fate of most of their order. " The Isle of Sena, now Isle de Sain[ts], off the coast of France, contained a college of Druidesses, who, like him of Skerr, had power over the winds, which they were in the practice of selling to credulous mariners. These unfortunate damsels fell at last victims to the sanguinary system of persecution, to which the votaries of bardism were everywhere subjected. Conan, Duke of Bretagne, in the fervour of his zeal, committed them to the flames."† The same writer, speaking of "those who acted so conspicuous a part, when in desperation they defended themselves against Suetonius and his legions in Anglesea," states that, "arrayed in black garments, they ran wildly to and fro, with dishevelled hair and drawn swords, forcing back, like the Cimbric females of old, those who were

---

* The reference is the "Foyer Breton," Vol. I. p. 155, which I quote from Mr. J. F. Campbell's "West Highland Tales," Vol. I. p. 24.
† Logan's "Introduction" to Mackenzie's "Beauties of Gaelic Poetry."

retreating." Here again, the black dress is seen to be common to the Lusitanians, to the people of the Cassiterides, and to the Druidesses of Anglesey. And if, as may be reasonably supposed, all these belonged to the same swarthy race, then, whatever position the Druids may have held among the rosy-cheeked, golden-haired Keltoi of the Greeks (to whom the "Barbarian Prisoner" and Ossianic Fingal were akin), they were at any rate quite unconnected by blood.

The Iberians are styled "swarthy," and "curly-haired." The word "swarthy" is rather elastic, for although literally *schwartz*, yet it is taken, I fancy, to mean something not quite so dark as the colour of a negro, in its usual acceptation. Perhaps this distinction does not exist. But, at any rate, if the "small dark Highlander" and the "Black Celt to the west of the Shannon" be assumed to be the descendants of Iberians, it may fairly be argued that, with so much intermixture with fairer races during the last two thousand years, the stock must now be lighter-skinned than then, and its representatives of the first century must have been actually as black as negroes. As a matter of fact, Pliny characterizes their complexion as *æthiopium*, that is, as black as an Ethiopian,—and it may be that the "curliness" of their hair was of the same nature as a negro's also. Thus the Negritos of Huxley, the owners of such skulls as those found in Caithness, may have been allied to the ancient Iberians. That the wild tribes of Ireland were black men is hinted by the fact that "a wild Irishman" is in Gaelic "a *black* Irishman" (*Dubh Eireannach*).* And that some of the natives of Scotland, as well as of England, were of this race also is evident when one remembers that, according to Skene, the powerful tribe of the Damnonii, which was the chief of the confederacy of the Mæatæ, or marsh-dwellers, who were a part of the Picti or Caledonii, were probably relations of their namesakes of South-Western Britain; which indeed is almost a certainty, if nomenclature goes for anything. Therefore the British Picts resembled the Ugrian Picts and the Tasmanian and other kindred Picts, not only in the using of

* Armstrong's Gaelic Dictionary.

similar customs and weapons, but also in their most striking physical features.

If the links of this chain of argument be held to be loosely joined together,—or even disconnected,—there can surely be little dubiety as to the evidence given by Claudian. There is a line of his which I have encountered in more than one antiquarian work, but by some strange oversight, one of its most significant words has, so far as I have seen, received no attention. In reciting the victories of the Roman general Theodosius, Claudian says—

> *Ille leves Mauros, nec falso nomine Pictos*
> *Edomuit—*

Now, when Claudian wrote, and for a long time after, *Maurus* signified a great deal more than "a native of Mauritania." (Or it may be more correct to say that Mauritania implied as much, though in a different quarter, as "Scythia" did.) Any Latin dictionary,—any old one, at least,—will tell you that *maurus* is "a moor," a "blackamoor," or "a tawny-moor." And Shakespeare uses the word "moor" as a synonym for "negro."* As that last word bears nowadays a somewhat restricted meaning, it may be better to take the old-fashioned "blackamoor," as the nearest English rendering of *maurus*, signifying thereby any black, or brown-skinned man.† Consequently, the translation of Claudian's line is this—

> *He subdued the nimble blackamoors, not wrongly named*
> *"the painted people"—*

and the British Picts, like those of other lands, stand out again as dark-skinned men.

A complementary witness with *maurus* is *gorm*, found

---

* *Merchant of Venice*, act iii. scene v.

† This usage outlasted Shakespeare by at least two generations. In a brief narrative of the encounters between the early colonists of New England and the native "Indians," I find it stated that ". . . . these unfortunate gentlemen were intercepted by 700 *Moors*, with whom they fought for the space of four hours, till not only they two, but Capt. *Sharp* and fifty-one Christians more lay dead upon the place." And again that "at Woodcock[s], ten miles from *Seconch*, on the 16th *May*, was a little skrimage betwixt the *Moors* and Christians, wherein there was of the later three slain and two wounded, and only two *Indians* kild." ("News from New-England," London, 1676; reprinted at Boston and Albany, U.S., 1850 and 1865.)

attached to the names of Highland (and other) chiefs and kings. This word is given in the Gaelic dictionaries as signifying "blue, of whatever shade; also green, as grass." And this recalls the fact that the indigenous tribes described by Cæsar were styled both "Virides" (green) and "Cærulei" (blue), from the woad with which they stained their bodies, the colour of which may come under either of these headings. Accordingly, when one looks again into the Gaelic dictionary, one finds that *gorman* is woad. Plainly, therefore, a man who is titled *gorm* is a *woad-stained* man. Now, although in the Gaelic of Scotland a negro is known as *duine dubh*, a black man, he is known in the Gaelic of Ireland as *duine gorm*, a blue, green, or woad-stained man. And while in the Scottish Highlands, the adjective *glas* is used to signify both "swarthy" and "green," in Wales it has the meaning of "green" or "blue"; and in the latter country the Gaelic *gorm*, here spelled *gwrm*, is equivalent to "brown." What possible explanation for all this apparent confusion of terms can there be, except the patent one that a brown-skinned man and a woad-coloured man were one and the same?*

Maurus is a word which suggests a great deal. It has this in common with the Ugrian word *Kara* or *Ciar*, previously glanced at, that it not only signifies swarthiness of skin, but it is radically connected with a marsh or morass, or carse, as it is called in Scotland. One meaning of *maurus*, in Latin, is *palus*, and the words *marsh, morass, marish, merse* (in Saxon), and *moor* or *muir*, are all different forms, clearly of one original root, whatever that may be. "The Apian land certainly meant the watery land, *Meer-umschlungen*, among the pre-Hellenic Greeks, just as the same land is called Morea by the modern post-Hellenic or Romaic Greeks from *more*, the name for the sea in the Slavonic vernacular of its inhabitants during the heart of the Middle Ages." So says Lord Strangford, speaking authoritatively.† In Gaelic, the sea is *mara* and *muir*, which suggests the Latin *mare*. Armstrong (who certainly excels in ferreting

---

* Compare with these expressions the archaic *green-man*, "a savage." (Halliwell.)

† Page 171 of his "Letters and Papers, &c.," posthumously published.

out an enormous number of kindred words, in this as in other cases, though sometimes with questionable success) gives a list of other forms, selected from nearly every European, and one or two African and Asiatic tongues.* And of *Carse* or *kerss*, which is defined as "low and fertile land; generally that which is adjacent to a river," Dr. Jamieson states that in one instance, at least, it means something very like a marsh. He quotes a historical passage, relative to the movements of the English army at Bannockburn, which shows that the Carse of Falkirk was then impassable for cavalry. (This district, it may be remembered, formed a part of the territory of the Mæatæ or marsh-folk, a thousand years before the Battle of Bannockburn.) Dr. Jamieson remarks upon this—"This connection would almost indicate some affinity between our *carse*, and C.B. *kors*, palus, a marsh; ...... Su. G. *kaerr* and Isl. *kiar*,† *kaer*, both signify a marsh." The Anglo-Saxon *cerse* or *kersc*, *i.e.*, cress, and also, perhaps, *gærs*, grass (in Scotland, *girse*), may be traced from this word; and it might fairly be argued that carse-land was simply cress-, or grass-land, and had no connection with *kara*, black,—which argument, however, hinges entirely upon the age of the word *cress* or *cerse*. In the absence of evidence proving it to be older than, and unconnected with *kara*, I prefer to regard it as an outcome of the time when the meadows and marshes were known as the *Karr's* Land, just as they were also known as the *Moor*-lands or *Muirs*, the *marshes*, *morasses*, the *Merse* (in Berwickshire), and the *Maghers* (in Galloway), from the race who dwelt among them, styled *kara* or *ciar*, and *maurus*.

But one cannot fail to see that as the *terra firma* of the modern *moor* and *carse* has succeeded the watery *morass* and *kors*, so also the *morass* (which, as Pytheas said, "was neither

* To wit: "*Lat.* mare. *Germ.* meer. *Sclav.* morie. *Dal.* more. *Island.* mar. *Teut.* maer *and* maere. *Corn.* mor. *Ir.* muir. *Arm.* mar, mor *and* var. Also *Sax.* merc. *Fr.* mer. In the South of France they say *marc*. *Du.* meer. *Dal. Croat. Boh. Lus.* more. *Sclav. Pol.* morze. *Goth.* marisaiv, *a pool*. *Du.* maras. *Fr.* mar-ais. *Eng.* mor-ass. *Tamoulic*, mari, rain. *Arab.* mara, *spring or spout, as water*. Arab. marakv, *a lake*. In some parts of Africa, marigots, *a marsh*. *O. Sax.* mars, merse, mere, *a lake*.

† It will be noticed that the Icelandic and the Gaelic forms are almost identical.

land nor sea") has succeeded *mare, meer, mor* or *muir, &c.*—the ocean itself. Therefore, if the word *mor* and its variations was primarily the sea and gave its name to a nation of sea-rovers, or if the case were reversed and the sea became associated with the name of a great sea-faring race, then a wider vista opens out before us. There has been much written about *Meer-minnen* and other "water-people,"* and the subject is usually treated mythologically, although capable, I venture to think, of being interpreted realistically. This view of the origin of *Maurus* must, however, be disregarded here, and our attention turned more directly to the dwellers among the moors and marshes. Whether they gave their name to these places, or were so styled because they inhabited them,—they were at any rate known as Moors. That is to say, this became the general pronunciation given to the word. The original root seems likelier to have been *mor*, as seen in Cornish, Armorican, and other languages. Jamieson, in his Scottish Dictionary, says of the word *moriave*, defined by him as "black, swarthy, resembling a *Moor*,"—"This word has certainly been used in Old English, as Cotgrave gives it as the sense of Fr. *more*, id. It is probably a contraction of Lat. *Mauritanus*, a moor." (It would, perhaps, be more correct to say that Lat. *Mauritanus* and *Maurus* are extensions of *Mor*.) He also connects this word with the *morion* that formed the head-piece of the mediæval man-at-arms. Another English word from this root is *murrey*, meaning dark red, or copper-colour.

The country of Moravia is said to receive its name from its chief river the Morava, March, or anciently Marus, and its first known inhabitants are stated to have been a people named Quadi, who emigrated in the fifth century to Gaul and Hispania. "The river Morava" is tautology; for *morava* is *Mor River*, whether *ava* be regarded as Celtic, or Gothic, or a language older than either. It is not unreasonable to conjecture that the "Quadi" who went into France and Spain may have borne this name "Mor," the other having been given to them by outsiders, or *vice versâ*. They seem to have been known to the Romans, against whom

---

* For example, in the *Contemporary Review*, 1881, in a series of essays by Karl Blind.

they fought, by the first of these names. Lempriere gives several nations bearing names beginning with *Mor:*—the Morei or Morienses in India, and the Moruni in that country also, and the Morini, a people of Belgic Gaul, on the shores of the British Ocean, are examples. The Mauri* of Mauritania are perhaps the most notable examples of a nation bearing this name, though in a slightly altered shape.

The consideration of this word, and of the localization of races thus named, is not irrelevant at this point. For although it may not be easy to trace their route hither, and the date of their arrival, a branch of this family did inhabit Britain, and are not only known as *Mauri* and *Moors*, but also as *Moravienses, Morienses* (identical with the name of those in India), *Murray-men*, and people of *Moray* or *Moravia*. This name *Moravia* was given to two districts in Scotland, one (the most important) in the north-central, and the other in the southern portion of the country. That the Picts, known to the Romans as Mauri, were finally divided into two sections inhabiting these localities, is a speaking fact which it is well to remember at this juncture. The smaller district in the south has been the name-father of a family distinguished in Scottish history, the Murrays of Philiphaugh in Selkirkshire, whose ancestor, Archibald de Moravia, was among those who subscribed the oath of fealty to Edward I. of England, in 1296. One of the estates of this clan bore the significant name of the Black Barony. Of course, the race of Archibald de Moravia may have been that of an intruding army, and not necessarily that of the Moravienses, as he was simply Archibald [lord] of Moravia. "Sir Charles a Murrè" who fought at Chevy Chase, of the same clan, shows the name in its modern form, or approximately.† But the principal territory of the Moravienses was,

---

* I see that Lempriere states their name to have been derived, "according to some authors, from their black complexion." This raises the question again as to what is the origin and primary meaning of the word.

† It is likely enough that this south-country family received their name in the same way as the Murrays of Tullibardine; whose ancestor, Freskine, is conjectured by Sir Robert Douglas (quoted by Burke) to have acquired from David I. "some of the most fertile districts in the lowlands of Moray" as a reward for his exertions in helping to quell an insurrection of the Moraymen in 1130. This lord *de Moravia* was of a different race from the people he fought against, being described as "a Flemish settler."

according to Mr. Skene, a large district of which Loch Ness was about the centre, the name of which he spells "Moravia" or "Moray."

These northern Morienses were a wild and turbulent race, and some septs of them are remembered as "the Moray rebels," having been apparently in almost constant rebellion during the tenth, eleventh, and twelfth centuries, although others of them proved loyal to the Celtic kings. They appear to have been finally subdued by Malcolm IV. in the year 1160. Before that time they were, as I have said, in a chronic state of rebellion. Malcolm MacDonald (more correctly Maelcolam, son of Domnall) king of Alban, was killed by them in the year 954 while endeavouring to quell them, then in revolt. The learned historian of Celtic Scotland says: "The Pictish Chronicle tells us that the men of Moerne slew him at Fodresach, now Fetteresso, in the parish of Fordun, Kincardineshire; but the later chronicles remove the scene of his death farther north, and state that he was slain at Ulurn by the Moravienses, or people of Moray. St. Berchan, however, places it with the Pictish Chronicle in the parish of Fordun, when he says—

> Nine years to his reign,
> Traversing the borders.
> On the brink of Dun Fother at last
> Will shout the Gael around his grave."

From this apparent confusion between the "men of Moerne" and the "Moravienses," it may be conjectured that they were one and the same people. The two names given to the scene of Malcolm's death may also refer to the same place. In 1130, there was a great rising of the Morienses, under their Mormaer, or Earl, Angus, who entered Scotia (at that period only the eastern portion of central and southern Scotland) with five thousand men "with the intention of reducing the whole kingdom to subjection." (The king of Scotia was then David I., son of Malcolm Ceannmor and Margaret, sister of Edgar Atheling, and he was also Earl of Northamptonshire "and had them both together, the kingdom of Scotland and the earldom in England," being, says Mr. Skene, the "first feudal Monarch" of Scotland.) "'Upon this Edward, the son of Siward, earl of Mercia in the time of King Edward, who was a cousin of King David and commander of his army, assembled troops and suddenly threw himself in the enemy's way. A battle was at length fought, in which Earl Angus was slain and his troops defeated, taken prisoners, or put to flight. Vigorously pursuing the fugitives with his soldiers elated with victory, and entering Morafia, or Moray, now deprived of its lord and protector, he obtained, by God's help, possession of the whole of that large territory.'" This engagement is thus recorded in the Ulster Annals, "Battle between the men of Alban and the men of Moray, in which fell four thousand of the men of Moray, with their king Oengus, son of the daughter of Lulag, a thousand also of the men of Alban in heat of battle."* Mr. Skene adds that in a eulogium of the day, King David is styled "that invincible king, who had subdued unto himself so many barbarous nations, and had, without great trouble, triumphed over the men of Moray and the islands;" and at the same period the natives of the Isle of Man, then under Norwegian rule, are spoken of as "the barbarous natives." (I mention this to show how the one race looked upon the other,—or the others.)

Some of the conquered Moraymen seem to have fought under King David's banner, as "Muravenses," a few years after this, but there were others of them still unsubdued in spirit. As previously stated, they rose against Malcolm IV. in the year 1160. This young king, though only twenty years of age, had during that year thrice invaded Galloway, finally conquering its inhabitants, who were Picts, and also the mixed race known as Gallgaidhel. He then turned his arms against the people of the north and invaded their country of Moravia. Indeed, it would scarcely appear that in this instance they could be termed "rebels," for it was more an act of aggression on the part of the king, with the aim of crushing all resistance out of them, which he succeded in doing. He then, to prevent any future trouble, "'removed them all from the land of their birth, and scattered them throughout the other districts of Scotland, both beyond the hills and on this side thereof, so that not

---

* Quoted in "Celtic Scotland," Vol. I. p. 462,—from which also (pp. 457-461) the preceding sentences have been taken.

even a native of that land abode there, and he installed therein his own peaceful people.'"* From this date, therefore, the Scottish Moravia became the home of another race than that which bestowed its name upon it, as the Austrian Moravia had done many centuries before.

But it remained a "debatable land" for a long time after its evacuation by the Moray-men. Whether there still remained an infusion of the native blood among the people of the lower ranks, or whether King Malcolm's "own peaceful people" were not very peaceful after all, the inhabitants of this province seem to have been regarded as Ishmaelites long after 1160. In Pennant's Tour in Scotland this fact crops out. He speaks of "a letter from Sir Ewin Cameron to a chief in the neighbourhood of the county of Murray, wherein he regrets the mischief that had happened between their people (many having been killed on both sides), as his clan had no intention of falling on the Grants when it left Lochaber, but only (!) to make an incursion into Murray-land, where every man was free to take his prey. This strange notion (adds Pennant) seems to have arisen from the country having been for so many ages a Pictish country, and after that under the dominion of the Danes, and during both periods in a state of perpetual warfare with the Scots and western Highlanders."

It has been seen that one of the modern forms of this word is "Moray" or "Murray."† Another form is "Morris," existing now as a surname, and remembered as associated with the morris-dance, common enough in this country during the middle ages, and still practised, I believe, by English country-folk. "Its origin is ascribed to the Moors, though the genuine Moorish dance (the *fandango* of the present day) bears little resemblance to it. The chief performer was the *hobby-horse*, so called from the light frame of wickerwork which was fastened round his body, and supplied with a pasteboard head and neck, so as to give him the appearance of a man on horseback. Bells were also attached to

---

* "Celtic Scotland," Vol. I. p. 472.

† And it is surely more than a coincidence that among an antipodean family of Australioids (those of Queensland) a "blackfellow" is a "murray." (*Journal of the Anthropological Institute*, Vol. III. No. II. pp. 262-4.)

his ankles, and the great art consisted in so moving the feet as to produce a rude kind of concord. The other principal actors, after a rude fashion, personified the characters of Maid Marian, the Queen of the May, Robin Hood, Friar Tuck, the Fool, &c.; and the performance was accompanied by rude music, and the clashing of swords and staves, and was the chief amusement at parochial festivals."* In its original form, it appears also to have been danced with wild leaps and bounds, more in keeping with the orgies round the earliest May-poles, than with the innocent revels of modern English rustics. This dance, then, which "bears little resemblance" to that of the mixed nation now called Moors, is one of the ancient dances of this country. Sir Walter Scott has this to say regarding it:—"Considerable diversity of opinion exists respecting the introduction of the Morrice-dance into Britain. The name points it out as of Moorish origin; and so popular has this leaping kind of dancing for many centuries been in this country, that when Handel was asked to point out the peculiar taste in dancing and music of the several nations of Europe—to the French he ascribed the minuet; to the Spaniard, the saraband; to the Italian, the arietta; to the English, the hornpipe, or Morrice-dance."† So that it was actually regarded as the *national* dance of our country! England has never been invaded from Morocco during historic times,—nor even is this dance the property of the people of Morocco. It is peculiarly British. And yet "of Moorish origin?" Yes,—but the date of its introduction into Britain by the Moors was the date of the landing of the Pictish people, whensoever that may have been.

Our language still retains the memory of their presence, under this name. In Shakspeare's time the audience at the Globe accepted the word as meaning "a black man," and either then, or later on, it became tautologically extended into "blackamoor." The common people of the country are not likely to have known much about ultra-British "Moors,"—not enough at any rate, to have made the word an everyday term for a black man. Nor can the Moors of heraldry be explained sufficiently by the theory that the founders of families bearing Moors as supporters, and Moors' heads as

* "Chambers's Encyclopædia." † "Fair Maid of Perth," Note S.

crests, had won their spurs in assisting the Spaniards to expel *their* Moors. The bearing is too common among ancient coats to admit of this explanation. And the heraldic representation of a "Moor or Negro-man" does not suggest Granada. The features are ugly and irregular, and the hair, though longer than that of a pure negro, is woolly. The head is encircled by a fillet or chaplet, and there are "pearls pendant" from the ears. The complexion is, of course, black. Such men are indifferently styled "Moors" and "Saracens." Their presence in the armorial bearings of ancient families can only be due to the cause which made "savages," "wild-men," or "wood-men" so common among the supporters of old North-European and especially Scottish shields,—the exploits of the founder of the family in the long conflicts with the people of "Heathenesse."

There is yet another form in which this name of Moor or Mor has reached us, and it is found in Galloway, a province in which the Picts remained until almost recent times, being known as Picts, and speaking their language, so lately as the reign of Queen Mary. In this district the word is "Morrow." And there is a tradition of the presence of one of this race living in some part of Galloway, at an uncertain period, which has been preserved by McTaggart, in his *Gallovidian Encyclopedia*. This straggling specimen, probably one of the last of unmixed blood, does not impress us favourably, and if the others of his race were possessed of similar characteristics, it is easy to see why they were remorselessly hunted down. He is locally remembered as the "Black Morrow," which of course is Black Moor, Moray, or Murray. "Tradition has him a '*Blackimore*,'" says the yeoman-chronicler, "and says he haunted the forests south of Kirkcudbright; there he stopped during the day, sallying out on the neighbouring country at night, and committing horrible outrages. Also, that having found his retreat, which was beside a cool spring, in the dark forest, yet called the '*Blackimore's Wall*' [that is, *Well*], a barrel of spirits was brought by the people, and poured into the spring-well one night when he was out on his rambles. Next day, having drank of the fountain, as usual, he became touched with the grog, and fell asleep, snoring profoundly; his foes then rushed on him, like the

Philistines on Samson, and '*dirked his heart wi' mony a deadly hole.*'" Such is the story told in the beginning of this century by a Galloway farmer, and likely enough to be true in all its details, even to the "grogging" of the well. He does not say anything as to the date of the incident, but as he states that it has "baffled the antiquaries," it is probably many centuries old.

In Gaelic, "Black Morrow" becomes "Mor Dubh." This is the shape in which the name appears in the quaint letter of John Elder, the "Redshank" priest, to King Henry VIII., often quoted by Scottish antiquaries, and printed at length in the *Collectanea de Rebus Albanicis*. He brings it in in the following passage:—" Now, and pleas your excellent Maiestie, the said people which inhabited Scotland afoir the incummyng of the said Albanactus (as I have said), beinge valiant, stronge, and couragious, although they were savage and wilde, had strange names, as Morewhow i. Mordachus; &c." Mr. Skene spells it "Morrdhow;"* but either spelling will stand for *dubh*, which, in certain conjunctions, and in different accents, is pronounced *doo, hoo* (the *whow* of Elder), and *yew*. The black warrior of the West Highland tales, *Mordubh*, is plainly another of this race.

Scottish history (using the word "Scottish" in its widest sense) is full of suggestions of conflicts and eventually of

* *Murdoch* is the modern form. It is probable that in cases where the surname *Murray* was never written with the qualifying *de* before it, an actual descent from Moray-men or Moors is possessed by the bearer of it. The names *More, Mure, Muir, Moir*, and *Morison* have clearly arisen from a connection with the "Moor," but not necessarily one of kinship. Several families so named "carry three Moors' heads in their armorial bearings, as having some allusion to their name." It seems likely that these forms are variations of the Gaelic genitive of *Mor*, and really signify *de Moravia*. Obviously, the heads would be borne by conquerors, not descendants, of Moors. It is also stated in Anderson's " Scottish Nation " (whence the foregoing extract is taken) that the name More is derived from " the Gaelic *Mor*, big or large." In all modern instances this must certainly be the case, but, *at the first*, it must have been derived from the *Mor* people. That *the adjective itself* also came from that source is a theory quite defensible, as I shall endeavour to show in another place. Anderson further says: " In a note [to a history of one of these families] the editor, William Muir, says, 'The surname *More* certainly occurs very early in all the three British kingdoms, and is most probable of Celtic origin.'" Such names as Mor-ton, Mor-ham, More-battle, may have come from this word when it meant a people and not moorland. So also Morville, in Picardy. Picardy itself suggests the Piccardach (Picts), as does the old name for Poitiers—Pictavium.

alliances between black, brown, and white races. Mr. Skene includes the terms *ban* and *finn* (white), *ciar* and *dubh* (black), *dearg* and *ruadh* (red), *liath* (grey), *glas* (green [also *grey*]), *gorm* (blue), *breac* or *brit* (speckled), among "the names of the primary colours which enter into the composition both of names, persons, and places." To these may be added *donn*, brown—which word is indeed no other than *dun* and *tawny;* and also *buidhe*, yellow. Now, of these terms it has been shown that green and blue, so often interchangeable with black and brown, relate to the woad-stained, dark-skinned races. *Breac*, translated "spotted" or "speckled," will be glanced at presently. But of the remainder, two are of uncertain meaning. These are *ruadh* and *buidhe*, usually rendered "red" and "yellow," and usually, also, held to denote the colour of the hair. But where the hair is not specified, as it is in *Haarfagr*, it is a little unwarrantable to assume that the adjective does not refer to the complexion. It is obviously absurd to suppose that the distinguishing agnomens *green*, *blue*, and *speckled* have to do with the hair. Why, then, should the other? As a matter of fact, I find that one who knows Gaelic intimately, both as a spoken and as a written language, translates *ruadh* as *tawny* in at least one instance.*
That it is now generally held to signify *russet* or *red-haired*, seems without doubt. But when it was used to distinguish the Red Comyn from the Black Comyn, and the Red Douglas from the Black Douglas—the "black" in each case having reference to *complexion*—it seems quite likely that the "red" branches of those families were *ruadh*, or tawny, being, by admixture of white blood, less swarthy than their black kindred. So also with *buidhe*, yellow. When one finds that in a Gaelic poem of the eleventh century† the phrase, "Mac Donncha datha Dreach *bhui*," is translated "Son of Duncan of *the yellow countenance*," and that the same king is also styled "Mac Donncha Dreach *ruire*"—"the son of Duncan of the ruddy countenance"—it is evident that a yellow or copper-coloured face is intended, and that in this instance *buidhe* and *ruadh* are interchangeable terms for *tawny*. The same expression occurs in the Prophecy of St. Berchan,‡

---
* Campbell's "West Highland Tales," Vol. II. p. 282.
† "Collectanea de Rebus Albanicis," pp. 76, 77.
‡ Skene's "Chronicles of the Picts and Scots," pp. 88 and 93.

though with reference to another king, about whose individuality there is some confusion. But as he, too, was "drechbhuidhe," or "yellow-faced," and as his successor in the throne of Alban is stated to have laid waste the country of the "Gaidhela geala," or "fair Gael," it seems likely that these two kings represented a race inimical to the whites—a race of yellow-faced Mongoloids. Of the same race, too, was Malcolm, son of Donald, who reigned over Alban in the middle of the tenth century. For he is described as "the Bodhbhdearg," *the dangerous red man*, in the Prophecy of St. Berchan. And in none of the cases cited is there any reference intended to red or yellow *hair*, by the use of the terms *ruadh* and *buidhe*.

Such colour-agnomens as these are very common in early history, and they point clearly to an era when greatly-differing races were encountering each other,—now struggling for the mastery, and now peacefully intermarrying. For example, we see one of the black people—the Moors of the Romans—in the person of a King of Alban of the tenth century. History knows him sometimes as Kenneth, sometimes as Dubh, and sometimes as Niger. "The version of the Pictish Chronicle in the Irish Nennius calls him 'Cinæd vel Dubh,'" and St. Berchan styles him "Dubh of the three black divisions." "The Picts seem to have preserved a tradition that the whole nation was once divided into seven provinces," and it would appear that "the three black divisions" over which Dubh, or The Black, held sway, formed that portion of the original seven which still remained untouched by the white races; in short, the Pictish provinces. He seems to have been constantly at war with Cuilean, or Caniculus, "The Young Dog,"* who is called Fionn, or White, by St. Berchan; and eventually White succeeded in driving Black out of the country, and reigning in his stead for more than twenty years after. A son, however, of the dispossessed Kenneth, or Dubh, known too as Kenneth (mac Dubh), regained the kingship in the year 997, reigning until

* The celebrated Cuchullin, whose era is placed eight centuries before this, is stated by Dr. McLauchlan to have been spoken of as "An Cu," or *The Hound*, "Cuchullin" meaning simply *The Hound of Cullin*. (Dean of Lismore's Book, p. 59.) Both he and the above Caniculus were probably identified with the totem of their clan.

1004. He is termed "the Donn, or brown, from strong Duncath," and since *Donn* implies a lighter shade than *Dubh* —being in fact *dun* or *tawny*—it is probable that Kenneth, son of the Black, was of white blood on the mother's side. A somewhat different race-mixture is perhaps indicated in the case of Conadh *Cearr* (Black Kenneth), whose father—a Pictish king—bore the name of Eochadh *Buidhe*, or Yellow Hector. Another son of this king was Domnall *Breac*. This Domnall (Donald) Breac is said to have succeeded his brother, Swarthy Kenneth, as King of the Dalriads in the year 629, and, according to the Annals of Ulster, he was killed at the battle of Carron, near Falkirk, in the year 642. And the introduction of his name brings us now to the consideration of the epithet *breac*.*

It is generally rendered "spotted" or "speckled," and in its aspirated form, *bhreac* (pronounced *vreck*), it offers itself very reasonably as the father of the modern *freckle*. Many words have been formed from it in Gaelic, and when it is now applied to a man it has the significance of "pimply," or "marked with the small-pox." But its original meaning seems to be "chequered, spotted, carved, embroidered," and out of one of these meanings has come the word *breacair*, "a graving tool, an engraver." Now, when one bears this in mind, and remembers that the nick-name *breac* was applied to a seventh century Pict by (presumably) a non-Pictish people, does it not almost amount to a certainty that the word was used in its sense of "engraved" or "chequered," that it bore reference to the "punctured" bodies of the Picts, and that, in short, "Domnall Breac" is nothing else than "Tattooed Donald"? †

The scene of Donald's death is closely identified with his people. But it is only here appropriate to make reference to one name in that locality—Falkirk. The first syllable, *Fal*, *Faw*, or *Fah*, is held to be Anglo-Saxon, and to signify "speckled, spotted, of many colours," and the word Falkirk is generally translated *the Speckled Church*. The Gaelic

---

* See "Celtic Scotland," Vol. I. pp. 231, 242, 366-8, and 382, for the facts stated in this paragraph.

† "The term Breac (says Mr. Skene) is usually associated with those of Pictish race." ("Celtic Scotland," Vol. III. p. 277.)

name for the same place is *Eaglais bhreac*, and the meaning is of course the same. It is possible that a church or temple once stood there, of which the distinguishing feature was some peculiarity of carving or of colouring. But, situated as it was in a district peculiarly Pictish, it is more than likely that it received its name, not from any outward characteristic belonging to it, but because it was the temple of the *tattooed* people. This epithet *breac* occurs so frequently in the topography of Scotland, and in such varying conjunctions,—attached as it is to islands, lochs, mountains, and, in this instance, to a church,—that its meaning cannot be reasonably solved by the supposition that the church, loch, mountain, or island presented in itself a "speckled" appearance. There are, for example, two little mountain-lochans on either side of Loch Awe known as the lochans *nam Breac-Buidhe*, or the lochans *Bhreac-Buidhe;* that is, the lochans of the "speckled-yellow" people. Now, it may seem at first to be destructive of what has been said above to state that the "people" here indicated are not human beings at all, but simply the little finny "folk" that abound in such lochans.* In reality, however, this supports the above theory. For the name does *not* refer to the water of the loch, but to its inhabitants. Whether in these and similar instances the name was originally given on account of the trout may be doubted, however. For one of these lochs is on a spur of *Beinn Bhreac* the Speckled Mountain (and the district in which both are situated abounds in suggestive names). Let this be compared with the name of the loch upon Coomroe, the Red Mountain, in the South of Ireland. This name is more explicit. It is the Lake of the Red *Women.* So that if, on the Red Mountain, the loch is named after the Red *people*, is it not likely that the loch on the Speckled Mountain is, or was originally, named after the Speckled *people* who inhabited the district? Again, however anxious one might be to discover an animal, or a bird, that by its appearance might reasonably have caused the qualifying adjective "speckled" to be attached to the district which it inhabited, it is difficult to find any except the human animal

---

* I assume that this is the signification of the names of these two particular lochans: at least, some similar cases are so translated, whether rightly or not.

that will suit. Beinn Bhreac, Lochan Bhreac, Carsebreck, Inchbreac, Eaglais Bhreac,—all of these, when taken collectively, cannot reasonably be derived from any other source than from the people who dwelt among them. Thus, although it is right to remember that, in the case of certain lochs, the "yellow-speckled" folk are not men, but fish, it by no means follows that those lochs were *originally* named after the fish. Nothing is commoner than for a peasantry to invent an explanation of this or that local name, when its origin is lost in the darkness of a great antiquity. But the theory that this class of epithets has derived its existence from the fact that "breac" or tattooed people once dwelt in those places in which such names most abound—offers the simplest and most natural explanation of their meaning. And that this is really the right explanation will, I hope, be made clearer after a few chapters.

CHAPTER IV.

THE savages, wild-men, or wood-men of heraldry, sometimes represented as white men, sometimes as black, are almost always naked, with the exception of a wreath round the head, and another round the loins. That they became part of the cognizance of certain families in token of conquests over real savages is indisputable, one notable example being that of an ancestor of the present Duke of Athole who received his supporters, and other more substantial honours, for defeating the army of a Lord of the Isles. The Picts, it is known, went naked, regarding the tattooed skin itself, with its representation of the totem of the owner's clan and sept, as more honourable than clothing. So at any rate they appeared in war, though it seems that, like the ancient Hungarians and other branches of the Ugrian people, they at other times wore the skins of animals. But, as the term is conventionally understood, they were naked savages. The Wild Irishmen, or Black Irishmen, presumably of the same race, were the same. "*Those*, says *Strabo*, *that now-a-days make a survey of the different countries of the world, find nothing to relate of any country beyond* Ireland, *which lies to the north, and near* Britain, *and is inhabited by men entirely wild.*"* There may be some doubt as to the island here meant, but whether it is Ireland or Scotland, the remarks just made apply equally well. Ireland had its Cruithnigh as Scotland had its Picts. (So also had England and half of Europe, as already stated, but one must narrow the limits in order to follow the discussion rightly.) If Father Innes meant that Ireland was inhabited *solely* by "men entirely wild," he was, I fancy, mistaken. There is too much evidence to the contrary to admit of such a belief. But the

* Innes's "Critical Essay on the Ancient Inhabitants of Scotland," Vol. II. p. 429.

existence of a race of wild people is told by the Irish legends themselves.

Fionn, the "firm chief of the Feinn," blue-eyed, golden-haired, marble-skinned,—whose knightly attributes were dwelt on in the preceding chapter, had, as many people know, as the chiefest of his followers, the equally heroic Diarmaid. And in one of the many legends regarding them (one which bears a striking resemblance to the Arthurian romance), the figure of one of these wild men appears for an instant upon the stage.

The story of the Pursuit of Diarmaid and Grainne, although so familiar to Celtic scholars, is yet not so widely known as to render it necessary to apologize for sketching it here. They are known as "the Venus and Adonis of Gaelic mythology," and many are the versions of the story of their flight. Mr. Campbell characterizes it as "one phase of a myth which pervades half the world;" and so it is. But underneath its mythological surface there are unmistakeable traces of incidents in the lives of real people, which took place "once upon a time;" how long ago, or in what locality, one can only surmise. It seems pretty certain, however, that the North of Ireland, and Western, and (perhaps) Central Scotland, formed the theatre in which the scenes were enacted. And "about the third century" is regarded as the era.

Grainne, who is perplexingly styled at one time "the wisest as well as the handsomest of women," and at another, as she who "never took a step aright," was the daughter of *Carmaig of Steeds, the King of the fifth of Ullin*. The hero Fionn, chief of the Feinne, who had vowed not to marry any lady but the one who could answer all his enigmatical questions,[*] found that lady in her, and wedded her. But their honeymoon was brief. For, after the great wedding-feast, which lasted seven days and seven nights, and at which were gathered all "the nobles and great gentles of the Feinne," there was made the feast for the hounds, and over

---

[*] Some of those "questions" and their answers are well worth repeating:— "What is sharper than a sword?" "*The reproach of a foe.*" "What is swifter than the wind?" "*A woman's thought betwixt two men.*" "What deed is the best of deeds?" "*A high deed and low conceit.*" "What is softer than down?" "*The palm on the cheek.*" "What is whiter than the snow?" "*There is the truth.*" "What is blacker than the raven?" "*There is death.*"

it, as dogs will, they fell out. And among those who parted them was Diarmaid. Now Diarmaid, handsome enough otherwise, bore on his forehead a love-spot which no woman could look upon and remain heart-whole. He, knowing this, and being a gentleman, used to hide the mark with his cap; but on this fatal day, his exertions in driving out the hounds displaced the cap, and Grainne looked, saw, and was lost. She does not appear to have beaten about the bush, or indeed to have been troubled with any qualms of conscience. She frankly told him of the state of affairs, and unhesitatingly concluded with :—"*Thou shalt run away with me.*" His answer was emphatic. "'*I will not do that,*' said Diarmaid." And, on her insisting further, he spoke with even greater distinctness. "'*I will not go with thee; I will not take thee in softness, and I will not take thee in hardness; I will not take thee without, and I will not take thee within; I will not take thee on horseback, and I will not take thee on foot,*' said he; and he went away in displeasure, and he went to a place apart, and he put up a house there, and he took his dwelling in it." But Grainne wasn't going to be baffled so easily, and one morning soon after this, Diarmaid heard her voice at his doorway, crying, "*Art thou within, Diarmaid?*" He, to silence her once for all, reminded her of what he had previously said, repeating the words again, for the sake of emphasis. But her ladyship had been too sharp for him. "She was between the two sides of the door, on a buck goat. '*I am not without, I am not within, I am not on foot, and I am not on a horse; and thou must go with me,*' said she."*

Diarmaid evidently realized that he would have no peace here, and besides, that Fionn would soon be on the track of his runaway wife, and not likely in a humour for listening to an explanation from her apparent partner in guilt, so he started off again, Grainne following. They travelled on and on, this better Lancelot and more shameless Guinevere, and never rested till they reached Cantire, in Scotland (so one account says), where Diarmaid decided to take up his abode. The very place is named, "Carraig an Daimh in Ceantire," a cavern by the sea-shore. Here, as on the journey, Diarmaid

---

* Mr. Campbell compares this incident with a similar one in the German story of "Die Kluge Bauerntochter."

kept his pursuer at arm's length, dutifully supplying her, however, with a share of the spoils of his hunting and fishing.

The various versions differ a good deal as to the incidents and localities at this portion of the tale, but they agree in bringing upon the stage another victim of Grainne's wayward fancy. This was a *ciuthach* (Mr. Campbell informs us that the word is pronounced *kewach*, and that the people so named are "described in the Long Island as naked wild men living in caves." He adds that the word is "supposed to be derived from 'CIUTH, long hair behind,' which word is applied in Islay to a pigtail. French, *queue*.") He appears to have wandered by the way of the cave, or weem, in which Diarmaid and, much to his vexation, Grainne were living, and to have been entertained by them at first in a friendly way, for it is stated they played with him at "wedges," or dice. How long the savage dwelt with or near them is not specified, but it was probably not more than a few days after his arrival that Grainne, having wearied of her fruitless, one-sided attachment for Diarmaid, and having wholly transferred her affections to the new comer (who fully sympathized with her views), arranged that her second love should slaughter the first, now become highly inconvenient. There was a sudden deadly struggle, and then Diarmaid, flinging off his assailant, sent his spear home into his naked bosom.

Of the subsequent events of their history, of their discovery by Fionn and his men, and of the way in which Fionn, believing Diarmaid guilty, brought about his death, it is not necessary here to speak. There is a vein of pathos running through the thing. For Fionn was loath to lose his favourite warrior, or to be himself the cause of his death. But he steeled his heart against him. There is a striking scene, sketched by Mr. Campbell, of the last moments of the hero.

. . . .

"Fionn took sorrow for him when he fell. '*What would make thee better, Diarmaid?*'

'*If I could get a draught of water from the palms of Fionn, I would be better.*'"

(These are the words of the narrator. The translator adds—)

"I well remember to have heard how Fionn held his palms to Diarmaid filled with water from a spring which is still shown, and how a draught from the hollow palms would have healed the dying warrior; but Fionn thought on Grainne, and opened his hands and let the water drain away, as he held his hands to Diarmaid's mouth, and Diarmaid died."

. . . .

And then—when it was too late—Fionn learned his grievous error. For, "when Diarmaid gave out the shout of death," the chief, turning to his faithless wife, asked bitterly:—

"*Is that the hardest shriek to thy mind that thou hast ever heard?*"

And she answered him:—"*It is not; but the shriek of the ciuthach, when Diarmaid killed him.*"

. . . .

Here then we have a glimpse of those men "entirely wild," of whom Strabo wrote, and tradition makes them out to be cave-dwellers. It does more. It calls them by a name which signifies "the wearer of a queue." Now, however different such men may have been from the courtly gentlemen who sported pigtails in this country a century ago, it must be remembered that this mode of dressing the hair is a distinctly Mongoloid custom, practised to-day by Chinese, North American Indians, and the tribes of Northern Asia, and Europe. I do not stamp this man as a queue-wearer, simply because of the Islay rendering of *ciuth*, although the traditional meaning seems deserving of all respect, and the word itself is likely akin to *queue*. But, in another version of the story, in which he is less romantically styled "a great sprawling old man," he is called by the narrator "*Ciofach Mac a Ghoill.*" This word *ciofach* will be admitted by anyone who knows Gaelic, as identical with *giobag*,[*] or *giofag*, a gipsy; and these again are virtually the same as *ciabh*, "a side-lock of hair, a ringlet," *ciabhach*, "hairy, bushy, having much hair, having ringlets," and *ciabhagach*, "bushy, having

---

[*] I take this word from Armstrong; and it may be mentioned here that all the Gaelic words introduced throughout this book will be found in one or other of these three dictionaries—Armstrong's, McLeod and Dewar's, and Macalpine's.

curls, ringlets, locks, or whiskers." *Goill*, again, which is the genitive singular and nominative plural of *gall*, a foreigner, means also "a hanging lip, a shapeless mouth, an angry or sullen look, a blubber cheek," while *goilleach*, derived from it, signifies "sulky, blubber-lipped or cheeked, having a swollen or distorted face," and *goillear* (*goill* and *fear*, a man) is "a blubber-lipped person." So that this "wearer of a queue" is also known as "the one with the ringlets, or locks, a scion of the blubber-lipped foreigner." This inelegant adjective (about which I shall have more to say in another place) is a very important one, for it describes exactly the "remarkably coarse and flexible lips" ascribed by Professor Huxley to the Ancient Egyptians (from whom *gipsies*, or *giofags*, claim to be descended, as do also some Scottish races, according to tradition), to the natives of the Dekhan, and to the Australians, all of whom he states to be of the same stock as the "maternal ancestors" of the *Melanochroi* of the British Islands. The connection between "bushy hair" and "ringlets" would seem to indicate something like the luxuriant and carefully curled hair of the ancient Egyptian statues.

But the pigtail, it was said, seemed to figure a Mongoloid, and not an Australioid? I do not pretend to do more than suggest,—and since both races have inhabited these islands, there is some excuse for supposing that they mingled. At any rate the wearing of the hair in long plaits, sometimes in a single queue hanging down the back, as among the Chinese, sometimes in two "tails," one on either side of the face, as among the American Indians and the Siberian Chukches, is one of the oldest known fashions in this country.

In the meantime, let us look more at the "wildness" of those tribes, chiefly as shown in their want of clothing, or their habit of not regarding clothing of any kind as a necessity, to put it otherwise. The heraldic savages, and the historical Picts, wore little or none. The historian Buchanan quotes this further information from the description of Solinus:—*" It [Ireland] is inhospitable on account of the cruel customs of its inhabitants; ... the natives are savage

---

* Buchanan's "History of Scotland," edited by Aikman, Glasgow and Edinburgh, p. 140.

and warlike. After battle, the victors stain their faces with the blood of their slaughtered enemies.* They make no distinction between right and wrong.... Those who study elegance, ornament the hilts of their swords with the teeth of sea-calves, which they polish as white as ivory, for the principal glory of the men consists in the brilliance of their armour." And from Herodian, he quotes:†—" In the first place, however, he [Severus] took care to cover the marshes with bridges, that his soldiers might stand securely, and fight on solid ground; for many places in Britain, are rendered swampy by the frequent inundations of the ocean; and through these marshes, the barbarians themselves swim or wade, sunk to the bellies in mud, and frequently naked, regardless of the slime, for they are ignorant of the use of clothes, but encircle their belly and neck with iron, thinking this an ornament, and a proof of riches, in the same manner as gold is with other barbarians; besides they mark their bodies with various pictures, and the forms of a variety of animals, on which account, they do not clothe themselves, lest they should cover the painting of their bodies; but they are a most warlike race, and rejoice in slaughter. Their arms consist of a narrow shield and lance, with a sword hanging by their naked bodies. They are almost entirely unacquainted with the use of a coat of mail, or a helmet, thinking these impediments in passing through the marshes, always covered with vapours, and dark with exhalations [the " blubber" described by Pytheas]."

These sketches are the presentment of what, in all conscience, is a savage people. The Mæatæ or marsh-folk against whom Severus fought, were Caledonii, nick-named Picti, known as Moors or black men, of the race of Damnonii who had curly hair (which may mean *ciabhagach*) and swarthy skins, which they tattooed with their family totems, —they wore nothing except their weapons, like Zulus or any other dark-skinned savages,—they smeared their faces with the blood of their foes,—if they, the Damnonii, were not

---

* The custom still survives in the Highlands, only the " slaughtered enemy" is a deer.

† Buchanan's " History"; Aikman's translation, pp. 141, 142.

cannibals, their nearest neighbours were ;—is not the whole picture one of the most utter savagery?

It is interesting to notice how long some of the habits, recorded by Herodian, have survived. Scott, in a note appended to *Rokeby*, regarding the lines——

> " Hiding his face, lest foeman spy
> The sparkle of his swarthy eye,"—

gives the following anecdote:—"After one of the recent battles, in which the Irish rebels were defeated, one of their most active leaders was found in a bog, in which he was immersed up to the shoulders, while his head was concealed by an impending ledge of turf. Being detected and seized, notwithstanding his precaution, he became solicitous to know how his retreat had been discovered. 'I caught,' answered the Sutherland Highlander, by whom he was taken, 'the sparkle of your eye.'" Here, therefore, is an example of the ancestral mode of warfare, or an incidental feature of it, practised fifteen hundred years after Severus. And the *dress* of Scott's rebel may also have been the same as that of his remote ancestor, excepting the ornaments. Spenser talks of "the naked rebels," and the only article of clothing he allows them is a "mantle," or plaid, which seems to have resembled the blanket of an Indian more than anything else; and while useful for sleeping in, or for wearing in ordinary circumstances, must necessarily have been cast aside as an encumbrance, during an engagement, leaving the warrior absolutely nude.

But the descriptions in the *Rokeby* notes are so interesting, and so illustrative of this subject, that it may perhaps be allowable to make several considerable extracts from them. The next picture is of the time of Queen Elizabeth, and it portrays the "karne," or commonalty, of at least one district of Ireland, about that period. The following quaint verses are quoted by Scott from Derrick's *Image of Ireland*.*

* * * * * *

> " With writhed glibbes, like wicked sprits,
> with visage rough and stearne;
> With sculles upon their poalles,
> instead of civil cappes;

* Note 2 R.

> With speares in hand and swordes besydes,
>   to bear off after clappes;
> With jackettes long and large,
>   which shroud simplicitie,
> Though spitfull darts which they do beare
>   importe iniquitie.
> Their shirtes be very strange,
>   not reaching past the thie;
> With pleates on pleates thei pleated are
>   as thick as pleates may lye.
> Whose sleaves hang trailing doune
>   almost unto the shoe;
> And with a mantell commonlie
>   the Irish Karne do goe.
> Now some amongst the reste
>   doe use another weede;
> A coate I meane, of strange deviss,
>   which fancy first did breade.
> His skirts be very shorte,
>   with pleates set thick about,
> And Irish trouzes moe to put
>   their strange protactours out."

Scott adds:—" Some curious wooden engravings accompany this poem, from which it would seem that the ancient Irish dress was (the bonnet excepted) very similar to that of the Scottish Highlanders.* The want of a covering on the head was supplied by the mode of plaiting and arranging the hair, which was called the *glibbe*. These glibbes, according to Spenser, were fit marks for a thief, since, when he wished to disguise himself, he could either cut it off entirely, or so pull it over his eyes as to render it very hard to recognize him. This, however, is nothing to the reprobation with which the same poet regards that favourite part of the Irish dress, the mantle.

"'It is a fit house for an outlaw, a meet bed for a rebel, and an apt cloke for a thief. First, the outlaw being for his many crimes and villanyes banished from the townes and houses of honest men, and wandring in waste places far from

---

* Probably one of the figures in a woodcut reproduced in the "West Highland Tales" (Vol. IV. p. 373), representing the Irishmen who fought in the German army during the Thirty Years' War, gives the same fashion of wearing the plaid as that referred to by Sir Walter Scott. This man has apparently nothing but his plaid, which is wrapped round him, and a bonnet covering his head.

danger of law, maketh his mantle his house, and under it covereth himself from the wrath of heaven, from the offence of the earth, and from the sight of men. When it raineth, it is his pent-house; when it bloweth, it is his tent; when it freezeth, it is his tabernacle. In summer he can wear it loose, in winter he can wrap it close; at all times he can use it; never heavy, never cumbersome. Likewise for a rebel it is as serviceable; for in his warre that he maketh, (if at least it deserve the name of warre,) when he still flyeth from his foe, and lurketh in the thicke woods and straite passages, waiting for advantages, it is his bed, yea, and almost his houschold stuff. For the wood is his house against all weathers, and his mantle is his couch to sleep in. Therein he wrappeth himself round, and coucheth himself strongly against the gnats, which, in that country doe more annoy the naked rebels while they keep the woods, and doe more sharply wound them, than all their enemies' swords or speares, which can seldom come nigh them: yea, and oftentimes their mantle serveth them when they are neere driven, being wrapped about their left arme, instead of a target, for it is hard to cut thorough with a sword; besides, it is light to beare, light to throw away, and being (as they commonly are) naked, it is to them all in all. Lastly, for a thiefe it is so handsome as it may seem it was first invented for him; for under it he may cleanly convey any fit pillage that cometh handsomely in his way, and when he goeth abroad in the night in freebooting, it is his best and surest friend; for lying, as they often do, two or three nights together abroad to watch for their booty, with that they can prettily shroud themselves under a bush or bankside till they may conveniently do their errand; and when all is over, he can in his mantle passe through any towne or company, being close hooded over his head, as he useth, from knowledge of any to whom he is indangered. Besides this, he or any man els that is disposed to mischief or villany, may, under his mantle, goe privily armed without suspicion of any, carry his head-piece, his skean, or pistol, if he please, to be always in readiness.'—SPENSER'S *View of the State of Ireland*, apud *Works*, ut supra, viii. 367.

" 'The javelins, or darts, of the Irish, which they threw with great dexterity, appear, from one of the prints already mentioned, to have been about four feet long, with a strong steel head and thick knotted shaft."

It is thus apparent that, with the exception of his "mantle" or plaid, which he and his Scottish kinsman seems to have used much in the same way as a Red Indian uses his blanket,—the Irishman of low rank three centuries ago was actually a naked man. Not, of course, *all* Irishmen, nor even, as Derrick's lines have just shown, all Irishmen of the "baser sort;"—but a large number, possibly of a perfectly different tribe from the two varieties pictured by Derrick, were "commonly" unclothed, or, if clothed, only by their plaid, which was to them "all in all." It must be remembered that the plaid of these Highland and Irish tribes was originally a very different thing from what it now is. It was one large mantle, wrapped round the otherwise uncovered body, and generally belted round the waist. The kilt, as now worn, did not exist.

Before crossing the Irish Channel, to look again into the question of the Scotch dress, which in some cases was identical with the Irish, I shall make another extract regarding the latter. As in it there is no reference to the fashion of *glibbing* the hair, spoken of by Derrick, and which was so much of a national custom that it had to be put down by law, it may be well to point out that this again is a Mongolian usage, and that this mass of thickly-plaited hair, so luxuriant that it served for a covering, hints strongly at the wearer's descent from those *ciuthachs* of a thousand years before.

From the same source (*Rokeby*) we get a picture of the customs of the nobles,—and this at a much earlier period,— two centuries earlier. Speaking of the bards or poets attached to the person of the chief, Scott says[*]:—"The household minstrel was admitted even to the feast of the prince whom he served, and sat at the same table. It was one of the customs of which Sir Richard Sewry, to whose charge Richard II. committed the instruction of four Irish monarchs in the civilization of the period, found it most difficult to break his royal disciples, though he had also much

---

[*] "Rokeby," Note 3 C.

ado to subject them to other English rules, and particularly to reconcile them to wear breeches. 'The Kyng, my souerevigne lord's entent was, that in maner, countenaunce, and apparel of clothying, they sholde use according to the maner of Englande, for the Kynge thought to make them all four Knyghtes: they had a fayre house to lodge in, in Duvelyn, and I was charged to abyde styll with them, and not to departe; and so two or three dayes I suffered them to do as they lyst, and sayde nothyng to them, but folowed their owne appetytes; they wolde sitte at the table, and make countenance nother good nor fayre. Than I thought I shulde cause them to chaunge that maner they woulde cause their mynstrells, their seruantes, and varlettes, to sytte with them, and to eate in their owne dyssche, and to drinke of their cuppes; and they shewed me that the usage of their cuntre was good, for they sayd in all thyngs (except their beddes) they were and lyved as co-men. So the fourthe day I ordayned other tables to be couered in the hall, after the usage of Englande, and I made these four knyghtes to sytte at the hyghe table, and there mynstrels at another borde, and their seruauntes and varlettes at another byneth them, wherof by semynge they were displeased, and beheld each other, and wolde not eate, and sayde, how I wolde take fro them their good usage, wherein they had been norished. Then I answered them, smylyng, to apeace them, that it was not honourable for their estates to do as they dyde before, and that they must leave it, and use the custom of Englande, and that it was the Kynge's pleasure they shulde so do, and how he was charged so to order them. When they harde that, they suffred it, bycause they had putte themselfe under the obesyance of the Kynge of England, and parceuered in the same as long as I was with them; yet they had one use which I knew was well used in their cuntre, and that was, they dyde were no breches; I caused breches of lynen clothe to be made for them. Whyle I was with them I caused them to leaue many rude thynges, as well in clothyng as in other causes. Moche ado I had at the fyrst to cause them to weare gownes of sylke, furred with myneure and gray; for before these kynges thought themselfe well apparelled whan they had on a mantell. They rode alwayes without saddles and styropes, and with great payne I made them to ride after our usage.'—LORD BERNERS' *Froissart*. Lond. 1812, 4to. vol. ii. p. 621."

What can one compare this with, but such a scene as is every now and then enacted, when a British officer or governor gives lessons in "deportment" (of the Modern British order) to a conquered Zulu King, or a Maori chief? Those Irish "monarchs" of four or five centuries back differed in no essential degree from the kind of men now called "savage" and "uncivilized." They rode their horses barebacked, themselves in a like condition, like the wildest Indians on the Plains. They had so little respect for clothing that they "dyde were no breches" and "thought themselfe well apparelled whan they had on a mantell." These are facts. It may well be disputed whether multiplicity of garments signifies increased refinement, or whether those naked men of five hundred years ago had not as high a conception of "honour," "bravery," and "brotherly love" as many a muffled-up specimen of modern humanity. They certainly could not have had among them any men of coarser calibre than a modern British "rough." If such differences mark "civilization" and "savagery" those men were savages. But so far as Sir Richard Sewry's evidence goes, this particular tribe or race was a vast improvement on some of those which preceded it.

At any rate, their fashions were those of what, rightly or wrongly, we call uncivilized people, whatever their natures were. It may be that even their predecessors of a thousand years before were not so savage altogether as some of the chroniclers make out. An enemy doesn't see the amiable side of one's character, and if they did some very fierce things, perhaps they did nothing much more barbarous than the blowing away of helpless captives from the cannon's mouth. And even the Irish of Solinus, who "made no distinction between right and wrong," might be matched in the present century without going very far from home.

However, these are points which may be decided according to preference. The fact remains that in outward seeming, all of the races glanced at in this chapter were "savages."

Nineteenth-Century "Survivals." 75

And it may be remarked, before leaving Ireland, that distinct traces of this savage and Mongoloid element exist in that island to-day, not only visible in deeds of bloodshed and cowardly murder, but also in less serious acts. I make a few extracts from the newspapers, chronicling incidents of a kind with which we have been lately too familiar. "Cork, Monday.—Another fatal affray has occurred in the south. A large party of men, disguised and armed, visited several farmers' houses in the district of Firess and Farranfore, near Tralee, on Sunday morning, and compelled the men to swear that they would pay no rents until Parnell was liberated. In some instances they assaulted the owners of the houses, and cut off their whiskers . . . . . The police state that they traced the raiders to Riordan's house, heard them cry out 'Boo,' and, seeing a flash of light, though they heard no report of firearms, they discharged two volleys." "Farther particulars respecting the arrest of Connell have been received here. . . Among the documents found in his possession is one containing a list of intended outrages on a number of persons, whose names, with their punishments, are given—one man, for paying rent, to be shot; another for a less aggravated offence, to have his ears cut off; a young woman, for having spoken to a policeman, was 'to have her hair cut to the bone.'" Another account, giving the particulars of the examination of the "Moonlight" raiders, states—"The evidence showed that on the night of the 7th December the house of Mrs. Fitzgerald, at the foot of Mushra Mountain, was broken into by a number of armed men. Mrs. Fitzgerald was struck with a gun, and an attempt was made to cut the hair off the head of one of her daughters. A man named McCarthy, a labourer, had his moustache cut off. . . . The informer . . . stated that . . . on the night of the outrage, 7th December, the party met at the Twohigs' house. . . . There were eleven persons altogether. The two prisoners were there. There were over a dozen hats, in which were holes for plumes, and they had foxes' tails for whiskers. . . . Another order read as follows :—'Regimental order by Captain Moonlight for appointed raids on 30th of 12th 1881. James Sullivan to be shot in legs, and his mother and daughter clipped for dealing with the Hegarty's. John Lineham, story telling, to be clipped," &c. &c.

These extracts are the records of an outburst of utter barbarism, and it is difficult to believe that the events took place within the British Islands in the year 1881. It is quite apparent that to the perpetrators of these acts, the cutting off of the hair meant an extreme degradation, and seemed to them as serious a deed (however puerile and grotesque in our eyes) as shooting a man in the legs. Mr. J. F. Campbell refers to the same idea when he says of a certain Gaelic phrase* that it " is explained to mean clipping the hair and beard off one side of the head," and that " the punishment was probably inflicted at some period, for the phrase occurs several times in Gaelic tales." The motive is identical with that which made the Huns shave their heads as a sign of abasement at the death of their king, and which makes the Chinaman resent so deeply the cutting-off of his queue ;— and it marks a race-connection most distinctly. The " holes for plumes " cut in the hats of the raiders is another clear "survival," and must date at least as far back as the naked horsemen of Richard the Second's time, and the " sculles " " instead of civil cappes " described by Derrick. And the cry of " Boo," which the police knew as a sign of battle, is yet another evidence, traceable farther back than the others (but all are equally stamped with the mark of a great antiquity). For this word " Boo " or " Bo," which survives in the larger island as a sound of terror to children, and also as an accompaniment of a " row " among noisy crowds, is really an ancient war-cry. It is usually spelt " Bu " in the Gaelic dictionaries, and usually defined "a sound to excite fear in children " (or some such phrase) but its original meaning is clearly seen where, under the form " Abu,"—which would be more correct if written " a-Bu " (the " a " being a mere preliminary breathing),—it is stated to have been " the war-cry of the ancient Irish." The words *Crom-a-Boo* (it has been pointed out to me since the above was written) form the motto attached to the armorial bearings of the Dukes of Leinster. The latter half of this legend

* "*Bearradh coin agus amadain.*" It is referred to in the " West Highland Tales," Vol. II. p. 474, and Vol. III. p. 205.

does not require explanation. With regard to the former, it may be stated that there was formerly a huge idol of gold, surrounded by twelve idols of stone "ornamented with brass," which stood in the "marsh" of Sleacht, in county Cavan, and which was "the god of all the people which possessed Erin till the coming of Padric." This central figure was known as the *Crom Cruach*, or the Red *Crom* ("while another idol .... in the western parts of Connacht was called '*Crom Dubh*,'" or the Black *Crom*). Thus, the cry of *Crom-a-Boo* would appear to belong to the same class as "*Allah!*" "*Saint George for Merry England!*" and others; being partly the invocation to a Deity and partly a tribal shout—and used in battle to intimidate the foe, as well as for mutual encouragement. The appropriation of such a motto indicates very clearly that the family using it is, to some extent, of Early-Irish origin. (For references to the *Crom Cruach*, see Dr. Angus Smith's "Loch Etive, &c.," pp. 241–2, and the second volume of *Celtic Scotland*, p. 112.) All these things combined, the naked, swarthy figures of the "wild Irishmen," their long and thickly-plaited hair, adorned (if to-day's custom has any meaning) with feathers, and sometimes covered with the human skull,—the angry, deep-bellowing war-cry,—all these make a picture of complete savagery, and argue a state of society, and a race, at no very remote period, closely resembling that which the early colonists found to exist on the other side of the Atlantic.

It was seen that the Scottish marsh-dwellers encountered by Severus, the black Damnonii or painted Moors, were, like the *ciuthachs* of tradition, "naked wild men," and not very different in appearance from the "Head-Hunters of Borneo" and the warriors of Zululand. It may be well, perhaps, to say something about the "native men" of Scotland generally, before making particular quotations, in case of any misunderstanding on the part of the reader.

In the *Collectanea de Rebus Albanicis*, there is a note appended to the "Obligations of Manrent by certain persons of various patronymical surnames, called the Native Men of Craignish, to their chief Ronald Campbell of Barrichibyan, then representative of the old Campbells of Craignish, with his Obligations of Maintenance in return, 1592-1595." This note runs as follows :—

"In all the instances which have come under the Editor's notice where *native men* are mentioned, it is evident that they were not, nor did they claim to be, of the blood of the individual whom they acknowledged to be their chief. They appear to have formed the bulk of the population of the Highlands, and to have descended from the ancient occupants of the soil; whilst the clan properly so-called consisted only of the blood relations of the chief. [For *clann* originally meant "children" or "descendants."] By degrees, however, the word clan received a wider interpretation, and embraced all who fought under the banner of the chief, among whom of course, were included all the able-bodied men dwelling on his lands, whether his *kinsmen* or his *native men*. In general it may be affirmed, that the former were the higher class, or aristocracy, and the latter the commonalty of a clan; the exceptions to this rule being very rare. The *Mac Colls*, and several other smaller septs, were *native men* to the Stewarts of Appin, and the proportion they bore to the Stewarts *proper* will be seen from the following abstract of a return of the killed and wounded of the Appin regiment, in the campaign of 1745-6."

The number of Stewarts proper given in the lists amounts to twenty-two killed and twenty-five wounded. The various commoners fighting under them were, of killed, sixty-nine, and of wounded, forty. Consequently, the greater part of the Appin regiment was made up of men of a totally different race from that of the chief and his kindred. The commoners in this list come under one or other of these names :—Maccoll, Maclaren, Carmichael, Maccombich, Macintyre, Macinish, Macilduie, Mackenzie, Maccorcadill, Macuchkader, Henderson, Macranken, Maccananich, Cameron, Macdonald, Maclachlan, Maclea, and Macarthur. With regard to the first of these, the Editor remarks—" So intimate was the connection between the Stewarts and the Mac Colls, that no single chieftain of the family of Auchnacone reposes in his tomb without a Mac Coll having been placed on each side of him." With regard to the other names, several of which were at that date borne by distinct Clans, themselves as honourable as the Stewarts of Appin, it is probable that while some were those of "native men," others were borne by renegades from other Clans who were perhaps not of "native" blood. Or they may have been *all* "native men," though bearing the names of other clans, in which clans they had been of the commonalty. Or again, their surnames may mean nothing particular, in the way of pedigree. Highland genealogy is rendered dreadfully uncertain and confused by the circumstance that two men, or a dozen men, might bear the same surname, and yet be of wholly different descent. *Any* son, or descendant, of a Donald was Mac Donald, *any* son of a carpenter was Macintyre. And although these, and many other similar names, did eventually become attached to certain particular tribes, yet the existence of such a fact makes it extremely difficult to trace out a lineage with any degree of certainty, and nullifies any sweeping statement about this or that surname, in a great number of cases.

However, the above testimony proves that the majority of the Highland people were subordinate to one or more invading races, whose chiefs stood to them in the relation of alien over-lords at the first, but who gradually and inevitably became identified with the native people. So many Highland pedigrees have an ultra-Scottish origin that it would be useless to attempt to specify these. But we saw that a Flemish settler of the twelfth century became transformed into a Highland Chief, and the very Stewarts themselves are said by Pinkerton to have "come in with the Conqueror," who gave to the first of them, Alan, the Shropshire barony of Oswestry. Such people in course of time became Gaels in speech, and some of them became partly Gaelic in blood. But some, I daresay, have actually none of the aboriginal blood in their veins.

A clear case of miscegenation is that of the Macraes, whom Dr. Johnson encountered. "The Macraes, as we heard afterwards in the Hebrides, were originally an indigent and subordinate clan, and having no farms nor stock, were in great numbers servants to the Maclellans, who, in the war of Charles the First, took arms at the call of the heroic Montrose, and were, in one of his battles, almost all destroyed. The women that were left at home, being thus deprived of their husbands, like the Scythian ladies of old, married their servants, and the Macraes became a considerable race."* Sir Walter Scott, however, in a note to Croker's Boswell,† says, in answer to Dr. Johnson's ejaculatory question, " what can the McCraas tell of themselves a thousand years ago?"—"More than the Doctor would suppose. I have a copy of their family history, written by Mr. John Mac Ra, minister of Dingwall, in Ross-shire, in 1702. In this history, they are averred to have come over with those Fitzgeralds now holding the name of McKenzie, at the period of the battle of Largs, in 1263 . . . . . ." This apparent contradiction is explainable by the assumption that the framer of the pedigree had traced it through the nobler, or maternal, stem,—a very common weakness among family historians in such cases. "The Maclellans of Bombie, a family at one period of great power and influence, supposed originally to have come from Ireland, were, in ancient times, sheriffs of Galloway. Duncan Maclellan is mentioned in a charter of Alexander II. in 1217." If the north-country Maclellans, therefore, were of this race, this is the explanation of the thing,—and I have little doubt that a further examination would prove the correctness of the hypothesis. That the Galloway Maclellans were of the conquering and non-aboriginal race is seen by the following extract from the same authority,‡ an extract which is of great importance also, as tending to confirm all that has been already said with regard to the indigenous Moors of Scotland. " Although the crest of the Maclellans was a Moor's head on the point of a sword, in allusion to their recovery of the estate of Bombie after being forfeited, by the slaying of a gipsy chief who infested Galloway, ... they sometimes used for crest a mortar-piece, with the motto, ' Superbo frango,' &c., &c." Here again, then, is evidence of a contest between an invading and presumably white people and a native and distinctly dark-skinned race, who are clearly regarded as " moors ;" and

---

* "Journey to the Western Islands of Scotland : Glensheals."
† 1848, p. 340.
‡ Anderson's "Scottish Nation."

it seems only to require investigation to show that the Macraes who were subjugated in the north-country, and the people who subdued them, were respectively related to the corresponding races in Galloway. Indeed, the mixture, in this instance, of two widely-separated families is indicated by Boswell in his journal, although at that date the process of amalgamation had been going on for more than a century. "There was great diversity in the faces of the circle around us; some were as black and wild in their appearance as any American savages whatever. [Plainly of 'native' stock.] One woman was as comely almost as the figure of Sappho, as we see it painted." [And she, it may be inferred, was the opposite of "black and wild."]* They were known as "the wild Mac Ra's" in the "Chevalier's muster-roll" of 1715.

It may be remarked here, parenthetically, that the "Moor" who was killed by Maclellan in Galloway was probably a precursor of the "Black Morrow" of peasant tradition, who was perhaps one of the last of that very clan. And further, the application of the terms "gipsy" and "moor" to the same individual reminds one that Diarmaid's *ciuthach* or *ciofach* was compared with *giobag*, a gipsy, and that the Kentish "black-tan" and the Gaelic *dubh-shiubhlach*, or black vagrant, were gipsies also.

Dr. Johnson speaks also of the Macquarries of Ulva as a tribe of great antiquity, that island having been possessed by the family of the then chief for nine hundred years. But this, of course, is not a long enough period to entitle them to be regarded as an aboriginal race. The name is said to be *Guarie*, and their descent is drawn from Guarie, Gor, or Gorbred, "said to have been 'a brother of Fingon, ancestor of the Mackinnons, and Anrias or Andrew, ancestor of the Macgregors.'"† This last clan is also stated to be very old, if not aboriginal, and to be of the Siol Alpin, or race of the Albanach. Probably they were hybrids. Their legendary descent is drawn from the father of Kenneth mac Alpin (King of the Picts, 844–860,) either through that monarch or through a brother of his. If this could be authenticated it would prove them to be half-breeds, for

---

* Croker's "Boswell," 1848, pp. 309-10, note.
† Anderson's "Scottish Nation."

such was Kenneth, so far as can be ascertained,—he being understood to be the son of a Scot, by a Pictish princess, through whom he derived his right to the throne, according to Pictish law. It seems, however that he really fought his way to the throne, his father Alpin having shown him the road. For the Chronicle of Huntingdon states that in the year of his accession to the Pictish kingship, "Kenneth encountered the Picts seven times in one day, and having destroyed many, confirmed the kingdom to himself."* And in all probability his hold on the sovereignty was maintained by the sword to the end of his days. "St. Berchan says of him :—

> Seventeen years of warding valour,
> In the sovereignty of Alban,
> After slaughtering Cruithneach [Picts], after embittering Galls [foreigners],
> He dies on the banks of the Earn."†

So that, if the Macgregors were sprung from the race of Alpin, they were only partly Pictish, and they owed their power and position not to the native race, but to the conquering Scots or Gaidhel.‡

It would be wearisome to search out the various so-called aboriginal clans, and to attempt to analyze their pedigrees. This, indeed, is a task which it would be utterly presumptuous for any but a scholar to undertake. But the random glances bestowed upon them have shown that the "native men" of a thousand years ago were, at that period and subsequently, undergoing a process of subjugation, and in some districts extinction, at the hands of invading Normans, Flemings, and others.

* Skene's "Celtic Scotland," Vol. I. p. 309.
† *Ibid.* p. 313.
‡ I have followed Mr. Skene so far in his belief that the Early Scots and the Gaels were one: it will be seen later on that there is reason for questioning the correctness of this assumption.

CHAPTER V.

IN addition to the Irish examples already given, there are many other relics of savagedom to be found throughout the United Kingdom, in the present as well as in the past. The horrible practice of disfiguring by cutting off the ears of their victims, perpetrated over and over again during the recent upheaval of the dregs of the Irish people (a practice which was also quite common in fifteenth century Scotland), is a slightly modified form of such barbarities as those performed on the dead bodies of the "men of Herefordshire" by the followers of "the irregular and wild Glendower," barbarities which were lately paralleled by the Zulus in the last war, as those who found the corpses of their former comrades know too well.* And one custom which proclaims a connection between the marsh-dwellers of Scotland and those of Borneo is the custom of "head-hunting,"—still practised in the latter country. As regards Scotland there are, or were at the date of Martin's Tour last century, tangible proofs of this. In describing one district in the Isle of Egg, he states:—" About thirty yards from the church there is a sepulchral urn under ground; it is a big stone hewn to the bottom, about four feet deep, and the diameter of it is about the same breadth; I caused them to dig the ground above it, and we found a flat thin stone covering the urn: it was almost full of human bones, but no head among them, and they were fair and dry. I enquired of the natives what was

---

* Shakespeare was not romancing when he made this reference. The details of this foul piece of savagery are given in the history of Thomas Walsingham (at "page 557," according to Dr. Henry, who transcribes the description in his "History of Great Britain," an eighteenth-century book), and they correspond exactly with the shameful insults to our dead in Zululand. It is quite possible that the ancestors of the Zulus were at that period (1402) inhabiting the fatherland of those Welsh tribes, and that the kinship between the two was, *at that date*, by no means remote. Whether—and to what extent—any of the present natives of Wales are the descendants of those savages is quite another question.

become of the heads, and they could not tell, but one of them said, perhaps their head had been cut off with a two-handed sword, and taken away by the enemy." Although not actually proving that the custom of "head-hunting" did at one time exist in that neighbourhood, the evidence of the headless frames, and the suggestion of the "native," point to the probability of such a thing,—though at a period so far back that the peasantry had almost forgotten it. But unmistakable testimony is afforded by an ancient poem to be found in the selection from "the Dean of Lismore's book,"* translated by Dr. McLauchlan of Edinburgh. The author of the poem is stated by the learned translator to have been "the most ancient of all the Ossianic poets," and "a contemporary of Cuchullin, who flourished, according to Irish historians, in the first century."

The poem is a dialogue between Conall and Evir, "who was either the wife or the betrothed of Cuchullin," and is chiefly made up of her questions regarding the heads of his enemies, which he was carrying upon a withe,†—and his answers. As the dialogue describes the physical characteristics of the people against whom Cuchullin fought, it is of some ethnological value, and deserving of quotation :—

* * * *

Whose is that hairy, black, great head,
With cheeks than any rose more red,
That which hangs nighest thy left arm,
The head whose colour has not changed?

That head the king of swift steeds own'd,
Said Cairbar's son of vigorous lance ;
In vengeance for my foster son,
I took that head and bore it far.

What head is that I see beyond,
Covered with smooth, soft, flowing hair,
His eye like grass, his teeth like bloom,
His beauty such as none is like?

* Pp. 58–62.
† They were no fewer than fifteen, and Conall not only has the assurance to say that he killed all their owners, but further, when Evir asks him how many men he had slain altogether "in vengeance for the head of Con," he replies —

Ten and seven score hundred men,
I tell the truth [?], *the number is,*
That fell by me, all back o'er back,
Fruit of my bravery and power.

Manadh, the man that own'd the steeds,
Aoife's son, who plunder'd every sea ;
I left his trunk 'reft of its head,
I slew his people, every man.

  * * * *

What fair-haired head is that to the east,
Whose hand might well have seized the heads ;
Well did I know his voice of old,
For he and I were friends awhile?

Down there it was the Cu did fall,
His body cast in fairest mould ;
Cu, son of Con, of poets king,
Among the last I took his head.

What two heads are those farthest out,
Great Connal of the sweetest voice ;
Of thy great love hide not from me
The names of them so dark in arms?

'Tis Laoghar's head and that of Cuilt,
The two who fell pierced by my arms ;
One of them had Cuchullin struck,
Hence his red blood my weapons dyes.

What two heads are those to the east,
Great Connal of the famous deeds ;
Alike the colour of their hair,
Than hero's blood more red their cheeks?

Cullin the handsome, and Cunlad brave,
Two who e'er triumphed in their wrath ;

  * * * *

What are those six hideous heads
I see in front facing the north ;
Blue in the face, their hair so black,
From which thou turn'st thy look, brave Connal?

These are six of Cuchullin's foes,
Calliden's sons, who triumphed oft,

  * * * *

Great Connal, father to a King,
What is that head, noblest of all ;
How bushy the golden yellow locks,
Covering it with so much grace?

The head of McFinn, McRoss the red,
The son of Cruith, slain by my stroke ;
Evir, he was King, chief of them all,
In Leinster of the spotted swords.*

  * * * *

---

* "Spotted" may here be taken to refer to the men who wielded the swords. An Irish annalist, quoted by Mr. Skene ("Celtic Scotland," Vol. I. p. 266),

Here then, we have head-hunting, pure and simple. It would be almost impossible to discover the nationality of the different slaughtered foemen, but they seem to have been of various races, chiefly white. The "six hideous heads," "blue in the face, their hair so black," whose owners are denominated "Calliden's sons," most probably belonged to the woad-stained "Moors," for the blue colour could not well have been anything like the lividness of a corpse. And, indeed, the redness of the other faces must have also been artificial, for an obvious reason.

Another relic of a barbarous era has lingered on in one or more districts of England to the present day. It is described in *Notes and Queries* of 10th September, 1881, the account being contributed by one whose evidence has all the weight of local experience, and it was evoked by other similar customs (such as that known as "crying the mare,") described in that periodical about the same date.

This curious performance is thus described:—

> We have, or rather had until the last few years, another harvest custom, which prevailed about Mobberley, Knutsford, Altrincham, and, in fact, in the central part of Cheshire generally, and which perhaps may only be another variant of those described. This was called a "shutting." When the last field of corn was cut, but not carried, the men used to come to the master and ask permission to have a shutting. Leave, was, of course, granted, and then they all adjourned to some open place, on high ground, if possible, so that their voices might be heard to a distance, where they formed a ring. One of them then acted as spokesman, and gave out the "nominy," which means in the Cheshire dialect an oration, or the text or burden of a sermon or song. I do not remember all the words that were used, though I hope to be able to obtain them and rescue them from oblivion. It began, if I recollect rightly, "Oh, yes! Oh, yes! Oh, yes! This is to give notice." One clause was that " Master So-and-so has given us forty gallons of good ale ;" another was to the effect that " Master So-and-so had finished cutting corn before his neighbours ;" and a third that he was thereby entitled to "send the old mare into somebody else's standing corn." Between each period of the "nominy" they all took hold of hands, and, bending forward, shouted at the top of their voices a prolonged and most unearthly " Wow—w! Wow—w—w! Wow—w—w—w!" The

---

speaks of "green swords." See remarks on "*breac*" and "*gorm*." The American Indians used the term "Long Knives" to denote the men who used them.

proceedings ended in a jollification, consisting generally of an extra allowance of beer, and sometimes a supper . . . "

Another kindred custom is the following* :—

North Devon has a curious custom at harvest time of "calling the neck." When the reapers have completed the reaping of the last field of wheat, a bundle of the best wheat is selected and arranged neat and trim. The reapers then crowd round it, take off their hats, and bow to the "neck," *i.e.*, the said bundle of wheat, and then begins a long, harmonious shout, "The neck!" three times, the men bowing and raising themselves at the same time. They then change their cry to "Wee yeu!" "Way yeu!" ("Yeu" means end.) After this has been done three times, they break out into a loud, joyous laugh, flinging up their caps and capering about. One of them seizes "the neck," and runs to the farm with it as fast as he can, trying to get into the house unobserved. If he is successful in getting in without being seen, he may demand tribute from the dairymaid, who stands at the door with a bucket in her hand; but if she sees him while he is trying to get into the house, she holds the right to souse him with the contents of her bucket.

In this connection, I shall also give some verses of a ballad included in Scott's *Minstrelsy of the Scottish Border*. He entitles it *The Fray of Suport; an ancient Border gathering-song from tradition*,—and regarding it he says—

Of all the Border ditties, which have fallen into the Editor's hands, this is by far the most uncouth and savage. It is usually chanted in a sort of wild recitative, except the burden, which swells into a long and varied howl, not unlike to a view hollo. The words, and the very great irregularity of the stanza (if it deserves the name) sufficiently point out its intention and origin. An Englishwoman, residing in Suport, near the foot of the Kershope, having been plundered in the night by a band of the Scottish moss-troopers, is supposed to convoke her servants and friends for the pursuit, or Hot Trod; upbraiding them, at the same time, in homely phrase, for their negligence and security. The Hot Trod was followed by the persons who had lost goods, with bloodhounds and horns, to raise the country to help. They also used to carry a burning wisp of straw at spear head, and to raise a cry, similar to the Indian war-whoop. It appears from articles made by the Wardens of the English Marches, September 12th, in 6th of Edward VI., that all, on this cry being raised, were obliged to follow the fray, or chase, under pain of death.†

* Described in *Notes and Queries* of 3rd September, 1881.

† Dr. Daniel Wilson, in his "Reminiscences of Old Edinburgh," throws discredit upon the authenticity of this ballad, which, he says, was compiled by Mr. Surtees of Mainsforth, "with the help of four widely-differing versions." But, even if this were so, the existence of various versons of such a song, current on the Borders, is not denied by the critic. And the above version may well embody their chief characteristics.

A few verses of the ballad will give an idea of its wild nature:—

* * * * * *

Weel may ye ken,
Last night I was right scarce o' men :
But Toppet Hob o' the Mains had guesten'd in my house by chance ;
I set him to wear the fore-door wi' the speir, while I kept the back-door wi' the lance ;
But they hae run him thro' the thick o' the thie, and broke his knee-pan,
And the mergh* o' his shin-bane has run down on his spur-leather whang ;
He's lame while he lives, and where'er he may gang.
  Fy, lads ! shout a' a' a' a' a',
  My gear's a' gane.
But Peenye, my gude son, is out at the Hagbut-head,
His een glittering for anger like a fiery gleed ;
Crying,—" Mak sure the nooks
Of Maky's-muir crooks ;
For the wily Scot takes by nooks, hooks, and crooks.
Gin we meet a' together in a head the morn,
We'll be merry men."
  Fy, lads ! shout a' a' a' a',
  My gear's a' gane.

* * * * * *

Doughty Dan o' the Houlet Hirst,
Thou was aye gude at a birst :
Gude wi' a bow, and better wi' a speir,
The bauldest March-man that e'er follow'd gear ;
Come thou here.
  Fy, lads ! shout a' a' a' a',
  My gear's a' gane.

* * * * * *

Ah ! lads, we'll fang them a' in a net,
For I hae a' the fords o' Liddel set ;†
The Dunkin and the Door-loup,
The Willie-ford, and the Water-slack,
The Black-rack and the Trout-dub of Liddel ;
There stands John Forster, wi' five men at his back,
Wi' bufft coat and cap of steil ;
Boo ! ca' at them e'en, Jock ;
That ford's sicker, I wat weil.
  Fy, lads ! shout a' a' a' a',
  My gear's a' ta'en.

* Mergh—Marrow.—(*Scott.*)
† Watching fords was a ready mode of intercepting the marauders ; the names of the most noted fords upon the Liddel are recited in this verse.—(*Scott.*)

Hoo ! hoo ! gar raise the Reid Souter, and Ringan's Wat,
Wi' a broad elshin and a wicker ;
I wat weil they'll mak a ford sicker.
Sae, whether they be Elliots or Armstrangs,
Or rough-riding Scots, or rude Johnstones,
Or whether they be frae the Tarras or Ewsdale,
They maun turn and fight, or try the deeps o' Liddel.
      Fy, lads ! shout a' a' a' a' a',
      My gear's a' ta'en.

*   *   *   *   *   *

Now, can there be found anywhere on earth, symptoms of more intense savagery than that displayed in these few examples of many like British customs ? Whatever changes and modifications they have experienced, they are rooted in the most ferocious barbarism. No Australian *corrobbaree* was ever wilder than the "harvest customs" of North Devon and of Cheshire, in their original form. No Comanchè war-whoop, that ever sickened the heart of a frontier house-wife, could surpass in thrilling *eerieness* those frightful yells that have sounded among the British Islands. It is difficult to say which of them is the most horrible,—the deep boom of *a-Boo! a-Boo!* the "prolonged and most unearthly" *Wow-w! Wow-w-w! Wow-w-w-w!* the fierce incitement of the Border fury, *Boo! Hoo! Hoo!* or the wild gathering-cry that answered her summons—*a' a' a' a' a'!* "swelling into a long and varied howl." The Englishwoman of Suport, whether she belonged to the era of buff-coats and steel-caps, or whether the song in its original form ante-dated these by centuries,—had inherited the blood of as fierce and savage a people as any in history. The flaming spear, and the throng of yelling warriors trampling after it, are the concomitants of a most barbarous age.

Other examples might be adduced, to equal and to endorse those already given. There is, for instance, an illustration in a comparatively recent number of the *Graphic*,* showing a Highland "Dance of Triumph," executed at night over a slaughtered deer. That the dancers were civilized gentlemen does not make the dance itself less wild. They bear flaming torches in their hands ; the pipers are playing an exciting strain ; and one has only to see in fancy the dress

* 22nd October, 1881.

of the seventeenth century Mull-men* instead of the modern garb evolved therefrom, and to imagine dancers of a hue as dark as a "moor's," in order to complete the likeness between this Braemar revel and the "Bison-Dance" of the American Indians. They may even have been originally identical in every detail. The dancers of the Bison-Dance wear the animal's shaggy head upon their own; and is there not a trace of such a usage in

> "What shall he have that kill'd the deer?
> His leather skin and horns *to wear*?"

Jaques says that "it would do well to set the deer's horns upon his head, for a branch of victory."

The savage element asserts itself in many legends and myths with great distinctness. This has been dwelt upon lately by Mr. Andrew Lang, and although the precise object of his essay† is rather to confute the interpretation given to this feature by the philological school, I take leave to borrow his words for the present occasion, for which they are eminently appropriate.

> In the study of Mythology one fact, at least, is universally accepted. As soon as a people reaches that stage of civilization in which science begins, men ask themselves the meaning of their own mythology. It is a puzzle to them. They cannot account for the strange and revolting legends of their own gods and heroes. The obvious inference is that mythologies, or rather that the crude and offensive parts of mythology, were developed at a time when people were in a different mental condition from that in which they find themselves when they begin to be perplexed by the extravagance of their own sacred legends. For modern inquirers, who are interested in mythology as part of the mental history of man, the question is—In what intellectual condition was our race when the stranger parts of mythology originated? There are many portions of mythology which seem intelligible. . . . But there is a strange element, namely, the presence of such lewd stories as the mutilation of Uranus by Cronus, and the swallowing of his children by the same god, which is common to all mythologies. The real difficulty of the mythologist is to explain this element, the 'silly, savage, and senseless' element, as Professor Max Müller calls it ('Selected Essays,' i. 578). Probably none but professed mythologists know what an abundance of silly, senseless, savage, and obscene tradition exists even

---

* Described in the next chapter.

† *Fraser's Magazine*, August, 1881; Mr. Max Müller's "Philosophy of Mythology."

in the legends of Greece. To explain it away, the earliest philosophers of Greece, Xenophanes, Theagenes, and the rest, constructed various theories, now simply accusing Homer of inventing lewd tales, now imagining that these tales contained moral or philosophical allegories. The effort to explain this side of mythology still occupies students. . . . .

. . . Mr. Müller starts from the observation that most of the ancient myths are 'absurd and irrational,' 'savage and senseless.' 'Among the lowest tribes of Africa and America,' he says, in speaking of the myths of Cronus, ' we hardly find anything more hideous and revolting.' How then were these legends invented by the ancestors of a people like the Greeks, and by the ancestors of Indians, Persians, Italians, Slavs, and Germans? 'Was there a period of temporary insanity, through which the human mind had to pass, and was it a madness identically the same in the South of India and in the north of Iceland?' Now here we must desert Mr. Müller for a moment to point out (what will elsewhere be proved by abundant evidence) that the 'madness' is 'identically the same,' not only from the south of India to the north of Iceland, but among Bushmen at the Cape, and Murri in Victoria or Queensland; among Eskimo and Kanekas—in fact, wherever human minds have produced a mythology. Indeed, as Mr. Müller elsewhere says, 'wherever we look, in every part of the world, we find the same kind of stories, the same traditions, the same myths.' . . . . . Now, as Mr. Müller well observes, the difficulty is, not to account for the preservation, but for the *origin* of loathsome and puerile legends. . . . Here let us interpolate one remark. If we find a savage trait in the manners of a civilized people—[examples of which are supposed] . . . how do we account for these inconsistencies? Simply by the hypothesis that the now civilized people was once savage, and that it retains its savage practices when these happen to be connected with a thing so tenacious of tradition as religion. Well, if we find that a people civilized in other matters retains 'savage and senseless' legends of its gods, why should we not suppose that these legends originated in an age of savagery, and were preserved by man's 'inborn reverence for the past?' . . .

This theory "that some myths were preserved by tradition from an age of low savagery, when men's fancies were almost incredibly puerile and hideous," is maintained throughout the article, as is also the argument that they are found all over the world, "from the Eskimo to the Australians." And the concluding words are these:—

The future student of mythology will ask, ' Is there any contemporary stage of thought and of society, in which the wildest marvels of mythology are looked on as the ordinary facts of experience, and as laws regulative of phenomena?' And they will find that condition of thought surviving among contemporary, and historically recorded of departed races of savages.

CHAPTER VI.

It was seen that the marsh-dwellers of the Forth district, who fought against Severus, were, according to Herodian, accustomed to dispense with clothing in time of war, although they may, at other times, have worn the mantle or plaid, like the Irish of a thousand years later; or more probably the skin-garments of the Hungarians and "the long-haired Getæ." This indifference to clothing was continued up to within comparatively recent times, among certain tribes, whose precise lineage it is difficult to determine. "Walter Espee, a great Norman baron (who came over with William the Conqueror in 1066), in a speech by him to the Anglo-Norman army, previous to the battle of Cowton-moor, after mentioning the former successful exploits by them against the Scots, added, that they should rather laugh than fear against such as the vile Scot, who half naked comes forward to fight, and that to the Norman swords and spears they oppose their naked hide, using a calf skin for a shield."* And the writer just quoted, who, curiously enough, is endeavouring to prove the "great antiquity of the Highland garb" *as now worn*, previously cites Herodian and also Dio, who, writing in the year 230 A.D., "says the Caledonians are hardly clothed and dwell in tents, and without shoes." He also gives the phrase used by Eumenius, in 296, "hostibus seminudis," or "half-naked enemies," adding that "Logan, in his work on the Gael, also quotes from the very ancient classical author (namely, Herodian) to the same effect that from the apparently scanty clothing of the Caledonian Gael, the expression naked was not inapplicable." (Assuredly not.) And he further states that Gildas, in the sixth century, "says that the Picts were only dressed with cloth round the

---

* Robertson's "Historical Proofs on the Highlanders," p. 237.

loins."* His argument is an astonishing instance of the force of preconceived ideas and *quasi*-national prejudice, for, by such quotations he believes that he is establishing the antiquity of the dress now called Highland. There is no confusion as to nomenclature, for he asserts that the Picts were the ancestors of the Gaels. And he, unintentionally, shows that so recently as the year 1688, the islanders of Mull wore the plaid as a mantle, and not in any fashion as a kilt. The evidence given is from the account of "William Sacheverell, Esq., Governor of the Isle of Man," who speaks of the dress of the Mull people in the following terms:—" The usual outward habit of both sexes is the pladd; the women's much finer, the colours more lively, and the squares larger than the men's, and put me in mind of the ancient Picts. This serves them for a veil, and covers both head and body. The men wear theirs after another manner, especially when designed for ornament: it is loose and flowing, like the mantles our painters give their heroes. Their thighs are bare, with brawny muscles. Nature has drawn all her stroaks bold and masterly; a thin brogue on the foot, a short buskin of various colours on the legg, tied above the calf with a striped pair of garters. What should be concealed is hid with a large shot-pouch, on each side of which hangs a pistol and a dagger, ... A round target on their backs, a blew bonnet on their heads, in one hand a broad-sword and a musquet in the other."† The writer of this account (Sacheverell) is perfectly unbiassed, and his attitude toward the people he describes is one of admiration, and not of provincial spitefulness; for he speaks in the highest terms of their noble qualities, their contempt of luxury and ambition, their courage, their temperance, and the "graceful modesty" of their women. But the dress of the men, as pictured by him, has some affinity with that of a Zulu warrior. The modern kilt does not form any portion of it; although, fortunately, the sporran does.

It seems doubtful whether the rival clans, in their famous duel at Perth, in the year 1396, wore anything more cumbersome than their weapons, and possibly (to give them the benefit of the doubt) the breech-cloth worn, according to

---

* Robertson's "Historical Proofs," p. 231. † *Ibid.* p. 252.

Gildas, by the painted Moors of the sixth century. The Perth combatants are stated by a writer of the reign of James II. of Scotland* to have entered the lists, "armed only with swords, bows and arrows, *without mantles or other armour except axes.*" A "mantle" is here clearly understood to be equivalent to armour, and the probability is that the custom among those tribes, as among the Irish of Spenser's time, was to "wrap it about their left arme, instead of a target," it being, in this shape, "hard to cut thorough with a sword." And since the Irish "karne" of Queen Elizabeth's day was, by this use of his plaid, left untrammelled by any other garment whatsoever, it seems likely that the kindred Highlandman of two centuries earlier, who followed the same usage, was also alike in other respects.

Other fashions, and likely other races, are described thus by "the Historian *John Major*, who wrote in 1512": "From the middle of the thigh to the foot they have no covering for the leg, clothing themselves with a mantle instead of an upper garment, and a shirt dyed with saffron . . . . . . In time of war they cover their whole body with a shirt of mail of iron rings, and fight in that." This description seems to be that of the semi-Norse Highlanders of the West, and it would appear that their chiefs only are so indicated. For the very next sentence says: "The common people of the Highland Scots rush into battle, having their body clothed with a linen garment manifoldly sewed and painted or daubed with pitch, with a covering of deerskin."† Here the plaid receives no notice at all, and the pitch-painted garment reminds one more of Falstaff's men in buckram suits than of a modern deerstalker, whose outward appearance has positively nothing in common with the "Highland Scot" just figured, unless the "covering of deerskin" be construed to mean a sporran, as it likely enough does. This pitch-painted dress seems to have been worn thirty years later by a contingent of Highlanders who, with a body of French auxiliaries, and with other Scots, besieged the town of Haddington, then garrisoned by the English. The Scottish portion of the army

---

* Bowermaker. The reference is taken from Robertson's "Historical Proofs," p. 241.
† *Ibid.* p. 242.

seems to have been half Norse, and the account given of their appearance tends to confirm the conjecture that the mail-clad warriors pictured in the above quotation were Islesmen of mixed breed. "A considerable body of Scots, from the islands of Orkney and the south, who were assembled at Edinburgh in obedience to the Queen mother's commands, joined the French camp . . . . . . 'They wore coats of mail,' says the journalist [Beague]: 'each had a large bow in his hand; and their quivers, swords and shields, hung as it were in a sling. They were followed by several highlanders; and these last go almost naked,—they have painted waistcoats, and a sort of woollen covering, variously coloured, and are armed as the rest with large bows, broad swords, and targets. There was not one of them but gave convincing proofs that they stood in no awe of the English.'"[*] In this case, the plaid is mentioned as well as the suit of buckram, but as to the disposing of the plaid there is nothing to show whether it was worn as a mantle only, or belted so as to form a kilt as well. The former fashion seems more likely, considering what has already been said. If it had been arranged as a kilt, the expression "almost naked" would be wholly unsuitable. Even when the kilt began to be evolved, its growth was gradual. There is a portrait of a Highland Chief of the sixteenth or seventeenth century prefixed to the history of his family,—one of some note,—in which the kilt he there displays is only about half as long as that demanded by modern fastidiousness. If a chief, then, dressed for a portrait-painter, was so scantily clad as regards his lower man, what sort of figures were his gillies likely to be, in their work-a-days suits? I fancy the old song stated a most apparent fact when it peopled the Highlands with "lang-leggit callants gaun wanting the breeks," and "without hose and shoon." This latter point is noted by Dr. Johnson as a feature in the appearance of the Highlanders of a time so recent even as his. He remarks, when at Inverness,—"The numbers that go barefoot are still sufficient to show that shoes may be spared; they are not yet considered as

[*] Miller's "History of Haddington," p. 82. The words "Scot" and "Scottish," as well as "English," are, of course, used here in their most comprehensive sense.

necessaries of life ; for tall boys, not otherwise meanly dressed, run without them in the streets ; and in the islands the sons of gentlemen pass several of their first years with naked feet."

Probably the earliest dress ever worn in these islands, as an advance upon the mere breech-cloth described by Gildas, and the leafy cincture of the heraldic savage, was that which found favour among "the nobles of the long-haired Getæ," and the ancient Hungarians of whom Gibbon speaks. This was the skin of some wild animal, which seems to have been worn much in the same fashion as that customary among the Dyaks of Borneo, except that the head of the animal was

Sinister Supporter of *Colville* arms. (From the "Pocket Peerage of Scotland," 1826.)

drawn over the head of the wearer of the skin. One of the supporters of the coat-armorial of the ancient family of Colville (probably intended to represent an actual savage slain by an ancestor of that family) gives one a good idea of the fashion. The above woodcut exhibits it.

Now this fashion, simple enough in its way, is really of great interest. For it is the very germ of heraldry. Or if that title belongs more to the tattooed emblem of the naked Pict,—at any rate, the wild beast's skin, thus worn, was the first *coat of arms*. The legendary heroes of the Highland tales used to wear a *cochal*, or "husk," which was believed to have the power of transforming them into animals of various kinds, but when the heroes came home to their dwellings, they put off this *cochal* and "became men."* Thus the *wearer* became identified with the *animal* whose skin he wore, and it is to this custom that we owe the origin of so many animal-names used as surnames. Mr. Grant Allen has pointed this out lately,† and shown that not only are there very many English towns and other localities, as well as family-names, still bearing the names of "birds, beasts, fishes, or plants," but also the bearers of such names did actually at one time believe themselves "to be lineally and literally descended" from the original of their family-totem. The birds, fishes, and plants must, of course, have been gradually assumed in course of time, and then only as *crests*. But the animal's skin was plainly (to judge from the tradition, and other evidence) the beginning of the idea; and, farther, it was apparently not worn at home, but only when "on the war-path," as the Dyak custom still is. It was a *coat of arms*. And the wearer was known to men of another tribe by the name of the animal of his clan. This is seen over and over again,—both in history and in legend. There was a King of Scotland (or, more properly, Alban) in the tenth century, who is known simply as *Cuilean* or *Caniculus*, The Whelp; and another as Kali Hundason, "the son of the Dog." The legendary Cuchullin, many centuries before the historic Cuilean, "is often spoken of simply as 'An Cù,' or *The Hound*," and sometimes as "Cù nan con," or "The Hound of [the tribe of] the Hounds," while one of the old Irish kings bore the title of "Cairbar of the Cat's-head." Mr. O'Curry states "that the 'Concheannaich or Dogheads were an ancient race who inhabited Magh O'Coinn-chinn [which seems to be The Marsh of the Dog-

---

* "West Highland Tales," Introduction, p. cxv. A survival of this may be seen in the New Year's custom described by Dr. Johnson when staying at Coll. "One man dresses himself in a cow's hide, upon which other men beat with sticks. He runs with all this noise round the house, which all the company quits in a counterfeited fright."

† "Old English Clans," *Cornhill Magazine*, September, 1881.

heads], now Moygonihy, in Kerry," and this race, along with a tribe of "Cats," and another wearing the hides of some white-backed animal, are evidently the actors in a very ancient Gaelic poem, in which the following lines occur—

> ' When three battalions were seen,
> Sons to the King of Rualay.
> Cat-headed one battalion was.
> Dog-headed was the one beside it ;
> The other behind them was white-backed,
> Brown the rest, though white the back.
>
> * * * * *
>
> The whole of the Catheads were killed,
> The Dogheads we seized to a man ;
> The whole of the Whitebacks fell."

The scene of this poem is laid in Ireland, and the reciters of it are supposed to be Finn, or Fionn, and his followers, who were (according to Mr. O'Curry) sworn enemies to the Doghead tribe. Other examples are to be found in the "Lugi" and "Mertæ" whom Ptolemy places in the modern county of Sutherland, and whose names are probably (thinks Mr. Skene) the Gaelic *Laogh*, a calf, and *Mart*, a heifer. A dynasty of the ancient Mormaers, or Earls, of Buchan, bore also the title of Mac Dobharcon, or "the children of the Water-Dog, or Otter." The "Cats," a race which must have at one time inhabited a large part of Europe, are still represented by the Highland Clan Chattan.*

And not only did this fashion of personating a real animal appertain to the days when men clothed themselves in the actual hide. It was continued after metal armour came into use. (Or it may be that the metal-using and skin-using peoples were contemporaneous.) At any rate, so far as the covering of the head is concerned. The ancient Gauls are said to have worn helmets which represented beasts ; not merely a crest worn *above* the helmet, but a helmet shaped into the semblance of a beast,—which, wholly enveloping the head of the wearer, made him visibly a "Dog-head," "Cat-head," or whatever his totem was. This

---

* See Dr. McLauchlan's translation of "The Dean of Lismore's Book," pp. 52, 59, 76, 77, 78, and 80 ; also Mr. Skene's "Celtic Scotland," Vol. I. pp. 206, 366–8, and Vol. III. p. 56.

is distinctly seen in certain bronze plates which were discovered some time ago in Œland, and which are represented in Mr. Du Chaillu's *Land of the Midnight Sun.** Two of the figures in these plates are intended either to denote the same individual twice over (for they are almost identical), or else two members of the same clan; and their crests, the complete figure of a boar, is only worn above the helmet. But of two others, one has his *head encased in* a metal boar's head, with eye-holes on either side, and his comrade is crowned with a large pair of cow's horns, apparently metal also. Specimens of such head-cases have been found in Scotland, and have been described in the " Rhind Lectures " of 1881. The one is a boar's head, like the Œland warrior's, and the jaws are contrived so as to open and shut, by hinges at each side. There are also eye-holes on each side, though it is likely the wearer would depend rather on the view obtained through the large, half-open mouth, lined with metal tusks. The other Scotch head-case has the horns of an antelope, or some animal of that kind.

Such head pieces, though only of skin, are to some extent worn among the Chukches of Siberia; " often . . . the skin of the hood is so chosen that the ears of the animal project on both sides of the head."† And this is apparently what is meant by an Irish tradition that, at a battle fought near Ballybeg Abbey, County Cork, " in the time of all the battles," there was " a giant killed there that had a horse's ears."‡

Indeed, this grotesque fashion explains away a great many things. The "furies" of heraldry, who have pointed brute-like ears, may have originated in this (unless they are witnesses to the truth of evolution). And all the otherwise-impossible stories, in West Highland and other tales, of "animals" speaking and associating with "men," of people assuming the shapes of various animals "by enchantment," of wer-wolves or men-wolves, of witches who become cats, of the dragons, and boars, and other "scaly monsters," against whom the heroes of old fought (the scales being, as Mr. Karl Blind suggests, scale-armour, worn by the Norwegian

---

* Vol. I. p. 371.
† Nordenskiöld's "Voyage of the Vega."
‡ *Journal of the Ethnological Society*, Vol. II. No. 4, p. 403.

and Danish conquerors);—all these are testimonies to the time when men, whether as individuals or as clans, were known by the name of the beast which was their totem. And it is in this custom, much more likely than in any mythological belief, that we shall find the solution of the antelope-headed, and otherwise brute-headed, human figures which are seen not only in Scotland and in Norway, but which are carved also upon the rocks of Egypt and of the Drakenberg. Such representations were the simplest and most natural way of betokening the kindred of the subject of the sculpture.

The cow-skin covering remarked upon by Dr. Johnson at the island of Coll, was probably worn by a race of men inimical to the forefathers of those who drubbed the temporary wearer of it, not knowing *why* they did so. Indeed it is a most likely hypothesis that, if the indigenous tribes of Interior England and Western Scotland wore their beast's-skin garments after the same fashion as the savage of the Colville shield, the particular hide most commonly used would be that of a cow or a bull. Because they are described as a pastoral, cattle-owning people. And in fact there is a traditionary proof that this was so. In the Cornish tale of *Tom the Giant* and *Jack the Tinkeard*, the garment of the latter is thus described :*—" It was made out of a shaggy black bull's hide, dressed whole with the hair on. The skin of the forelegs made the sleeves, the hind quarters only were cut, pieces being let in to make the spread of the skirts, while the neck and skin of the head formed a sort of hood. The whole appeared as hard as iron; and when Tom hit the tinkeard, it sounded, as if the coat roared, like thunder." "Such a coat (it is said) was never seen in the West Country before," which makes it still more likely that this "tinkeard" (*tincaird* or *tinker*) belonged to the aborigines of the interior. It is further stated in the legend, that after the "tinkeard" had fraternised with Tom and his family, he taught his hostess how to make a similar coat for her son. "So a bull-calf's skin was put on to the boy, and Jane had special instructions how she was to allow the coat to dry on his back, and tan and dress it in a peculiar way. The skin thus treated would shrink and thicken up until it came to

* Hunt's "Popular Romances of the West of England."

his shape." In this way, the wearer of such a hide would resemble the animal itself as closely as a man could possibly do. If he wore a wolf's skin, he was to all appearance a man-wolf (a *wer*-wolf); if a cow's skin, he was a cow. And so, as we have just seen in the Gaelic examples, and as more than one scholarly investigator has lately shown with regard to Southern Britain, certain tribes became known by the names of certain beasts, which it was their fancy to resemble as nearly as possible in appearance. And hence, *inter alia*, the talking "animals" of the legends.

But the cow-headed warrior of the Œland bronzes represents a development of this idea. For, though still faithful to the brute similitude, he is cased in metal instead of hide. This is evident at a glance,—so far, at any rate, as the headpiece is concerned. And it is the fellow of the bronze boarheads and others which have been found in Scotland. And of the presence of such men in Scotland there is yet an echo. The "scaly monsters" of folk-lore were, Mr. Karl Blind suggests, no other than the invading Norsemen and Danes, clad in their scale-armour. Now, those "scaly monsters" are otherwise known to the Scottish peasantry by the name of "Shelly-coats," a name plainly given by a people unacquainted with scale-armour. A "Shelly-coat" became, after a long interval of time, dimly remembered as a wild creature emerging from the sea, and regarded, with too good reason, as an especial object of fear to the maidens of Britain. This, which is vehemently asserted in tradition, is discernible in a line of Allan Ramsay's—a line which also identifies the "shelly-coat" with such a man as the cow-helmed figure of Œland. It occurs in *The Gentle Shepherd*, and the occasion is the abrupt flight of Jenny from her suitor. "She fled as frae a shelly-coated *cow* ;" the lover complains. And you will find in Dr. Jamieson's Dictionary that a *cow* is still a Scottish equivalent for a bugbear, or object of horror.*
Farther still, it is more fully styled a *bu-cow*, and this recalls the shout of *Bo, Boo,* or *a-Bu,* said to have been the war-cry of the "ancient Irish." Now, this sound of *Bo* or *Boo*, which has given rise to the Gaelic name for a cow—*Bo*—is nothing

* It may be, also, that the verbs "to bully" and "to cow" are derived from this source.

else than the bellow of cattle, and it is quite legitimate to assume that those tribes of "ancient Irish" who used this war-shout did so *because* it was the roar of the creature they represented, and that such "Irish" were substantially the same people as the cow-warrior of Œland and the "tinkeard" of Cornish tradition. But the "shelly-coated cows" and "scaly monsters" of our peasantry were intruders and foreigners, and Mr. Blind identifies them with the Norsemen and Danes. The latter, I should think. For the Scottish peasant-girl fled from the "shelly-coats," actuated by the same fear that made the Prioress of Coldingham counsel her nuns to mutilate their faces and so render them repulsive to the Danish banditti,—the fear of outrage. The salient features of the brutal Dane of history and the quaintly named "shelly-coat" of peasant tradition are identical. Thus, the so-called "Irish" to whom the war-cry is attributed were only "Irish" in a sense. Their "war-cry" is the property of the larger island as well, where it has been long embalmed in a popular saying.

Thus we see that various tribes in Scotland and Ireland, as well as in England, whether in history or in legend, are known by the names of the totems they bear. And that some examples of such tribes are the Dogs, Cats, Boars, Cows, Heifers, Calves, and Otters. Another clan is suggested by the old name of that part of Ross-shire called the Black Isle,—which was formerly, if not now, "Edderdail,"— or the country of the Adders. And this name again gives rise to another suggestion. The coloured amulets of glass and vitreous paste, which are found throughout the country, are known among the peasantry as "Druids' beads," and also as "Adder stones." There is an ancient, but manifestly absurd belief, that these are in some mysterious way made from the saliva of serpents. This has been stated and re-stated in many forms, one of which I shall quote from the *Gallovidian Encyclopedia;* that valuable, if somewhat motley, collection of the wreckage of a remote Past.*

* "The portion of the Pictish people which longest retained the name were the Picts of Galloway. Completely surrounded by the Britons of Strathclyde, and isolated from the rest of the Pictish nation . . . . . they maintained an isolated and semi-independent position in a corner of the island, and appear as a distinct people under the name of Picts as late as the twelfth century, when

"ADDER-BEADS."—Beads made by Adders. Such beads are common now in museums, and other repositories of rarities; they are mostly about the size of a hazel-nut, oval shaped, of an amber hue, but full of specks of other beautiful colours. The hole through them is about half an inch in diameter, and large enough to admit a child's little finger. That the Adders make them is never doubted, but how, is as yet never exactly known: the country people say it is gone about in this way. Seven old Adders, with manes on their backs, have a meeting in some snug heather bush, before the sun; with them is also a long small white one; operations are begun by the hairy reptiles, putting forth from their mouths a glutinous matter of a honey colour. The white Adder moulds this into a certain shape, forming the hole by creeping through it—and still as it creeps in-through and out-through the matter, the old ones keep salivating it—so the bead is constructed. and left to harden in the sun.

"But (add the peasantry) it is impossible to stand at any time, and behold them thus at work in their bead manufactory—as at these times they are full of wrath and swiftness; so that if the observer be seen by them, he has little chance to get off alive."

Now this, as it stands, is sheer nonsense. But it may easily be the confused remembrance of a time when people of a wholly different race observed, from some hiding-place, the fierce and alien tribe of "Snakes." mixing up the paste of which those amulets are formed. Ordinary adders do *not* have "manes on their backs,"— but *ciuthachs* have; and if these latter detected one of the opposite race watching their movements from behind some cover, it is quite likely that they would be "full of wrath and swiftness," and that the inquisitive observer would have "little chance to get off

---

they formed one division of the Scottish army at the battle of the Standard. If any part of the Pictish people might be expected to retain their peculiar language and characteristics, it would be the Picts of Galloway; . . . . . We find, therefore, that in this remote district, in which the Picts remained under their distinctive names as a separate people as late as the twelfth century, a language considered the ancient language of Galloway was still spoken as late as the sixteenth century." (Skene's "Celtic Scotland," Vol. I. pp. 203-4) Whatever the language was, it is evident from the facts just quoted that the traditions of this Galloway district are of deep interest.

alive." That there should be a "white one" among them is not surprising at a time when a great mixture of races was going on;—or if one remembers that among the invading Mongolian hordes there were both white Huns and black Huns. So that, all things considered, it becomes very probable that the makers of the "Druids' beads" were "Snake Indians," and that the memorable campaign of Patrick was against the same people.

Buchanan, the distinguished tutor of James VI. of Scotland, in the course of his description of the ancient inhabitants of Scotland, remarks as follows :*—

> There are, besides, two ancient nations, the Mæatæ, and Attacotti, placed by the Roman writers within the limits assigned to the kingdoms of the Scots and Picts . . . . . . The Attacotti, according to Marcellinus, appear to have been those who were for some time, excluded by the wall of Adrian, but upon the extension of the Roman empire, by the wall of Severus, were included within the province, as in the Book "De Castrensibus Officiis Romanorum Per Provincias," on the Camp services through the Roman provinces, among the foreign auxiliaries, I find some cohorts of the Attacotti, as well as the Britons. I am, therefore, at a loss whether to admire more the effrontery or the stupidity of Lloyd—his effrontery, in affirming the Attacotti to have been Scots, not only without any authority, but without the smallest shadow of a probable conjecture ; or his stupidity, in not perceiving, in the very passage he quotes from Marcellinus, that the Scots are distinguished from the Attacotti ; for Marcellinus says, "that the Picts and Saxons, Scots and Attacotti, harassed the Britons with constant miseries."

And Aikman, in a foot-note, adds

> The Attacotti are only mentioned by the ancient writers, whom Buchanan quotes, and by St. Jerome, who characterizes them as delighting in the taste of human flesh. "When they hunted the woods for prey, it is said they attacked the shepherd, rather than his flock ; and that they curiously selected the most delicate and brawny parts, both of males and females, for their horrid repast." Jerom. tom. II. quoted by Gibbon . . . . . The character given by the Saint, whose veracity, Gibbon says, " I see no reason to question," must of necessity have belonged only to some scattered savages ; it never characterized the whole Scots, and corroborates the assumption that they, the Attacotti, were a distinct tribe. A modern writer, however, Richard of Cirencester, whose work has appeared since the days of Buchanan, differs in his statement, as to the boundaries, from our author . . . . . According to

* "History of Scotland" : Aikman's translation. 1827. pp 91-3

Richard, the Attacotti inhabited from Lochfine to Lochlomond, comprehending the whole of Cowal in Argyleshire, and the greater part of Dunbartonshire.

Who the Attacotti were, and the etymology of their name need not be here discussed. It is sufficient that in them we have one of those tribes, regarding whom reports of cannibalism were current in the days of Strabo.

The practice of cannibalism must to some degree have continued for many centuries after the days of the Attacotti. Sir Walter Scott's story of Richard Cœur de Lion and the Saracen's head, and the reputed cannibalism of the seventeenth century, of which he speaks in Woodstock, quoting the incident of the "fine squab children" who figure in the play of the *Old Troop*, need not be historically true. But, the very currency of such tales, and the fact that they were not scouted as utterly incredible, seem to suggest a substratum of truth underlying the fiction. Not only can we look back to those Argyleshire *Attacotti*,—plainly pictured as cannibals, by a writer "whose veracity, Gibbon says, 'I see no reason to question,'"—but all over the country we have traditions of Ogres, Ughres, or Ugrians, who carried off—*and ate* children; while in Scotland there are several traditional instances of cannibalism, within comparatively recent times. One of these is of a family of cave dwellers, on the coast of Forfarshire. This rocky coast is, in many places, hollowed out into large caves. "In one of these most dismal caverns, there lived, in the fourteenth century, a cannibal and his family, who allured young men and children to his haunt, and there devoured them. Pitscottie gives a very quaint account of the whole family being 'burned quick' for their crime."* Another, and somewhat later example—being placed in the following century—is that of a Galloway clan, or family, who also inhabited a sea-side cavern. These people were savages of the most degraded character. "As soon as they had robbed any man, woman, or child, they used to carry off the carcase to the den, [it is previously stated that "they never robbed any one, whom they did not murder,"] where cutting it into quarters, they would pickle the mangled limbs, and afterwards eat it; this being their only

* Dawson's "Statistical History of Scotland;" parish of St. Vigeans.

sustenance: and notwithstanding they were at last so numerous, they commonly had superfluity of this their abominable food, so that in the night-time they frequently threw legs and arms of the unhappy wretches they had murdered into the sea, at a great distance from their bloody habitation; the limbs were often cast up by the tide in several parts of the country, to the astonishment and terror of all beholders, and others who heard of it."*

Here, then, is one of the most repulsive traits of savagery carried down to the very days of Chaucer—and farther. It is plain, from the context of each of these recitals, that the cases were isolated. But they were survivals of what had been a common practice of certain Scottish tribes. The most pleasing reflection for every one now living in these islands is, that those two families particularized cannot be numbered among "Our British Ancestors." Because in these, as in most other similar instances, in which revolting savagery asserts itself among civilized people, the savages are not permitted to leave any posterity behind them. Nevertheless, we have no assurance that the very people who looked with such horror upon the anthropophagous tribes of Scotland and elsewhere, were not themselves, the remote descendants of cannibals. There are well-educated and refined people in Polynesia to-day, who do not require to look farther back than one generation, to find the same custom practised by their own people, and to whose children the fact will scarcely seem credible.

. . . . . .

A year or two ago, there was a report—contradicted afterwards, and subsequently re-affirmed—that the King of Ashantee had caused two hundred young girls to be slain, in order that their blood might be used for mixing up with the mortar employed in the building of his new palace. It was understood that the girls had been captured from some neighbouring tribe, into whose territory the King's brother had made incursions, in order to procure the required number of victims. Whatever horrible superstition may have given rise to such a bloodthirsty custom,—it was also practised by the

* Nicholson's "Historical and Traditional Tales, connected with the South of Scotland": Kirkcudbright, 1843: p. 72.

savage "blackamoors" of Early Scotland : if any faith is to be placed in tradition. Sir Walter Scott, in a note to *The Cout of Keeldar*, tells us, that—"castles, remarkable for size, strength, and antiquity, are, by the common people, commonly attributed to the Picts, or Pechs, who are not supposed to have trusted solely to their skill in masonry, in constructing these edifices, but are believed to have bathed the foundation-stone with human blood, in order to propitiate the spirit of the soil." And Hugh Miller, wandering among the ruins of Craighouse, in Cromarty, encountered the same belief. This ruin, he states, was then supposed to be haunted by a spirit ; regarding which, he says :—" I remember getting the whole history of the goblin . . . . . . from a sun-burnt herd-boy, whom I found tending his cattle under the shadow of the old castle-wall. I began by asking him whose *apparition* he thought it was that could continue to haunt a building, the very name of whose last inhabitant had been long since forgotten. '*Oh, they're saying*,' was the reply 'it's the spirit of the man that was killed on the foundation-stone, just after it was laid, and then built intil the wa' by the masons, that he might *keep* the castle by coming back again ; and *they're saying* that a' the verra auld houses in the kintra had murderit men builded intil them in that way, and that they have a' o' them their bogle. '"

It is impossible to believe that such a custom as this was of spontaneous growth in early Scotland and in modern Africa. That, in each case, the perpetrators were of the black-skinned races, renders the assumption doubly sure, that the common custom of these physically-similar people had one common origin.

. . . . . .

Let me point out another "coincidence." The high priests of certain races among the ancient Britons regarded the mistletoe with the greatest reverence, and the traditional honour bestowed upon this plant at the present day (by a nation composed chiefly of "dark whites") shows the strength of the feeling. But of what *race* were the men who first reverenced the mistletoe ? Perhaps the following quotation may help to answer the question :

"The times of offering sacrifice were in the spring and

fall. . . . Then, the victim, self-appointed, or determined by lot, as the case might be, repaired to the tent of the senior prophet, who, aided by his four junior associates, painted the face and adorned the body of the favoured victim with a covering of the mistletoe, that being the holiest and most rare of evergreens."

But this is not the description of a religious ceremony among the *British* priests: it is a faithful account* of an immemorial custom practised by a Mongoloid nation on the other side of the Atlantic. That the mistletoe could be seized upon as "the holiest of evergreens," by two races that had never been connected, is so unlikely, as to be almost incredible. The readiest solution lying to hand is, that this circumstance is a relic of the time when "one homogeneous people occupied, if not a ring round the world, at least one reaching from Britain to Kamskatka."

. . . .

The same parallel is observable in a custom described by Martin, in his Description of the Western Islands of Scotland. "All the inhabitants [of Barray, an island of the Hebrides, "Barr's Isle,"] observe the anniversary of St. Barr, being the 27th of September; it is performed riding on horseback, and the solemnity is concluded by three turns round St. Barr's church." These islanders are even yet described as of tawny complexion, and if their physiognomy resembles that of many other Hebrideans, they are Mongoloids. And, just as the North American priest, sacrificing with the rites of the sun-worshipper, and the sacred plant of the mistletoe, bears a startling resemblance to the British priest of eighteen centuries ago, so the solemnity of making the circuit, sun-wise, of any sacred place (for to go *against* the sun was simple profanity, in the opinion of certain natives of Scotland, at quite a recent date,)—a certain number of times,—forms another connecting link between the inhabitants of the same two countries. Indeed, the ceremonies of the American "Indians," as pictured in the book just quoted from, are almost identical with those of certain of the early

---

* "Antiquarian Researches," by W. Pidgeon, New York, 1858. (From a description of the rites practised by certain "Indians," in the Sacrificial Pentagon, Wisconsin.)

races of Britain. This likeness, however explainable, exists in a marked degree: but enough, for our present purpose, has been said regarding it.

. . . . .

At least *one* tribe of Ancient Britons employed poisoned weapons in warfare. It may be remembered that the traditional Agathyrsi or Geloni, arriving in Ireland from Thrace by the way of France, received a tract of country from the King of Leinster as a reward for slaughtering a certain tribe. This was the tribe of the Tuath Figda, who are spoken of by the chroniclers as "hateful horrid giants," and "the giants of high Banba (Ireland)." "Any man wounded by them died, and they carried nothing about them but poisoned iron." It is therefore, satisfactory, on the whole, to learn that "the Tuath Figda were all killed afterwards."*

. . . . .

Such are a few of the traits characterizing certain among our forefathers—or, at any rate, forerunners—in these islands. To what extent these were our ancestors, it is impossible to decide. But they were as thorough savages as any race now living upon the earth.

* Skene's "Chronicles of the Picts and Scots," p. 326.

CHAPTER VII.

LET it once be understood that the Picts of history were "blackamoors,"—the question next arises, "Could they have been related to the Scandinavians, as some aver?" Keightley says that the Picts, who "early seized the Scottish Lowlands," were "akin to the Scandinavians;" and Martin, in his Description of the Western Islands of Scotland, says that "it is generally acknowledged that the Picts were originally Germans, and particularly from that part of it bordering upon the Baltic Sea." While another last century voyager, Pennant, in speaking of the round tower at Brechin,* remarks thus :—" The learned among the antiquaries are greatly divided concerning the use of these buildings, as well as the founders. Some think them Pictish, probably because there is one at Abernethy, the ancient seat of that nation; and others call them Danish, because it was the custom of the Danes to give an alarm in time of danger from high places."

The writers I have quoted are rather old-fashioned and unscientific, but the opinions they repeat are held at the present day. Therefore, it becomes evident that some race of Scandinavians must have been Black Huns also, with physical characteristics approaching those of the Pictish Moors, either in the Australioid or in the Mongoloid direction. And since the Mongoloid belt stretches generally north of the Australioid, it seems likely that any possible Scandinavian Picts belonged to the former, rather than to the latter type. There really happens to be a tradition of a "Hungarian" invasion of Scotland. "Hector Boece, in referring to this legend, tell us that while some write that they were Hungarians, others say that they were a company collected

* Pennant's "Second Tour."

from Scots and Angles."* This was in the year 875, the date of a Danish invasion of Scotland. But this statement recalls the Huns proper, of whom something has already been said. They, it will be remembered, united in their persons the qualities of the two great types under consideration. They were "of a dark complexion, almost black ; deformed in their appearance, of uncouth gesture, and shrill voice. 'They were distinguished,' says Gibbon, ' from the rest of the human species by their broad shoulders, flat noses, and small black eyes deeply buried in the head ; and they were almost destitute of beards.'" They had attained to such a degree of power in the fifth century that they were able to exact an annual tribute from Rome, so that the Empire might be secured from further injury. They had previously " occupied all the territories that had been abandoned by the Goths," " whose dominions reached from the Baltic to the Euxine." After the death of Attila, in 454, their power waned, and gradually, as Huns, they disappear from sight.

Many centuries before the days of Attila, the provinces of Rome had been invaded from the north by hordes of barbarians, one section of which resembled the Huns in several particulars. Towards the end of the second century before Christ, the Romans, under Marius, had to repel the attacks of the Ambrones, the Teutones, and the Cimbri, who poured into Italy in immense numbers, only however, to suffer defeat. It is said of the Cimbri, that " 140,060 were slaughtered by the Romans, and 60,000 taken prisoners," and this overwhelming defeat most effectually put a stop to their inroads. But before that, they had in one battle " destroyed 8,000 Romans." Lempriere (whose words have just been quoted) describes them as "a people of antient Germany [*i.e. Scythia*], who at one time inhabited that part of the country which now forms the modern kingdom of Denmark. They were very powerful, and in their invasion of the Roman empire were so courageous, and even desperate, that they fastened their first ranks each to the other with cords." A quainter recorder than Lempriere† has this to

---

* Skene's "Celtic Scotland," Vol. I. p. 321.
† The "Cambridge" Dictionary of 1693, previously quoted from.

say of the Cimbri:—" Cimbri, qui lingua Gallicà *latrones* dicuntur, Fest. vel à *Gomero*, à quo originem deduxerunt. *People of* Denmark *and* Holstein, &c. *Men of vast bodies and dreadful looks,* Juv. *They made an inrode into* Italy, *with a design to take* Rome, *but were beaten and routed by* Marius. Anno U.C. 640." So that, about the period when one branch of the Hiong-nou was invading the Chinese empire on the east and south-east, another branch was carrying fire and sword through the countries to the west and south-west? There is scarcely enough evidence to fully warrant this conclusion, but there are some resemblances between the two barbarian hordes. Both were "Scythian" (though this does *not* mean much), and the "vast bodies and dreadful looks" of the Cimbri suggest the "broad shoulders" and other "dreadful looks" of the Huns. The Huns were "of a dark complexion," and so also were the Cimbri, as shall be afterwards seen. Both were plainly of a warlike and nomadic disposition: they were both in fact *latrones*, freebooters, pirates. It seems likely, in short, that the Hiong-nou were in Europe several centuries *before* the date assigned by De Guignes, although fresh hordes swarmed westward out of Asia in the early part of the Christian era.

The country inhabited by the Cimbri was, it is stated, the modern Denmark and Holstein, which, indeed received from them the name of Cimbrica Chersonesus, or the Peninsula of the Cimbri. But those Cimbri are said* to have been known by another name: "Dani, iidem qui Cimbri. *The Danes.*"

It now begins to appear possible that the tradition of a "Hungarian" invasion of Scotland, cotemporary with an inroad of "Danes," is the memory of the arrival of one nation under two names. If this be the case, then the comely, fair-skinned people now inhabiting Denmark are out of the question, as having nothing in common with the Dani of "vast bodies and dreadful looks." If it can be shown that the "Danes" who invaded and overran the British Islands in the eighth and succeeding centuries, and who were distinctly *latrones*, or pirates, were also dark-skinned like the Black Huns, then the identification of the eighth-

---

* The "Cambridge" Dictionary of 1693, previously quoted from.

century Danes (who are confused with "Hungarians") with the Dani or Cimbri, and again with the more or less Mongoloid Huns or Hiong-nou, will be strongly suggested, if not established.*

"It is necessary, in steering one's way through the numerous invasions of the Northmen, to distinguish clearly between Norwegians and Danes. This is evidently done in the Pictish Chronicle, the Norwegians being called Normanni, and the Danes, Danari."† "Ever since the Danes, or Dubhgaill, first came to Ireland there had been a contest between them and the Norwegians or Finngaill for superiority, and in 877 a battle took place between them, in which the Norwegians had the victory. The Danes, being for the time driven out of Ireland, went to Alban or Scotland."‡ The mere fact of jealousy and warfare existing between the two does not of itself warrant one in concluding that the Northmen and the Eastmen (as Danes and Saxons together were styled by the Franks) were different in race, but it shows that they regarded themselves as different in nationality. Probably the name Vik-ing also belongs to the Danes, and not at all to the Normans. It is as Danes and Vik-ings that the piratical hordes that plundered, burnt, and destroyed along the Scottish sea-board, are chiefly known, and it was by a treaty with the king of *Denmark* (in 1014) that the Scottish King Malcolm succeeded in obtaining the withdrawal of these marauders from his country. However, the two peoples, Northmen and Eastmen, Norwegians and Danes, are also known by other names. "Besides the general term of Gentiles (says Mr. Skene), that of Gall, the Irish word for stranger,§ was likewise applied to them, and two nations were distinguished as Finngaill, white or faired-haired Galls, and Dubhgaill, black or dark-haired Galls—the former being

---

* It is stated, in an account of their great defeat by Marius ("Chambers's Encyclopædia," art. "Cimbri"), that "when the battle was lost, the women, who remained in the camp formed of the waggons, killed themselves and their children." This waggon-laager reminds one of Attila's similar camp on the plain of the Marne five or six centuries later. From the fact that they carried their women and children about with them, even when "on the war-path," it is evident that the Cimbri or Dani were, like the Huns, a nomadic people.

† "Celtic Scotland," Vol. I. p. 376.

‡ *Ibid.* p. 327.

§ Compare the name given to the Abyssinian *Oroma, Gall-is,* or "invaders."

Norwegians, ... and the latter, Danes." But the typical Dane of to-day is *not* a black-haired man; quite the reverse. And *dubh* means *black*, without any word of *hair*.*
These two sections of invaders were also known as Finn Gennti, and Dubh Gennti, White Gentiles and Black Gentiles; and as (according to Armstrong), Fionn-Lochlinneaich, and Dubh-Lochlinneaich, White and Black "Lochlinners" or Scandinavians. And, in "the wars of the Gaedhil and the Gaill" (Gaels and Galls), the Danari are styled "black Danars," or "black Danes." In none of these terms is there any hint that the colour of the hair is indicated. But the expression used by St. Berchan in speaking of the Norwegians leaves no room for doubt. He calls them "the Gentiles *of pure colour*."† The Danes, then, were *not* "of pure colour." They were *dubh*, black. As black, at any rate (let us suppose), as the Black Huns, who were "of a dark complexion; almost black."

There can be no question about it. The designation given by the common people of one race to another is almost invariably founded upon some physical feature, and the most natural distinction is that of colour where the races differ in complexion. The invading whites styled the "Indians" of America "Red-skins," and these again called their conquerors "Pale-faces." A native Australian is a "black-fellow" to the modern Briton (who, after all, is his exceedingly distant kinsman). Other "Blacks" are roughly spoken of by us either under that title or, under its other form, as "Negroes." Therefore, when the white races of Britain styled the Danes "Black heathen," they simply made use of the most natural term that could occur to them.

It was not only in Scotland that the Danes received this name, but throughout the British Islands. Let me give a few extracts from the Annals of St. David's, in Wales, (*Annales Menevenses*), which I obtain from Archbishop Baldwin's *Itinerary*, translated and annotated by Sir R. C. Hoare.‡ It is a record of murder and rapine, a sample merely of what was happening throughout the greater part

---

* This point has already been touched upon.
† Skene's "Chronicles of the Picts and Scots," p. 85.
‡ Vol. II. : annotations on Chapter I.

of these islands at that period, and before and after it, when a peaceful and partly-Christianized people had to suffer every indignity at the hands of a ruthless and brutal race of pirates. The extracts are these:—

A.D.
812. Combustio Meneviæ.
986. Godisric filius Harald cum nigris gentibus vastavit Meneviam.
1000. Menevia vastatur à gentilibus.
1011. Menevia vastatur à Saxonibus, sc. Edrich et Umbrich.
1071. Menevia vastatur à gentilibus.
1078. Menevia vastatur à gentilibus, et Abraham Episcopus occiditur.
1086. Scrinium Sancti David de ecclesiâ furatur, et juxta civitatem ex toto spoliatur.
1088. Menevia frangitur et destruitur à gentilibus.

. . . .

[The learned annotator continues, farther on]—As the account given by Powel in the Welsh Chronicle differs somewhat from the above, I shall insert his tradition:

"In the year 810, Saint David's was burnt by the West Saxons. In the yeare 911, there came a great navie from Tydwike, with Uther and Rahald, and past by the westerne sea to Wales, and destroied Saint David's. A.D. 981. Godfryd the son of Haroald did gather a great armie, and landed in West Wales, where spoiling all the land of Dyvet, with the church of Saint David's, he fought the battell of Lhanwanoc.

A.D. 987. The Danes landed in South Wales, and destroyed Saint David's Lhanbadarn, Lhanrysted, and Lhandydoch (which were all places of religion), and did so much hurt in the country besides, that to be rid of them, Meredyth was faine to agree with them, and to give them a penie for everie man within his land, which was called, 'The tribute of the blacke armie.'

A.D. 1078. Menevia was all spoiled and destroyed by strangers.

. . . .

A.D. 1090. The Normans landed in Glamorganshire, and spreading themselves over different parts of South Wales, put an end to the predatory incursions of the Danes and other pirates. [These words are Sir R. C. Hoare's.] 'The Normans in great companies landed in Dyvet, or West Wales, and Cardigan and builded castels there, and so began to inhabite the countrie upon the sea-shore,' and to their protection the church and town of Saint David's probably owed the tranquillity which they afterwards enjoyed."

Here there is perfect unanimity. The "cum nigris gentibus" of the Annals, and Powel's "blacke armie," are at one. Thus, we have as evidence these terms—*dubh* (used with four different nouns), *niger* and *black*—all applied in the most natural and matter-of-fact way to the Danish pirates by men of presumably white race. Can anything be clearer?

What may be called genealogical evidence of the existence of black-skinned races existing in Scotland within historic times, has already been adduced in considering the "Moors." And it is difficult to decide whether the examples given ought to be styled Picts (so-called) or Danes. Because both were "Picts," and contemporaries. And the very district which still bears the name of the ancient "Moray" men, was also the very district in which the "Danes" lingered longest (that is, excluding the Isles). For which reason, it had become the hunting-ground of the fair-skinned victors, descendants of Freskine the Fleming, Berowald the Fleming (founder of the powerful Innes family), and others of kindred race. Therefore, when a black man is discovered on a family tree of a thousand years ago, he may be either a "Dane" or a "Pict." Of those, however, who are better known by the former name there may be specified an ancestor of the Macleods of Macleod, that family being held to be descended (at the date of Martin's visit to the Western Islands, and in his words,) "from Leod, son to the black prince of Man," which island was for a long time under the rule of the Danes. The father of this Leod was in all probability Olafr Svarti, or Olave the Swarthy, mentioned in the Flateyan manuscript, who was King of Man during the thirteenth century. A certain branch of the Campbells had also a similar lineage.

Pennant* speaks of "Sir Colin . . . , ancestor of the Breadalbane line, the famous knight of Rhodes, surnamed from his complexion and from his travels Duibh na Roimh, or Black Colin of Rome;" and "in a manuscript history of the Campbells, written about 1827," the author says "that Righdeirin dubh Loch Oigh (the Black Knights of Loch Awe) was the name then used by old Highlanders in mentioning the chiefs of the Duin (Campbells),'' who, or their followers, were probably the "swarthy men from Lorn" introduced in one of the Legends.† They must have been latterly displaced by a totally different race, as that member of the clan whom I have just quoted states that the Campbells now-a-days boast of their yellow hair.

Another and more distinctly visible member of this race may be seen in the beginning of the eleventh century, in that memorable ship that carried the Northmen to the American coast. "Now in Thorvard's ship was one Thorhall, who had been the huntsman in summer, and in winter the steward of Eric the Red. He was, it is said, 'a large man, and strong, black, and like a giant, silent, and foulmouthed in his speech, and always egged on (*eggjadi*) Eric to the worst; he was a bad Christian."‡

But a still more notable Black Dane, was Earl Thorfinn, son of Sigurd, "the most distinguished of all the earls in the Islands." His deeds are recorded, with some minuteness, in the *Orkneyinga Saga*, and he is also referred to in the *Saga of Saint Olave*. "Earl Thorfinn was very precocious in his education, and in every improvement. He was a strong man, and ugly, and of great stature. When he grew up it was manifest that he was avaricious, harsh, and cruel and sagacious." "Now Thorfinn became a great chieftain, one of the largest men in point of stature, ugly of aspect, black haired, sharp featured, and somewhat tawny, and the most martial looking man; . . . He was then five winters old when Malcolm, King of the Scots, his mother's father, gave him an earl's title, and Caithness to rule over; but he was fourteen winters when he prepared maritime expeditions from

---

* "Second Tour: Pinkerton's Voyages," Vol. III. p. 368.
† "West Highland Tales," Vol. III. p. 280.
‡ Bryant and Gay's "History of the United States, Vol. I. p. 48.

his country, and made war on the domains of other princes." On the day of his great, and victorious engagement with the army of Kali Hundason, King of the Scots, his appearance is thus described:—"He had a gilt helmet on his head, and was girt with a sword, a spear in his hand, and he hewed and cut on both sides. It has been related that he was the foremost of all his men."

"Earl Thorfinn held all his *rikis* till the day of his death, so that it was said that he was the richest of all the Earls of Orkney. He was possessed of nine earldoms in Scotland, the whole of the Sudreys, and a large *riki* in Ireland. Earl Thorfinn was five winters old when Melkolf [Malcolm], King of Scotland, his mother's father, gave him the title of earl, and he was earl for seventy [or sixty, according to Saint Olave's Saga] winters. He died in the end of the reign of Harald Sigurdson, and was buried in Christkirk, in Birgisheradi, which he had caused to be built."*

Thorfinn's widow, Ingibiorg, is said† to have married "Melkolf, King of Scotland, who was called Langhals. Their son was Dungad, King of Scotland, the father of William, who was a good man. His son was William the Noble, whom all the Scots wished to take for their King." It is difficult to reconcile this genealogy with those given by

* From the *Collectanea de Rebus Albanicis* pp. 340, 346. Mr. Skene places the battle against Kali Hundason at Burghhead on the Morayshire coast. He identifies this Kali Hundason with the Shakespearean Duncan, and he states that Thorfinn and Macbeth were probably allies, if not actually one and the same person (for there is more than one instance of a confusion between these two names, pointing to such a conclusion). It is curious to reflect that if Thorfinn and Macbeth were one, then the memorable duel in the play was between "the son of a black" (himself either a "black" or a mulatto) and an "ugly, black-haired, sharp-featured, and somewhat tawny" giant!

I have quoted a few more sentences than were necessary to the proving that Thorfinn was not a "fair white," because it is important to bear in mind, what the Sagas and Mr. Skene's maps reveal, that Scotland was for several centuries a dependency of this mixed, semi-Mongoloid race. About the period of Thorfinn's exploits this nation ruled over the greater part of Scotland—over the present counties of Sutherland and Caithness, a large part of Ross and Inverness, the whole of Argyleshire, Galloway, the Northern Islands, the Hebrides, and the Isle of Man; besides large districts in England and Ireland. Caithness was so identified with the Danes that until within recent times ("Coll. de Reb. Alb." p. 307) it was known to the Highlanders by the name of *Gallibh*. "The Islands of the Galls" (the Hebrides), Galloway, and Galway have all received their names in this way.

† *Orkneyinga Saga*; *Coll. de Reb. Alb.* p. 346.

Feuds and Inter-Marriages.

Mr. Skene, but it serves to show how the Danes and one or other of the Scottish races were so closely allied as to make it a question whether they were not actually the same people.

What this syllable "finn" (or "find," as the Irish Annals have it) precisely denotes, it is not easy to determine. It occurs in a large number of names, and is translated "white," which is probably the correct rendering.* But it is found, in at least one instance, along with a Mongolian characteristic. A celebrated leader under Harold the Fair-haired was "Caittil Finn," who is also called "Caittil the White." But he was known besides as Caitill or Ketill "Flatnose," which points to the possession of Ugrian blood.† This Ketill Flatnose was of noble descent, and was despatched to the Hebrides by Harold, to bring these islands under subjection, which he succeeded in doing. (There is some discrepancy as to this, one account stating that he subdued the Hebrides independently of Harold.) He attained to great power, and a daughter of his, "Audur the Wealthy," was married to Amlaiph or Olaf the White, King of Dublin, who had previously been at war with his wife's father, for the Irish Annals record, in the year 857, a "victory by Ivar and Olave over Caittill the White, with his Gallgael [the mixed Scandinavian-Gaelic people of the Hebrides], in the lands of Munster."‡ A son of this marriage is known as Thorstein the Red, which, if this term indicates the complexion, seems to suggest a mixed lineage. This same Olaf the White seems afterwards to have married a daughter of Kenneth mac Alpin, who was himself of mixed blood.§ Indeed, whether one looks at the question from the Pictish or from the Danish side, one sees plainly that a great fusion of races was going on during a period of several centuries. Thus

* At any rate, it is so translated by all the highest authorities. And yet Thorfinn or Finntuir (as he is elsewhere called) was *not* white, but "somewhat tawny."

† One is almost tempted by this to construe *Finn Galls* and *Dubh Galls* into white and black *Huns*, thereby explaining the disputed etymology of the name Finn as applied to the Finns of Finland. It will be seen in another chapter that there is other evidence tending to support this theory. But the great objection to it is the fact that the Finn Galls are stated to have been the Northmen or Normans, who are understood to be pure *Xanthochroi*.

‡ "Collectanea de Rebus Albanicis," p. 257.

§ "Celtic Scotland," Vol. I. pp. 311, 312, 323-326.

also, Harold Haarfagr himself (whose appellation alone would hint that "fair hair" was an exceptional feature among his people) was the son of Halfdan Svarte, or the Black, and it is therefore to be presumed that the "fair hair" was inherited from a white mother. And since Harold II., surnamed Graafel, or Greyskin, was the son of Eric Bloody-axe, who was of the Finn Gennti, it is as evident that the "greyskin" came through a tawny mother.

(Feuds between near relations seem to have been quite usual at this time. Not only did Olaf the White war against his father-in-law, Ketill Flatnose, but also, in the year 865, he, along "with his gentiles laid waste Pictavia, and occupied it from the kalends of January to the feast of St. Patrick," the then King of the Picts being the brother of his other wife, Kenneth mac Alpin's daughter. It was only a natural thing, therefore, for Constantin—his brother-in-law—to kill him in the following year as he was "withdrawing with his booty." This Olaf must have been a restless and daring warrior, for at another time the stronghold of Alclyde [Dumbarton] "was besieged by the Northmen under the same Amlaiph, along with Imhair [Ivar], another of their kings, and destroyed after a four months' siege. . . . On this occasion they appear to have also attacked both the Picts of Galloway and the Angles of Bernicia, for in the following year we are told that Amlaiph and Imhair returned to Dublin from Alban with two hundred ships, and a great booty of men, Angles, Britons, and Picts, was brought with them to Ireland in captivity."*)

It is apparent, then, that the "fair whites" and the "dark whites" were much more widely separated by physical characteristics at the time of the Danish Conquest than at the present day. So widely separated, indeed, that "dark *whites*" were only beginning to make their appearance, or had not been on the scene for very long. The titles *Finn* and *Dubh* were still more frequent than *Donn*. "White" and "Black" occur very frequently. Not only were there the "white foreigners" and the "black foreigners," but the Pictish Chronicle has also mention of a native race which Mr. Skene decides were "the white Tisians, a white people

---

* "Celtic Scotland," Vol. I. pp. 323-5.

of the Tees,"* And on the other side, one of the pedigrees accredited to Olave the White—for there is a want of unanimity as to his lineage—states that he was the grandson of "Frodi the gallant, whom the Svertlings killed." That is, "whom the Black Dwarfs killed."†

The Danes, then, were like the "Moors"—black. Like them, too, they were Picts, as more than one eminent writer has proved. The title of "gorm" (woad-stained) is not confined to Highland genealogies: it was the actual name of a grim old pagan Dane who ruled over Denmark in the earlier part of the tenth century, and the word survived lately in that province of the Black Gentiles, Northumberland, where it bore the significance "to smear; to daub."‡ So also were the Picts (known as such) at home on sea as well as on land, like the Danes. In the year 729, the Irish Annals record that "three ships of the Piccardach were wrecked this year on Irrois Cuissine," and ten years previously there had been fought "the maritime battle of Ardnesbi, between Duncan the son of Becc with the tribe Gabran, and Selbhac with the tribe Lorn, . . . in which battle certain chiefs were slain." Whether as "Danes" or as "Picts," they were a swarthy, piratical race. And it is interesting to notice that the custom of tattooing has survived longest in their *professional* descendants, our own seamen. It is stated, I see, that "although this practice was condemned in the year 785, it was not wholly rooted out of England till after the Norman conquest."§ It is really not "wholly rooted out" yet.

But before leaving the consideration of the complexion of the Danes, it may be well to make a few more remarks thereon.

The islands which were specially their home (in Scotland) since an unascertained epoch, are or were known to the people

* "Celtic Scotland," Vol. I. p. 364, note.
† From the "Laxdaela Saga," as quoted in Coll. de Reb. Alb. p. 67. In the Scandinavian "mythology," there is mention of a race known as the Ynglings. If the syllable *yng* be taken as equivalent to *ing*—which Halliwell defines as "a meadow, generally one lying low near a river"—then these people would be *Mæatæ*, like the swarthy Damnonii or Moors. And if "ling" be accepted in its diminutive sense, then the Ynglings were Marsh-dwarfs. That they were probably one with the Svertlings, or Black Dwarfs, will be pointed out afterwards.
‡ Halliwell's Dictionary.
§ "Comprehensive History of England," Vol. I. p. 168.

of the mainland as Inchegall or Innse-Gall, the Isles of the Foreigners, and to this day "an islander" (*innseanach*) means "an Indian." And although the "black heathen" were expelled from these islands many centuries ago, and although, as a distinct race, they have almost vanished from Europe, yet there may be traces seen of them even yet, in the physique and the complexion of their descendants, whether in the Hebrides or elsewhere. It would be impossible to decide with certainty who are their descendants and who are not, but so far as complexion goes, the "moors" are still largely represented throughout the British Islands; although of course the crossing and re-crossing of thirty generations, while increasing the number of descendants, has lessened the intensity of the resemblance to the ancestral stock. But the swarthy hue asserts itself still, though in a modified degree. Last century, when Martin described the *Western Islands of Scotland*, he remarked that the complexion of the natives of Skye was "for the most part black;" of the natives of Jura he said that they were "generally black of complexion," and of Arran that they were "generally brown, and some of a black complexion." The inhabitants of "the Isle Gigay" presented a greater mixture: they were "fair or brown in complexion."* And Pennant, speaking of the Islay people, describes them as "lean, withered, dusky, and smoke-dried."

In their memorable tour through the north and west of Scotland, Johnson and Boswell several times took notice of the swarthy colour of some of the natives.† It will be remembered that Boswell said of the mixed race of the McRaes:—"There was great diversity in the faces of the circle around us; some were as black and wild in their appearance as any American savages whatever." And he may have had their complexion before his mind's eye when he said of some of the Islanders:—"Our boatmen were rude singers, and *seemed so like wild Indians*, that a very little

---

* He also repeats an anecdote of "a gentleman," "a native of Skye," who "did, when a boy, disoblige a seer in the Isle of Rasay, and upbraid him for his ugliness, as being black by name and nature. At last the seer told him very angrily, 'my child, if I am black, you'll be red 'ere long,'" which saying was next day accepted by the boy as the prediction of a cut on the forehead which he then received by some accident.

† Croker's "Boswell," 1848, pp. 309, 310, 316, 352.

imagination was necessary to give one an impression of being upon an American river;" and when he particularized, at another time, "a Macleod, a robust, black-haired fellow, half naked, and bareheaded, something between a wild Indian and an English tar."*

A later writer than Boswell, writing forty or fifty years ago, speaks thus of the people of Harris. "In general the natives are of small stature... Scarcely any attain the height of 6 feet, and many of the males are not higher than 5 feet 3 or 4 inches.... There is nothing very peculiar in the Harrisian physiognomy; the cheek bones are rather prominent, and the nose is invariably short, the space between it and the chin being disproportionately long. The complexion is of all tints. Many individuals are as dark as mulattoes, while others are nearly as fair as Danes [modern Danes, of course]. In so far as I have been able to observe, the dark race is superior to the fair in stature and strength. .... In respect to intellect, they are acute, accurate observers of natural phenomena, quick of apprehension, and fluent in speech. In their moral character they are at least much superior to the population of most of the lowland parishes."†

And finally, one who has every right to speak upon the characteristics of the Western Islanders, gives us the following picture of a Highland girl:—"In the warm nook behind the fire, sat a girl with one of those strange foreign faces which are occasionally to be seen in the Western Isles, ... a face which, at the time, reminded me of the Nineveh sculptures, and of faces seen in St. Sebastian. Her hair was as black as night, and her clear dark eyes glittered through the peat smoke. Her complexion was dark, and her features so unlike those who sat about her, that I asked if she were a native of the island, and learned that she was a Highland girl [that is, from the mainland]."‡ She did not differ in *complexion* from the people beside her, who were the "short, dark natives of Barra,"

---

* This Macleod was a true descendant of the black Prince of Man. What "an English tar" of Boswell's day resembled will appear in another place.

† *Edinburgh New Philosophical Journal*, No. VII. pp. 142, 143. (Quoted from Dawson's "Statistical History of Scotland," p. 550.

‡ "West Highland Tales," Vol. III. p. 144.

and the difference in feature is accounted for, says Mr. Campbell, by the supposition, generally current there, that she and others like her, are "the descendants of the Spanish crews of the wrecked armada." There is no reason to discredit such a belief, which, if correct, would place this girl out of court as a witness to Danish blood—("the short, dark natives of Barra" being indeed themselves sufficient). But it may not be necessary to go so far away from the Hebrides to find an explanation of a gipsy face among the people of these islands, or of the neighbouring Highlands.

Whether we look, therefore, at the Danes of history, or at the people who to-day have the best claim to be regarded as their descendants, we see before us men of swarthy skin. And what is more, we see that Meredith and the Southern Welsh of the tenth century were, by inference, *Xanthochroi*. And the extracts proving this, have also shown, to those of us who were previously in ignorance, that the "Welsh" of Cardiganshire and other parts of West Wales are largely, if not wholly, Normans. And since Pembroke was, in the twelfth century, partly peopled by Flemings, there must also be a considerable infusion of Flemish blood among the Pembrokeshire "Welsh" of to-day. So that in Wales, as in the Scottish Highlands, an immense number of people who believe themselves to be Celts, and who are full of enthusiasm on the subject of the Celtic languages, which they regard as the immemorial speech of their forefathers, are in actual fact the descendants of Flemings and Normans of eight or nine centuries ago. And a Welsh Jenkin (Jan-chen), whose ancestors have intermarried with Watkins and Wilkins (Wat-chen and Will-chen), has as little to do with the Briton of a thousand years back as have his Scottish kinsmen who descend from Freskine, or from Innes, or from Fleming. In trying to discern the lineaments of this or that variety of "Ancient Briton," we must disregard such "Celts" altogether. And they are not few in number. "I am convinced," says Professor Skeat, in the *Brief notes* prefaced to his Etymological Dictionary, "that the influence of Dutch upon English has been much under-rated, and a closer attention to this question might throw some light even upon English history ...... We read of Flemish mercenary soldiers being employed by the Normans, and of Flemish settlements in Wales, 'where (says old Fabyan, I know not with what truth) they remayned a long whyle, but after, they sprad all Englande over.'" . Like the Norman and other immigrants, they gradually identified themselves with the people of the district in which they settled, and so became Welshman, Englishman, and Scot, their descendants fighting against each other under these names, fully believing themselves to be—as by intermarriage they to some extent were—Welshman, Englishman, and Scot. If blood relationship counted for much, they would not have lost their nationality so easily. But the ties of mutual interests are vastly stronger than the ties of blood, and the American of next century will not stop to consider his lineage, if his country should happen to fall out with any other power. So the Fleming—as the Norman—became eventually a clannish, Gaelic-speaking Highlander, or a bigoted Welshman, or, picking up a few new words, dropping a few old ones, and modifying his accent, he became an Englishman.

To return to the swarthy people. If the earliest races of Picts or Moors were expelled from the districts in which we now find dark people, or were wholly exterminated there, such people will become the probable descendants of the "black strangers" who overran our islands at a later date. And thus the "small swarthy Welshman"—the "small dark Highlander"—and the "Black Celts to the west of the Shannon"—are, as likely as not, the living representatives of the Danes.

While, on the other hand, it is evident that the Flemings, the Norsemen ("Gentiles of pure colour"), their kin the Normans, and the Celtic tribes represented by Prince Meredith, the "Fionn" of tradition, and the "barbarian prisoner" of South-British race, are all substantially one people, the *Xanthochroi* of Professor Huxley, and the fair-skinned Germans of the Romans.

CHAPTER VIII.

BEFORE going on to consider the various consequences of regarding the Danish pirates as a swarthy, half-Mongoloid people, it is advisable to discover, if possible, what traces they have left of their complexion in the topography, and the language, of this country. They, and any other black race.

It has been remarked, incidentally, by an American writer, that "Indian Creek is a sort of John Smith in the nomenclature of western streams;" and this, of course, is the result of the fact, that for many years after a frontier district has been settled (though not thickly) by white pioneers, scattered bands of the native tribes have lingered on, in a harmless gipsy-fashion, beside their old riverside camps. And thus the name of "Indian Creek" has been the most natural name that could be given to those streams beside which they lived. (For I think it will be found that localities are oftener named after the people who inhabit them, than from any other distinguishing association.)

There is no word better entitled to be called the "John Smith" of the nomenclature of British localities than the word "Black." Undoubtedly there are cases where this adjective has been applied because it denoted some apparent and striking feature in the landscape;—as for example in the case of the gloomy "Black Country," or where some craggy peak asserts itself distinctly as a "Black Rock." But in most instances, no such explanation is satisfactory, and it is apparent that the real origin of the name dates from the days when certain portions of Scotland were distinctly recognized as "black divisions;" for the simple reason that they were peopled by black races, over whom, in the latter half of the tenth century, there ruled Kenneth MacMalcolm, known to his contemporaries as *The Black*.

At this present time, certain districts in the Southern States of America are called "the black regions," for a similar reason. And since the waters of the Black Sea are *not* black,—it is more than probable that the savage tribes whose presence upon its coasts once made it known as the Axine, or "inhospitable" sea, were also black. The Egyptians who dwelt by the Red Sea depicted themselves as *red*, —which the sea itself is not. And though it may be argued that the White Sea was so named on account of the snowy ice-floes that cover its surface the greater part of the year,—what is one to make of the more Arctic *Kara* Sea? It may be left, however, to others to settle whether those seas, and various European rivers and districts (of which latter the Black Forest* is an example), originally received their titles from the presence in their neighbourhood of a black people, or from some striking natural feature. There are plenty of names for our present purpose within the limits of the British Islands.

One of the most convincing of these is the Black Isle of Ross-shire, otherwise known as Edderdail, which, it has been already presumed, is a token of the presence there of the "Adder" tribe. This "black isle" is not really an island, but "a peninsular territory" "between the two seas, or the Cromarty and Moray Firths," "consisting chiefly of two great ridges parallel to one another, and running nearly from S.W. to N.E., including the N. slope of the 'Maolbuy' (or Yellow Hill) . . ." "There are several old castles and numerous traces of Danish camps." It may be added that it formed a part of the ancient *Moravia*. It was almost the last part of the Scottish mainland in which the Danes lingered, and their expulsion, and the battles preceding it, were contemporaneous with the struggles between the Scottish monarchs (assisted by Normans and Flemings) and

---

* "As they bowled along in the deliberate German express train through the Black Forest, Colonel Kenton said he had only two things against the region : it was not black, and it was not a forest." (Mr. Howell's "At the Sign of the Savage.") It may be objected that the district was once clothed with an actual forest of dark and gloomy pines. This may be so ; but if so, it is difficult to see why this particular forest should have been distinguished from the many equally sombre pine-forests of Central Europe. It is much more likely that the true explanation of the name is to be found "at the Sign of the Savage."

the "Moray rebels." So that whether the Moray-men and the Danes are to be regarded as one and the same, or only as akin to each other, there is quite sufficient reason for that particular corner being styled the "black isle,"—without endeavouring to prove that its scenery is black;—*which it is not*.

The lochs which throughout Scotland are named "Black" are too numerous to specify. (Those which are styled "Yellow" and "Red" are also numerous, but for more than one reason they cannot be held as undoubtedly named after the dwellers along their shores. The Lake of the Red Women on Coomroe mountain, in county Kerry, Ireland, speaks for itself.) Not only are lochs and streams in Scotland designated "black" in English, but—and they constitute the majority—a large number bear the Gaelic title of *dubh*, often hidden from a casual observer by its pronunciation of *yew*, which it receives when aspirated (*dhubh*). *Loch Ewe* and *Pool Ewe* are examples of this. This aspirated form is also disguised in some districts by the sound of *hoo* which it receives. Sometimes, also, it becomes *doov, duffie* and *duff*. It is perhaps a mistake to say that, in its English form, "black" is a *common* title of Scottish lochs, although a glance at an Ordnance Survey Map is sufficient to show how common it is in Gaelic. But I see there is a "Black Loch" in the parish of Mearns, Renfrewshire, and another near Slamannan, in the county of Stirling. It may be said that Highland lochs are really black, in their peaty depths. And this is so far true. Why, therefore, should one loch be distinguished from another by this title, when all are alike black? So also it may be said that "Pool Ewe" or "the black pool," might be applied to many a sullen and gloomy river-bayou. But the places so named in Ross-shire are formed by the sea, which is *not* black. And if the many Black Rivers in the United Kingdom got their titles from the sombre aspect of their depths, what is one to make of the not infrequent Black-ford? For, of course, a ford is the shallowest and *whitest* portion of a river; and the several "black fords" cannot well have been designated after their colour. Much more likely did they become known as "the black fords" for a reason akin to that which (to cite one

Examples.   129

modern example) has given to the Indian ford on the Bow River, Saskatchewan, the title of "Blackfoot Crossing."*

"Black Waters" are quite common in the British Islands. There are at least five in Ireland, and one in Essex, while the towns of Blackburn and Blackpool bespeak their origin. These are well-known instances, but it is probable that the Ordnance Survey Maps will reveal a great many more. In Scotland, a Black Water and a Ciaran (*Little Swarthy*) Water together form the River Leven, which skirts the northern border of the famous Black Mount deer-forest; a Black Water runs down Glen Shee in Perthshire; there are two Black Waters in Kirkcudbrightshire; two Black Burns in the adjoining county of Wigtown (in which district there are many other "black" names); and, in Sutherlandshire, the Black Water of Clyne has, on its banks, "an ancient Pictish fortress"—known as Cole Castle—to testify to the presence there of the "blackamoor." "A so-called 'Picts' Work' [*i.e.* Moors' Work], a circular structure of large stones strongly fortified by a wall," which stands on the left bank of the Black Burn, a mountain stream in the parish of Castleton, Roxburghshire, proclaims, with equal distinctness, that the river owes its title to the swarthy people who once dwelt beside it. Besides other Black Burns, there is a village of Blackburn in Linlithgowshire, a village of Blackford in Perthshire, and another in Midlothian. This last is situated in the neighbourhood of *Mor*-ton-hall, where there are several tumuli, and near at hand are the Pent-lands (*i.e.* Paint-lands, formerly Pict- or Pight-lands, a name which still clings to the north-eastern limit of Scotland, once known as *Gallibh*, or "the land of the *Galls*," or Foreigners, —who, whether early "Picts," or later Danes, were painted "Moors"). The River Forth, from Aberfoil upward, is *Avondow*, "the black water,"—and no one who has visited the charming little valley through which it sparkles, would dream of saying that the name is derived from the colour of

---

* It is almost unnecessary to point out that the recurrence of the word "black" in the name of this particular tribe of Indians is a mere coincidence, and has nothing to do with the question under discussion. Any other ford that may be named after a tribe accustomed to use it will suit equally well. Had "Blackfoot Crossing" been named "The Redskin Crossing," the parallel between it and "The Black Ford" would have been more exact.

the stream. But any one who looks at the "lie" of the country will see how naturally that mountain-guarded valley would become the last retreat of a defeated people,—who might even hold their own there for several generations, until that section of the Forth that passes through their fastness (and *only* that section) had for ever become associated with them; going down as "the Black River" to generations that knew them not.*

Of other Scottish rivers, showing a like pedigree, there may be named—the Black Esk, the Black Cart, the Blackadder (each of which has a companion White stream of the same name)—the Black Devon, and the Black Megget-water, each of which has a companion bearing no distinctive forename. And it may be noted that the Blackadder flows through the district known as The Merse (*merse* or *marsh*), and that the Avondow was one of the chief rivers of those marsh-dwellers, or *Mæatæ*,—the swarthy Damnonii.

Of miscellaneous "black" names, there are a great many. Without leaving London, one can see Blackwall and Blackheath, neither of which is any blacker than the rest of the metropolis. The latter is less so : but the *Danes* encamped upon the heath during the year 1011 A.D. which will easily account for the origin of its name. In Cumberland, there is a Black Combe,—and in Brecknockshire are the Black Mountains and the Black Forest. Such names as the Black Lions, of which, as of Black Heads, there are two,—and Black Rock and Black Ball Head—all in Ireland—may, and probably do bear only a superficial meaning. But there can be no doubt as to the paternity of the appellations attached to the following places in Scotland :† "*Black Cairn*, a hill surmounted by a large cairn, in Rayne parish, Aberdeenshire. . . ." "*Blackcastle*, the northern summit of Cocklaw Hill, in Innerwick parish, E. Haddingtonshire. It takes its name from remains of an ancient fort." "*Blackcastle*, an ancient camp in Greenlaw parish, Berwickshire, on a precipitous bank at the confluence of Faugrist Burn and the Black-

* One guide-book states : "The Avon Dhu is properly the Forth, but receives here the name of Avon Dhu, or 'black river,' from the sombre appearance given to it by overhanging woods and heights." An explanation less satisfactory than this could scarcely be found.

† Described in the *Ordnance Gazetteer of Scotland*, edited by F. H. Groome.

adder... An entrenchment commences opposite to it, on the right bank of the Blackadder; ... and, in the southerly reach of it, is called Black Dikes." "*Blackchester*, an ancient oval camp in Lauder parish, *Berwickshire*..." "*Black Hill*, a hill in Crawfordjohn parish, Lanarkshire... Two consecutive circles are traceable on it..." "*Blackhouse*, a range of mountains, on the natural border of Selkirk and Peebles shires... This region, from so early a period as the time of Malcolm Ceannmor, belonged to the family of Douglas [*Dubh-glas*, or Black-Swarthy], and appears to have been used by them as both a fastness and a hunting-ground..." "*Blacklaw*, a ruined tower of the Douglases* of Fingland..." "*Black Quarter*, the teritory now forming Portpatrick parish, Wigtownshire..." Several of these places, and some other "black" names, are within the limits of the *Picts'* ["blackamoors'"] *Dyke*, "a long line of ancient fortification in Galloway and Dumfriesshire, commencing at Loch Ryan near Innesmessan.... and extending.. to the upper part of the Solway Firth... It separates the fertile lands of the seaboard districts from the irreclaimable wastes and wild fastnesses of the mountains...."† And that this particular district should teem with relics of the black people is not surprising, since—according to Mr. Skene—the Picts of Galloway retained their individuality longer than any other division of their kindred.

Blackness, on the southern shores of the Firth of Forth, is clearly an example of those names which have not been derived from any natural feature; and another such is Blackcup Scars, in the Moorfoot Hills, where "a circle of tall stones, 70 or 80 feet in diameter, and three large rings or ditches, about fifty paces in diameter," remind one that

---

* There must always be a little uncertainty attending such surnames as this. Its original meaning was undoubtedly "black-swarthy," but a time came when it ceased to denote complexion, and passed into the class of ordinary meaningless family names. For example, Ballyduff in the north of county Kerry, and Balduff near Alyth, Forfarshire, each signify "the Black Town." But Dufftown, in Banffshire, is more likely "the town of the Duffs," the name having been given at a period when this had become a clan-name, irrespective of complexion.

† Along the line of this rampart there are several Black Lochs and White Lochs in juxtaposition. Only those acquainted with the neighbourhood can decide whether any striking physical characteristic has given rise to the distinctive title in each case. But this seems very unlikely.

the dusky Australioids of Tasmania and the Dekhan have reared such monuments as these. "Several remarkable cairns or tumuli," and "a distinct Druidical circle" in the neighbourhood of the Black Craig at New Cumnock, Ayrshire, point to a like comparison. In this vicinity, too, one of the Black Waters finds its source, and another hill bears the somewhat puzzling name of "Black Larg." Near Morebattle, Roxburghshire, there is a Blackdean Hill,—and a Blackwood Hill in Nithsdale. Finally,—to complete this "black list"—there are such places as Blackcarnside, in Fife; Blackrig, in Dumfriesshire, and Blackridge, in Linlithgow; and in Peeblesshire, Blackbarony,—the ancient home of the family *De Moravia;* while, among the mountain-peaks that enclose Glen Almond, Perthshire, there are two bearing the names of *Meal na Dhu* and *Craig na Dhu,*—that is to say— "the hill" and "the craig of the Blacks."*

Here, then, we have a large class of names, of which most of the samples just given are quite meaningless if they do not bear reference to the inhabitants of the districts they denominate. It is true that in many similar cases the designation "black" refers solely to some natural feature,—and that, in some others, the application of the term is doubtful. But, after considering the majority of the instances already cited, it is impossible to reach any other conclusion than the one arrived at. And this being so, it is not necessary to surrender those names whose etymology is uncertain; since it is extremely probable that they, too, owe their fatherhood to the dusky complexion of the people who dwelt beside the places they designate.

In addition to such topographical evidences, of which the foregoing specimens only form a fraction, there are cases where this qualifying adjective is still attached to objects not wholly, and sometimes not at all, inartificial. Dr. Jamieson

---

* In addition to these, the following have subsequently come under my notice:—*Ross-dhubh,* "the black promontory," on the shores of Loch Lomond; and in the parish of Watten, Caithness, Blackisle, Blacklass, the Black Pools, and *Druimdubh,* "the black mount"—all of which latter places are contiguous, while to the south of them, and quite near, are various *Dubh Lochs.* No feature of the landscape can possibly explain the unanimity of these names. It is unnecessary to cite further examples; but the Ordnance Survey Maps abound in such cases.

mentions, in his Scottish Dictionary, that in Argyleshire a certain kind of mill is styled a "black mill." It is, he says, "the designation unaccountably given to a miln of the ancient construction, having one wheel only." (*Really*, quite as accountably given as the name of any Black-ford or Black-barony, in the country.) Again, the Iona guide-book tells you that "the Black Stones of Iona, on which the Highland chieftains made oaths of alliance and mutual contracts, have all been carried away." They had not been removed when Martin visited the island last century, and he remarks of them: "A little further to the west lie the black stones, which are so called, not from their colour, for that is grey, but from the effects that tradition says ensued upon perjury, if any one became guilty of it after swearing on these stones in the usual manner." Here, the title was confessedly not given from the colour of the stone; and the traditional explanation is no explanation, since the supposed result of forswearing oneself was to blacken the face of the perjurer, without affecting the stone,—or, indeed, whether the oath had been taken on a stone or not. The apparent deduction is that "tradition" has here performed a not unusual feat. The true origin of the name has been forgotten, and since *some* reason must be given to inquisitive travellers, "the effects that tradition says ensued upon perjury" has been dragged into service. So might the peasantry of the Avondow valley gravely inform the traveller of the twentieth century that the upper reaches of the River Forth were one time as black as ink. I do not know whether the perjury fable clings also to a "huge mass of rock, called the Black Stone of Odin," to be seen in the Orcadian island of Shapinshay.

The dictionaries, archaic and Gaelic (which is living-archaic, so to speak), are full of memories of the black people. And these chiefly relate to the time when they were underfoot,— "the servants of servants." To this period belong the phrases which have been already introduced,—the time when "a girl of the lowest rank of peasantry" was *dubh-chaile*, a black wench; as is the case in Georgia or the Carolinas at the present day. (And like the Southern-Negress,[*] the

---

[*] According to the unbiassed judgment of the author of "Studies in the South," *Atlantic Monthly*, February 1882.

British *Dubh-chaile* was too often *dubh-choitchionn*,—so that, indeed, the two designations became interchangeable.*) Similarly, the talk of the mob is still called *dubh-chainnt*, or black speech; and there remains also the military term, *dubh-chléin*, the flank, to remind one that the Picts assisted ultimately in fighting the battles of their conquerors, and, as Dr. Skene tells us, "formed one division of the Scottish army at the battle of the Standard." It seems quite a tenable theory, also, that the "black-men," defined by Halliwell as "fictitious men, enumerated in mustering an army, or in demanding coin and livery," represent another phrase-witness of the time when a minority of our troops were really black men; the phrase having long out-lived the date when the black element—as distinctly such—became absorbed in the overwhelming white element. Another of Mr. Halliwell's archaic terms—" black-money "—seems, in one way or another, to be connected with his " black-men." He explains this term to denote " money taken by the harbingers or servants, with their master's knowledge, for abstaining from enforcing coin and livery in certain places, to the prejudice of others." Or it may, perhaps, be more reasonable to conclude that this expression is something equivalent to the still-surviving " black-mail,"—used at the present time in our daily speech, without any consideration of its radical meaning.

But, however lightly we may use it now, this term is intensely significant. It links the Black Danes and the Black Huns together, by a tie of common custom as well as by a common hue. The expression applied by the inhabitants of Wales to the tribute exacted from their prince, Meredith, by the Danish pirates of the year 987 A.D., virtually signified " black-mail." And, moreover, " the tribute of the blacke armie " precisely phrases the tax paid by Theodosius to Rugilas, King of the Huns, five centuries before. It was *black*-mail. That is the origin of the term. *Dane-gelt* was *black-mail*, equally with the tribute paid to the black Huns by the Romans.

The earliest instance of this term, in its English form, seems to be in an act of James VI. of Scotland, of the year

* *Dubhadh* also indicates something of this sort.

1567, where it is used in its modern sense,—that is, without any reference to the complexion of the people to whom the mail or tribute was paid. This is the earliest *date* given by Dr. Jamieson in his Scottish Dictionary, where he further states: "This term was also used to denote a certain rate of money, corn, cattle, or other consideration, paid unto some inhabiting near the Borders, being men of name and power, allied with certain known to be great robbers and spoil-takers within the counties; to the end to be by them protected and kept in safety, from the danger of such as do usually rob and steal in those parts.'" The words occur in an act of Queen Elizabeth's reign, by which time the phrase must, of course, have lost its first signification. But the reason of the phrase clinging to that particular district may be traced to the fact that "the Danes of Northumberland belonged to the branch of the Northmen called Dubh Gall, or Dubh Gennti, that is, black strangers;"* and it is probably owing to this that (according to Armstrong) "a Lowland Scot" and "an Englishman" were also Dubh Galls, to the white-skinned race of Highlanders who opposed them.

Dubh-chis, or *-chios*, is the Gaelic equivalent, rendered in the dictionaries "a tribute," and "black-mail," this last being of course the strict interpretation of the term. In its Gaelic form it is a memorial of the time when two-thirds of Scotland owned the sovereignty of the Danes. The memory of this time runs through the West Highland (and Irish) tales; and, indeed, it was to free their people from this oppression that the traditional league of the Feinne was formed. "There was a king on a time over Eirinn, to whom the cess which the Lochlanners had laid on Alba and on Eirinn was grievous. They were coming on his own realm, in harvest and summer, to feed themselves on his goods; and they were brave strong men, eating and spoiling as much as the Scotch and Irish (Albannaich and Eirionnaich) were making ready for another year."† And so, as the story goes, the oppressed peoples were roused into a bold effort to throw off the yoke.

In looking over the lists of "black" names in the archaic

---

* "Celtic Scotland," Vol. I. p. 364, note.
† "West Highland Tales," Vol. III. p. 331.

vocabularies, one is constantly reminded of the deformed bodies and equally deformed moral natures of the Huns. The "Chunorum impudica" asserts itself everywhere. Not only in the *dubh-chaile* and the *dubh-choitchionn*, but also in such words as these—*dubhaile*, "vice, wickedness," *dubh-fhocal*, "a bad expression," (literally, "a black word,") *dubh-ghràin*, "extreme disgust, abhorrence;" all of which terms render it likely that the "foul-mouthed" black man who accompanied the Vinland expedition, and who is emphatically put down in the Saga as "a bad Christian," was a thorough-paced Black Dane,* or Hun. The words just given have shown the deformity of the moral nature,—which the English "blackguard" and "black" ("mischievous, malignant;" *Halliwell*,) may be said to do in a less marked degree,—and the last of these, *dubh-ghràin*, shows the physical deformity as well. For it also means "deformity." And another word, *duaichnidh*, signifies "deformed, ugly, dismal, black;" in which connection it is curious to note that the black man in the ship of Eric the Red was "ugly" as well as "foul-mouthed," and therefore a most typical Hun, or Sarmatian, or Dane;—for of all these branches of the race, ugliness of soul and body seem to have been the distinctive features. The worst horror of a Danish inroad was not the burning of churches, and sacking of treasuries; and the Danish oppression of the eleventh century was most keenly felt where it affected neither life nor property. And it may be remarked in passing, that it is through this "Scythian" channel that we have most probably received the "strange and revolting legends" of European "mythology," previously referred to.

A tradition of a black man living in Scotland within the memory of man, was noticed in treating of the "Moors," who are in all probability of the same race, substantially, as the other black Europeans, under whatever name. A counterpart to the Black Morrow of Galloway is to be seen in a traditional "Black Knight," who is said to have lived near Ashton-under-Lyne, "holding the people in vassalage,

* It was noticed, some chapters back, that *duine dubh* (a black man) and *duine gorm* (a blue or woad-stained man) were one and the same. It is pertinent to the present theme to notice that we have still, in the dregs of our language, two words which are applied to *dubh-fhocal*—the one signifying the quality *dubh*, and the other *gorm*.

and using them with great severity."* This legendary "blackamoor" must ante-date the Galloway ruffian, for the latter evidently belongs to a period when he and his race were almost wholly subdued, and only able to commit their outrages under cover of night, whereas the former was distinctly "the lord of the manor." There is a hint of another Scotch "lord" of this sort, who was presumably of the same race as him of Lancashire, but as in his case the complexion is not specified, he need not be more than alluded to in this place.

In one of the Notes to *Ivanhoe*, Sir Walter Scott adduces an instance which indicates the existence in our islands of a considerable black population within historical and comparatively recent times.

The critics had been objecting to "the complexion of the slaves of Brian de Bois-Guilbert, as being totally out of costume and propriety." This objection he meets by citing "an instance in romance" which shows that, not only were there black people in England during the dark ages (*dark* in a double sense), but also that they constituted, or at least formed a recognized part of, the class of wandering minstrels and mountebanks. The case in point is this :—

"John of Rampayne, an excellent juggler and minstrel, undertook to effect the escape of Audulf de Bracy, by presenting himself in disguise at the court of the King, where he was confined. For this purpose, 'he stained his hair and his whole body entirely as black as jet, so that nothing was white but his teeth,' and succeeded in imposing himself on the King, as an Ethiopian minstrel. He effected, by stratagem, the escape of the prisoner. Negroes, therefore, must have been known in England in the dark ages." (*Ivanhoe, Note B.*)†

* See Halliwell's Dictionary ; *Black-Lad-Monday*.

† Those who believe in the tremendous force of inherited custom (more powerful far in *communities* than in *families*, for the longest-lived family is at the best ephemeral) will see another hint of the memory of a black race in the following incidental feature of the regatta of the Mediterranean Fleet, held in October, 1881, and described in the *Illustrated London News* of the 15th of that month :—

"One amusing feature of the regatta was a procession of 'copper punts,' the punts so-called because they are chiefly used for men to clean the copper of the ships' sides. These clumsy punts were so rigged as to represent their respective ships. They were manned by parties of seamen with blackened faces and arms,

Now, this "instance in romance" (or history?) not only fully corroborates what has already been said with regard to the *presence* of black people, but it also agrees with several other word-witnesses. For example, the Gaelic *dubh-fhocal*, or black word, which means "a bad expression," has other varieties of meaning. It signifies as well—"a dark saying, a riddle or puzzle, a parable." And *dubh-chleas* is "a feat in legerdemain or in black art." And magic or necromancy *is* "black" art. All of which things are connected with strolling jugglers and charlatans. To the same people must belong a dance once known as Black-Almain (*Halliwell*), which is perhaps nothing else than the Morris-dance. And it was possibly danced amid the din of the Blacksaunt or Black Sanctus, which Wright, in his Dictionary of Provincial Phrases, defines as "any confused or hideous noise," and of which Halliwell says that it is "a kind of burlesque hymn, performed with all kinds of discordant and strange noises."

But all this tends to bring to mind a race of people of whom something has already been said. It will be remembered that Maclellan of Bombie became entitled to bear the Moor's head in his arms *because* he had slain a gipsy chief who was ravaging the south of Scotland. And also that the Gaelic name for "a gipsy" was seen to be only another form of the name of the wild savage whom Diarmaid killed. Farther, this savage, and the Galloway gipsy, and the "Irish rebels" described by Derrick are all *ciuthachs*, or men with plaited hair, and the two last are known as men of swarthy skin, which may be predicated of the first as well, since *ciuthach-gipsy;* in short, the three names describe one people. And this swarthy, nomadic race is possessed of precisely the same characteristics as the black-skinned "jugglers and minstrels" who formed part of the substratum

variously disguised, and using coal shovels instead of oars, while singing comic songs, accompanied by fife and drum . . . . "

In a sketch of this by an officer of the *Téméraire*, the men are seen to be using the shovels as paddles, and this, with their black faces and arms, their "disguises," the wild strains of the music, and the din of the "comic songs," must have produced exactly the effect of a war-party of savages in their canoes. And if the prototypes of these "savages" were sea-faring Picts or Danes, then the "comic songs" would probably be found to be quite unfit for printing, and to contain many words whose meanings were wholly unknown to the singers.

of the English nation in the dark ages,—if there be any truth whatever in the adventure of John of Rampayne. It becomes, therefore, of importance to discover what is known as to the date of the arrival of the Gipsies in Europe, and to glance, as hurriedly as may with advantage be done, at their most striking features.

... The Scandinavian and Low-German *Tatare* identifies Gipsies with the Mongolian hordes, the terror of Europe in the thirteenth century; and their French name *Bohémiens* was probably due either to a confusion of some such form as *Secani* with *Czech*, or to the belief that Gipsies originated in Bohemia. To the same class belong *Walachi, Cilices, Uxii, Saraceni, Agareni, Nubiani*, &c., cited by Fritschius (1660). ... Their Scotch name *Tinkler*, which occurs in a charter of William the Lion (1165-1214), is commonly held to be a mere variant of *tinker*; but if its initial *t* correspond to *z* (*cf* English *ten*, German *zehn*), it comes very near the Italian *Zingaro* or *Zingano*,* which like the German *Zigeuner*, Czech *Cingan* or *Cigán*, and Magyar *Cigány*, is a form of the most widespread of all the Gipsies' appellations—Bulgarian *Atzigan*, modern Greek 'Ατσίγκανος or 'Αθίγγανος. ... Less dubious seems an extract from the Georgian *Life of Giorgi Mtharsmindel* (eleventh century), which describes how at Constantinople certain descendants of the race of Simon Magus, *Atsinkan* by name, sorcerers and famous rogues, slew wild beasts by their magic arts in the presence of Bagrat IV. ...

... Other documents might be cited, but these are enough to show that in the fourteenth century Gipsies existed in the Balkan peninsula and islands of the Levant; that in Wallachia they were reduced to a state of bondage (from which they were only freed in 1856); and that nowhere were they regarded as new comers, so that by these documents it is impossible to fix the date of the first Gipsy immigration. More than this, a metrical German paraphrase of Genesis, made by an Austrian monk about 1122, preserved at Vienna, ... goes far to prove that Gipsies were known in Austria three centuries before the commonly-accepted date of their appearance in that country. A passage relating to Hagar's descendants (Gen. xvi. 15) runs :—" So she (Hagar) had this son; they named him Ishmael. It is from him the Ishmaelites descend.

---

* Scotch children have a game which they call *Jing-ga-ring*, of which a particular description might be given here, were it not that it would entail a further digression. It seems to be without doubt an ancient marriage ceremony (indeed the *aim* of the thing is to marry a pair of very young lovers, and the verses chanted throughout constitute the marriage-service), and the various stages of the solemnity are marked off by a circular, sun-wise dance. The similarity between these words *Jing-ga-ring* and *Zingari* is strong; and it is not difficult to believe that in this children's game we really have the marriage ceremony of this ancient people.

Possibly also the dance of the *Zigeuner* has come down to us as a *jig*.

They journey far through the world; we call them *Chaltsmide* (lit. cold-smiths).... "That here by *Chaltsmide, Ishmaelites*, and *descendants of Hagar* Gipsies are meant, scarcely admits of doubt....

Late in 1417 there came to Lüneburg a band of 300 wanderers, "black as Tartars and calling themselves *Secani*."... Next comes a long notice of a troop of fully 100 lean, black, hideous Egyptians in the *Chronica di Bologna* (July 18, 1422), which tells how the sorceress, "Duke" Andrew's wife, could read the past and future of men's lives;....

... We find them in England in 1514 (*a Dyaloge of Syr Thomas More*, 1529), but nothing is known of the date of their landing; and in Scotland the earliest certain record of their presence is an entry in the books of the Lord High Treasurer: "Apr. 22, 1505. Item, to the Egyptianis, be the kingis command, vij lib."... In a "King of Rowmais" (? *Rômas*, Gipsies), twice mentioned in entries of July 1492, as also in the "Erle of Grece" (1502), "King Cristall" (1530), and the "King of Cipre" (1532), one dimly recognizes four Gipsy chiefs; and with Gipsies perhaps the Saracens may be identified, whom a tradition represents as making depredations in Scotland prior to 1460 (Simson, p. 98).*

The Gipsies, then, whom we have already seen described as "Moors," were also known as "Saracens," the terms being indifferently used in heraldry and in the old romances. "Nothing is known of the date of their landing" in England, while "a tradition represents them as making depredations in Scotland prior to 1460." The piratical races who are known to history under various names, and who "made depredations" throughout the British Islands at various dates "prior to 1460," were also, as Scott remarks, styled "Saracens," and it has been noticed that a "Hungarian" and a "Danish" invasion of Scotland took place, according to tradition, at the same time. The Gipsies, also, under their Scandinavian title of *Tatares*† are "identified with the Mongolian hordes, the terror of Europe in the thirteenth century."

---

* "Encyc. Brit." 9th edit. art. "Gipsies."

† It does not appear that our own Gipsies—known as "Gipsies"—were ever styled "Tartars," but it is pretty certain that *thieves* were. (And "thief" and "gipsy" were synonymous terms at one time, if not now.) The Host, in "The Merry Devil of Edmonton," says: ".... there's not a Tartarian, nor a carrier, shall breath upon your geldings;" and this calls forth the following remark, in Dodsley's edition :—"*Tartarian* seems to have been a cant word for thief. In 'The Wandering Jew,' 1640, p. 3, the hangman says, '..... and if any thieving *Tartarian* shall break in upon you, I will with both hands nimbly lend a cast of my office to him!'"

The Bataillard Theory.

Thus, the Moors or Saracens, the Danes and other kindred races, and the Gipsies are virtually the same people under different names.

In believing this, it is of course impossible to agree with the theory (never substantiated) that there were no Gipsies in Europe until a few centuries ago. But it is an easy matter to agree with a French scholar, Bataillard (author of *Les Origines des Tsiganes, Les Tsiganes de l' Age du Bronze, &c.*), in the conclusion which he has reached by another route. " He now believes the Gipsies to have existed in Europe from immemorial times,—a conclusion to which he is led by the absence of any record of their passage across the Bosphorus, by their enslaved condition in Wallachia in the fourteenth century, by the casual notices . . . of their presence at a still earlier date, and by their present monopoly of metallurgical arts in South-Eastern Europe." [For he argues that the ancestors of the Gipsies are the people of the Bronze Period; and although " it is a mighty leap from the Athingani of the ninth century A.D. to the Sigynnæ of Herodotus (v. 9)," these are the people " whom Bataillard claims for the ancestors of the Gipsy race."]*

In the matter of dress, Mr. Crofton . . . infers that "Gipsies formerly had a distinctive costume, consisting of a turban-like headdress of many colours, together with a large cloak, worn after the fashion of a toga, over a long loose under-skirt " . . . The English Gipsy woman may be known by her bright silk handkerchief, her curiously-plaited hair, her massy rings, her coral or bead necklace, and by the *monging guno*, a tablecloth arranged bagwise over her back. . . On the other hand, the dress of the children upon the Continent is simple, not to say scanty. . . . (In warm countries the gypsy children go perfectly naked for the first few years of their life. . . . In England the females are generally distinguished by a cloak, grey or red, and a coloured kerchief tied around the head.)†

Outwardly as within Gipsies present strong contrasts, some being strangely hideous, others very beautiful, though not with a regular conventional beauty. . . . The hair, black or dark brown, inclines to coarseness, is often frizzled, and does not soon turn grey; the complexion, a tawny olive, was compared by the Plymouth Pilgrims (1622) to that of the Indians of North America. The teeth are of dazzling whiteness and perfect regularity, the cheekbones high; and the aquiline nose is overhung by a strongly-marked brow, knit often in deep lines of thought.

* "Encyc. Brit." 9th edition, art. "Gipsy."
† *Ibid.* 8th edition, art. "Gypsy."

But the most striking feature is the full, dark eye, now lustreless, then changing to an expression of mysterious childlike sorrow, presently blazing forth with sudden passion. (The Gypsies, like the Pariahs, are very disgusting in many of their customs; such as, for instance that of eating the flesh of animals that have died of disease. . . . They marry very early; boys of fourteen and girls of twelve are often man and wife; nor is the closest propinquity any bar to their union. . . . In mild climates they dispense with tents, and congregate in companies in forests and deserts. In cold countries they find shelter in caves, or build huts sunk in the earth, and cover them with sods laid on poles. In Spain, and also in Hungary and Transylvania, there are some gypsies who follow trades. They are innkeepers, farriers, and dealers in horses; smiths, nail-makers, tinkers, and menders of old pots and kettles; makers of wooden spoons, spindles, &c.; and occasionally they engage in the labours of the field. They have a certain degree of natural talent for music, and are often respectable performers on the violin, flute, Jew's-harp, &c. Their skill in this art is confined to instrumental music, particularly of the dance kind. In many place the gypsies support themselves by rope-dancing and tricks of legerdemain; while the women find occupation in fortune-telling, the interpretation of dreams, and the like. In the earlier part of life, particularly in Spain, the women are dancers; and when they grow older, they invariably practise fortune-telling and chiromancy.)*

Although these extracts may seem needlessly ample, they contain many statements whose importance will appear in the next chapter, if not in this. In this Zingari race, then, we see much to identify them with the vast pre-historic European people, of whom the Black Huns are a good enough type. Because, whether as gipsies or as Black Huns, they seem to unite the Mongoloid with the Australioid races. They are swarthier than Mongols; and although the "curiously-plaited hair," the high cheekbones, and the aquiline nose, combine with their complexion to render them European counterparts of the races encountered by the Pilgrim Fathers in North America,† yet the strongly-marked brow of most, and the "strangely hideous" physiognomy of some of

---

* "Encyc. Brit.," 8th edition, art. "Gypsy."
† Other resemblances between the British "Moors" and the North American tribes have already been pointed out, as, for instance, the reverence paid to the mistletoe, the riding three times round a building as an act of solemnity, and (of course) the use of war-paint. The similarity of features and complexion was remarked by the Puritans of the seventeenth century. As a matter of fact, the scattered bands of tame Indians who wander among the settled districts of the United States and of Canada, occasionally working and oftener begging, are nothing more or less than Gipsies.

them, connect them again with that low type of man which has been classified as Australioid by Professor Huxley. And there is a great deal in the foregoing description to remind one of what has already been said regarding Ancient Britons, with whom, as Moors, Saracens, and Hungarians, or Ogres, or Cimbri, or Danes, they are historically identified. While the "naked wild men living in caves," who were "blubber-lipped," and men with "plaited hair," against whom the Celtic legendary heroes fought, are in all these respects gipsies: and under either name are one with the naked Wild- or Black-Irishmen, with their "glibbed" locks, described by Derrick and Spenser. And again, the ugly Moors of heraldry, with their black skins, thick lips, and "pearls pendant," are virtually the same as the ear-ringed black and hideous Egyptians who trooped into Bologna about five centuries ago.* (Those "Egyptians" were in all probability a branch of "the pagans of Prussia" who are said to have besieged Dantzic, under Udislaus Ingello, in the year 1389.) So that the strolling mountebanks and minstrels of the days of John of Rampayne, whether descended from pre-Roman "Moors," or from later "black heathen" invaders, were pretty clearly of this race. The legend shows them to be black, and to this very day you may see the racial characteristics in the ear-rings and gay colours of the nomadic, open-air juggler, with his oily, plaited hair, and perhaps also in the long side-locks which are still dear to the "Putney Pet" fraternity; and in the half-*salaam* with which the circus acrobat greets his patrons round the ring.

Such conjectures as these are entirely corroborated by the statements made in a very faithful record of gipsy life— Simson's *History of the Gipsies.* It is there (p. 39) stated, on authority, that, of the fourteenth century gipsies of Samarcand, "Some were wrestlers, others gladiators, others pugilists." While a description of certain English gipsies runs thus (pp. 93-4) :—"This chief and the two females were the most swarthy and barbarous looking people I ever saw.... [The man had] a profusion of black, greasy hair, which

---

* In such desultory glances over such a great extent of time, every allowance must be made for changes in dress, customs, and *physique*, resulting from intercommunication and commingling with other races.

covered the upper part of his broad shoulders. He wore a high-crowned, narrow-brimmed, old hat, *with a lock of his black hair hanging down before each ear*, in the same manner as the Spanish gipsies are described by Swinburn ... His visage was remarkably dark and gloomy."

This man, then, connects the "Putney Pet" with the *ciuthach* of the Hebrides—greatly separated though these are in time. And, in an account of the gipsies of the Pyrenees (quoted by Simson, p. 88), one sees again the same "blubber-lipped" race, the Saracens and Moors of tradition and of heraldry. "The Gitanos are tanned like mulattoes ... Their features are irregular .... They have the mouth very wide, thick lips, and high cheekbones." All these Mongoloid features remind one again that the Scandinavians know the gipsies as *Tartares*, which identifies them with the Ugrian races of Huns and others. And the following sketch of an Ugrian family, the Siberian Samoyeds, recals Mr. Howorth's injunction to study them and their characteristics if we would know more about the pre-historic races of Britain :—" Those who have seen them affirm, that no people on the earth make such shocking figures: their stature is short ; their shoulders and faces are broad, with flat broad noses, great blubber hanging lips, and staring eyes; their complexion is dark, their hair long and as black as pitch, and they have very little beards."* The "flat Tartar faces" remarked by Thackeray in the south of Ireland (and visible elsewhere in the United Kingdom) may be derived from earlier Agathyrsi or later Danes, it has been suggested. For the Agathyrsi or Geloni, who were a tattooed, nomadic people, were also Tartars. They "are otherwise called Getae and Tartari" says the *Dictionary* already extracted from (which though not entitled to be quoted as an authority, is a useful repository of some seventeenth-century ethnological beliefs) ; and the writer adds "some take them for the Walachians or Moldavians." Which last two names agree with the *Walachi* of Fritschius, and the *Bohémiens* of the French—two of the titles by which the gipsies are designated. And an old statute of Denmark which curtly ordains

---

* "Encyc. Brit." 3rd edition, art. "Samoieda." This picture is almost a copy of Gibbon's description of the Huns.

that "The Tartar gipsies, who wander about everywhere, doing great damage to the people, by their lies, thefts and witchcraft, shall be taken into custody by every magistrate"—indicates a firm conviction as to their nationality.

Their qualities and attributes are everywhere the same. "Sorcerers and famous rogues" at Constantinople in the eleventh century,—jugglers, and minstrels, and mountebanks during the middle ages (*teste* John of Rampayne),—wrestlers and prize-fighters in the fourteenth century at Samarcand. In the reign of James II. of Scotland, they come under the heading of "*sorners* (forcible obtruders), fancied fools, vagabonds, out-liers, masterful beggars, *bairds* (strolling rhymers), and such like runners about,"* and their descendants, whether known as such or not, still practise some of these crafts. Their "witchcraft" is referred to over and over again. Scott has an incident of a gipsy who "exercised his glamour over a number of people at Haddington," once upon a time; while it is said of the followers of the famous Johnny Faa, who carried off the Countess of Cassilis,—

"As soon as they saw her weel-far'd face
They coost their glamourie owre her."

But under the name of "gipsies," we are accustomed to regard them only as vagabonds, fortune-tellers, tinkers, basket-makers, and suchlike. When they are strolling jugglers, we call them so, and not gipsies. When, as prize-fighters, they show a faint trace of their origin in the long, black side-locks, they are, nevertheless, "prize-fighters," and nothing else. This arises from the fact that, by a long lapse of time, this or that calling may have gradually drifted into the hands of a different race from those who first practised it, although they unconsciously keep up the usages of their predecessors.† And there is one most striking instance of this—that of the "fancied fools" of the time of James II. of Scotland.

That the commonalty of the conquered black people

* Simson's "History of the Gipsies," p. 99. The name of *Baird* (bard) is now a common surname in Scotland, and argues Gipsy blood. So also is *Caird*, another name for this people, signifying "tinker" or "smith."

† Thus a mountebank, or a prize-fighter, or a tinker, *need* not have a drop of the black "Saracen" blood in his veins.

should sink from the position of dreaded foes to that of servants and wandering players, was almost inevitable. We see that the tribes of North America, once so terrible to Europeans, have now fallen to such a level (except where the finer blood has turned into courses of modern refinement and civilization). When the Governor-General of Canada visited the territory of the North-West, he was shown the Bison-dance for his amusement. So, when the Prince's sons took a run up-country in Australia, the colonists got up a native "corrobboree." And the leisure hours of our Indian officials are often filled in by witnessing the feats of native magic-workers and jugglers. In short, wherever a conquering race has once established itself, and after its foes have once been thoroughly subjugated,—the games and customs of the lower class of aborigines become gradually used as spectacles for the amusement of their governors. And that this is what has happened in Britain, is told to us by Sir Walter Scott's half-historical anecdote, and by the evidences still visible to our sight.

But, as generation succeeded generation, this swarthy and once-alien people would begin to lose its individuality. Just as any incoming race inevitably allies itself, to some extent, with the indigenes, so the fair-skinned Britons (whether entitled to be styled "invaders" or not) would become gradually amalgamated with the dark-skinned races that were their contemporaries (whether aborigines or not). And indeed that this was so is shown by a thousand recorded instances of intermarriage. So that, in course of time, although the sports and dances of the common people would still be maintained for the entertainment of their over-lords, it would become more and more difficult to find full-blooded "blackamoors" to enact them. And their places would, at first occasionally only, be filled by others. Until this curious result would eventually come about: we should see men of white skins putting on the white pigment with which their swarthy predecessors had bedaubed their faces: we should see them painting over this the black and vermilion characters that marked the ancestral caste (on the cheeks and head, like the Redskins,—on the forehead and between the eyes, like the Hindus): because the ugly, wide, "blubber-lipped" mouth had gradually vanished, we should see them widening theirs and thickening their lips by artificial means: because they no longer shaved their heads or cut their hair fantastically, we should see them wearing tufted cowls, or wigs of strange and grotesque fashion:—and to these men, as also to the clumsy and inferior castes employed as serfs and labourers, there would still attach the common appellation—*clowns*.*

In the words "clown" and "buffoon," one sees plainly the low satyr-nature of the Huns,—or of their forefathers, the "demons" of the Scythian desert. The primary meaning of the first of these words seems to have been "a man of brutal disposition,"—although, nowadays, the uncouth gestures and misshapen limbs of the race so styled (as exemplified in the Huns of Gibbon, and last century's Samoyeds) are the only features indicated by the word, as applied to awkward people of any descent. So also a "buffoon" meant originally something more than a mere *farceur*. Dr. Johnson gives, as one meaning of the word, "a man that practises indecent raillery," and he supports this definition by a couplet of Garth's—"The bold buffoon" ("bold" signifying, of course, brazen-faced) "their motion mimicks, but with jest obscene." The pantomimes, or dumb-actors, who performed before the ancient Romans, bore precisely the same character; so much so, that, in speaking of "the language, plays, and ludicrous expressions" of the Osci (a nation of buffoons inhabiting the district "between Campania and the country of the Volsci"), Lempriere states that "from their indecent tendency some suppose the word *obscenum* (*quasi oscenum*) is derived." And since this low-natured race was of black complexion,—known as such in its Black-Hun and Samoyed branches, and presumed to be so elsewhere—it is no wonder that, as we have seen, the adjective "black," whether in Gaelic or in English, has, in one of its phases, become a synonym for everything debased. Even yet you will see in such a modern dictionary as Ogilvie's—although

---

* Since the above was written, I have observed that Mr. Tylor, in his "Anthropology," states that the circus-clown is, in all probability, a survival of Pictism. While, therefore, the above deduction is not a novel one, it has at least the value of an independent conclusion.

the expression is surely half-forgotten—that "black-mouthed" signifies the "using foul or scurrilous language." It is the English equivalent of the quality expressed by the Gaelic *dubh-fhocal*. It betokens again the *Clunorum impudica*.

These monkey-natured, dimly-seen European races have happily disappeared as a distinct type. They have bequeathed to us some of their "absurd and irrational," "savage and senseless," "hideous and revolting" tales and fancies, but they themselves are extinct as a separate people. It may be that their lowest qualities are inherited by a few straggling representatives, but these can be referred to hereafter. It would be utterly absurd to entertain for a moment the idea that swarthiness of skin, among modern British people, indicates anything whatever of that evil nature. Whencesoever their brown complexion has come to them, the *Melanochroi* of this century have nothing of the moral deformity of the Hun in them. No more than the *Xanthochroi*, at any rate. One cannot look into the records of the last century travellers among the Scottish Highlands and Isles without seeing that, wherever the swarthy skin of certain tribes has called forth a remark, there is almost invariably on the same page an involuntary tribute to their courage, virtue, and high-mindedness. There is no higher type than theirs anywhere.

Such an ancient race-river as the Black European has, without doubt, spread out into a many-branching delta long before our time. And Clowns and Gipsies are only two of its channels. The former, it is true, only represent certain characteristics without inheriting the blood.* But the

---

* That a society or profession may continue the customs of its founders, long after their descendants have died out, is so evident that it is almost unnecessary to cite other examples of this tendency. No better one than our navy could be found. In Alfred's days (says an authority on the subject, Mr. Grant Allen) it had to be wholly re-established, having gradually dwindled away to nothing prior to his time. And Alfred's new navy was manned entirely by one race—the Frisians. Thus it is that British sailors have inherited many customs and phrases peculiarly their own, and not belonging to landsmen at all. These they inherit by virtue of office, and not of blood. Whatever be the lineage of a British sailor, so soon as he becomes a sailor he acquires certain customs—notably that of tattooing—traditions, and forms of speech. The Frisian *people* are nowhere; but their customs have survived a thousand years.

latter, though in a modified and fragmentary fashion, do retain a good many of the distinctive features of character, of *physique*, and of custom, belonging to their Negrito-Mongoloid ancestors. The Druidesses of two thousand years ago, who arrogated to themselves the power of forecasting the future, were certainly the prototypes of the fortune-telling gipsy-wives of to-day; and both of these have a strong affinity with those descendants of the race of Simon Magus, *Atsinkan* by name, "who were accounted sorcerers and famous rogues" in the eleventh century, when they "slew wild beasts by their magic arts" at the court of Constantinople. The Gaelic speech asserts this affinity strongly. *Druidheachd*, literally "Druidism," is rendered nowadays "witchcraft;" and *Ban-draoidh*, "a Druidess," is also "a witch."

But Gipsy hags are not the sole repositories of the mysteries of the Druids, although they and their acquirements represent a certain phase of the Druidical system. Just as the swarthy colour of the Pictish Moors—while forming a distinctive characteristic of their Gipsy descendants—asserts itself also in all the dark-skinned millions of educated and peaceable people in the modern British nation: just as the arts that distinguished the Austrian "Cold-smiths" and the metal-workers of Cornwall—while still possessed by the wandering Tinker—are displayed in their real strength, and in a vastly greater degree, in the great ironworks and armouries that have made us famous: so, although the most despicable element of the Druidical system is retained by the illiterate vagrants who possess the greatest share of the dusky Pictish blood, yet the highest and noblest attributes of Druidism are to be found in our schools, and universities and churches.

CHAPTER IX.

It has been seen that the topography of our country, and many other word-witnesses in our speech, all testify to the presence of a black race not yet blended with the white. And other evidences—of history, of legend, and of custom—have been adduced. But of the traditional memory of the "blackamoor," still visibly impressed upon the minds of our peasantry, very little has been said. The Black Morrow, who, from his forest den, ravaged the neighbouring country, and the Black Knight of Lancashire, who "held the people in vassalage," and "used them with great severity," were two distinct specimens. But they can be matched with many others.

The popular tales of the West Highlands are full of dark-skinned people, whose deeds are often recited by people half-unconscious of the fact that they, too, are anything but white. In the Tale of the Shifty Lad, there is the *gadaiche dubh* of Aachaloinne, who is perhaps identical with the Black Robber (*an gadaiche dubh*) of the Barra fisherman's story. "Two tawny women" figure in the Tale of the Soldier; and The Widow's Son is variously described as a "slender dark lad," a "black lad," and a "black rough-skinned lad;" while Iain the Soldier's Son encounters a "black fisherman," who lives in an island cave. The song of The Yellow Muilearteach mentions the "three sons of the dusky black king Dhuinne," and also introduces "Ciar Dhubh (Dusky Black), Prince of Lomhann;" and the "Gruagach" who figures in the Lay of the Great Fool is of brown complexion. The King of Iospainde, who is a prominent figure in the Story of Conall Gulban, is a "slender, black man" in one version, and in another "lean-boned, savage and swarthy." The black warrior *Mordubh* (that is, Black Mor, Morrow, Moray, or Moor) has already been spoken of;

and Mr. Campbell further states—in remarking upon British traditions—that "a great black giant with a club" appears in many Gaelic and Breton tales; and, in the same chapter, he also speaks of the *nighean dubh na luideag*, or "black girl of the clouts," as well as of certain "bald swarthy youths." In addition to these, there is (in the tale translated, "The Sharp Grey Sheep") a "bald black-skinned girl" introduced. The hero of the Lay of Osgar—"brown Osgar of the Alba"—and a "big, black girl" who figures in an anecdote suggested by the Song of the Smithy, complete my tale of West Highland specimens.

That is to say, of specimens not regarded as historical. Of those that are historical, perhaps as good an example as any will be found in the person of Allan Mac Ruari, a "black heathen" of the fifteenth century. We are told "that Allan Mac Ruari, great-grandson of Ranald, and chief of clan Ranald, was one of the principal supporters of Angus, the young Lord of the Isles, at the battle of the Bloody Bay; and that he also followed Alexander of Lochalsh in his invasion of Ross and Cromarty in 1491, receiving a large share of the booty taken on the occasion." His portrait is preserved in a Gaelic song, composed after his death, and written down afterwards by the famous Dean of Lismore, in whose *Book*, as translated by Dr. McLauchlan, the lines may be read. The poem, or song, is a hearty outburst of relief at his death, and exultation over his probable fate. It begins thus—

"The one demon of the Gael is dead,
A tale 'tis well to remember,
Fierce ravager of Church and cross,
The bald-head, heavy, worthless boar.

And he is apostrophised in another place in this fashion—

"MacRuari from the ocean far,
. . . . .
Bald-head Allan, thou so faithless.
That thou hast, not thine only crime,
Ravaged I and Relig Oran.*
. . . . .
Thou art Inche Gall's great curse."

* Iona, and the church of St. Oran in that island. This account is from "The Dean of Lismore's Book," pp. 143-5.

It is probable that he was called a "boar," from the shape of his head-gear and armour, presumably fashioned after the manner of the Œland sculptures, and the bronze, beast-shaped headpieces found occasionally in Scotland. This name is plainly given to him for some reason or another, because in another line he is again styled a "boar";—and the reason just surmised seems the likeliest. But in the second reference of this kind he receives another epithet: he is "the *black-skinned* boar." And it is stated that "many were the devils in his train." Now, this term of "devil" was at one time quite commonly used to denote certain races of black men, as will be more distinctly pointed out hereafter. So that the black-skinned Allan and his band of swarthy "devils" were simply so many *dubh galls*.

The race to which Allan belonged was styled *Mac Ruari;* that is, "the sons, or kindred of Ruari, Rory, or Roderic." It is difficult to decide—when considering old surnames—the exact date at which this or that name has become meaningless. For, of course, all names were once given *for a reason;* although, as we now employ them, they are only convenient signboards, used without any reference to their etymology. But in this case the sons of Ruari were well named. For *Ruari, Ruaidri,* or *Roderic* may be rendered *The Tawny Chief;* being a compound of *ruadh* (Germ. *roth,* Old Gael. *rotan,* Eng. *red* and *ruddy*) and *ri, ric,* or *righ* (in gipsy, *riah*), a kinglet or chief.* It might have been doubtful

---

* This word is often translated "king," but a *ri* was not exactly what we now understand by the word "king." That swarthy warrior, Thorfinn the Dane, possessed a great number of *rikis* in Orkney, Scotland, and Ireland at the time of his death, as the Sagas tell us, but these were not, properly speaking, kingdoms. Even "earl" seems too high a rendering of *ri,* since Thorfinn's earldoms gave him his highest title. "Chief" is perhaps as suitable a synonym as any. The title appears in many names of individuals, *e.g.,* Ala*ric,* Theodo*ric,* Herman-*ric,* Rode*ric,* Os*ric,* Sit*ric,* &c. In all these cases the whole name seems capable of being translated after this fashion. Carlyle states (I presume, at second-hand) that *Dietrich* or *Theodoric* "signifies *Rich in People.*" But this will not do. Else we should have Hermanric = *Rich in Germans,* Roderic = *Rich in Tawny People,* and so on. It may well be that the adjective *rich,* being expressive of a quality belonging to a *ri, riah* or *righ,* really comes from the same root as the noun. But the simplest and most natural meaning of the word, where it terminates a proper name (originally appellative), is that rendered by "king" or "chief." In this way the first Hermanric was a king of the Germans, the first Theodoric a king of *the* People or Teuts (see Strangford's "Letters," &c., pp.

whether *ruadh* in this instance signified *tawny*—and not *rosy* or *ruddy-faced*, or perhaps *rea-haired*,—this might have been doubtful were it not for the fact that the poem, just quoted from, distinctly reveals those men as black-skinned. That "ruadh" *does* sometimes signify "tawny" we have already seen, the authorities for this rendering being Dr. Armstrong and Mr. J. F. Campbell. Therefore this etymology and the contemporaneous picture both agree in depicting those Sons of Ruari as "the clan of the Tawny Chief." (Or, perhaps more correctly,—"the clan of the Chief of the Tawny People.") Moreover, their genealogy also concurs with this deduction. For this pedigree shows that the Clan Ruari and the Clan Dubgaill, or Dougal ("black heathen"), are descended from brothers. And the reason why one division of this tribe should be *ruadh*, or tawny, and the other *dubh*, or black, may be guessed from the mixture of "whites" and "blacks" that form the family tree, there being a "Ranald the white" in two different generations. In other words, the "Gentiles of pure colour" and the "black heathen," known in history as the Norsemen and the Danes, had in this particular family become amalgamated. That the dark blood greatly predominated during the fifteenth century in the Ruaidri branch, is shown by the Dean of Lismore's book. Whether this dark blood came wholly from the Danes, or partly from their kindred, the earlier Moors, may be questioned. There is more than one *Ruaidri* in the pedigree of an ancient race, supposed to be that of the old Maormors or Earls of Moray, towards the beginning of the eleventh century.* But "Moor" and "Dane," ethnologically regarded, are very much alike.

Thus, the legends and the history of the Scottish Highlands are both witnesses to the existence of purely black people. The Welsh traditions bear a similar testimony. The hero Peredur, Son of Evrawc, discovers a company of "bald, swarthy youths," sitting at the hall-door of a black

172-3), Wolfdietrich a king of the Wolf(-totemed) People, Hugdietrich a king of the Boar (?) tribe, and so on. There may be many opinions as to the proper translation of the clan-names indicated by this somewhat numerous class of names, but it is difficult to see how their terminative syllable can be otherwise translated than by "chief" or "king."

* See *Collectanea de Rebus Albanicis*, pp. 59 and 61.

giant, playing at chess. This giant is styled the Black Oppressor, and seems to have been of the same genial nature as the "black knight" of Ashton-under-Lyne. He very frankly informs Peredur that "for this reason I am called the Black Oppressor, that there is not a single man around me whom I have not oppressed; and justice have I done unto none." (And, though it does not bear upon the present question, it is, therefore, satisfactory to repeat the conclusion of the dialogue between him and Peredur. "'Since thou hast, indeed, been an oppressor so long,' said Peredur, 'I will cause that thou continue so no longer.' So he slew him.")

While sitting in the tent of the "Empress of Cristinobyl the great," Peredur "beheld a black man enter, with a goblet full of wine in his hand," and shortly after, "there entered a black man of larger stature than the other, with a wild beast's claw in his hand, wrought into the form of a goblet and filled with wine." At another time, when he and other Round Table knights were in Arthur's hall at Caerlleon, "they saw a black, curly-headed maiden enter." Her aspect is characterized as "rough and hideous." "Blacker were her face and her two hands than the blackest iron covered with pitch [—they must have been *very* black—]; and her hue was not more frightful than her form. High cheeks had she, and a face lengthened downwards, and a short nose with distended nostrils. . . And her teeth were long and yellow. . . . And her back was in the shape of a crook. And her figure was very thin and spare, except her feet, which were of huge size." In short, she had the race-marks of the Negritos and Australioids of Professor Huxley; and in a more pronounced and hideous degree than may be seen in any living representative of these types.

Kynon, the son of Clydno, encountered another of those black people, a black giant with an iron club,—and such giants swarm throughout the Welsh tales. "The Mabinogion (says Mr. Wirt Sikes). . . are full of black men, usually giants, always terrible to encounter." And they are all extremely ugly. In which respect they resemble the misshapen and swarthy Huns, the foul-mouthed and ugly Black Dane who went to Vinland in the eleventh century, the ill-favoured Moors and Saracens of heraldry, the hideous Egyptians who rode into Bologna in the year 1422, the deformed and "shocking" Samoyeds of last century, and the "blubber-lipped" *ciuthach* whom Diarmaid killed. The black, crisp-haired wench that came to Caerlleon-upon-Usk was assuredly hideous. And the other "giants" are invariably ugly. Mr. Sidney Lanier (in his Introduction to the "Boys' Mabinogion") speaks of one of the Welsh worthies as having lips "so large that he was accustomed to draw the lower down for an apron and to lift up the other for a hood." The description is, of course, a monstrous and ludicrous caricature, drawn by others of a handsomer race, but it is plainly founded upon the "remarkably coarse and flexible" lips of the Australioid; and the equally exaggerated picture of the man "whose eyebrows hung over his eyes to such a degree that they had to be propped up with forks" again suggests the shaggy eyebrows of the same race. But all those grotesque and fanciful figures were once real men, though their deformities (horribly real at the best) are magnified and distorted to us, who look at them through the dim mists of many centuries. The giant Gwrnach, who was slain by Kai and the Arthurian knights, and whose castle and treasures they appropriated, was once an actual "black gentile," living in one of the many Black-castles whose names still speak of their former lords. So the shaggy-browed Yspaddaden Penkawr, who,—like the so-called black "Serpent," or serpent-crested black man, slain by Peredur—is pictured as throwing poisoned arrows, or darts, at his enemies, is pretty clearly one of those "hateful horrid giants," known to the Irish chroniclers as the *Tuath Figda*, who "carried nothing about them but poisoned iron."[*]

Although certain divisions of this primitive black race are now only known—in Wales and elsewhere—as quasi-supernatural beings, yet the blurred pictures that still remain to us are painted the proper colour. In Welsh tradition (says Mr. Wirt Sikes), "the Bwbach is usually brown, . . . and

---

[*] The Welsh extracts are from Mr. Sikes' "British Goblins" (pp. 133, 177-9, and 219), and also from Mr. Sidney Lanier's "Boys' Mabinogion." The West Highland figures are, of course, taken from Mr. Campbell's "Popular Tales." The *Tuath Figda* are met with in Mr. Skene's "Chronicles of the Picts," &c., pp. 326-7.

the Coblynau are black or copper-coloured in face as well as dress." And of the "Gwrach,"—which word he translates "hag" or "witch"—he states that she was the wife of the "Avagddu." Now, this word "Avagddu" is the Welsh—and phonetical—spelling of what in the Scottish Highlands is *Abhach Dubh*. And the English of *Abhach Dubh* is the Black Dwarf. So that the name given to the male "Gwrachs" is only another term for the Svertlings, or Swarthy Dwarfs, who are stated, in the Laxdaela Saga, to have slain Frodi the Gallant, the grandsire of Olave the White. And, what is more, this term connects the *Svertlings* with the *Ynglings*, *Ing-lings*, or *Marsh Dwarfs*. For, although *Abhach* is one of the Gaelic words for a dwarf, it radically means a "water-man,"—being made up of the now obsolete *Abh*, water, and *Ach*, a termination (as in *ciuth-ach*, hair-man,) signifying a person.* Therefore, *Abhach Dubh*, or *Avagddu*, when analyzed, is seen to be literally "Black Water-Dwarf." And, consequently, the name generally given to the females of this race, by the modern peasantry of Wales, is quite appropriate; for the *Gwragedd Annwn* are simply "Water-Hags, or Witches." Further, all these names remind one that the earliest forms of the words *Maurus*, *Mor*, &c., and *Kors*, *Carse*, *Ciar*, &c., formerly touched upon, are closely associated with the sea and marshlands, as well as with the swarthy tribes they designate.

The Welsh tales, it has been said, are full of black "giants," against whom the Arthurian warriors fought. An inference from this is that Arthur's followers were white. Because the *blackness* of their foes would not have been particularised, had they been of the same hue themselves. Now, the Arthur of history is said to have been himself of swarthy, Silurian blood: but the Arthur of romance has never been wholly identified with him, and indeed he is altogether difficult to localize in time and place. The legendary Knights of the Round Table may fairly be assumed to have been of the civilized, Christianized, and *Xanthocroic* stock of Provincial Britons, who, if represented

---

* *Acharadh*, another word for a dwarf, may either be taken as a diminutive of *ach*, in the sense of *person*, or as a compound of *agh* or *ach*, a meadow (? once a marsh), and *fear*, a man.

by the "Barbarian Prisoner" of the sculpture, were, in face and figure, strikingly handsome. And their enemies, who are usually styled "the heathen," are seen in the Welsh traditions to be black. That is they were "black heathen," —like the Danes. Or like the Moors.

For the black people, as we know, ante-date the Danish branch of that stock by many centuries,—how many, no one can tell. Professor Huxley, speaking on this subject, says " that probably in the time of Cæsar, and certainly in that of Tacitus, there existed in these islands two distinct types of population :—the one of tall stature, with fair skin, yellow hair, and blue eyes ; the other of short stature, with dark skin [as dark as an Ethiopian's, says Pliny ; as dark as a "Moor's," says Claudian,] dark hair, and black eyes. We further learn that this dark population, represented by the Silures, bore considerable physical resemblance to the people of Aquitania and Iberia; while the fair population of parts of South-East Britain—the present counties of Kent and Hants—resembled the Belgæ who inhabited the North-East of France and the country now called Belgium. These Belgæ, again, were closely akin in physical characters to the tall fair people who dwelt on the east bank of the Rhine, and were called Germani. These two distinct ethnological elements (continues Mr. Huxley) probably coexisted in these islands when the country was discovered by the Romans ; and the subsequent invasions to which Britain has been subjected have not introduced any new stock, but have merely affected one or other of the pre-existing elements."*
Accepting this conclusion, then, as, in the main, correct,† we have before us undeniable evidence—historical and ethnological—of the immemorial presence of the blacks in this

---

* "On the Ethnology of Britain," *Ethnological Society's Journal*, Vol. II. No. 4.

† "*In the main*, correct," because the assumption that Western Europe remained unvisited by any "new stock," during a long stretch of sixty generations, is somewhat sweeping. To assume this is to forget that Britain, in its first historical millenary, was in the position of modern Australia, or the Western States, the *recipient* of the overflow of other nations, and not—as it now is—a great imperial centre. It is to overlook the fact that a thousand years ago our islands were overrun by a race whom certain mid-Europeans styled Ostmen, or Men of the East ; which race, though *akin* to certain tribes of Britons, must inevitably have brought with it a large infusion of alien blood.

country. Other confirmatory statements have been made in the foregoing chapters, and additional evidence of a traditional kind has just been adduced.

In most of the examples cited, of whatever nature, the two great types appear as enemies; which was their natural attitude. And a great number of the legendary instances preserve the memory of this mutual enmity. The black "giants" of the Welsh, and other tales, are "hateful" and "horrid." The Welsh Black Oppressor, and the Black Knight of Lancashire are fierce tyrants, the cruel foes of all white people. At a later date, when the whites were gaining the ascendancy, and the blacks were cut up into straggling bands, or lurking, like the Black Morrow of Galloway, in solitary dens and forest-shades, out of which they issued by night, intent on murder and rapine,—even at this stage of their history, the blacks were the dreaded enemies of the whites. Indeed, it is of this epoch that the popular imagination has most retained the impression. The days of the "black oppression" are so remote that their memory only lives in half-forgotten legends. Not so the time when the black castles were owned by another race, and their former masters were skulking among woods and caves. So vivid was the fear of them, and so lasting its impression, that children of the nineteenth century, peering into dark recesses, timorously,—or peasant girls, seeing suddenly their own image, reflected by the candle from the dark window-pane,—shiver all over with apprehension at the vision of the dreaded "black man"—a mere imaginary bugbear to them, but a real terror to those from whom they inherited the feeling.

But this state of things could not last for ever. No two races—however antagonistic—could inhabit the same territory for countless generations, without amalgamating. Such a thing is an impossibility. Whether in an authorised fashion or not, a mixed race eventually comes into being. And this is what we see in our own history. Long ages ago, —and in spite of a gradually dwindling party of "Irreconcilables,"—the two great sections may be seen uniting here and there. As early as the Norse and Danish invasion, and earlier than that, this had happened at various points. *Fionn* and *Dubh* did not always war against each other.

Occasionally, they united in friendlier mood: and the result was *Donn*, or *Ruadh*. At what date the first approach was made, it is impossible to say; though the earliest legendary record seems to be that of the story of Diarmaid. There we see the "fair whites," in the persons of Diarmaid and Grainne (who, as the friend and the wife of *the* Fionn, are presumably white also,) amicably associating with their black contemporaries, as represented by the *ciuthach*,—whose violent death was preceded by several days of chess-playing and love-making. Of historical instances after that date, enough has been said. But of traditionary examples it may be convenient to say more.

In those districts which were colonized by white races,—such as the Dutch, or Flemish, and the Norman,—at a period subsequent to the latest "black" invasion, it is likely that a "blackamoor" was to many people a being undreamt of, because never seen. And when a straggling specimen of the swarthy races did, by accident, become visible to one of such a community, he would naturally be regarded as something uncanny. A case of this sort is presented to us in an old Welsh story, repeated by Mr. Wirt Sikes in his interesting collection; and it cannot be many centuries old. It is of a young woman, who, while "going one evening to milk the cows," saw, "as she passed through a wood, ... a horrible black man standing by a holly tree." She describes him as "very big in the middle," but says nothing of his features, which she was probably not near enough to see. To her great relief, he took his departure quietly—walked "towards a spring ... where ghosts had been seen before," crossed the stile into the road, whistled loudly, and then disappeared. This "Welsh" girl must, of course, have belonged to a white community, and may have been of the blood of either of the two races named above, or of earlier White British blood, —that is, Celtic.

Another kindred instance is that of the experience of certain Scottish Covenanters, not much more than two centuries ago. In one of his *Notes* to *The Heart of Mid-Lothian*, Scott tells of the encounter between the once-celebrated "prophet," Alexander Peden, and a "devil," in a lonely, moorland cave. He also puts into the mouth of

Douce Davie Deans, the recital of a terrible episode of similar nature; a real incident of Covenanting times. He "used to tell with great awe . . . how he himself had been present at a field-meeting at Crochmade, when the duty of the day was interrupted by the apparition of a tall black man, who, in the act of crossing a ford to join the congregation, lost ground, and was carried down apparently by the force of the stream. All were instantly at work to assist him, but with so little success, that ten or twelve stout men, who had hold of the rope which they had cast in to his aid, were rather in danger to be dragged into the stream, and lose their own lives, than likely to save that of the supposed perishing man." [But "famous John Semple of Carspharn" having told them it was no other than "the Great Enemy," who couldn't drown]—" Sae we let go the rape," said David, "and he went adown the water screeching and bullering like a Bull of Bashan, as he's ca'd in scripture."

Now, this story does not show the entire non-acquaintance with black people that the Welsh girl's adventure does. For the black man of the Covenanting story was at first regarded as a fellow-man, and even as a possible participator in the worship of the conventicle. But he was enough of a rarity to make his would-be rescuers accept "famous John Semple's" nonsense as truth; never reflecting that any supernatural being would hardly allow himself to be swept away by the current, calling out for help, after they had left him to his fate. And since the story is said to be true, we may believe it as a fact, that on a certain day in the middle of the seventeenth century, the corpse of an unfortunate Moor, or gipsy, went swirling down a Lowland river to the sea: thanks to the wisdom of famous John Semple.

Here, then, a black man was not regarded, at first, as extra-human, though perhaps not a very familiar object to the natives of certain districts of Scotland, six or seven generations back. There must, however, be many memories of the time when the two opposite types were losing their individuality by peaceful inter-communion. The simple existence of a particular class of mills known as "black "mills" (already quoted) points to this, not to speak of many other "black" terms of like nature, implying the same result. Of Highland and Welsh—and, I fancy, of Irish—tales, in which there are numerous evidences that the blacks were not always enemies, there is no lack. And this cannot be wondered at, since it is in particular localities of Ireland, Scotland, and Wales that the black blood shows itself the most emphatically at the present day. But even in other neighbourhoods there are manifold tokens of this phase. For example, among the floating literature that used to delight the rustics of a byegone day—those coarsely-executed, and often coarsely-worded tracts, once hawked throughout the country, and known as "Penny Chap Books," —there is one sheet which sets forth to us *The Comical History of Simple John and his Twelve Misfortunes.* With John and his misfortunes we need have nothing to do, but his wife is deserving of some transitory notice. For her father is casually introduced as "the black butcher on Ti'ot side," and the physical attributes of his daughter are quite in accordance with her lineage. Therefore this black butcher of Teviotdale may be taken as a representative of the peaceable, prosaic, workaday "blackamoor,"—just as the wild and savage gipsy represents, or did represent, the fiercer qualities of the race. The epoch of *Simple John* is not revealed by anything in the narrative: we can only say that this particular black man lived "before now," as the Gaelic phrase is. But he and his like must have been very numerous at one period; for, had all their kindred shared their ferocious nature of the old-time gipsy, these British Mic-macs would be now the only survivors that their out-numbering, white-skinned enemies had left,—and the *Melanochroi* of to-day would only number a few thousands.

But the traces of our black ancestry are visibly existent in a hundred surnames. Some of these denote complexion, —others do so, but indirectly. The first class includes a great many. There are the clans Ruari and Dougal (spelt Dubgaill, or "black strangers," in their own genealogy),— there are all the varieties of Dubh (black),—such as Duff, Dow, Macduff, and others,—there are Donns, Carrs, and Dargs,—with their equivalent Dunns, Browns, Greys, and Blacks. All these are colour names, showing a black or tawny ancestor. So also is the name of Dubh-glas, or

Douglas,—literally Black-Swarthy; and that of Murray, with its kindred forms of More, Moore, &c., *but these only where the original name did not signify de Moravia, whether in Latin or in Gaelic.*

Such are the kind of names that directly point to a descent from the Moors. (Of those that do so indirectly, nothing need be said here.) But, in saying this, it is not meant that such names, *nowadays*, necessarily indicate that the bearers of them had one or more Pictish ancestors. Because it is well known that the surname of the feudal superior was given, in many cases, to his vassals, though wholly unconnected by blood. Consequently, many of the unwilling followers of a Black Oppressor might transmit to their descendants a surname that denoted a complexion vastly different from their own. Nor is it to be supposed, either, that a real descendant of a Black, or a Macduff, must of necessity be found in the ranks of the " dark whites." For a patronymic indicates nothing more than a descent from a certain individual,—one ancestor out of myriads. They say that in the Southern States a man is counted a "nigger" if he have ever so slight an infusion of negro blood in his veins. Nothing but the most paltry prejudice could so define him. When a man is ninth-tenths white, or nine-tenths black, he is white, or black, before anything else. But if the negro ancestor of such a nine-tenths white man had lived amidst a white population whose ideas with regard to nomenclature were as primitive as those of our ancestors a thousand years ago, his* offspring would have eventually become known by some such name as Black, or Negro, *used as a surname.* Precisely the same thing has actually happened here. We know, as a historical fact, that a *Niger vel Dubh* has lived, and reigned over certain "Black divisions" of our island—and probably over white divisions also,—and that a race known as "the sons of the Black" succeeded him in history. But, just as our hypothetical octoroon family on the other side of the Atlantic might for

---

* It would have been more in accordance with facts had I supposed the Octoroon's Negro ancestor to be a woman. But the parallel would not have been so obvious, as the name inherited would be that of a white man. In this country the blacks were not always a servile race. Hence this superficial difference.

ever after continue to intermarry only with their white kindred, so might our British octoroons have done likewise: with the result, in either case, that the far-down posterity of the negro, or Moor, would be so "white" that no ethnologist could detect the presence of any other blood. And yet, in both cases, the male descendants would bear the surname first given to their remote authors,—a surname signifying "the black man."

The fact is, that most of our surnames are so old that while they argue, with considerable force, that this or that man is descended from such-and-such a race, they give us no help in finding out the predominating blood. Every one—unless the child of cousins-german—is possessed of eight great-grandparents, but the patronymic only shows the descent from one of them. The other seven are wholly ignored. So that, if one's pedigree is not complete enough to point out clearly, *and with authenticity* (a feature which, though the most important, is perhaps the oftenest disregarded) every line of the descent, back to the days when each surname had a meaning, the genealogy is only of partial value in any argument of this kind.

Nevertheless the names exist. And, with those of topography and of usage, already quoted: and, with many a record in written and oral history, they emphatically tell us of a large section of our ancestry, whose complexion was black.

CHAPTER X.

UNQUESTIONABLY, the most recent Black-European races must be looked at under their guise of Gipsies. And it is startling to reflect *how* recent they are,—as actually black people. The tawniest gipsy now in Europe is probably but a half-blood, and most of them are something like quadroons. Mr. Simson says (in his *History*, p. 374), "I may, indeed, venture to assert, that there is not a full-blooded gipsy in Scotland ; and, most positively, that in England, where the race is held to be so pure, all that can be said of *some* families is, that they have not been crossed, *as far as is known ;* but that, with these exceptions, the body is much mixed." In all the older references to the race, they are spoken of as purely black, not tawny. It is said that Scottish peasant-mothers soothe their children with the couplet—

> " Hush nae, hush nae, dinna fret ye ;
> The *black* Tinkler winna get ye "*

And, in the song of *Johnny Faa*, the Countess sighs—

> " And now I must lie in a auld tenant's barn,
> And the *black* crew glowring owre me."

Mr. Simson states, also, that when gipsies quarrel, they begin to question each other's lineage ; and one, " having more of 'the blood,' will taunt his acquaintance, with some such expression as 'Gorgio like' (like the white)." — To

---

* Simson's " History," p. 45. This recalls Sir Walter Scott's account of the taking of Roxburgh Castle, and the song of the Englishwoman to her baby—

> "Hush ye, hush ye, little pet ye,
> Hush ye, hush ye, do not fret ye,
> The Black Douglas shall not get ye."

And, like the Tinkler, Douglas was himself a black man.

which the other returns—" And what are you, you black trash ? Will blood put money in your pocket ? Blood, indeed! I'm a better Gipsy than you are, in spite of the black devil that every one sees in your face!"*

The farther back one looks, the more do the Gipsies become visible as armed marauders and not as mere vagrants ; suggesting a time still farther back when they formed a vast Tartar confederation. And quite recently they have been used as auxiliary troops. "In the thirty years' war, the Swedes had a body of them in the army; and the Danes had three companies of them at the siege of Hamburg in 1686. They were chiefly employed in flying parties, to burn, plunder, or lay waste the enemy's country." (They formed in fact, the "black men" of Halliwell, and the *dubh-chléin* of the dictionaries.) And again,—" Francis von Perenyi, who commanded at the siege of Nagy Ida, being short of men, was obliged to have recourse to the Gipsies, of whom he collected a thousand. These he stationed behind the entrenchments, while he reserved his own men to garrison the citadel. The Gipsies supported the attack with so much resolution, and returned the fire of the enemy with such alacrity, that the assailants—little suspecting who were the defendants—were compelled to retreat. But the Gipsies, elated with victory, immediately crept out of their holes, and cried after them, 'Go, and be hanged, you rascals ! and thank God that we had no more powder and shot, or we would have played the devil with you!' 'What!' they exclaimed, bearing in mind the proverb, 'You can drive fifty Gipsies before you with a wet rag,' 'What! are *you* the heroes?' and, so saying, the besiegers immediately wheeled about, and, sword in hand, drove the black crew back to their works, entered them along with them, and in a few minutes totally routed them."† Thus the outcry against the use of black troops in Europe, whether these are drawn from Algeria or from India, cannot be raised on the ground that such a practice is an innovation in European warfare.

Without going back so far as the "black divisions" of Scotland, one finds also in recent times a hint of certain

* Simson's "History," p. 195.
† *Ibid.* pp. 359-60, note.

stretches of territory belonging to the Gipsies, or rather which had belonged to them at an earlier date. Wiessenburch " notices that in Hungary the gangs assumed their names from the countries which they chiefly traversed, as the band of Upper Saxony, of Brandenburg, and so forth. They resented, to extremity, any attempt on the part of other Gipsies to intrude on their province; and such interference often led to battles, in which they shot each other with as little remorse as they would have done to dogs."*
"In Romania, a large tract of Mount Haemus, which they inhabit, has acquired from them the name of *Tschenghe Valken*—Gipsy Mountain." (As, for a similar reason, has the Black Mount district of Argyleshire acquired its name.) And "in Poland and Lithuania, as well as in Courland, there are an amazing number of Gipsies."†

Now, although these statements only *suggest* a former ownership of the soil, this suggestion is confirmed in one instance, at any rate. It must first be remembered that a common, if unpleasant, epithet applied to the black race, is that of "devil." The fifteenth-century Gaelic poem, previously quoted, speaks of the pirate, Allan MacRuari, as "the one demon of the Gael," saying also—

> "Then, when came the black-skinned boar,
> Many the devils in his train,"—

(the title of "boar" being presumably given to him on account of the boar-like shape of his headgear and armour). The fairer of the two wrangling gipsies of Mr Simson's description, taunts the other with the "black devil in his face." And there are other and more notable cases of such "devils," to be more particularly looked at in another place. The name seems to have been chiefly applied to the black Tartar tribes. "About the time of Gengyz," says Dr. Gustav Oppert, in a paper on the *Kitai* and *Kara-Kitai*, "these tribes passed under the name of Tatars, and as they behaved like children of hell, they were considered to have come from Tartarus." Accordingly, there cannot be much doubt as to the meaning of the figures in one particular por-

---

* Simson's "History," p. 80.
† *Ibid.* p. 75. Quoted from Grellmann.

tion of a fifteenth-century chart or planisphere, described by Sir Walter Scott.* The territory in which these figures are placed embraces "Esthonia, Lithunia, Courland, and such districts," the very districts in which Grellmann states that there is yet "an amazing number of Gipsies." This part of the map, then, "exhibits rude cuts of the furclad natives paying homage at the shrines of demons, who make themselves visibly present to them; while at other places they are displayed as doing battle with the Teutonic knights, or other military associations formed for the conversion or expulsion of the heathen in these parts. Amid the pagans, *armed with scimitars, and dressed in caftans,* the fiends are painted as assisting them, pourtrayed in all the modern horrors" generally ascribed to "devils." Now, this map was made in the very century that the "band of 300 wanderers, 'black as Tartars and calling themselves *Secani*'" arrived at Lüneburg, and the "troop of fully 100 lean, black, hideous Egyptians" reached Bologna. Moreover, it was from this very neighbourhood that, two centuries earlier, "innumerable multitudes of these barbarians [Tartars], headed by their Khan Batto, or Battus, after ravaging great part of Poland and Silesia, broke suddenly into Russia, where they committed the greatest cruelties."† So that this fifteenth-century map represents nothing else than this,—a furclad, and probably Ugrian people inhabiting the southern and south-eastern shores of the Baltic,—this people thoroughly dominated in certain districts by a black, Tartar race,—and in other districts (most likely the western), the rulers and the ruled uniting to repel the forces of the white-skinned Christians of the West. To such Christians those Tartars were "the children of hell;" they were "devils." And it is clearly from them that the "amazing number" of Lithunian and Courland gipsies are descended.

The Gipsies, then, looked at as *Gipsies*, were fierce in nature and swarthy in skin, as far back as the conventional limit allows us to see them. Their warlike nature is most apparent in Simson's book. The first sketch he gives of them is in the Maclellan story of *circa* 1460, where, as

* "Letters on Demonology and Witchcraft," pp. 78 and 79.
† "Encyc. Brit." 3rd edit. art. "Russia."

"Moors," or "Saracens," they ravaged the southern districts of Scotland. And, although he forgets this fact—strangely enough—when contradicting a statement that they greatly "annoyed the country in the fifteenth century," his contradiction only bears upon the epoch, which he places in "the three following centuries" after the fifteenth. "So formidable were the numbers of the nomadic Gipsies, at one time, and so alarming their desperate and sanguinary battles, in the upper parts of Tweeddale and Clydesdale, that the fencible men in their neighbourhood, (the *countryside* was the expression,) had sometimes to turn out to quell and disperse them." "A writer in Blackwood's Magazine mentions that the Gipsies, late in the seventeenth century, broke into the house of Penicuik, when the greater part of the family were at church. Sir John Clerk, the proprietor, barricaded himself in his own apartment, where he sustained a sort of siege —firing from the windows upon the robbers, who fired upon him in return. One of them, while straying through the house in quest of booty, happened to ascend the stairs of a very narrow turret, but, slipping his foot, caught hold of the rope of the alarm bell, the ringing of which startled the congregation assembled in the parish church. They instantly came to the rescue of the Laird, and succeeded, it is said, in apprehending some of the Gipsies, who were executed."

Inter-tribal battles, such as that between the Fawes and the Shawes at Romanno, in Tweeddale, in the year 1677, and the "Battle of the Bridge," fought at Hawick a century later, by the Kennedys and Taits, reveal this people to us in the same red light. This fierce and warlike disposition of theirs, evinced in their constant attacks upon each other, as well as upon any peaceful whites who came in their way, gives them almost exactly the same appearance, in our eyes, as the half-subdued North American tribes of to-day; a resemblance which, in many other respects, is most striking. One sees this similarity, again, in reading such an anecdote as that of the Yetholm minister's adventure. Riding home one evening in the gloaming, he took a short cut through a desolate tract, following a path that led by an old deserted cottage. Suddenly he discerned a "grim visage" staring at him from the cottage window, " and also several 'dusky figures' skulking among the bourtree-bushes that had once sheltered the shepherd's garden. Next moment, there was a hand on his bridle, and a gruff voice demanding his money. Fortunately, the minister was able to recognize the voice, and to discover, in the uncertain light, that it issued out of "the great, black, burly head of his next-door neighbour, *Gleid Neckit Will* (Will Faa), the Gipsy chief." The recognition being mutual he was allowed to pass unharmed, as a friend of the tribe. The scenery and many of the accessories are different, but the incident suggests the reservation of a half-wild Indian tribe, rather than any part of the British Islands, at a period within the memory of people now alive.

Such adventures have gradually become less common, until now they have ceased altogether. Gipsy banditti do not now ravage the country with fire and sword, or engage in savage and frequent clan-fights, or carry off the children of the whites, or waylay and murder travellers, or—as in more than one instance—strip an unfortunate countrywoman and leave her naked among the hills. These things have ceased with us, as they will have done across the ocean in the course of another generation or two.

Mr. Simson insists very strongly upon the large amount of Gipsy blood that is flowing in the veins of the ordinary population of Scotland, through intermarriages extending over (as he believes) the last three or four centuries. Some villages in the south of Scotland are, he says, "almost entirely occupied by Gipsies. James Hogg is reported to say" (he adds) "that Lochmaben is 'stocked' with them." And he introduces such examples as that of the Falls of Dunbar—a branch of the celebrated Faw clan—to show how gipsies have become peaceful, industrious citizens, and have mingled their blood with many families of high rank.* In short, the people whom he styles *gipsies*, using that term comprehensively, correspond exactly with the *melanochroi* of Professor Huxley. And this view of the matter explains very clearly all the "black" allusions which have been made heretofore. The "black butcher" of the Teviotdale story thus becomes nothing more than one of the peaceful members

* The preceding extracts are from Mr. Simson's " History," pp. 125, 190, 195, 237, 353, and 381.

of the Yetholm bands, and all the other black men spoken of here and there are only gipsies, prior to their intermixture with the whites.* Further, this view of the question allows us, also, to advance the limit of "black" nomenclature almost up to the present day. "Black-mail," for example, is an appropriate term not only when applied to the tribute exacted by the Black Huns and the Danes, but also when it is employed in such an instance as that related of Henry Faa, chief of his clan in the latter part of last century, to whom "men of considerable fortune paid a gratuity, called blackmail, in order to have their goods protected from thieves." Of course, this phrase had lost its original aptness before Henry Faa's time, *as usually employed*, but the ratio of its aptness must have increased more and more as it receded from his era. A "black-fisher," also, defined by Dr. Jamieson as "one who fishes illegally by night," was evidently at one time so-called *because* he was a black man, or gipsy. The other explanations offered for this term are quite unsatisfactory. One says that "*black-fishing* is so called because it is performed in the *night* time," and another that it is because "the fish are then *black*, or foul." It appears to be a name for the form of fishing pictured so graphically by Scott in "Guy Mannering," namely, the spearing or "leistering" of salmon by torchlight; and the presence, on that particular occasion, of a number of gipsies among the sportsmen, is peculiarly appropriate; although it is probable

* The views expressed by Hogg and Simson are fully shared by another writer—one whose statements, in this respect, ought to be held decisive, since they express the experience of a man thoroughly acquainted with Border life. John Mackay Wilson, in his "Tales of the Borders," writes thus of the Faws :— "Since waste lands, which were their hiding places and resorts, began to be cultivated, and especially since the sun of knowledge snuffed out the taper of superstition and credulity, most of them are beginning to form a part of society, to learn trades of industry, and live with men. Those who still prefer their fathers' vagabond mode of life—finding that in the northern counties their old trade of fortune-telling is at a discount, and that thieving has thinned their tribe, and is dangerous—now follow the more useful and respectable calling of muggers [that is, makers of pottery or *mugs*], besom-makers, and tinkers." Simson's testimony is identical with this :—"Many of the Gipsies now keep shops of earthenware, china, and crystal. . . . . These . . . . . stone-ware merchants are scarcely to be distinguished as Gipsies; yet they all retain the language, and converse in it, among themselves. . . . . Among them there are tin-smiths, braziers, and cutlers, in great numbers." ("History of the Gipsies," p. 347.)

they were introduced by the writer more from instinct than otherwise.

The gipsies, then—not to go further into details—when accepted as numerous, warlike, and distinctly black people, living an individual existence in various districts of the British Islands during the past few centuries, but gradually becoming mingled with the white races, announce themselves very clearly as the progenitors, on one side, of all the *melanochroi* of our country. So far, this is very well.

But M. Bataillard will not accept the fifteenth, or the fourteenth, or even the eleventh century as the date of arrival of the gipsy races in Europe. Nor is there any reason why he should do so. It is not necessary to follow out his own particular line of argument in order to see this. The existing gipsies of Lithuania and Courland are—it will be denied by few—quite evidently the descendants of those black pagans who, "armed with scimetars, and dressed in caftans," are depicted upon the fifteenth-century map just spoken of. And these, it will be as readily admitted, are, to some extent, the posterity of the thirteenth-century Tartars of Gengyz Khan; as, indeed, the Scandinavian appellation given to them indicates. But these were not the *first* Tartars that lived in Europe. It is true that, in the thirteenth century, we see them regarded as intruders by the Christian chivalry of the West, to whom they were "Saracens," "Moors," "devils," "heathen," and "pagans;" and, as such, warred against with unceasing vigour until, in Prussia, they were almost totally exterminated. But, whether the European Tartars of that period were wholly, or only partially, invaders, and whether their characteristics were Mongolian, or only partly so, still, they had been preceded by countless swarthy hordes. That kindred peoples are to be found in the Austrian "Ishmaelites" of the twelfth century, and their predecessors, the *Atsinkan* of the eleventh, there can be little doubt. As clearly were these akin to the black-skinned jugglers and minstrels of the mediæval story, who at that time were living in England. Earlier still, in the eighth century, we see the same stock—in the Huns, the Bulgarians, the Pagans of Saxony—whom Charlemagne, after many fierce insurrections, overcame. Of such kindred were the heathen against whom he fought in Spain and Southern France; such were the Saracens and "pagans" that swarmed around his knights at Roncesvalles; and, in the half-historic, half-romantic *Song* that tells the battle, the lines—

> "When Roland sees the cursèd heathen folk,
> As black as ink—all black except their teeth,"

reveal their lineaments to us again. The great Charles's grandsire, Charles Martel, had to encounter a like confederacy in the revolted Saxon pagans, and the Saracens, whose conquering progress he checked before they reached the English Channel. Earlier yet, in the fifth century—three hundred thousand of their tawny corpses lay on the plain beside Chalons-sur-Marne; a portion only of Attila's great host. And farther back in time than this, whether as, accidentally, in the persons of Cæsar's Numidian archers, or as Chuni, Sarmatians, and Tartar-Agathyrsi, dwelling in the vaguely-defined regions of Scythia, those swarthy and kindred nations inhabited Europe.

But it is not so much with the Continental as with the British gipsies that we are concerned. These, it is said by one of their historians, regard themselves as a compound of many races,—"dreadfully mixed," is the expression they employ. "Pharaoh's folk," "Egyptians," and (as often) "Ethiopians," are the racial titles they apply to themselves in Scotland; and the resemblances even yet borne by them to these ancient peoples are many. That they were present in Scotland in great force during the fifteenth century is admitted by all. That they were there, also, at a far earlier period, and in overwhelming numbers, I am endeavouring to show, by the evidences both of history and tradition.

The mountebanks and minstrels of John of Rampayne have declared to us their presence in England during the Middle Ages. By what historical name their ancestors were known cannot easily be determined. Because there are so many to choose from. About the time when Charles the Great and his knighthood were struggling against such "Saracens" on the right hand and on the left, their northern branch is discernible, under various names, sweeping out from the Cimbric channels, "swarming o'er the northern sea," and pouring their wild hordes into Christian Britain, ravaging and spoiling as they came. The fiercest division of these, and apparently the most recent in time, was that of the Danes, or Cimbri, remembered by the Christianized races of Britain as "the black heathen," the *nigræ gentes*, the *dubh galls*. But although such invaders as these may be claimed as, in some respect, the progenitors of the mingled people whom we now call gipsies, yet—like their Continental kindred—the gipsies of Britain had far earlier British ancestors than these. Scotland was overrun, in one district, by "Moors" of the fifteenth century; but five centuries earlier the Kings of Alban were Moors: and one of the most celebrated of these, Kenneth, or *Niger*, or *Dubh*, ruled over certain districts known as "the three black divisions." How long before, and after that, the ascendency remained with his swarthy nation, and what were the probable fluctuations of colour throughout the island, it is impossible to ascertain, and premature to discuss. But, at any rate, the Moorish races, "*nec falso nomine Pictos*," were among the chief opponents of the Romans, when they marched through Britain, eighteen hundred years ago.

The traces left by these people in our folk-lore, and our language, have already been dwelt upon. They are remembered in many a tradition of the days when Christendom was battling against Heathennesse. They were ultimately overcome; and as separate and distinct nations they no longer exist.

CHAPTER XI.

THE resemblances between the British Moors of the old historians, and the least mixed among their descendants of to-day—whom we call *Gipsies*—are many. Those Moors of Scotland, for example, who lived among the fens and sea-lagoons that stretched across the now solid and fertile Carse of Stirling, were Mæatæ or Marsh-dwellers; and, indeed, an etymological connection between such people and such places was pointed out. "The Gipsies, in general (says Mr. Simson), appear to have located themselves upon grounds of a flattish character, between the cultivated and uncultivated districts; having, on one side, a fertile and populous country, and, on the other, a heathy, boggy, and barren waste, into which they could retire in times of danger." The burning of the dead, seen, by our ancient burial-grounds, to have been once a custom in this country, and known to have been formerly practised by the native tribes of North America, was also a custom of the Gipsies in former times. "In England, it was customary with the Gipsies, at one time, to burn the dead"—states the writer whom I have just quoted (p. 128)—"but now they only burn the clothes, and some of the effects of the deceased." The "Scythian" oath upon the knife is at once a solemnity of the Gipsies, and of their differently-named kindred in the Highlands. The common Gipsy occupation of working in iron and other metals—so common as to have given rise, in Hungary, to the proverb, "So many Gipsies, so many smiths"—so characteristic of them that it forms the unassailable basis of Monsieur Bataillard's argument; so long their property that we can trace their possession of it from the era of the iron-girt enemies of the Roman Severus, down to the present century, when, in the neighbourhood of St. Andrews (Simson, p. 140), a small foundry, known as

"Little Carron," remained peculiarly their own;[*] this distinctively *Gipsy* occupation is one of the most striking memories of the Scotch Highlands. "The smelting and working of iron was well understood, and constantly practised, over all the Highlands and islands from time immemorial," says a somewhat unamiable Highlander of last century.[†] "Instead of improving in that art, we have fallen off exceedingly of late years, and at present make little or none. Tradition bears, that they made it in the blomary way; that is, by laying it under the hammers, in order to make it malleable with the same heat that melted it in the furnace. There is still in the Highlands a clan of the name of Macnuithear, who are descended from those founders, and have from thence derived their surname. I am likewise well informed, that there is in Glenorchy, in Argyleshire, a family of the name of Macnab, who have lived in the same place, and have been a race of smiths, from father to son, for more, perhaps, than three hundred years past." This evidence is further confirmed by the late Mr. Cosmo Innes, who says [‡] :—"In our own Highland glens I have heard more legends of supernatural smith-work than ever I could gather of Ossian. We must not wonder, then" (he adds) "that the family of *Smith* is large, nor that it assumes many forms of spelling in our low country talk, as well as the shape of *Gow*, and probably *Cowan*, among those whose

---

[*] It is very likely this *Little Carron* that is alluded to in "The Monymusk Christmas Ba'ing" (written by the Rev. John Skinner, Langside, Aberdeenshire, in the latter part of last century), in which the following lines occur :—

"Afore he cou'd step three inches back,
The millart drew a knife,
A curst-like gullie and a snack [ready],
Some blacksmith's work in Fife."

A *gully* is (in Scotland and Northumberland, if not in other parts of the country) a large knife with a curved blade. It is now applied to large pocket-knives of such a description; but I am inclined to think there may be evidence showing that it once meant a hooked *scimitar*. Possibly the word is akin to *gall*, a foreigner. At any rate, the *gullies* manufactured in Fife last century had evidently a distinctive character that separated them from ordinary blades, and rendered them recognizable in Aberdeenshire.

[†] McNicol, in his " Remarks " on Dr. Johnson's " Journey."

[‡] Quoted in the " Proceedings of the Society of Antiquaries of Scotland," 1880–81, p. 354.

mother-tongue is Gaelic." And Mr. J. F. Campbell corroborates both phases of these statements, in his collection of the "Popular Tales of the West Highlands," in which there are many "magical" smiths—as Loan Mac Libhinn, "the dark smith of Drontheim," and Balcan or Bhalcan, a "sea-smith." There is a hint, also, of this "magical" property in the very name of *Magus* Moor, beside which the gipsy foundry of Simson was formerly situated. Dark—"magical"—metal-working,—these so-called Celtic and Danish smiths possess three of the chief attributes of the Gipsies.

One other example may be taken here. Scott tells us that the Morris-dance was regarded by Handel as the distinguishing dance of Britain. This dance, as the modern jig, or hornpipe, is a greatly modified version of the dance of the ancient Morris, or Moorish men. But we have a glimpse of it in something like its original aspect in the picture drawn by the Scotch historian of the Gipsies,* where we see the chief of a Fifeshire gang, with his half-dozen concubines, in the full swing of their satyr-revel.†

These are a few of the characteristics common to the Gipsies, known as such, and to certain of our British predecessors, not *called* Gipsies. But the most striking comparison has yet to be made.

Lempriere's Sarmatians — the Agathyrsi, Tartari, or Geloni—

"who delight
Their hardy limbs with iron to imprint,"—

the long-haired Getæ, whose "bodies bore the seamy ornament of many a scar"—the Mauri of Claudian, on whose dying limbs the Roman soldiers "saw the rude figures, iron-graved"—the "scarified" Hungarians of Gibbon,—all these were *Picts*. I use this term in its widest sense, including by it both "tattooed" and "painted," although in all but the first of these cases the former custom is clearly meant. Of these tribes, then, the Agathyrsi, Geloni, or Tartari are

---

* Simson's "History," pp. 180-182.

† So that when the distinguished author of "The Sketch-Book" made his Gipsy chief—"Starlight Tom"—to possess the reputation of being "the best morris dancer in the country," his selection was singularly apt, and in no likelihood fortuitous.

believed to have come to Ireland, in the *Annals* of which country their tattooing finds a place; as it had also done in the verses of Virgil and Claudian, before this nation quitted its Thracian home. Therefore, since, in the terminology of Modern Denmark, *Gipsy = Tartar*, this invasion was an invasion of tattooed *Gipsies:* and, consequently, these Gipsies were *Picts*. Again—because the fifteenth-century Gipsies of Galloway were "Moors," and the Moors were Picts, "*nec falso nomine Pictos*," these Galloway Gipsies were Picts. But a less equivocal evidence than either of these is that afforded by Hoyland's description of a Gipsy troop that entered Paris in the year 1427. "The men were black, their hair curled;* the women remarkably black, *and all their faces scarred.*" Here, beyond every doubt, the Gipsies were Picts.

These French Gipsies were tattooed, like their Irish kindred, the Agathyrsi, like the scarified Hungarians, and like other branches of their race. The Scottish divisions, in some cases were tattooed, in others painted. The Roman soldiers "saw the rude figures, *iron-graved*," on the bodies of the Stirlingshire Moors; and one of their chiefs, slain near Carron in the seventh century, was known to his enemies as *Domnall Breac*, or *Tattooed Donald*. But, in this same district—the home of the Moors from the very dawn of history, and, even yet the haunt of their purest descendants —the Stirlingshire bands, described by Simson — in this same locality, there were also painted sections of the race. For one of the chief centres of these fen-lands bears the nickname given to a most powerful Gipsy sept; the Faas, Faws, or Falls already spoken of. This place is Falkirk, or *Eaglais bhreac;* literally, "the church of the speckled, or parti-coloured people." The modern form of the name owes

---

* Mr. Simson (from whose "History," p. 70, this is quoted) adds these remarks :—" Dr. Hurd . . . . says that the hair of these men was 'frizzled,' and that some of the women were witches, and 'had hair like a horse's tail.' . . . . I have myself seen English female Gipsies with hair as long, coarse, and thick as a black horse's tail." All this is quite in accordance with what has already been said, both with regard to the possession of magical powers and the physical characteristics of the race. In the "curled" and "frizzled" heads of these men one sees their connection with the "glibbed" Irish rebels of the sixteenth century—the Wild or Black Irishmen of the Gaelic dictionaries.

its origin to a word, believed to be Saxon, which is variously spelled Fah, Faw, and Fal; and its meaning is "of many colours." On the other hand, the form of *Eaglais bhreac*, as pointed out in a previous chapter, indicates not *painting* so much as *tattooing*; a conclusion arrived at from the etymology of *bhreac*. Thus it would appear, either that Falkirk was inhabited by a tattooed clan, at a period prior to the time when it became "the church of the Faws,"* or else that the two varieties of decoration were practised by the same clan.

The Gipsy Faas, or Falls, then, be it observed, received that name, at first, merely as an equivalent for "Pict"; although, in the course of time, it adhered to them as a surname—like the parallel surnames of Black, Brown, or Dunn. Thus a Faw, originally, might have borne any other special name. Or, to put it otherwise, Gipsies now bearing various surnames may be as much the descendants of the Faws as any representative of the family ultimately distinguished by that name.† Such a "Faw" is distinctly visible in the person of a celebrated Galloway chief, whose fame is preserved in more than one record. He went by the familiar name of "Billy Marshall"; and Mactaggart, in his *Gallovidian Encyclopedia*, states that his family had "been tinklers in the south of Scotland time out of mind" (like the

---

* Falkirk, or Fawkirk (as it is still pronounced), is invariably called "*the Fawkyrk*" in Harry the Minstrel's "Wallace," Book X., where the place is mentioned several times. In one line (90) Jamieson has "South *hald* Fawkyrk"; but in the edition of 1594 the words are "South *the* Faukirk"—which is every way preferable to Jamieson's rendering.

† The correctness of this deduction is proved by the following statements encountered after the above was written :—

"One thing is certain—that the name *Faa* not only was given to individuals whose surname might be *Fall*, but to the *Winters* and *Clarkes - id genus omne*— Gipsy families well known on the Borders." (Wilson's "Tales of the Borders," "The Faa's Revenge.")

"*Faw*. An itinerant tinker, potter, &c." (Wright's "Provincial Dictionary.")

"FAW-GANG. A gang of faws. *Cumb*. Francis Heron, *King of the Faws*, was buried at Jarrow, 13 Jan. 1756, Chron. Mirab. p. 6." (Halliwell's "Dictionary.")

The word is also used in Mr. Walter Besant's Christmas novelette (1882):— "There were waggoners to talk with, friendly hawkers, whom the people call muggers and faws, or tinkers, who are too often robbers and pilferers."

And this particular is, further, most clearly established in a recent publication "The Yetholm History of the Gypsies"—by Mr. Joseph Lucas.

Argyleshire Macnabs mentioned by McNicol). Mactaggart calls him "the chief of the most important tribe of vagabonds that ever marauded the country." But the most pregnant statement he makes about him is this. He says that Marshall and his followers, when embarking on a certain adventure (one of little moment in itself, and quite irrelevant here), "painted their faces with *keel*," or ruddle. This is stated by Mactaggart in the most casual way, and he does not refer to it again, showing thereby that there was nothing remarkable in a thoroughbred gipsy of ninety years ago putting on his war-paint before going into action. The thing is intensely significant. It connects this tawny "Billy Marshall" with any "Billy Ross" now living in the Indian Territory. And it proves him, also, to be a lineal descendant of those Ancient Britons of whom Jornandes speaks; who smeared their faces over with the red iron ore; the identical "keel," or ruddle, of their remote posterity in Galloway.

It is pretty surely from this usage that the word "keelie" has come—defined by Dr. Jamieson as "a thief." Simson states that the bands of young gipsies, who used to pass through North Queensferry on plundering expeditions, "were all known at the village by the name of 'Gillie Wheesels,' or 'Killie Wheesh,' which, in the west of Fife, signified 'the lads that take the purses.'" This word *keelie, killie*, or *gillie* is very familiar to us, now-a-days, although it is pronounced by non-Gaelic-speaking people as *gilly:* and wrongly pronounced, since the spelling, *keelie*, gives the proper sound. It signifies, of course, a servant. Sir Walter Scott introduces the same word when he speaks of "a combination of young blackguards" in Edinburgh, who "termed themselves the *keelie gang.*" It may be questioned whether this term was self-applied, or given by the youthful enemies of the said "combination." For the word is by no means obsolete in this application, and is used contemptuously, as to a humble caste. At any rate, whether as *keelie*, or as the inoffensive *gilly*, this word denotes people of low rank. And, in this way, it presents itself as if primarily given by a non-painted, conquering race, to the people whom they overcame, and, as a natural consequence, reduced to servitude, and who were painted people, or Picts. For this word *keel*, in its sense of *ruddle*, exists among obsolete Gaelic words, under its form of *cil*, which, like its other form, *gille*, is pronounced *keel*, or *keelie*. Thus, although the word has long outlived its primary significance, a *keelie*, or "red-stained man," was, to a certain race, the equivalent for a servant. (A parallel case is apparently found in the *gorm-mhac*—literally, "a woad-stained son"—which Shaw defines as "a brave servant, a sturdy domestic.") It would also seem from this, that the reason why *ruadh*, "red," should come to signify "tawny," is precisely similar to that which made *duine dubh*, "a black man," and *duine gorm*, "a woad-stained man," to be interchangeable terms; or to that which made such words as *glas* and *gorm*, or *gwrm*, be used in Scotland and in Wales, in an, apparently, most contradictory fashion—signifying in the one place "green," or "blue," and in the other "brown," or "swarthy": the explanation in all these cases being that the swarthy people were also *ruadh*, or red-stained, and *gorm*, or woad-coloured.

"Billy Marshall," the famous gipsy chief of Galloway,—who was clearly an eighteenth century representative of the marauding "Moors" that ravaged that district in the fifteenth century,—and a distant kinsman of the savage "Blackimore" of local tradition,—and as clearly a descendant of the remote, red-smeared natives pictured by the sixth century historian, was also, by this barbarous custom, the fellow of any vermilion-dusted Wasaji, now camping on the feeders of the Arkansaw. In looking at the gipsies, one is constantly reminded of this resemblance. It would be as absurd to assert that the two peoples were identical as it would be to expect that they should be so. For the British Indian has had a vastly different history from his American cousins. A much earlier contact with Christian civilization, an alliance, or repeated alliances with other varieties of the dusky races, and a greater numerical force with which to meet the advances of the whites (thereby saving himself from extermination,)—have all combined to render the gipsy different from the Indian in several ways. But, notwithstanding all this, the likeness is a striking one. This has already been insisted on sufficiently, but since the

pages that treat of the doings of the "gillie wheesels"*
suggest the likeness again, it may be permissible to say a
few words farther on the subject. The picture given, while
it shews the points of contact between the two peoples, also
reveals their dissimilarity. It refers to the earlier part of
this century, or perhaps, more exactly, to the century before.

"Great numbers of these gipsy plunderers, at one time,
crossed the Forth at Queensferry, for the purpose of stealing
and robbing at the fairs in the north of Scotland. . . . They
were, in general, well dressed, and could not have been
taken for gipsies." (Because they were in a country that
included, among its people, great numbers of peaceable
Melanochroi, as swarthy as their wilder kindred now were.)
At the inn where they used to put up, "no fewer than fourteen of these plunderers have frequently been seen sitting at
breakfast, with Captain Gordon, their commander, at their
head . . . . I believe they were among the best customers
the landlord had. Gipsies, however, are by no means
habitual drinkers, or tipplers; but when they do sit down,
it is, in the phraseology of the sea, a complete *blow-out* . . . .
At these meetings the landlord's son frequently heard them
talking in the gipsy language . . . . It was sometimes the
practice with the young bands to leave their reckoning to be
paid by their chiefs, who were not present, but who, perhaps
next day, came riding up, and paid the expenses incurred by
their men. I am informed that two chiefs, of the names of
Wilson and Brown, often paid the expenses of their bands
in this way." "The young gipsies, male and female, of
whom I have spoken, appear to have been the flower of the
different bands, collected and employed in a general plundering at the fairs in the north . . . . These wanderers were all
known at the village by the name of 'gillie wheesels,' or
'killie wheesh,' which, in the west of Fife, signified 'the lads
that take the purses.' "

Discounting, then, such differences as their power of
identifying themselves with the ordinary population, in
every respect (which is not a characteristic of the *marauding*
Red Indian), these "gillie wheesels" have much the appearance of a band of young braves on the war-path. By the
time that Mr. Simson, senior, knew them, the custom whence

* Simson's "History," pp. 171-173.

their name of *keelies* came had evidently fallen into desuetude. But suppose them a century or two earlier,—when they were armed to the teeth; when they were bold enough to besiege a mansion house in open day; or ferocious enough to engage in savage tribal fights; when, on such a marauding expedition, their dusky faces were ruddled with iron ore; and when (as there are good grounds for supposing) they were nearly as naked as their forefathers who fought Severus;—and what is the picture but a Red Indian foray?

That they were nearly naked, during comparatively recent times, may be assumed for several reasons. As long as they were out-and-out *Picts;* as long, that is, as the painting was not confined to the visage, so long would they be unclothed. Herodian says of their ancestors that "they do not clothe themselves, *lest they should cover the painting of their bodies.*" Under their Gaelic name of *ciuthach, ciofach, giofag,* or *giobag,* they were "naked wild men, living in caves." Their "glibbed" kinsmen in Ireland, during the sixteenth century, were "naked rebels." "In Ireland, a few centuries ago, (says Captain Burt, in his *Letters* from the North of Scotland) the *lower class* seldom encumbered themselves with dress of any kind within doors; and there is every reason to suppose that this was also the case among their brethren in Scotland." Gipsies, generally, in warmer climates than ours, are represented as partially clothed,—their children as wholly naked. And there is a strong hint in their own language that, at one time, English gipsies were themselves "naked wild men." The writer just quoted from speaks of the "*Abraham-men,* and sturdy beggars of all sorts," who "were in England, after the suppression of the monasteries," supported by the benevolence of the public. But what was an *Abraham-man?* In a list of gipsy words, annexed to the *Life* of Bampfylde-Moore Carew, this adjective is thus defined: "ABRAHAM, naked, without clothes, or scarce enough to cover the nakedness." Thus, out of their own mouths, the gipsies of comparatively modern times are proclaimed to be in this respect—as in many others—true descendants of the "semi-nude" "blackamoors" that fell before the Roman legions.

In effect, then, those British Moors, Picts, or gipsies of two or more centuries ago were very much like the modern

American Indian. They have been so gradually subdued in this country, and so imperceptibly blended with the general population (of which they form a great part,) that we do not see this so clearly as we should do, if they had been photographed and written up half as much as their Transatlantic kindred. We think that because they bear familiar surnames they must be very much the same as ourselves. But their nature—when it was allowed to show itself—was the wild Tartar's, or "Indian's." This Billy Marshall of Galloway recalls most forcibly a sketch of Mr. Hepworth Dixon's, so *à propos* that it may well be quoted here :—

"'A gang of Cherokees, under Billy Ross, their savage chief, are coming up the country, swearing they will burn out the white men and carry off the white women from Vinita, that is what's going to happen,' growls a settler on the Kansas plain.

"'But surely,' I venture to put in, 'those Cherokees under Billy Ross are civilised people, not wild animals like Cheyennes and Osages. Are they not settled on the land? Have they not farms and sheep-runs, schools and chapels? Are they not dressed in caps and coats, and called by Christian names? Billy Ross does not exactly smack of tomahawk and scalping knife.'

"'Ha, ha!' roars the Kansas settler, 'bully for you. I see you'll bite. Then tell me, stranger, what is the difference whether you call a savage Flying Hawk or Billy Ross? Will a name wash off war paint, or turn the Indian's yep-yep into Home, sweet Home? Guess Billy Ross is a savage, like the fathers of his tribe.'"*

There is something very appropriate in the locality of this latest gipsy-Pict. "The portion of the Pictish people which longest retained the name were the Picts of Galloway . . . . they maintained an isolated and semi-independent position in a corner of the island, and appear as a distinct people under the name of Picts as late as the twelfth century, when they formed one division of the Scottish army at the battle of the Standard. If any part of the Pictish people might be expected to retain their peculiar language and characteristics, it would be the Picts of Galloway ; . . . . Reginald of Durham, writing in the last half of the twelfth century, mentions, in 1164, Kircudbright, as being in 'terra Pictorum,' and calls their language 'sermo Pictorum.'"†

* "White Conquest," Vol. I. c. xxvi.
† Skene's "Celtic Scotland," Vol. I. pp. 203-4.

In pointing out a few of those places whose names still bear the memory of their black inhabitants, several examples were taken from this particular neighbourhood; and it was observed that these—and others, not specified—are situated in the vicinity of the Picts' Dyke: which, it may be convenient to notice, bears the alternative name of the *De'ils' Dyke* (the name of *devil* being a common, if inelegant, epithet of the black races,—as already observed). This dyke of the painted people, or "devils," is defined as "a long line of ancient fortification in Galloway and Dumfriesshire, commencing at Loch Ryan near Innermessan ... and extending ... to the upper part of the Solway Firth ... It separates the fertile lands of the seaboard districts from the irreclaimable wastes and wild fastnesses of the mountains."

This wild and remote district was thus the home of that portion of the "painted people" which longest retained its distinctive nickname. They were so characterized as lately as the twelfth century: at which period they formed an important division of the Scottish army, in its invasion of Northumbria. Their name of *Picti* having, apparently, lapsed—we see them, three centuries later, ravaging various districts of Galloway, under their alternative name of *Mauri*, or Moors. Lastly, their power and their proportions sadly contracted, they are visible to us about ninety years ago,—under the leadership of Billy Marshall, "the chief of the most important tribe of vagabonds that ever marauded the country." At which period,—if they had lost their distinctive *title*,—they had at least retained "their peculiar language and characteristics;" and that portion of Kircudbrightshire which was their chief resort, could still with all fitness be denominated, *Terra Pictorum*.*

---

* That the British gipsies, generally, so recently as last century, were Picts, is seen from the following statement of the antiquary, Grose (which I had not met with at the time the foregoing conclusion was arrived at). Of the gipsies, in general, he says:—"They pretend that they derive their origin from the ancient Egyptians, who were famous for their knowledge in astronomy and other sciences; and, under the pretence of fortune-telling, find means to rob or defraud the ignorant and superstitious. To colour their impostures they artificially discolour their faces, and speak a kind of gibberish peculiar to themselves." (Grose's "Classical Dictionary of the Vulgar Tongue.") It is a very strange circumstance that Sir Walter Scott—who was of the same century as Grose, though a much younger man, and who was of age before Gipsy Marshall died—says nothing whatever of this most striking fact.

CHAPTER XII.

OF all the clues by which men try to thread the mazes of the past language is the most likely to lead to a false conclusion. To suppose that, because two peoples speak one language, therefore they are closely allied in blood, would be utterly erroneous, in many cases, as we can see by looking around us at the present day. No greater diversity of type could be found, living side by side, than that of the planter aristocracy of the Southern States, before the war, and the dusky serfs they employed; yet their common language was English. And, if an antiquary of a thousand years hence, learning this fact, jumped to the conclusion that *therefore* the planters and their serfs were nearly akin, he would form an impression of the ethnological situation in that territory, during the nineteenth century, which would be as mistaken as it could possibly be. Accordingly, if we were to learn that this or that portion of the British Islands was inhabited by a Celtic-speaking population, at, say, the date of the Roman invasion; and if, from this, we were to conclude that the people of that territory formed a homogeneous Celtic nation, we might be making a blunder of as gross a nature as the hypothetical one we have just supposed.

But, although all this is true, there are nevertheless certain lessons to be learned from the examination of various British forms of speech; and, although none but philologists are rightly able, or entitled, to discuss linguistic questions, yet there are certain facts of this nature which bear closely upon the present theme, and to which one may fairly draw attention.

The leading ethnologists of the present day are agreed in this—" that, probably in the time of Cæsar, and certainly in that of Tacitus, there existed in these islands two distinct types of population: the one of tall stature, with fair skin, yellow hair, and blue eyes; the other of short stature, with dark skin, dark hair, and black eyes. We further learn (continues Professor Huxley) that this dark population, represented by the Silures, bore considerable physical resemblance to the people of Aquitania and Iberia; while the fair population . . . . resembled the Belgæ who inhabited the north-east of France and the country now called Belgium." Another writer* states the same thing in these words: "Two main stocks of Britons certainly lived in the southern part of the island at the date of the Roman invasion. One of these was the Aryan race of the Kelts, almost beyond question a light-haired, light-eyed, and light-skinned people. . . . The other was the Euskarian race of the Silures, almost beyond question a dark-haired, dark-eyed, and dark-skinned people. . . . On the whole, it seems .. . . probable that a body of conquering Keltic warriors had crossed over to Britain long before the dawn of history . . . . but that they were numerically very weak, and that they lived on thenceforward as a military Keltic aristocracy, in the midst of a servile population of Euskarian or half-Euskarian aborigines. The long-headed Kelt Euskarian *plebs*, ruled over by the round-headed Aryan Keltic chiefs and soldiers, form, in all probability, the mass of the historical Britons, at and after the date of the Roman invasion." These statements, then (more fully quoted in the opening chapter), have been, in the main, borne out by all the observations made heretofore.

Thus, the "British," whom the Romans encountered, were made up of ingredients as greatly different from each other as are the component parts of the present population of the United States. They were, *at least*, fair whites, dark whites, and blacks.

Of the fair whites, or *Xanthochroi*, the Celts or Kelts formed a part. Race names are rather dangerous weapons to work with, because a white Celt, or a white Norseman, might easily become as swarthy (almost) as a Euskar or a Dane, after repeated intermarrying with these races for some

---

* Mr. Grant Allen, "The Welsh in the West Country," *Gentleman's Magazine*, August, 1882.

generations; and yet he would be, politically, a Celt or a Norseman. But, at any rate, the pure Celt of, say, two thousand years ago, was a "fair white." This is held to be "almost beyond question." So that the pure Celt, the pure Norseman, and the pure Belgian, of a distant, and not easily defined, epoch, were probably near kinsmen: while the swarthy Silurian, or Moor, or Pict, and the equally swarthy Dane, were much more closely related to each other than to any branch of the *Xanthochroi;* from whom they were separated by an enormous gulf.

The Celts, then, formed one division of the pure whites; the Moors, or Picts, of the pure blacks; and both were living, side by side, in Britain, when the Romans came. That the Silures were *Picts* seems clear. "Tacitus mentions the painted countenances and curled hair of the *Silures*, as an argument that they were of Spanish origin."* (From which one may see, also, that ancient Spain, too, was Pictish.)

But, at present, it must be remembered, we have in view the question of *language*. Speaking of this politically-united, racially-divided nation, Professor Huxley says:— "Evidence may be adduced to show that the language spoken by both these types of people in Britain, at, and before, the Roman conquest, was exclusively Celtic. This evidence is furnished, not only by the statements of Cæsar and other early writers, but also by the testimony of ancient monuments and local names." And Mr. Grant Allen repeats this dictum. "Speaking the Keltic language, and, no doubt, considering themselves as much Kelts as their masters, they were yet, as far as blood went, almost pure dolichocephalic Euskarians." But, in spite of Cæsar's statements, and the testimony of ancient monuments, let us consider if this conclusion is a just one.

The Celtic language was that spoken by the white invaders. The very name of one branch of that language, the Gaelic, corroborates this. For, according to one writer, the word "Gaelic" signifies "the language of the white men."† Now, on looking into that language, what do we find? We find, that just as a "girl of the lowest rank of the peasantry"

* Huddleston's edition of Toland's "History of the Druids," p. 336.
† Captain Burt's "Letters," &c., Vol. II. p 82.

is a "black hussy," so is "the vernacular" or "the speech of the mob" literally (as it was once actually) "black speech." Here, then, we have at once an emphatic denial to the received belief.

But it may be said that the Gaelic words which style the language of the people "black speech" are so old that they antedate the coming of the Romans, by which time, it is said, the Celtic aristocracy (though supposed to be numerically weak) had imposed their speech upon the whole inhabitants of Britain, black or white. At the first glance this seems defensible, but it will not bear investigation.

Like race-names, language (as already remarked) is not a perfectly reliable weapon in warfare of this speculative kind. It was observed, a few sentences back, that the term "Celt" might come to be applied to one who has inherited only the least possible infusion of Celtic blood. We see this misuse of nomenclature in a most marked form to day, when the "Black Celts to the west of the Shannon," and other tribes of non-Celtic descent, are distinguished by the race name of their conquerors, whose blood they scarcely share at all. If the original Celts were really pure *Xanthochroi*, it is evident that no dark-haired, or dark skinned man can be a genuine Celt. So is it with language. Just as the white races have intermingled with the swarthy "native men," so has "the language of the white men" become amalgamated with the "black speech" of the Moors, until at length it is difficult to decide what "Gaelic" really is.

To judge from what has been said of it by several eminent men, one might reasonably conclude that it is a patchwork of all the tongues of Babel. "There is scarcely a language in the world" (says Dr. Sullivan, in his Preface to Ebel's *Celtic Studies*) "between which and the Celtic some one has not attempted to prove a connection." And he states that various theorists, with varying success, have traced a distant kinship between it and the language of the Jaloffs, an African tribe, the Leni Lenappe of North America, the Lapps, Ostiaks, and other North Siberian tribes, the Jews, and the Phœnicians, all which supposed connections he regards with something like contempt. But Mr. Howorth's Ugrian-Celtic words, and the evidences of common physical features, agree in indicating the wide ramifications of the Turanian or Mongoloid family, to which the so-called Celts, in a measure, and several of the nations just enumerated, distinctly, belong. Nor is there anything strange in the statement that many Gaelic words are of Jewish and Phœnician kindred, since both of these nations sent traders to our coasts. Again,—Professor Blackie announces as the result of an analysis of Armstrong's Gaelic Dictionary, "that of the four Aryan languages with which I compare it, the Gaelic presents the strongest affinity with the Latin, after that, with the German, and the Teutonic element of the English, including Scotch, least of all with the Greek." That Gaelic should closely resemble Latin, in certain words, is not surprising, when one learns from Mr. Skene that, in the eighth century, Latin had "become common to all" in Britain (the Venerable Bede being his authority for the statement), or when one reflects upon the great and long-continued influence of a Latinized clergy, and the presence, for several centuries, of a dominant Latin caste. The Gaelic annals, indeed, seem to have been largely written in a Gaelic-Latin *patois*. Speaking of a seventh century entry, Dr. McLauchlan remarks:—"It is, *as usual*, a curious instance of Gaelic and Latin." And, in the list of Latin words picked out, at random, by Professor Blackie, the great body of them, he says, are clearly borrowed direct from the Latin, such as *sagart* from *sacerdos*, *eaglais* from *ecclesia*, and *sraid* from *stratum*, all of which are simply the Latin words pronounced according to certain local accents. Another form of *stratum* is the better known *strath*, a word which many of us believe to be peculiarly the property of the Scottish Gael, although (like *street* and *sraid*) it is quite likely nothing more than a development of *stratum*.

It is curious, indeed, to discover—as one may do by glancing in the most superficial fashion at any of the authorities on this subject—that very many of our popular beliefs, in this respect, are ludicrously erroneous. The irregular use of the letter "h"—generally spoken of as a Cockneyism, or as, at least, confined to certain districts of England—is as common a Celticism. For example, one may say either *aon* or *a h-aon*, in pronouncing the Gaelic numeral, *one*,—*ochd* or *a h-ochd*, in pronouncing *eight*,—and the word *uile* (*all*) may be aspirated or not, according to choice. Words, also, that are quite as much "English" as they are "Gaelic" may be picked out of the dictionary with little trouble. Not modern English words Gaelicised, but Old English. Thus, *teanga* and *tunge* (tongue), *bogha* and *boga* (bow), *mòd* and *mote* (court), *gruamach* and *græme* (grim), are specimens of the words claimed equally for the Gaelic and Anglo-Saxon languages. But perhaps the oddest instance of all is one word which, like the pseudo-Gaelic *strath*, is identified with the Celtic family—in the popular fancy. This is the prefix *Mac*. One learns from the vocabularies that this is no other than the Anglo-Saxon *mæg, mecg*, or *maga*, and the Dutch *maag*. The form *maga* is almost identical with the Gaelic, for it seems that in certain districts of the West Highlands, if not elsewhere, a final "a" is tacked on to the "Mac" in conversation. And we see this "Dutch" spelling in the Irish-Gaelic "Book of Rights" (O'Donovan's Translation, p. 131) in the surname *Mag Dubhain*. So that there is no real difference between the "Celtic" prefix, as it is seen in this instance, or when it occurs in the West Highland Tales in such cases as *Mac-a-Ghoill* and *Mac-a-Rusgaich*, and the "English" prefix as it is found in the *Maga Healf-denes* of Beowulf. And such names as *Macnab*, *Macvicar*, and *Macpherson* have quite as much a right to be called "English" as "Gaelic," since, in either language, they signify "the son of the abbot—the vicar—and the parson." Another name of this sort is *Macleod*. The first of the family so designated is supposed to have been a son of Olave the Swarthy, "the black prince of Man," one of the race of Danes, *dubh galls, nigræ gentes*, or "black strangers." *Leod* is an Old English word signifying "prince:" the "son of Healfdane" was "Leod Scyldinga," "Prince of the Scyldings." *Macleod*, therefore, is simply Old English for "the son of the prince."

The identity of certain "Gaelic" words with "English" is often concealed by the orthography; but the pronunciation at once reveals it. Such words, for example, as *deacaid*, *cuite*, and *geola*, look very strange to the eye of the modern Englishman, but their pronunciation—and signification—is simply *jacket*, *quit*, and *yawl*. "English" of this kind is merely Phonetic Gaelic.* No doubt there are words, now called Gaelic, which are nothing but modern English Gaelicised. How many of these neutral words are nineteenth-century English, Gaelicised, and how many are Old English which never changed into New English, must ever be a matter of uncertainty. It seems likely, however, that the class to which *geola*, or *yawl*, belongs, cannot be included under the heading of Modern English, Gaelicised. For words of this sort are very common in Anglo-Saxon, as well as in Gaelic, and they seem to indicate such an utterance as that of the slow-speaking Hungarians described by Gibbon, since the vowel which terminates each word—otherwise a monosyllable—is little else than a drawl. Some examples of this feature are the following (the words in italics being the Scotch-Gaelic forms): *Ata*, hat; *apu*, ape; *bata*, boat; *bocsa*, box; *bogha*, bow; *boma*, bomb; *capa*, cap; *canna*, can; *cota*, coat; *cupa*, cup; *druma*, drum; *iarla*, earl; *geola*, yawl; *grota*, groat; *geata*, gate; *gunna*, gun; *peata*, pet; *poca*, poke; *roca*, rock; *ropa*, rope; *teanga*, tongue; *tunna*, tun; and *unnsa*, ounce. Four of these examples are duplicated in Anglo-Saxon in the words *boga*, *bât*, *eorl* and *tunga*; while that language exhibits the same tendency in such words as *horsa*, horse; *steorra*, star; *tima*, time; *manna*, man; *eahta*, eight; *wyrhta*, wright; and others. That these words are originally Ugrian is probable, since *cota*, a coat, cot, or cote—radically, a *covering* or *enclosure*—is found in the Lapp *cota*, a tent; and the Lapp *svaka*, a pack-saddle, proclaims its kinship with the English-Colonial *swag*.

Made up, as it is, of so many different languages—what is it that forms the main body of the Gaelic speech? In his *Language and Literature of the Highlands of Scotland* Professor Blackie makes this statement: "I have gone through Armstrong's Gaelic Dictionary very carefully twice, arranging all the roots alphabetically in columns, and placing in a line parallel to each column of Gaelic roots the real or probable corresponding roots in Greek, Latin, German, English, and Scotch. My list includes about eight hundred words, and from a rough comparison with another list which I made I should say it leaves two-thirds of the simple

* When it is not " Phonetic English "—from the Gaelic point of view.

vocabulary of the language unconnected with any known form of Aryan speech." This estimate, he warns us, is only approximate, but, as the result of a scholarly investigation, it is surely of some value—even though approximate. Another authority—Dr. McLauchlan of Edinburgh—says:— " Our earliest written [Scottish] Gaelic is, without doubt, the ' Book of Deer;' our earliest printed Gaelic is with as little doubt, ' Carsewell's Prayer-Book.' The former of these is probably of the eleventh or twelfth century, and the latter is of the sixteenth; and a remarkable thing is that the language of both is far more alike than is the language of either to modern Gaelic. I do not know what dialect the people spoke in those bye-gone ages, but the dialect which they wrote and read was very different from that written and read now." The learned writer does not indicate the direction in which this difference leads, but it would be of great importance to know.

The consideration of any language, however, by one who is not a scholar, can lead to little. The chief impression that one gets from consulting the Gaelic dictionaries, therefore, is that the Gaelic speech is a mosaic of other tongues. The pre-Roman *clachan*, or stone-circle,* which was the equivalent for our modern word *church*, has given place to the Latin *eaglais* and *teampull* (*ecclesia* and *templum*). The officiating priest of the *clachan*, once a *cairneach*, is now a *sagart* (*sacerdos*), or a *ministeir*. These words are Latin, pure and simple, though slightly altered by a local accent. And, as everybody knows, they are not solitary instances. Nor is it any wonder that the Gaelic speech has been greatly Latinized, when one remembers the widespread influence of monas-

---

* An eminent Scottish archæologist has just decided that the stone-circles were places of interment rather than of worship. But the probability is that they were both, since the custom of burying in " sacred ground "—whether outside a church or within its walls—is of great antiquity in this country. A *clachan*, or "place of stones," is held (I think by the best judges) to signify primarily "a burying-ground," whence it has been transferred to the village that usually sprang up in the neighbourhood of the sacred place. But while "a place of stones" bore this meaning, it also signified "a church." We are told that "Are you going to *the stones?*" used to be the usual Highland query on a Sunday, though now it is "Are you going to *church?*" Thus, there is every reason to believe that the ancient stone-circle, like the parish church of yesterday and the Abbey of to-day, was equally a burying-ground *and* a church.

ticism, felt throughout all our islands for a thousand years. We have seen that the Annals of Tighernach, compiled in the seventh century, were written in "a curious mixture of Gaelic and Latin;" while Bede, in the century after, states that Latin, "from the study of the Scriptures, has become common to all" in Britain. The very character in which "Old Irish" is written is the Roman letter.

And the same character is also known as "Saxon," which language, we have seen, has also some right to be styled "Gaelic," as it claims, equally with the latter, a considerable number of words, not the least famous of which is the familiar *Mac*, or *Maga*, "a son." And again, this word has displaced a much older one, *Bar*, which, though now obsolete, is included in Dr. Armstrong's Gaelic Dictionary. *Bar*, it is hardly necessary to observe, also signifies "a son" in a very ancient and celebrated language, the Hebrew; and it is only one out of a thousand Hebrew words that are claimed by the Gaelic lexicographers. Which reminds us that several other forms of speech—now called "Oriental"—are also identified in some degree with Gaelic.

Thus, as the Magi of the East and the Magi of Britain were, according to Pliny, closely akin in their mysteries and observances, so the oldest—or one of the oldest—languages in Britain has many words that belong to the very language of those Eastern Magi. But it has been seen that the British Magi, or Druids,—from an ethnographical point of view,—were *gipsies*, or something very like the hybrid people we now know by that name. Therefore, if the language spoken in Britain, "at and before the Roman Conquest, was exclusively Celtic" (as some believe)—then the gipsy speech must be a branch of the Celtic family of languages. Now, this is exactly what Mr. C. G. Leland has discovered is the case,—in one instance. He has ascertained that the dialect used by the Tinkers (who, be it remembered, are only one division of the gipsy people), and known by their kindred as the *Minklers Thari*, or *Shelta Thari*, is nothing else than a Celtic tongue, though different from any of the other well-known varieties of that speech. Wherein it differs from them—and to what extent—will be seen when it, and all the other dialects of this neglected group of languages, have been more carefully studied by scholarly men than they have yet been. If it should appear that *all* the gipsy dialects of Britain belong to the Celtic family, then (and then only) will the statement that the British language was "exclusively Celtic" in Cæsar's time be proved to be true.

In the meantime, however, let us suppose that—with the exception of the *Shelta Thari*—the gipsy dialects are far removed from any Celtic form of speech. That is to say, the language of the Picts, Moors, Euskarians, Druids, gipsies (or whatever name one may use to designate the non-Xanthochroic Britons of the Roman period) was vastly different from that used by the Celts. If this be the case, then the "exclusively Celtic" argument—whether founded upon Cæsar's imperfect knowledge of the country, or upon the also imperfect "testimony of ancient monuments and local names"—this argument falls to the ground. Not only because "the language of the white men" distinctly tells us that "the speech of the mob," or "the vernacular," was "black speech." Not for this reason alone; because the word that tells us this may have become fossilized long before the Romans came. But chiefly for this reason: the language of the Moors, or Picts, or Magi, has not yet become extinct, and is spoken by the very descendants of those people at this present moment. If, then, it has lingered on till now, in spite of layer after layer of other and newer languages, how much more general must it have been in the days of Cæsar!

The pure Pictish tongue is still spoken. And not one dialect of it only, but many. "If any part of the Pictish people might be expected to retain their peculiar language and characteristics, (says Mr. Skene,* speaking of Scottish Picts,) it would be the Picts of Galloway." That they retained one of their most peculiar characteristics until the beginning of this century was visibly demonstrated to us by the ruddled cheeks of the famous Galloway Pict—"Billy Marshall." And though that custom seems to have vanished now, it is not likely his descendants have forgotten the language of their forefathers. Nor is it likely that the Faws who still wander among their ancestral haunts in Stirling-

* "Celtic Scotland," Vol. I. p. 203.

shire have altogether forsaken the speech that has come down from the far back marsh-dwellers whose blood and customs they inherit. Nor, indeed, that any other branch of the Pictish people, that still keeps up its ancient habits, has forgotten its ancient tongue.

But there is yet another aspect of this question. The modern writers, already spoken of, believe "that a body of conquering Keltic warriors had crossed over to Britain long before the dawn of history," that they had conquered the swarthy, aboriginal tribes, and that—although numerically weak—they had established themselves as "a military Keltic aristocracy," ruling over a mixed, but chiefly Euskarian, Silurian, Moorish, or (to use the punning term that denotes their common custom) *Pictish* population. And such writers assume that the Keltic language had been imposed by the conquerors upon the conquered by the time that Cæsar came. Now, in a previous chapter, it was supposed that these white conquerors—acting much in the same fashion as the white, or quasi-white conquerors of to-day—had amused themselves, in their idle moments, with the games and antics of their swarthy subjects—"not wrongly named 'the painted folk,'"—who formed the bulk of the rustic population, and who were—*clowns*. And these—it was also assumed—are still represented, in many ways, though not necessarily in blood, by the clowns and jesters of our own time.

In two thousand years, however, many of the games, customs, and occupations that belonged peculiarly to the subject races may have passed out of their hands into those of the heterogeneous nation that now makes up the "Modern British." That this has really happened, and is happening before our eyes, has recently been noticed. The workers in pottery, or in metals, in this present generation need not have any "Moorish" blood in their bodies ;—neither need the clowns just spoken of. All these *may* be of a wholly different race from those Pictish Moors (though they are more likely to belong, in some degree, to that particular type,—not only because of their proclivities,—but because the *Melanochroi* are believed to form the majority of our people). Circus-clown and itinerant mountebank, therefore, *may* have little or nothing of gipsy blood. But there is one professional caste that, even in our time, seems only partially, if at all, severed from the race with which it was once identified.

One of the distinguishing occupations of the black people was that of minstrel, or wandering harper. In the mediæval episode of the escape of Audulf de Bracy,—recited by Scott, and previously quoted,—John of Rampayne had to stain "his hair and his whole body entirely as black as jet, so that nothing was white but his teeth," before he could pass himself off as a minstrel. (And it is possible, if not probable, that it was by a similar method that Alfred was able to mingle with the swarthy Danes, undetected, when he, too, "disguised himself" as a strolling harper, and ventured into their camp.) There is no record, in the story, of the particular language spoken by those mediæval minstrels, though surely their mother-tongue cannot well have been anything but *dubh-chainnt*, or "black speech." But, to learn the language of a minstrel, we need not go back all the way to the Middle Ages. The race of harpers is not yet extinct. At any rate, the *caste* of harpers exists: whether their blood is pure or mixed.

The "gipsy" article in the *Encyclopædia Britannica*, from which some extracts have been made, states that the dialect of the Welsh gipsies, "generally unintelligible to the English gipsy, is one of the most perfect, as it has also been the least studied, of all the dialects" of the gipsy speech. And examples of this interesting tongue are there given. An intensely interesting dialect it is; because, since the Galloway gipsies are the Galloway Picts, this Welsh dialect of "gipsy" is a Welsh dialect of Pictish. But what gives an added interest to this fact, and what links the preceding paragraph to this, is the statement made, relative to these examples of Welsh "gipsy." They "are derived from letters and stories written by John Roberts, the oldest living harper, whose thorough knowledge of his language is probably unique." Now, since he has attained the eminence of such particular notice, there can be little harm in regarding this venerable minstrel more closely. Whatever his physical features may happen to be, if he descends from a long line of Welsh harpers, he ought to be, in complexion, the darkest of the Melanochroi. At any rate, he is a true representative of the caste, whatever his lineage. It is one of those castes that, in the Middle Ages, and earlier, ministered to the pleasures of the Norman aristocracy; and, earlier still (by hypothesis) amused the leisure of the Keltic nobles. This venerable harper represents one of these castes—of the black people—whatever be his own pedigree. What, then, is his language? He may speak English,—no doubt he speaks Welsh,—but what is "his language?" It is gipsy.

CHAPTER XIII.

SINCE we see that the people known to us *specially* as "Picts" (the *Picti* of Claudian) were of black complexion, it becomes a question whether their chief allies—the Early Scots—were not of a kindred hue. The two nations are invariably linked together, in all records of the Roman Conquest, and their chief historian at the present day seems to regard them as akin in blood. He tells us, also,* that the Pictish inhabitants of ancient Argyle were, by one writer, styled *Scoti Picti*, or Painted Scots; and that the occasion on which the Scots Proper first make their appearance in history is when, in conjunction with the nation particularly styled "Picts," they began a series of fierce incursions into Roman Britain, in the year 360 A.D. The districts of the main island which the marauding Scots selected as the scene of their depredations, "consisted of part of the mountain region of Wales on the coast opposite to . . . . Ireland, from whence they came."

It is now known by most people that the Early Scots had, at first, very little to do with that portion of our islands now distinguished by their name. "That Scotia, prior to the tenth century, was Ireland, and Ireland alone," is one of those propositions which, Mr. Skene maintains, "lie at the very threshold of Scottish history." And Gildas, writing of the Scots two centuries after the date of their first recorded advent, characterizes them as "shameless Irish robbers."

This expression of the British monk would appear to hit off their chief characteristics very fairly, and it is under this guise, as "land-pirates and water-pirates," that the Scots Proper, like their fellow-robbers, the "Picts," are visible everywhere in history and tradition. Their appellation, *Scot*,

---

* Skene's "Celtic Scotland," Vol. III. p. 104; also Vol. I. pp. 3, 97, and 98.

is believed by some to have been given to them by their civilized foes, and to be a contemptuous term, signifying "vagabond." Gildas, at any rate, has no respect for them, as the following quotation will show: "The Romans being drawn home, there descend in great crowds from the little narrow bores of their *Caroghes*, or *Carts*, wherein they were brought over the Stitick Vale, about the middle of summer, in a scorching-hot season, a duskish swarm of vermin, or hideous crew of Scots and Picts, somewhat different in manners, but all alike thirsting after blood; who, finding that their old confederates (the Romans) were marched home, and refused to return any more, put on greater boldness than ever, and possessed themselves of all the north and the remote parts of the kingdom, to the very wall, as if they were the true native proprietors."* These references of the South British monk suggest several things, not the least important being the impression conveyed by the last words of the preceding sentence. It is evident that Gildas regarded himself as the descendant of a race that had dwelt in Britain —or, at least, its southern portion—long before the arrival of either Scot or Pict. It is true that this may mean nothing more than that, in his eyes, Ireland and North Britain were foreign countries; and the expression, "transmarine nations," used by him and by the Venerable Bede (in speaking of Picts and Scots), is, indeed, held to refer to their residence in Ireland, and that part of Scotland lying to the north of the Forth and Clyde, which—being at that date almost separated from the larger and southern part of the island—was nearly as "transmarine" as Ireland itself. But the words of Gildas may bear a wide significance. The latter portion of the sentence just quoted is translated thus by another writer:†— "The Romans having left Britain, they (the Scots and Picts) eagerly land from their curroughs (skin boats), in which they passed over the Scythian Valley [*Scythicam Vallem*]." The "carts" of the first rendering is thus an obvious mistranslation, and the vehicles in which those "Scuits," or vagabonds, conveyed themselves were the well-known *coracles*, still seen in Wales and Ireland, and used, until within recent

---

* Maule's "History of the Picts," p. 115.
† Huddleston, in his edition of Toland's "History of the Druids," p. 425.

times, by the people of the Hebrides,* to whom they were known as *curachs*. They were used also, at the date of the first inroad of the Scots, by the inhabitants of another country, that, to a South Briton such as Gildas, was transmarine. This was the Oestrymnic Archipelago, which lay to the north of Spain, and of which, it has been supposed, the present Scilly Isles form a fragment. A Latin writer of the fourth century has left us this account of the shipbuilding powers of those islanders:—

> "They know not to fit with pine
> Their keels, nor with fir, as use is,
> They shape their boats; but, strange to say,
> They fit their vessels with united skins,
> And often traverse the deep in a hide."†

It is pretty clear that, although allied to the open coracles still used in Wales, and fashioned of the same materials, yet the skin-boats in which those various piratical races ventured out to sea and performed voyages of several days' duration could not have been of the same egg-shell formation, or they would have been swamped by the first "chopping sea" they encountered. Let it be remembered that, by several lines of argument (indicated to some extent in a previous chapter), scientific men have reached the conclusion that a race "not unlike the modern Eskimo," inhabited certain parts of western and north-western Europe at about the dawn of the Christian era, and it will be seen that if those sea-coracles were themselves "not unlike" the *kayaks* of the modern Eskimo, or even exactly like them, there would be nothing surprising in the fact. That this was really the case I shall point out subsequently. In the meantime it is sufficient to be content with the assumption that the Eskimo kayak and the "Scythian" sea-coracle were identical, grounded on the fact that no other shape of skin-boat could live in a tempestuous sea.

Thus the Picts and Scots may have been "transmarine nations" in a very wide sense, since, by many links, they are connected with other "Scythian" nations more remote from Southern Britain than they were. The Silures and the

---

* According to Dr. Armstrong (under *Curach* in his Gaelic dictionary).
† "Celtic Scotland," Vol. I. p. 168.

Spaniards of their time were seen to be both "Picts," and they (along with other indigenous British tribes, inhabiting Interior England and a large part of Modern Scotland, as well as the black and painted races of Ireland) were also shown to have possessed many common characteristics, and to have closely resembled each other in several physical traits. And the Picts and Scots — specially so named (although each title appears to have been a general nickname and nothing else)—may thus have been "transmarine," not only because they dwelt on the further side of the Irish Sea and the "Firth of Darkness" (that, save for the mountain-range that skirts the eastern side of Loch Lomond, would have severed the bulk of Scotland from the larger section of the island); not only because they were apparently the kindred of the more distant Picts of the Spanish Peninsula and the Islands of the Oestrymnides; but also because they themselves—the Picts of the British Islands—are traditionally said to have come originally from that part of "Scythia" lying on the eastern side of the North Sea; the exact locality fixed upon by some being no other than "the *Chersoness Cimbrica*, that promontory that is now called *Jutcland*,"* out of which, some centuries later, issued the Black Danes, or Cimbri. So that the Picts Proper and the Black Danes, being both Picts and both Moors, and both being "black strangers," or *dubh galls*, in the sight of the white races of Britain, coming, as they appear to have done, from the same locality, present themselves as not improbably akin.

So far, however, we have only decided, with regard to the early Scots, that they were the associates of swarthy, piratical, painted races,—of a Black-Eskimo, or Negrito-Mongoloid strain,— without reaching the conclusion that the Scots themselves were of the same complexion. But this seems to be distinctly pointed out by Gildas, when he chronicles the arrival of "a duskish swarm of vermin, or hideous crew of Scots and Picts, somewhat different in manners, but all alike thirsting after blood." The indifferent translation which I have quoted from does not enable us to see those invaders as clearly as we might, but another version is more exact. The precise words used by the monkish chronicler

* Maule's "History of the Picts," p. 60.

are these—*tetri Scotorum Pictorumque greges*—"the black herds of Scots and Picts."* There is no ambiguity in the words. The writer—himself, it is almost certain, a white man—was recording an event that had happened only two centuries before his time. He was in the position of a twentieth-century Briton describing the Battle of Plassey, or of a Bostonian of to-day picturing an attack of the Wyandots, or the Narragansetts. Better than these, he had likely enough seen one or more members of the race he was describing; which either of these supposititious historians might easily have failed to do. Therefore, when he speaks of the *black* herds of Scots and Picts, we have every right to believe that in so speaking of them he depicted them truly.

The fourth-century Scots, then, being undistinguishable from the general "black herd" that made up the Scoto-Pictish army, were themselves of the same complexion as the Picts Proper. That is to say, they, also, were *Mauri*, or Moors.

But this is tantamount to saying that the Scots were gipsies. Now, it is important to remember that although there are *traditions* of gipsy invasions of Scotland (at a time when a gipsy was an armed foe, and no mere vagabond), yet there is no *historical* record of such invasions. That is to say, the invading foes were not called "gipsies" by the historians. But such invasions could not well have happened, and within the memory of the people, without there being some recorded notice of them. *Unwritten* history tells us that bands of wild, marauding *gipsies* came into Scotland from Ireland, and the gipsies themselves assert the same thing. "Almost all the Scottish gipsies (says Mr. Simson), assert that their ancestors came by way of Ireland into Scotland." *Written* history tells us that *Scots*, also wild marauders, "shameless Irish robbers," says Gildas, came over from Ireland; and the very district that especially tells us of their fierce and turbulent nature is full of stories of "the Wild Scots o' Gallowa'." It is true that the gipsies

---

* In this, as in every other quotation from the writers of antiquity, the statement is here made at second-hand; but there seems no reason to question the soundness of the information thus conveyed.

do not style themselves "Scots;" and true, also, that the gap between the sixth-century "robbers" of Gildas and the fifteenth-century gipsies of the Maclellan story is immense. But it is held by some writers—as stated a page or two back—that the title "Scot" was given in contempt by the enemies of this people, and that it signified *Scuit*, a vagabond; while there is no proof that the fifteenth century witnessed the *first* advent of the gipsies in Scotland. Farther, the wild, Black-Irishman of Queen Elizabeth's reign, with his plaited hair, his swarthy skin, and his fen-land haunts, was virtually a gipsy; and his island was the mother-country of the Scots. The speech of the Scots of Galloway was the *sermo Pictorum*,—the Moors were Picts, the gipsies (whether as "Moors," or as "gipsies") were Picts,—by all these names substantially the same people are intended. The Scots *were* gipsies.

However contradictory this deduction may appear, it must never be forgotten that the people who made Scotland an independent nation were *not* Scots. The Bruces, the Wallaces, the Stewarts, and many other lesser names, were Normans and Flemings. It is true they identified themselves with the earlier races, and readily assumed the name and some of the ideas of their adopted country—(for men are very chameleons in their aptitude for taking on local colour). But they were not Scots. The rank and file of their followers *may* have been Scottish. Some of the leaders were so. For example, "the good Sir James," the most loyal of all Bruce's knighthood. But he came of a race that boasted its ancient, aboriginal blood, and that bore a surname which signified "the black man." And he himself, although by his time the family of Douglas had, likely enough, made more than one alliance with the whites, he himself was "of a black and swart complexion," according to Godscroft. For which cause, he was known to his foes as "the Black Douglas." Thus, although his high birth, and all the chivalrous qualities attributed to him by Barbour, rendered him a splendid specimen of a brave and courteous gentleman, and although he died in battle with the Saracens of Spain, he was actually, in some degree, a Moor or Saracen himself. And farther, this "Moorish" blood must have run in the veins of the chiefs of his house for fully a century after his death. For the Black Douglases, or those of Liddesdale, retained the headship of their clan until the year 1455, when they were overthrown, and their estates forfeited in favour of the younger and rival branch of Angus. "And it became a saying, in allusion to the complexion of the two races, that 'the *red* Douglas had put down the *black*.'"

But although the Douglases, and other tribes, belonged to a race that, by one name or another, preceded the Normans, yet the prime movers in the struggle that ended in "Scottish" independence were not "Scots." The two great heroic figures of that era were not "Scots," neither was the first of the royal Stewart race. At Bannockburn Norman fought Norman, and Fleming Fleming. And when the Bruces had reached the summit of their power, and Edward Bruce made the haughty discovery that "Scotland was too little for his brother and him also," his chief generals in the Irish campaign were kindred Normans, such as Sir Philip Mowbray and Sir John Stewart, or others of the race of Sir Neil the Fleming. Of course, it is not to be understood that these two were the only white races at that time in the country, or that they constituted the greater portion of the two armies at Bannockburn. Centuries before this period Britain was known to be inhabited by swarthy Moors,—whether these were found among the Cornish Damnonii and their Scottish kindred of the Forth marshes, or elsewhere in the British islands;—and coeval with them were the fair-haired Keltoi, and men of the stamp of the white-skinned "Barbarian Prisoner." These, again, had been reinforced from time to time by inroads of black heathen and white heathen —more or less akin to either party—and the mingled nations had fought and intermarried, had formed leagues of amity, and broken them, during all the fourteen hundred years that stretched from Cæsar's landing to the achievement of Scottish* independence. And consequently our predecessors of the fourteenth century must have belonged to many varying types, whose differences were at that time sharply defined. Sharply defined in those of unmixed blood, and blended in every

---

* It is difficult to avoid confusion in the use of this and other race-names, which eventually were used to denote the most heterogeneous peoples.

possible permutation in the hybrid population that must have inevitably arisen. So that, at the battle of Bannockburn, the combatants on either side must have belonged to many races, whether they fought in the ranks of the so-called English army or of the so-called Scottish. That in the latter army there were many pure "Scots" cannot be doubted, the most distinguished of these being the swarthy Douglas knight. But historical records tell that their leaders belonged to other races, and these races must have been largely represented in the ranks also. Professor Skeat draws attention to the fact that Dutch, or Flemish mercenary soldiers helped to fight the battles of the Normans, and that these Flemings settled in great numbers in various parts of England; while a glance at certain "Scottish" pedigrees reveals that in North Britain also the Flemish invaders appear as the allies of the Normans, with whom they shared the fruits of conquest—land and power. In Mr. Skene's sketches of Galloway during the century prior to Bannockburn he indicates a similar movement there. The Scots of Galloway, like the Moors of Morayshire, are seen rising up in rebellion against Norman barons, the vassals of a partly Norman king; and, whether in the north or in the south, the rebellion is crushed, and great numbers of the rebels slain. The country now called Scotland had not yet attained a national existence, but, in its most important parts, a new power was making itself felt. And the Normans and the Dutch were among the chief ingredients of this power.

The Battle of Bannockburn, then, was not won by Scots Proper alone, but by a greatly mixed multitude, of which they formed a part. Many of the leaders were, no doubt, Scots,—although the more distinguished were chiefly non-Scottish: and none among them, of whatever race, excelled that famous Scot, "the Black Douglas." It would be difficult to find a better example of the Scot Proper, and accordingly it is worth while to look at him and his lineage a little more closely.

He belonged to the oldest sept of his clan, that known as the Black Douglases, a term which proves to be tautological when analyzed, since *Dubh-glas* signifies "the black swarthy" man. Their origin is shadowy, but one tradition states that the first of the family distinguished himself by his bravery, in a battle against Donald the White, a Norseman of the eighth century. From this half-mythical figure down to "the good Sir James" who fought at Bannockburn there is a fall of nearly six hundred years. Time enough for any amount of changes in the race. Indeed, there is a hint that such took place, and a suggested alliance with the Flemish Freskin of Moray, during the twelfth century. However this may be, it is evident that Sir James Douglas inherited the blood of his swarthy ancestors, whether he was a lineal descendant of the eighth century Dubh-Glas or not. Quite likely he was not, but only a scion of the same tree. Barbour has enough to say of him, from the days of his youthful "thowlesnes" in Paris, down to his gallant death in Spain. But it is only with Barbour's description of his complexion that we have to do here. And this, he says, was "sumdeill grey," his hair being "blak." As already stated, Godscroft remarks that "he is said to have been of a black and swart complexion," an expression somewhat stronger than that used by Barbour. This dusky skin earned for him, say the historians, the title of *The Black Douglas;* and although "the good Sir James" to his friends, he was such a terror to his foes that their most troublesome children could at once be hushed into good behaviour by a single threat of a visitation from that dreaded bugbear, *The Black Douglas.*

So say the run of historical writers. But—without throwing any doubt upon the complexion of "the good Sir James"—it may be well questioned whether this title was his peculiar property. There is, indeed, every reason to believe that it served no more to distinguish him from other Black Douglases than "the black man" would separate one out of a whole tribe of black men. We see this by looking at the chiefs of his clan, without even taking their followers into consideration. For not only was "the good Sir James" known as *The Black Douglas,* but so also was his grandson, a son of Archibald *The Grim.* So, apparently, was the eighth earl of this line, who was killed at Stirling in the year 1452, by King James the Second. More than this, it seems very probable that Archibald *The Grim,* who has just been referred to, was really so called because he was Archibald *The Black*. This is actually stated by one writer,* who says that "on account of his swarthy complexion [he] was commonly called 'the grim :'" which statement brings to light an obsolete meaning of this adjective, a meaning which must only recently have passed out of use.† Accordingly, we have three successive chiefs of this clan, and another in the following century, all styled *The Black Douglas*,—or what is equal to that,—on account of their swarthy complexion.

There is thus no room for doubting that the chiefs of the Black Douglas tribe were styled *The Black Douglas* because of their dusky skins,—and not from any accidental circumstance, such as that which (it is said) gave rise to the epithet attached to the young hero of Crécy. Wherever you encounter *The Black Douglas* in history or tradition you find that he is a black man. The following example is one out of many, and whether the romance in which it occurs be wholly fictitious, or almost wholly true, the expressions used denote the prevalent inherited opinion regarding the complexion of *The Black Douglas* :—

"By your father's crown," cried Ramorgny, "I see nothing for it but to obey. The difficulty lies in the selection, : for, if I am able to appreciate the beauty of women, thou wilt have to choose between a crow and a rook. Elizabeth of Dunbar is the descendant of Black Agnes, who defended that old castle, in the days of the Second David, against the arms of the Duke of Salisbury; and Elizabeth of Douglas cannot fail to have in her some portion of the blood of the black Earl, who fell in Spain, trusting to the protecting charm of Robert's heart, which he carried with him in a casket. So thou seest the black choice thou hast got ; . . ."‡

It is plain, then, that several (at least) of the chiefs of the

---

* The editor of "a very ancient Gallovidian ballad," "The Battle of Craignilder." This statement is made by the editor (Capt. Denniston) in one of his appended *Notes*, and he seems to make it on the authority of Fordun.

† In touching upon the etymology of the *Grampian Hills*, in his edition of Toland's "History of the Druids" (p. 362), Huddleston talks of "our vulgar phrase, *grim-puss* (a black cat)"—which again makes *grim* = *black*. The root from which *grim*, and its cognate *grime* (our nearest approach to *black*), have sprung seems to be claimed by the Danish, Saxon, and Gaelic tongues, taking the shapes of *grim, gram, grüm, grame, gruaim, gruamach*, &c.

‡ "The Prince of Scotland; or, The Rivalship of March and Douglas": Wilson's "Tales of the Borders."

Black-Douglas clan were themselves black skinned men. They could not well have continued to be so for very long after the period at which they begin to appear in history as veritable flesh and blood; as distinguished from the fictitious creations of mediæval genealogists. Because their first authentic appearances coincide with the time when the barrier between black and white had been broken down in many places, and the two opposite types had greatly intermingled. This movement is seen in their own history, which tells of intercourse, political and matrimonial, between them and such white races as the Normans and the Flemings. Eventually, this tendency resulted in the disappearance of the pure *Black-Douglases* from place and power; the last of them being James, the ninth earl, whose tribal sceptre was thenceforth swayed by the chiefs of the half-blood offshoot known as the *Red Douglases*.

This last chief of the black division of the Douglases, the main stem of the Douglas tree, was James, ninth earl. He had succeeded his elder brother in 1452, and his first act, after assuming the chiefship, was to take up arms against his king, James the Second, in order to avenge the deaths of his brother and the sixth earl, both slain by the king or his partizans. Or, rather, his direct aim was to settle, once for all, whether Scotland should be ruled by Norman Stewarts, or by "Moorish" Douglases, a question which this proud and powerful caste had practically been putting for several generations. The struggle ended in his utter discomfiture, and the complete downfall of his race; their estates passing wholly away from them, and being, soon after, bestowed upon their distant kindred, the Red, or Angus, Douglases, who had assisted in bringing about the ruin of the ancient stock. "The Red Douglas had put down the Black."

The eighth lord of this terrible family is thus oddly sketched by Mactaggart, in his Galloway book: "BLACK DOUGLAS."— Perhaps the greatest villain ever known in Galloway. His den was the Castle of Thrave, a befitting keep for the tyger; he keep'd the country round him in awe for many a day; even the Scotch kings could make nothing of him. He caused Lord Kirkcubrie, McLellan, to be hanged by a rope from a projecting stone in his castle wall, yet to be seen, and took his dinner calmly, while his hangmen were doing so. Some say he was '*durked*' in Annandale, but how he came by his death is uncertain; however, he did not die a natural death." From whatever source Mactaggart obtained these statements they are not in accordance with those made in history, and are evidently only half-truths. For this is the earl who was stabbed by King James at Stirling, in 1452, and the Maclellan whom he hanged from his castle wall was no " Lord Kirkcudbright" (the title being a subsequent creation of Charles I.), but the tutor, or guardian, of the young Laird of Bombie, of whom we have heard, and who was ancestor of the Lords Kirkcudbright. The story of Douglas's treachery towards Maclellan, and his own subsequent death, as related in the "Tales of a Grandfather," thus reconciles the local tradition with recorded history, though in a partial degree only.

Two years after the death of this cruel earl, his brother, the last lord, was confronting the army of King James in the open field. The king's army had laid siege to one of the Douglas castles, that of Abercorn, and Douglas himself had marched an army of forty thousand men to raise the siege; when, suddenly, he found himself one morning deserted by all his vassal lords and their forces, who, by dissension and jealousy, or by the diplomacy of the royal party, had gone over in a body to the king. He then appears to have fled southward into Annandale, where he lurked until the following spring, 1455. In the meantime, his brothers, the Earls of Murray and of Ormond, had headed the other sections of the Black Douglas confederacy, and offered a determined resistance to the king; but their army was completely crushed in the May of 1455, themselves slain, the Douglas castles besieged and reduced, and, finally, the Douglas estates forfeited, and the main body of the race overthrown for ever. *The Black Douglas* himself escaped into England, out of which he made one or two raids into his old domains; but he never achieved anything, and, finally, died a prisoner in the Abbey of Lindores, in the year 1488. Thus, the legendary version of the Galloway peasants is incorrect in many particulars, though preserving faithfully the feelings with which this haughty despot was regarded by a certain section of his subjects.

At the time when the Black Douglas was hiding in the recesses of Annandale the royal forces were everywhere attacking the Douglas strongholds, and altogether stamping out the Douglas power. King James, in person, is said to have headed that division of his army that besieged Threave Castle, the "den" referred to by Mactaggart, and the scene of the base murder of Maclellan, three years previously. There is a local tradition to the effect that, when the king arrived in the neighbourhood, he was presented by the Maclellans with a heavy piece of ordnance (sometimes confounded with the "Mons Meg" at Edinburgh Castle), with which to batter down the walls of the Douglas castle, the home of their hereditary foe*. And it is evident that, at this particular juncture, the hatred which the Black Douglas had inspired in the Maclellans must have been deep. Only three years before, his brother had treacherously killed the temporary head of their family, the young laird's guardian, and

---

* Mactaggart, in his odd way, thus describes this celebrated stronghold :—

"CASTLE O' THRAVE.—The strongest castle in Galloway, and the most famous. It is a large square building, with horn-works, on an island in the river Dee. . . . . It was anciently an infernal place, and many were the foul deeds there done ; . . . . It was the seat of the *Black Douglas*, one of the most horrible devils that ever appeared in Scotland ; he made his very king tremble for him, and hanged McClellan, Lord Kirkcubrie, against his order."

The following verses will serve to show how this Black Castle and the "Black Oppressor," who owned it, were regarded by a portion of the Galloway people. The lines are probably Mactaggart's own, but they reflect a certain inherited feeling :—

> On a bonny green isle in the water o' Dee,
> As it rows frae the ken to the Solway sea,
> Stands the tower of the baron, the fell bluidy knave,
> And the name o' his keep is the Castle o' Thrave.

> He has strung Lord Kirkcubrie ower his castle wa',
> The worthy McClellan o' wild Gallowa ;
> The dumb sough o' vengeance we hear frae his grave,
> And it shall be answered at Castle o' Thrave.

> Mons Meg we'll drag out, and we'll thunder him down,
> We'll skelp him to hell, where his frien's will him crown,
> We'll show him what's honour, and how we'll behave,
> By dashing destruction on Castle o' Thrave.

> Let him rally his rebels through a' Gallowa,
> We care for them not, we shall conquer for a' ;
> We'll rush on our faes like the far-fetched wave,
> And sweep to damnation the Castle o' Thrave.

this for no other reason than that he had refused to join the Black Douglas confederacy in the attempt against the Stewart power. In return for this foul action the Maclellans had invaded the Douglas territory with fire and sword; but, for the time being, with evil results to themselves. For it is stated, in their history, that, as a punishment for so doing, their office of Sheriff of Galloway, so long held by them, and also their family estate of Bombie, became forfeited to the crown. Now, this is a curious statement: for being over-zealous vassals of the crown, the crown deprived them of their rights! And it is equally remarkable that King James had been roused into indignation by this very act of the eighth Lord Douglas, indicating, as it did, the extent of the league that had been formed against his sovereignty, and also an insolent indifference to the king's opinion. Stung by this culminating action into making a decisive movement, he had (by means of craft and unworthy dealing) inveigled the eighth Douglas to Stirling Castle, where he killed him with his own hand. This happened immediately after the murder of Maclellan. Now, it is very unlikely that at such a crisis the king would deprive a loyal family of their possessions, and that for an excusable act of revenge against a rebel; nor is it likely that he would do so to conciliate the new Lord Douglas, the brother of the traitor, for this other Douglas was as fierce a rebel as his brother, and his very first act, it is stated, was to take up arms against the king. The likeliest solution of the question is, that the Bombie estate and the Sheriffship of Galloway had been wrested from the Maclellans *by the Douglases*, immediately after the murder of Maclellan and the ensuing raid made by that clan into the Douglas country. The "crown" to which these honours were forfeited was not the nominal one, that of the Norman Stewarts, but the real one (real so far as Galloway was concerned), that of the Scottish Douglases, then on the eve of revolt.

Of whatever stock the Maclellans were—and, in speaking of the Ross-shire Macrae-Maclellan mixture, it was suggested that they were no other than the Norman Fitzgeralds—they had been faithful adherents of the Stewarts. So that, when King James had destroyed the Castle of Threave (in doing which he was assisted by the Maclellan artillery), and after he had overthrown the Black Douglas league, it would have been only a natural consequence of these events had he restored the Bombie lands to their rightful owners. He did do so; but the exact date seems unobtainable. It must have been prior to 1460, the year of his death, and it cannot have been before May, 1455, the date of the great Douglas defeat. The most natural time and place for this act of restitution would be when he was personally present in the neighbourhood of Bombie, elated with his complete success in the recent struggle for the throne, in which he had all along been aided by the loyal Maclellans.

But the family tradition does not say that this was the case. It tells us that the estates were recovered at this very time, 1455–60; but it states that they were given as a reward for the death of a Moorish or Gipsy chief, who had been terrorising the Galloway district, and for whose person, dead or alive, the king offered, as a reward, the barony of Bombie. This the young chief of the Maclellans himself succeeded in obtaining, slaying the gipsy, and bringing his head to the king on the point of his sword; in commemoration of which incident he thereafter bore, as his crest, a Moor's head on the point of a dagger, with the motto, "*Think on.*"

So, then, Galloway was devastated, in the year 1455, by *two* separate black-skinned races? The one, the historical race of the Black Douglases; the other, a traditionary company of Moors, Saracens, or Gipsies. Both were the enemies of King James the Second; both were enemies of the Maclellans. So important were the robbers in the eyes of the king, that he issued a royal proclamation, and held out a spacious barony as a reward for their destruction. The hero who slew the robber chief was the dispossessed heir of Bombie, and, in killing him, he regained the lands of his forefathers. He had not received any token, whatever, of kingly gratitude for the unswerving loyalty of his race during the perilous days of the Douglas ascendancy. He was not rewarded in any way for the aid which he and his clan had rendered the king in this final assault upon the fastness of the arch-rebel. For the slaying of a wretched bandit, he had been restored to all the honours that were his birthrigh

In return for the loyalty that had cost him these honours, he received—nothing.

Is this credible? Were there *two* different races of Moors existing in Galloway at this time, both so hateful to the Stewart king, but only one of them recorded in history? Or, are these not two different versions of the same story? It is hardly reasonable to believe otherwise. Young Maclellan's motto of "Think on" means nothing, if it does not bear reference to the cowardly slaughter of his guardian three years before, with the consequent ruin brought upon his family, and a fixed resolve on his part that "wrong should be right" one day. Even had such a hypothetical rival confederacy of Moors attempted to ravage Galloway on their own account, the absolute power of the Black Douglas would have crushed them at once. Or, on the other hand, if they *could* have existed in spite of the Douglases, would they have been foes of the Stewarts as well as of the Douglases, at a time when the whole district belonged to one side or the other? But the notion is untenable. The Douglases *themselves* were a gang of black, marauding Moors, or Gipsies; certainly on an extensive scale. So extensive, indeed, that the injured king might well put a heavy price upon the head of their leader dead or alive.

Who this leader was is not quite certain. He could not have been the nominal head of the clan, for he was not one of the actors in the closing scene; having then, or soon after, made his escape into England. Besides, his end was, after all, a peaceful one, and he did not die until thirty-four years after Maclellan's sword had severed the "gipsy's" head in Galloway. And in this there is a certain fitness. Because, although the titular head of the Black Douglas sept, this last earl had inherited some share of the white Norman blood; and, consequently, a *Moor's*-head crest would not have been a wholly appropriate emblem had his been the head that Maclellan brought to the King.*

The leaders of the Black Douglases when finally brought to bay were the chief's brothers—the Earls of Moray and of

---

* Possibly, however, a fifteenth-century herald would have held that the conventional "Moor's-head" was the proper bearing, even although the "Moor" in question was not strictly one in complexion.

Ormond. Thus, the Gipsy, or Moor, of the Maclellan story was, in all probability, one of these. It may be that he was the Earl of Moray, who was killed at the crushing defeat of Arkinholme, or Langholm—"'durked' in Annandale," as the local tradition has it.* But it is much more likely that he was the third brother, Hugh, Earl of Ormond, who is not said to have been slain on the field of battle, as was Moray, but to have been "taken prisoner *and afterwards beheaded.*"

The fact that the aristocracy of this race were great nobles, possessed of lands and dignities in France as well as in their own country, the leading figures in Scotland for several generations, and almost the occupants of its throne—this fact in no way affects the ethnological deduction just arrived at. The eye of the peasant sees only the most apparent characteristics of the local over-lord: the peasant understanding knows nothing of his historical attitude. This may be seen in a thousand instances. Therefore, to a certain section of the peasantry of Galloway (presumably those of Norman, Flemish, and Celtic blood), *The Black Douglas* was simply a swarthy tyrant, like the "Black Oppressor" of Welsh tradition, or that other "black knight" recorded by Halliwell, whose sway extended over various districts of Lancashire, where he "held the people in vassalage, and used them with great severity." And, in the diction of the past, a black man was a "Moor," so that when *The Black Douglas* and his brothers, with others of their tribe, had retreated to the wilds of Annandale after the defection of their allies, in the year 1455, they were virtually a band of marauding Gipsies, or Moors, as the legend of the Maclellans testifies. They had been utterly discomfited—their power and position in the country was gone for ever, another had taken their "bishopric"—from that time forward they were outlaws and rebels, cut up into separate bands, and lurking in mountain fastnesses and the intricacies of the Border "Mosses"; as a political power in the country, or as nobles under a semi-Norman monarchy, their days had come to an end. And *precisely* at this point of time, when the last vestige of Pictish, or Moorish, power had crumbled away, and the

---

* Langholm (formerly Arkinholme) is not, however, in Annandale, but in the neighbouring valley of Eskdale.

latest representatives of Moorish nobility had sunk into the position of hunted bandits and outlaws, the *Gipsies* of Galloway make their appearance. From that date onward, a "Black Douglas" was an equivalent for "a Gipsy."*

This is seen in another way. Claudian's lines have revealed to us that the historical *Picti* of Britain were, ethnologically, *Mauri:* being *Picti* only by custom. Therefore the Picts of Galloway were the Moors of Galloway. Now, in detailing the chief ingredients of the army of King David of Scotland, at the Battle of the Standard (1138 A.D.), Mr. Skene makes this statement:† "The first body of his army was composed of the 'Galwenses' or people of Galloway, who still bore the name of Picts, and who claimed to lead the van as their right." Four or five centuries after this, in 1593, at the Battle of Glenlivet, the Earl of Angus—head of the *ruadh*, or tawny Douglases, that younger and half-blood branch to whom, in 1455, had come all the hereditary Douglas honours—"*claimed the leading of the vanguard, ... alleging that this honour, of right, belonged to him, being the ancient privilege of the Douglases.*"‡ Whether, therefore, we view them as twelfth-century Moors of Galloway, or as sixteenth-century representatives of the *dubh-glasses*, or black men of Galloway, we see distinctly the same stock. As historical Moors they are Picts, or painted men. As historical Douglases, they prove the correctness of their family name by claiming the right of the historical Moors of Galloway, as their own "ancient privilege:" therefore, either as Moors or as *dubh-glasses* (synonymous terms), they are Picts, or painted men. As traditional Moors, they are Gipsies: and thus, on the showing of Grose the antiquary, and by the ruddled skins of Gipsy Marshall and his gang, the traditional Moors of Galloway are painted men. Moors, Picts, Gipsies, Faws—all were *dubh-glasses* of Galloway.

The Black Douglases were taken as examples of the Scot Proper, or Early Scot: but this, we have seen, is equivalent

---

* Annandale, into whose wild glens and fastnesses the vanquished Black Douglases of the fifteenth century were driven, is a distinctly "gipsy" district; and "the thieves of Annandale" were proverbial.

† "Celtic Scotland," Vol. I. p. 467.

‡ Anderson's "Scottish Nation," Vol. II. p. 419.

to Moor, or Early Pict. "The black herds of Scots and Picts" were all alike to British Gildas. The Picts of ancient Argyle were *Scoti Picti*, Painted Scots: "shameless Irish robbers." *Scot* was, to certain races, a synonym for "vagabond:" the Scots and Picts were simply "black herds of *vagabonds* and *painted men*," in the sight of the civilized Britons. The characteristics of the "Wild Scots of Galloway" are identical with those of the Picts, or Moors of Galloway. And the worst side* of these characteristics is exemplified in the hated chief of those *dubh-glasses*, whose abode on the island of the river Dee, in Galloway; is spoken of as "an infernal place," where "many foul deeds were done," and the owner of it characterized as "one of the most horrible devils that ever appeared in Scotland." It is immaterial, therefore, whether we call those older Douglases (not the mixed *ruadh*, or tawny section) by the style of Scots, or Picts. They were substantially the same.

Thus, as Moors, or Scots, or Picts, the purest specimens of the *dubh-glasses* of Galloway were *gipsies* and *faws*. And a *Douglas*, or, latterly, a *Black Douglas*, was a generic term.

This fact explains the confusion that has arisen concerning "the Black Douglas." Mactaggart, of the *Gallovidian Encyclopedia*, is dreadfully "mixed" with regard to the chiefs of this name, for he evidently supposes that only one of them was so designated. He errs in good company, as Sir Walter Scott seems also to regard "the good Sir James" as *The* Black Douglas, whereas we know that no fewer than four of the Douglas earls bore that title, while their very clan-name, strictly considered, signifies "the black man." That "a Black Douglas" must at one time have been a term interchangeable with "a black man" or "a gipsy," is indicated also by the rhyme which Scott places in the mouth of the soldier's wife at Roxburgh castle—

> "Hush ye, hush ye, little pet ye,
> Hush ye, hush ye, do not fret ye,
> The Black Douglas shall not get ye."

* Of the best side, the gentle and refined side, "the good Sir James" is a splendid example. Between him and the treacherous savage that murdered young Maclellan's guardian there is the wide gulf that separates civilization from barbarism.

This very rhyme is said by Simson to be sung by mothers to their fretful children, at the present day, with this significant variation, that the last line runs—

"The black *Tinkler* winna get ye."

Therefore, for this reason also, a "Black Douglas" was only a synonym for a "Moor." And when one or other of the chiefs of this race was styled "*The* Black Douglas," the article so prefixed was employed exactly as it is yet done in Ireland and in Scotland, to distinguish the head of the clan from the rest of his clansmen, all of whom bear the same tribal name.

It has been hinted that the movement which ended in the final overthrow of the Black Douglases was a last effort of the "Moorish" races to recover their lost sovereignty; and there does seem some reason for believing that race-hatred entered largely into the motives by which the participators in the struggle were actuated. Be this as it may, there is no doubt that the first celebrated Black Douglas was on the side of the Norman Bruce. But at that time—a century and a half before the Black Douglas collapse—all difference of race was sunk by every one who really wished to further the new-born desire for a united national life in Scotland, and the high-minded knight portrayed by Barbour would be the last to trade upon racial spite. After this independence had been actually gained, and the fever of patriotism had cooled, and when the noblest of their leaders had long been dead, it is conceivable that the attitude of the Black Douglases may have considerably altered. Or, indeed, had "the good Sir James" been framed of baser materials, like his unworthy descendants, he might have placed himself at the head of the anti-Norman party in Scotland, a large portion of which consisted of the Picts of Galloway, who were, of course, Black Douglases. "Many of the people of Galloway were unfriendly to Bruce. They lived under the government of one McDougal, related to the Lord of Lorn, who . . . . had defeated Robert Bruce at Dalry, and very nearly killed or made him prisoner. These Galloway men had heard that Bruce was in their country, with no more than sixty men with him; so they resolved to attack him by surprise, and for this purpose they got two hundred men together, and brought with them two or three bloodhounds." Now, these Galloway men were, as stated, Picts—for the Picts of Galloway were popularly known as Galloway men, or Galwegians.* As Galwegians, or Picts, they had led the van of King David's army at the Battle of the Standard, nearly two centuries prior to Bruce's day. Therefore, it is not to be wondered at that their leader was styled McDougal, since that name signifies "the son of the black stranger." And if divisions of them were at that time, or subsequently, styled Douglases or Mac-Dougals, the names were the natural outcome of their descent from "the black strangers." Whether, as Mr. Skene appears to indicate, they were the posterity of Early Picts, or whether, as Scott hints, they were related to the McDougals of Lorn, they were literally *Douglases*. As Picts, as Scots, or as Black Danes, they were—in the eyes of men of the race of Gildas—"black foreigners," or *dubh galls*, the offspring of what originally were "transmarine nations." The chances are, that such colour-names were used in a very shifty fashion, even at so recent a period as the days of Bruce, and many of those Galwegians would be indifferently called Douglases, MacDougals, or one or other of a hundred various names that set off some peculiarity of complexion, or of figure; or that denoted the occupation of the individual.

Those Galloway men that tried to surprise Bruce, then, were Picts, whether they were the spray of the waves named Pictish, or Scottish, or Danish. And, of course, they were "Moors." The splendidly graphic description of this scene, given to us by Barbour, reveals them to us as horsemen and archers; and it shews that they, if not naked, were devoid of armour. Because, when Bruce hastily decided, with even more than his usual hardihood, to defend, single-handed, the narrow gully in the steep bank that rose up from the ford, he encouraged himself with the reflection that he need not fear their arrows "since he was furnished with armour." And, if this does little more than insinuate that his enemies were *not* mail-clad men, that assumption is proved to be fact

---

* "Celtic Scotland," Vol. I. p. 467, note.

by the subsequent passage, which tells how easily they were slain by the thrusts of the king's spear. Again, if they were like their fellow Picts, who fought Severus in the marshes of Stirlingshire, they were naked men, save for the usual loin-cloth. Or, if they resembled their kindred in Ireland, of the previous century, the wild, "glibbed," Black Irishmen, described by Froissart,* their only garment, the plaid or mantle, was at that moment wrapped round the left arm, and they rode their horses without saddle or stirrup. Or (which is likelier still), if their manners resembled those of their own forefathers, a hundred years before the days of Bruce, they were devoid of any clothing whatever.† As already remarked, those savage warriors were more akin to Cheyennes or Comanches than to any variety of modern European, *except the gipsy;* and this encounter with the Christianized Norman hero was an early scene in a drama that has been enacting ever since. Like their contemporary kinsmen in Ireland, or like the so-called Indians on the other side of the Atlantic, those races may be regarded as the drift of an older civilization than the Christian, and, therefore, "savages" or not, according to individual notions of "civilization." But the picture of Robert Bruce defending the narrow pass above the ford has been copied over and over again, with very little variation, all over the globe. And never was the battle fought against greater odds; and the conqueror never achieved a more brilliant victory. On the one hand, the throng of mounted warriors, trampling through the shallow water with wild war cries; the moonlight gleaming on their dusky skins and ruddled faces; and in front of them, bestriding the narrow pathway in the bank, the solitary impregnable figure of the king.

The Black-Douglases of history were thus the ancestors of certain families of modern gipsies; the name of Douglas

---

* Appendix to "Rokeby," note 3 C.—formerly quoted.

† "Ralph de Diceto thus describes the Galloway men who served in the army of William the Lion, King of Scotland. They were fleet, naked, remarkably bold, wearing on their left sides small knives, formidable to any armed men, very expert in throwing and aiming their javelins at great distances, setting up for a signal when they go to battle a long lance." ("Historical and Traditional Tales connected with the South of Scotland," John Nicholson, Kirkcudbright, 1843; page 39.)

being, in one of its phases, an equivalent of *Tinkler*.* Their language would naturally vary to some extent, as it was influenced by circumstances; such as their blending with other races, the influence of other forms of speech introduced into the country, and the inevitable attrition of time. Their nobles, during the days of Black Douglas ascendancy, would assuredly speak the language of chivalry and of courts. "The good Sir James," while listening to the romances with which the king beguiled the time, during their enforced idleness among the hills,—the tales of Oliver, of "worthy Ferambrace," and of the Twelve Peers of France,—or, while conversing with the ladies of Bruce's refugee court in the Aberdeenshire Highlands, no doubt would speak in Norman French, or, in the language of his biographer, Barbour, "the Inglis toung." A result of his high birth, and his wide experience, must have been to make him familiar with both of these languages; to both of which his mingled ancestry may have given him an inherited claim. But, in speaking to the mass of his followers, the *gillies* of the Black Douglas clan, he must have employed another language; what that was may be more easily surmised than ascertained, since it is confessed by scholars that the so-called *gipsy* tongues have not hitherto received the particular attention they merit. But we shall not go very wide of the mark if we suppose that the common speech of the fourteenth century Pict, or Black Douglas, of Galloway, known locally as the "Wild Scot o' Gallowa'", was something very like the *Shelta Thari*, just discovered by Mr. Leland to be at once "the language of the Tinkers" and a dialect of the Celtic tongue.†

---

* It is noteworthy, in this connection, that the *Tinklers* are referred to "in a charter of William the Lion (1165-1214)." ("Encyc. Brit." 9th edit. art. "Gipsies.")

† Since a great number of gipsy words are incorporated in the conglomerate speech which we call Slang, and which a former generation termed *cant* or *thieves' Latin*, there must, consequently, be many slang words which are really Celtic. To adduce an instance of this, Mr. J. F. Campbell points out that the slang verb, *to twig* (comprehend), is nothing else than the Gaelic *tuig*. Other examples may be seen in *Dad* or *Daddy* (father), which is in Welsh *Tad*, and in certain parts of Ireland *Dada*; and such words as *Libbege* a bed, *Buss* a kiss, *Dag* a gun, *Gob* a lump, and *Baubee* a halfpenny—all of which are given in lists of "cant" terms, but which are easily identified with the Gaelic *Leaba*, *Busach*, and *Dag* (a pistol), with the Welsh *Gob*, and with the so-called Scotch *Baubee*. It is

Thus the tribe to which the name of Douglas, or Black Douglas, eventually adhered, identifies the Early Scots and Early Picts with one particular division of the Modern Gipsies, namely, those inhabiting Galloway and other districts in the south of Scotland. In a less marked degree, these races are identified with the "dark whites," or *Melanochroi*, of the same districts. Lochmaben, which is said to be "stocked" with people of "gipsy" descent, is situated in a district peculiarly associated with the Douglases. And the other places in the same neighbourhood, particularized by Mr. Simson, have, no doubt, received much of their semi-gipsy population from the Black-Douglas source.

But it must be remembered that this name originally meant nothing more than "the black man," and that it only clung to one special tribe, by the same accidental process that has made such names as Black, Duff, Dow, Brown, Donn, Dunn, and others, become the distinguishing surname of other families. To attempt to trace the history of those various names, with a view to cite them as companion examples to that of Douglas, would be exceedingly tedious and unnecessary; but it may be allowable to consider one or two others that naturally present themselves before us.

In noticing those Douglas lords that were unmistakably styled *Black* because of their complexion, it was observed that one of them, a son of "the good Sir James," was surnamed "*the Grim*." And, since both his father and his son bore the special epithet, *the Black*, attached to their ordinary names; and, also, because this adjective, *grim*, did, until very lately, signify *black*, as well as *ugly* or *stern*, there is every reason for believing that, in the case of this earl, his contemporaries had merely selected an alternative adjective, denoting the same quality as that which characterized his father and his son. Whether this nickname ever became the actual surname of others of his children (unknown to history), does not appear, although this is quite probable. At any rate, it did become a very well known clan name in various parts of

probable that this last word, like many other similar "cant" terms, denotes a real coin—perhaps the *Gally halfpenny* (? Galls' or Foreigners' halfpenny) that is stated in Halliwell's "Dictionary" to have been "an inferior foreign coin" prohibited by Henry VIII.

the country, and quite independently, so far as one may judge, of this "grim" earl.

It is difficult to learn what the earliest form of the word was. Dr. Armstrong gives an obsolete Gaelic *grim*, meaning *war*, and also *gruama*, "*moro*se, dark, gloomy;" while Professor Skeat includes *gram*, "wrathful," and *grim*, "ugly, grim," along with the kindred *grim* or *grüm* (lampblack, grime), among Danish roots. The antiquary, Pinkerton, derives the name of the Grampian Hills "from the Danish *gram*, a warrior." All of these meanings could, no doubt, be reconciled. If the name was originally the property of the Danes, or other *dubh galls*, to whom it signified *war*, and *warrior*, it is easy to see how the same word would mean, to their opponents (once they became acquainted with it), *ugly, wrathful,* and *black;* the chief features of those "black strangers," wherever we get a sight of them (from the opposite side) in history or tradition. And that its signification of "black" survived until a generation ago, was shewn by two quotations on a previous page. The chief associations of the word, then, were blackness, ugliness, and surliness; and its history in this country seems clearly to prove its connection with one division or another of the "black foreigners." The wall that Antoninus built, between the firths of Forth and Clyde, to keep back the Scoto-Pictish Moors, is popularly known as the *Grimes'* Dyke. In the counties of Hampshire, Wilts, and Berks, a similar wall, with a somewhat similar history, is locally called the *Grims'*-dyke. A *Carr*-dyke in Norfolk, and, at least, two other *Black* Dykes in Scotland, have apparently all received their names for similar reasons, Grim, Carr (Celt. *ciar, car* or *ker*), and Black, all denoting the complexion of the people against whom (or, possibly, *by* whom) they were erected. *Grimsby, Grimsthorpe, Grimsbury,* in England, and *Græmsey,* in the Orkneys, are some examples of bays, thorpes, boroughs, and islands, once noted as the resort of such *Græmes*. At the eastern end of the Scottish Grimes' Dyke, or Grahams' Dyke (for the word is thus variously spelt), and on the northern, or Pictish, side of the wall, there is a *Grahams'* Town. It is situated in a district which has been very closely associated with the Moors from the earliest times. This neighbourhood, now dry land, was the *habitat* of the Pictish marsh-dwellers, against whom Severus fought: those swarthy, almost naked savages, who fought, like modern Zulus, with spears and long narrow shields, who (like modern Esquimaux, or North Siberians,) shot their light skin canoes through the intricate channels of this "Scythian Vale," and swarmed, in a "black herd," across the wall. Here it was that the great Pictish king, *Tattooed Donald*, fell in battle in the year 642. Beside this *græmes'* town once stood the temple that was known to another people as the Faw Kirk, or *Eaglais bhreac*,* the church of the "speckled" people: and even at this remote day, some of their vagabond descendants still range the district, one clan of them still bearing the appellative name of *Græme;* while two of the most distinctive "gypsy" industries, *mugging* and *tinkering*, have developed (possibly in other hands) into the celebrated pottery and iron works of Dunmore and Carron, situated in the neighbourhood of this *Græmes' Town*.

Those *græmes*, being *moors, blacks, browns, carrs, dows* or *duffs, dubh-glasses, dubh-galls*, and *faws*, may readily have branched out into numerous families bearing those names; which, though at first appellative, would gradually become fossilized into ordinary surnames, devoid of any literal meaning. This, no doubt, has happened. But we are considering them at a date prior to the era when their names had reached the "fossil" stage; at a date when a *græme* was so known *because* he was a grim or black man—a moor. Speaking of these græmes of the Forth marshes, Dr. Jamieson says (in a note to his edition of Blind Harry's *Wallace*): "A fabulous antiquity has been ascribed to this family; it having been asserted that the wall of Antonine vulgarly received the name of *Graham's Dike*, because in a very early period of our history it was penetrated by a valorous chief, from whom those of this celebrated name had their origin." It is scarcely correct, perhaps, to say that Dr. Jamieson is speaking of the marsh-dwelling *græmes*. At the period to which he refers —the thirteenth century—the marshes of Stirlingshire were

---

* In the Latin records this is translated *Varia Capella*. Obviously this rendering has been first made by some one ignorant of the real meaning of its alternative names—*Eaglais Bhreac*, and *Faw* or *Fall-Kirk*.

becoming dry land, and the *mæatæ*, or marsh-dwellers were under the rule of an alien race. And it is of that later race that Jamieson is thinking, when he speaks of "this family." Its founder appears to have been one of the Anglo-Norman followers of David I. of Scotland, during the twelfth century, and his title of "*de* Græme," probably signified nothing more than that (like the first "*de* Moravia") he ruled over a territory of *græmes*, or *moors*. One of the descendants of this William *de* Græme, was the celebrated Sir John, the Græme, the devoted companion of Wallace: and his complexion is denoted by Henry the Minstrel's reference to his "pale face," as he lay dead. However, it is likely enough that this ruling caste may have afterwards intermarried with the subject race; as the Norman MacLellans are reported to have done with the subject MacRahs of the north. At first they appear to have allied themselves with fellow-Normans; but it is probable that rulers and ruled would become, to some extent, mingled. So that the traditional connection between their clan-name and the *græmes'-dyke, blacks'-dyke, moors'-dyke,* or *picts'-dyke*, would be correct enough; so far as one division of their ancestry was concerned.

Mr. Simson has a good deal to say of the "gypsies" of Stirlingshire, and that neighbourhood; and of their fierce marauding habits. And the present writer has been informed by a man who lived in the town of Stirling during the early years of this century, that, not only did they indulge in savage fights at the weekly markets held in that town, but that, on one occasion, they took forcible possession of several outlying farm-houses; from which they were eventually ousted by the town guard of Stirling (then a somewhat important entity). Their haunts, at that period, were the mosses and moors of the Menteith district; of Sheriffmuir; of the Ochils; and of the Lomonds.

It would appear from Scott that the *græmes* of the Debatable Land were the descendants of those of the Forth district. "Their chief (he says) claimed his descent from Malice, Earl of Stratherne." The same writer has often referred to them, and their wild intractable nature, in several of his writings; as most people know. Their territory is described* as "a

---

* "Chambers's Encyclopædia"; articles "Border" and "Debatable Land."

tract of land, chiefly level and of a moory character, but now in course of improvement, on the western border of England and Scotland .... The upper half was adjudged [in 1542] to Scotland, and the more eastern part to England. Yet the Debatable Land continued long after to be the residence of the thieves and banditti to whom its dubious state had afforded a refuge .... After the accession of James [VI. of Scotland] to the English throne, a sweeping clearance of the Scottish border was effected .... At the same time, the Debatable Land was cleared of the Græmes, a daring sept of freebooters, who were transported to Ireland, and their return prohibited under pain of death." Thenceforward coming under the heading of Wild Irishmen (*Dubh-Eireannaich*), or, to use an expression equally inexact—Black *Celts*, or otherwise, as Irish "gypsies."

As in Stirlingshire, and in Scotland generally,—there floated upward from this mass of *græmes*, an element of refinement, of education, and of chivalry, which, along with all that was best in a thousand other British tribes, has constituted the educated population of the British Islands. But with these we have nothing to do here. Whatever of the marsh-dwelling *græme* blood they may have inherited, has been so mixed with that of other races, and its original character has been so completely refined away, that even could any one of this sort prove a descent from the Moors that crossed the wall of Antoninus, it would be impossible to regard such a one as representative of those archaic Picts: since the same man cannot represent both the second century and the nineteenth. Not that it can be said that "gypsies," even, represent a period so far back as the second century; but, at least, they are many generations behind their fellow countrymen.

The whole of the *græmes* of the Debatable Land cannot have been sent into Ireland, in the reign of James I., because they still retained their hold upon those uncultivated tracts until the time of George III., if not later. During the latter half of last century, Lord Tankerville and others of the Border magistracy proceeded one day to survey, for the purposes of settlement and agriculture—" some uncultivated land called the *Plea lands*, or *Debatable lands*, the pasturage of which was generally eaten up by the Sorners and vagabonds on both sides of the marshes." By "threats and entreaties," the chiefs of these tribes, and their followers, had been induced to keep away from the scene of action; but they stationed themselves on the higher grounds, not far off, from which position they watched the proceedings. "At first they were very quiet. But when they saw the English Court Book spread out on a cushion before the clerk, and apparently taken in a line of direction, interfering with what they considered to be their privileged ground, it was with great difficulty that the most moderate of them could restrain the rest from running down, and taking vengeance, even in sight of their own [?] Lord of the Manor.

"They only abstained for a short time, and no sooner had Sir David [Bennet], and the other gentlemen taken leave of each other . . . . and had departed to a sufficient distance, than the clan, armed with bludgeons, pitchforks, and such other hostile weapons as they could find, rushed down in a body; and before the chiefs [the modern gentry] on either side had reached their home, there was neither English tenant, horse, cow, nor sheep left upon the premises." (*Hoyland*, pp. 107–109: *Simson*, pp. 249–250.)

Scenes of this description are taking place to-day in New Zealand: and, in either country, it is the protest of the savage against civilization; of the "native man" against those who would wrest from him the fatherland of his race.

All these examples have been taken as specimens of Early-Scottish, Pictish, or Danish tribes. Necessarily, there must be uncertainty as to the exact pedigree, but since all three branches were connected (or, at least, since none were of the Xanthochroic type), their particular lineage is, so far, of little importance. The Douglases, however, were brought out to show that while the Early Scots were seen, *in the mass*, to be akin to the Early Picts, so individual cases might be found proving the same thing. But, since the "trees" of families and tribes cannot be traced, authentically, to a period prior to the latest invasion of *dubh galls*, that of the Black Danes, neither Douglases nor Græmes can be accepted as positively proving the swarthy complexion of the Early *Scots*. Nevertheless, it is manifest that the Black Douglases, the Galwegians Proper, or Galloway Picts, and the *Wild Scots o' Gallowa'*, were one and the same people. In this way, the Douglases, as a tribe of Scots, demonstrate that the Early Scots were Moors; or, as we now call them, "gipsies."

There must thus have been Scots and Scots. In the one acceptation of the word—and that the oldest—they were wild piratical marauders, whether by land or sea; in the other and more catholic sense, they were the ordinary inhabitants of modern Scotland. There is nothing exceptional in such a twofold use of the same word. When one talks to-day of a New Zealander, it is not a matter of certainty that the word is *not* used as Macaulay used it. "Australians" are either Colonists or Aborigines, according to the nature of the society in which the word is uttered. In a club of squatters the former meaning is taken for granted; at an ethnological meeting the latter is as naturally assumed. It is not so very long ago that "an American" meant "a Red Indian": Wesley, I believe, somewhere calls the native people "dark Americans." And this distinction of Wesley's corresponds exactly with that existing between "Irishmen" (itself a far too comprehensive word) and "Wild Irishmen," which is in Gaelic "Black Irishmen." Accordingly, we find that Scottish people, generally, have traditions of a fierce Galwegian race, whom they—though Scots (and indeed Galwegians) themselves, in the widest sense of those terms—remember specially as the Wild *Scots* of Galloway. As "shameless Irish robbers," or Early Scots; as Picts of Galloway and as Black Douglases; those people were Moors, or gipsies, as just stated.

There is no doubt that "Scot" has been used in a national sense for very long. Barbour, who wrote in the "Inglis toung" (at that time—the days of Chaucer—scarcely a whit different from modern English), speaks of "Scottis" and "Inglis" men in the same comprehensive geographical way as we now do. The Picts or Wild Scots of Galloway, he distinguishes as "Gallowaiss." But, although this usage dates so far back, yet the word Scot had a definite, restricted signification nearly three centuries after Barbour wrote. This is seen from the following newspaper paragraph, written *at Edinburgh*, in the year 1662:—

"The Scots and moss-troopers have again revived their old custom, of robbing and murthering the English, whether soldiers or other, upon all opportunities. Within these three weeks we have had notice of several robberies and murders, committed by them. Among the rest, a lieutenant, and one other of Col. Overton's regiment, returning from England, were robbed not far from Dunbarr. A lieutenant, lately master of the customs at Kirkcudbright, was killed about twenty miles from this place; and four foot soldiers of Col. Overton's were killed, going to their quarters, by some mossers, who, after they had given them quarter, tied their hands behind them, and then threw them down a steep hill, or rock, as it was related by a Scotchman, who was with them, but escaped."

Here the distinction between *Scots* and *Scotchmen* is marked. The first are the associates of mossers, or moss-troopers,—*are* mossers, or moss-troopers,—the others are peaceable lieges. Though written at Edinburgh, the paragraph uses the pronoun *them*, in speaking of the Scots. In short, "a Scot" and "a moss-trooper, or mosser," were synonymous terms in 1662.

But what manner of men were mossers, or moss-troopers? The same newspaper records, in the following year, that "The Parliament, October 21, passed an Act, declaring any person that shall discover any felon, or felons (commonly known or called by the name of moss-troopers), residing upon the borders of England and Scotland, shall have a reward of ten pounds upon their conviction." The mossers, then, were felons. They are further described by Sir Walter Scott, in these terms:—"But, on the middle and western marches, the inhabitants were unrestrained moss-troopers and cattle drivers, knowing no measure of law, says Camden, but the length of their swords. . . . Various proclamations were in vain issued, for interdicting the use of horses and arms upon the west border of England and Scotland. The evil was found to require the radical cure of extirpation. Buccleuch collected under his banners the most desperate of the border warriors, of whom he formed a legion, for the service of the states of Holland, who had as much reason to rejoice on their arrival upon the Continent, as Britain to congratulate herself upon their departure. It may be presumed, that few of this corps ever returned to their native country. The clan of the Græme, a hardy and ferocious sept of free-

"*Felons, commonly called Moss-troopers.*"

booters, inhabiting chiefly the Debatable Land, by a very summary exertion of authority, was transported to Ireland, and their return prohibited under pain of death. . . . . Numbers of border riders were executed, without even the formality of a trial; and it is even said that, in mockery of justice, assizes were held upon them after they had suffered. . . . By this rigour, though sternly and unconscientiously exercised, the border marauders were, in the course of years, either reclaimed or exterminated ; though nearly a century elapsed ere their manners were altogether assimilated to those of their countrymen."*

Those moss-troopers, or mossers, are thus revealed to us as a race of men so different from the civilized inhabitants of Scotland, that the bulk of them could not be tolerated,—but were either killed or transported ; while those that succeeded in clinging to their native land did not become civilized until the process of assimilation had been going on for three generations. The treatment they received was so analogous to that experienced by their kindred across the Atlantic, that the resemblance hardly needs to be pointed out. This is distinctly visible as far back as the twelfth century. At that time (Dr. Skene tells us) the country of the Moors or Moray-men of the North was colonized by Norman-Dutch people, under the supervision of David I., and his grandson (and successor), Malcolm IV.† The native "Moors" or

---

* See the earlier pages of Scott's Introduction to "The Minstrelsy of the Scottish Border."

† This *Plantation of Moray*, as it was called, was distinctly a feudal prototype of the Plantation of Virginia, or any other colony of comparatively recent times. David I. of Scotland was the youngest son of Malcolm Ceannmor, by his second wife, Margaret, sister of Eadgar Aetheling. Whatever of the fierce Saxon blood she had inherited, had long before been mellowed by refinement, civilization, and Christianity ; and she herself was singularly gracious and noble. Her share in the civilizing of Scotland can hardly be over-rated. This, then, was the mother of David I. of Scotland. He, again, had been brought up among the young nobles of Henry the First's Norman Court, and had been "as William of Malmesbury expresses it, 'polished from a boy by intercourse and familiarity with us.'" His wife was a grandniece of William the Conqueror, and by her he "obtained during her life the earldom of Northampton and honour of Huntingdon." His reign is pronounced to be "the true commencement of feudal Scotland," and "under his auspices . . . . its social state and institutions became formally assimilated to Norman forms and ideas, while the old Celtic element in her constitutional history gradually retired into the background. During this and the subsequent reigns the outlying districts, which had hitherto

"Indians,"—who may have been of Early-Pictish, or of Danish stock—were first overcome, after many severe conflicts. When this was finally accomplished, Malcolm IV. "removed them all from the land of their birth, and scattered them throughout the other districts of Scotland, both beyond the hills and on this side thereof, so that not even a native of that land abode there, and he installed therein his own peaceful people." In Transatlantic parlance, the Indians were placed upon reservations and the country opened up for settlement,—by people who were presumably, if not certainly, "fair whites" (in the main); and whose ideas of life were, in essence, the same as those held by our modern colonists. This Malcolm IV. had, at the same time, many encounters with the painted "Moors" of Galloway, whose descendants, a century and a half later, were momentarily discerned assailing King Robert Bruce, at the river-bank. By the year 1587, such people were wholly forbidden from entering the districts occupied by the civilized inhabitants of Scotland, unless they could "find security for their quiet deportment." (Just as "Indians" are permitted to leave their reservations, after receiving a "pass" from the autho-

---

maintained a kind of semi-independence under their native rulers, and in which they were more tenaciously adhered to, were gradually brought under the more direct power of the monarch and incorporated into the kingdom." (Skene's "Celtic Scotland," Vol. I. pp. 454-472.) One of the "outlying districts" referred to was that of Galloway, and the arms of these Scoto-Norman monarchs were there, as in Moray, directed against a Moorish people In either district the so-called *natives* were made up of various combinations of *dubh galls* or black *foreigners*, although their settlement in the country for many generations gave them a certain right to be styled "natives." How far the customs of such "natives" were Celtic, is quite another question. In the latter part of the tenth century two kings are believed to have ruled jointly over the "Kingdom of Alban." These were known to the chronicler, St. Berchan, as *Dubh* and *Fionn*, or Black and White. Dubh, who only reigned over "the three black divisions," was eventually dispossessed by Fionn. Of whatever race Fionn was, his victory meant a "white conquest," and so prepared the way for the twelfth-century colonization above spoken of. Even the vast scholarship of the author of the dubiously-named "Celtic Scotland" is not able to disentangle (at length) the confused pedigrees of chiefs, whose very existence and position he has been greatly taxed to set forth. But whether *Fionn* was descended from "white strangers" or from Early Britons, his reign shows the gradually-waning power of the *Moors*, and the slowly-increasing power of the *Whites*. So long as Scotland was wholly or chiefly Pictish, so long was it Moorish. Therefore, the extent of its pre-Norman "Celticism" is doubtful.

rities.) But, in the following century, owing to a temporary dominance of the intolerant and merciless spirit that is yet displayed by the white rowdies of the fast-vanishing "frontier" in the United States, those Moors that still infested the borders were subjected, as we have seen, to a more despotic treatment. Some were formed into regiments (like the Hungarian gipsies mentioned by Simson), and sent to find a speedy death in Continental battles ;* others, as, for instance, those specially known as *Græmes*, were deported to Ireland, —then, in some parts, a species of *Indian Territory ;*—and others, like many an ill-starred Peigan, or Seminole, were killed without any show of mercy or justice.

Their habits are thus further described. They are stated to have ridden "horses of a small size, but astonishingly nimble, and trained to move, by short bounds, through the morasses." Those horses were variously styled " Galloway nags " and "Irish hobbies "† by the contemporary *non-moss-trooping* population, and they seem to have been akin to the small breeds of Orkney, Shetland, and the Hebrides. Their riders were "so much accustomed to move on horseback, that they held it even mean to appear otherwise" ; " hence the name of prickers and hobylers, so frequently applied to them." Camden, writing in the sixteenth century, says of them :— " They sally out of their own borders, in troops, through unfrequented bye-ways, and many intricate windings. All the day time, they refresh themselves and their horses, in lurking holes they had pitched upon before, till they arrive in the dark at those places they have a design upon. As soon as they have seized upon the booty, they, in like manner, return home in the night, through blind ways, fetching many a compass." " Like Falstaff (says Sir Walter Scott), they were 'gentlemen of the night, minions of the

---

* One of those mossers that were sent to Holland as *enfans perdus* did return to his native land, and his descendants are numerous at the present day. He was the only survivor of his regiment, after an attack upon the ramparts during the Siege of Namur, and in this engagement he saved the life of his captain, a Scotch laird. "Out of gratitude to his faithful follower," the laird—on his return to Scotland—settled this man upon his estate ; where his posterity still live. The place is Kirk-Yetholm in Roxburghshire, and the descendants of this moss-trooper are styled *Gipsies*. (See Simson's " History," &c., p. 252.)

† See Dekker's "Gull's Hornbook," edit. 1812, pp. 93 and 109.

moon,' under whose countenance they committed their depredations."

The surnames which gradually became attached to various sub-divisions of those mossers are many. One of the personages in "a curious drama," by Sir David Lindsay, mentions several of these. The speaker is himself a moss-trooper, about to be hanged, and in his dying speech he is made to apostrophize his fellow moss-troopers, thus:—

> Adew! all theeves, that me belangis;
> Baileowes, Erewynis, and Elwandis,
> Speedy of flicht, and slight of handis:
> The Scotts of Eisdale, and the Gramis,
> I haif na time to tell you namis.

Of these names, the first is regarded by Mr. Simson as peculiarly a "gipsy" name. It is borne by two "Egyptians," or "*Faws*," named in an act of James V., quoted in the "History of the Gipsies." It is said to be the same as Baillie, and if so, it suggests a descent from the form Balliol,* which also has been changed to "Baillie." The Bailyows in the act of James V. are there stated to be Faws and Egyptians. They were also—using the names *literally*—Moors, Douglases, Græmes, and Scots,—by virtue of their complexion.

Now, this last surname reminds one of a curious fact, namely, that the very man who has written so much about the Borderers, was himself, by descent, of this identical race of Early Scots. He had, without doubt, inherited the blood of twenty other races, but he inherited his surname from the marauding Scots of the fourth century, who were, in the estimation of their Christianized contemporaries, so many "black herds" of "shameless Irish robbers." If, with the surname of Scot, or Scott, he had also inherited the blood of the founder of the clan particularly named "Scots," then the

---

* The first historic Balliol, or Baliol, is said to have been a fellow-Norman and contemporary of William the Conqueror, and to have been the owner of a place in Normandy, called *Balleul*, whence he derived his designation De Balleul or De Balliol. But this does not interfere with the supposition that the first Balliol was of the same "Moorish" stock as the Scots, Picts, and Danes. It has been pointed out that the first ancestor of a family surnamed Murray was a Fleming of the name of Freskine, who, receiving a grant of land in the conquered district of the Moors or Moraymen, was styled De Moravia, and subsequently Moray. Such may have been the origin of the first De Balliol family.

most illustrious bearer of that name was, in some degree, of this "Scythian" origin. This is seen, not only by regarding the manners of the Scots proper, whether as early Scots or as later Moss-troopers, but also by examining the alleged origin of the Scott clan. They are understood to be descended from "John of Galloway," one of "two brethren, natives of Galloway," who were "banished from that country for a riot, or insurrection," during the latter part of the ninth century. It is likely enough that this "riot, or insurrection," was one of many others taking place at that time in Galloway, and resulting in the possession of the throne of Alban by Kenneth Mac Alpin, who seems to have been strongly supported by the Scots of Galloway; from which district, indeed, he, himself, is said to have come. At any rate, Kenneth Mac Alpin is the king who is stated, in the family legend, to have transformed this Galloway Scot into "John Scot of Buccleuch." Thus, the tradition that draws the origin of the Selkirkshire Scots from the Wild Scots of Galloway, is strictly in keeping with the characters of both races. What the Scots or Picts of Galloway were like we have already seen; and Sir Walter has himself acquainted us with the chief features of their posterity in Selkirkshire. He shows us that a Scot and a moss-trooper were once synonymous terms. This, indeed, is a fact that is recognized everywhere. "The Scotts of the south of Scotland (says the author of 'The Scottish Nation') were among the most noted moss-troopers of their time." And of one branch of this clan, the same writer says:—"The Scotts of Tushielaw in Ettrick, at one period a powerful section of the clan Scott, were, like all the race, reavers and freebooters. . . . . The exploits of Adam Scott of Tushielaw, one of the most famous of their chiefs, and usually called 'King of the thieves' and 'King of the border,' with the excesses of the other border barons, roused the wrath of James V., and in 1528 he 'made proclamation to all lords, barons, gentlemen, landwardmen and freeholders, that they should compear at Edinburgh, with a month's victuals, to pass with the king where he pleased, to danton the thieves of Teviotdale, Annandale, Liddisdale, and other parts of that country; and also warned all gentlemen that had good dogs to bring them, that he might hunt in the said country as he pleased.' In the course of this excursion, guided by some of the borderers, the king penetrated into the inmost recesses of Eusdale and Teviotdale, and seizing Cockburn of Henderland and Scott of Tushielaw, one morning before breakfast, summarily hung them in front of their own strongholds."

This proclamation of James the Fifth's was made about seventy years after James the Second's fiat, uttered for the breaking up of the Black-Douglas league ; and it can scarcely be doubted that many of the remnants of that "broken clan" formed no inconsiderable portion of "the thieves of Teviotdale, Annandale, and Liddisdale." And just as the once-powerful Black-Douglases of history are preserved in the popular memory as Moors or Gipsies,—so were their representatives two generations later known as thieves and moss-troopers ; one of their principal leaders being styled the " King of the Thieves," a term that, in the sixteenth century, was synonymous with " King of the Gipsies." In short, it is difficult to find any distinction between the edicts issued two or three centuries ago against thieves, moss-troopers, and the like, and those issued against " Egyptians ; " and it is almost certain that a study of such ancient acts would disclose the fact that no real difference between the two ever existed. " Proclamation shall be made (quotes Scott, from the ' Proceedings of the Border Commissioners,' 1505,) that all inhabiting within Tynedale and Riddsdale, in Northumberland, ... east and west Teviotdale, Liddesdale, Eskdale, Ewsdale, and Annesdale, in Scotland (saving noblemen and gentlemen unsuspected of felony and theft, and not being of broken clans, and their household servants, dwelling within those several places before recited), shall put away all armour and weapons, ... and shall not keep any horse, &c. .... upon the like pain of imprisonment." This proclamation was made fully twenty years before James V. made his raid upon the border thieves, whose chiefs he summarily disposed of. It is observable that a distinct line is drawn between the members of " broken clans " and those who were men of good repute ; and it is under the former heading that such tribes as the now-vanquished Black-Douglases fall to be placed. That this line of demarcation did, to a great extent, define a difference of race, is most likely: the "broken clans" and "thieves," on the one hand, representing the last remnants of Pictish nationality; and the king's-men (like the Maclellans of the previous century) representing the Normanized governing power. By acts subsequent to those just cited, and issued in the later years of the sixteenth century, "such clans as had no chieftain of sufficient note to enter bail for their quiet conduct, became broken men, outlawed to both nations." "They were in truth (says the same distinguished writer*), ... a kind of outcasts, against whom the united powers of England and Scotland were often employed." In short, ever since the overthrow of the black nobility in 1455,—or (to go far farther back) ever since the tenth century, when a white king displaced a black one on the Pictish throne,—those Moors who refused to accept the laws of the new civilization, and who refrained from mixing their blood with that of the white races, had been sinking lower and lower in the social scale; until, in the sixteenth century, they had become outlawed banditti, mossers, or gipsies.

The accession of James of Scotland to the British throne marked (says Scott, as already mentioned) a crisis in the state of affairs on the Borders. The *moss-troopers* were sent as soldiers to Holland, were transported for life to Ireland, and, in many cases, were hunted down in their own country, without mercy. At exactly the same period (says Mr. Simson), the *gipsies* received the same treatment. In the words of Baron Hume—"All ordinary means having proved insufficient to restrain so numerous and so sturdy a crew, the privy council at length, in June, 1603, were induced to venture on the more effectual expedient .... of at once ordering the whole race to leave the kingdom by a certain day, and never to return under the pain of death."

The moss-trooping *græmes*, or black-men, had been transported to Ireland for the rest of their natural lives. Speaking of them and other border moss-troopers, a seventeenth-century writer† says:—"They dwell in the bounds, or meeting

---

* Scott, from whose notes to "The Lay of the Last Minstrel" and his introduction to "The Minstrelsy of the Scottish Border" these extracts have been made.

† Dr. Fuller: quoted in Note N. of the Appendix to "The Lay of the Last Minstrel."

of the two kingdoms, but obey the laws of neither. . . . . Amounting, forty years since, to some thousands, [they] compelled the vicinage to purchase their security by paying a constant rent to them [black mail*]. . . . . [But, being now declared outlaws, and having lost all their former power]: Thenceforward (after that they are outlawed) they wear a wolf's head, so that they lawfully may be destroyed, without any judicial inquisition, as who carry their own condemnation about them, and deservedly die without law, because they refused to live according to law." Thus of the *moss-troopers*. Speaking of *gipsies*, Mr. Simson states that, by a statute of 1609, it was declared "lawful to condemn and execute them to the death, upon proof made of the single fact 'that they are called, known, repute and holden Egyptians.'"

The Act of 1609 deals with "common thieves, commonly called Egyptians;" and, three years later, the king "entered into a contract with the clan Scott, and their friends, by which the clan bound themselves 'to give up all bands of friendship, kindness, oversight, maintenance or assurance, if any we have, with common thieves, and broken clans, &c.'" A chief of that clan (Scott of Tushielaw) had, in the previous century, been known as the King of the Thieves, and, as such, hanged before his own door. He may be taken as one of the latest specimens of the gipsy who yet retained the rank of his ancestors; who was a pure-blooded *Scot*, a chief of a minor clan, the holder of a territorial title, and yet the King of the Gipsies. In his person one sees the decay of his race illustrated. Born the chief of a clan yet distinguished by its historical surname, he was hanged as a " common thief "—a mosser—a gipsy.

A genuine Scot—like a genuine Douglas—was thus of the mingled people whom we now call gipsies. While the Scots remained tolerably pure in blood, we do not usually see them styled gipsies. At that period their position and

---

* The point we have now arrived at—the recognition of the border mossers as black men—greatly modifies the remarks made in a former chapter as to this term. It is now evident that the acts of the reigns of Elizabeth and James employ a perfectly appropriate word when they designate as "black-mail" the tribute or mail "paid unto some inhabiting near the Borders, being men of name and power, allied with certain known to be great robbers and spoil-takers within the counties."

power was so great that it was national and historical: during that period, therefore, they are known by their historical name. But whenever they declined to the grade of "broken clans," as did the Black Douglases in 1455, and Scott of Tushielaw, a century later, they are styled "common thieves, commonly called Egyptians." The exact date when the popular name began to be used in the statutes can only be learned by painful research. But it must have been a popular name for many centuries, since Dr. Skene tells us that the pedigree of the early Scots of history was deduced by some from an Egyptian source.

However, we are at present trying to limit our gaze to the Border Scots, apart from the general race of early Scots, throughout these islands. We have seen that a contemporary writer describes the Borderers as always making their expeditions during the night, and lying in concealment during the day. This Sir Walter also corroborates. And it is also a characteristic of the Black Morrow, or Blackimore, of Galloway tradition, who may have been of the Black Douglas clan. It is a characteristic, also, of all the "blackmen," once so greatly feared by timorous peasant-girls and young children; although such black men—as belonging to a distinct type—are now non-existent, or nearly so. Such black robbers were all, in the often-quoted words of Falstaff "minions of the moon." "Hence the emblematic moons and stars (says Scott), so frequently charged in the arms of border families." Now this is precisely one of the distinguishing features of the gipsies. Washington Irving's "Starlight Tom" was no exceptional gipsy. The name by which they are known in the "cant language" is *Moon Men*.*
Thus, in this particular, as in so many others, the Scots proper are seen to be a division of the gipsy race.

It may be remembered that the Black Douglases of 1455 are not only styled "Moors" in local tradition, but also

---

* Grose's "Classical Dictionary of the Vulgar Tongue." It need not be insisted that such a title *originally* arose from the moonlight depredations of the Gipsies. Mr. Leland explains the term *Zingan*, or *Tchenkan* (by which they are so often known), to signify the "moon-sun" people; and thus the "moon-men" may have been so styled because they worshipped "the host of heaven." But the same theory would apply to the favourite bearings of the Border mossers, or Scots.

"Saracens." Now, there was probably some difference between a "Moor" and a "Saracen," although in heraldry there does not seem to be much distinction. The Algerine pirates who made occasional descents upon our coasts, were probably the latest wearers of this title. "The opinion which has been most generally supported, and prevails at the present time, is that the word was originally *Sharkeyn*," an Arabian word signifying "eastern people," and used in contradistinction to *Maghribé*, or "western people," the Moors of Morocco. While, therefore, all Saracens were Moors, all Moors were not necessarily Saracens. But, at any rate, the term "Saracen" has been applied to the piratical invaders of this country from a very early period.* It has also been applied on the Continent to various races, one of which the article quoted from the *Encyclopædia Britannica* identifies with gypsies. So that when the Scots, or Gypsies, of the Borders were distinguished by the Saracenic symbols of crescents and stars, such symbols were quite in accordance with their supposed descent from such Saracens and Moors as the Scots and Picts of Galloway. It is necessary, however, to defer to another chapter the consideration of such people, under the designation of Saracens.

One of the oldest branches of the clan Scot, or Scott, is that of Murdockston, or Murdieston. And this is very appropriate. For it was noticed (in quoting from Elder's letter to Henry VIII.), that Murdoch, Mordhow, and Mordubh, were all forms of the same word: and that that word is applied to a black warrior in the West Highland tales, being in his case simply an appellative name. For Mor Dubh is Black Moor, Morrow, or Murray. Therefore, that the Black Moor's Town should become the headquarters of an Early-Scottish chief is not a matter for surprise. Similarly, another branch of the same clan, also of ancient lineage, was Scot of *Fawsyde*; which, of course, was only another name for Murdockston.

The name of Scot has thus come to signify three different kinds of *Scots*. First, the piratical Scot of the early centuries, who was, in the main, one with the Wild Scot of Galloway, and the moss-trooping Scot, or gipsy of later times: then

* This fact is one which modern writers, generally, appear to have overlooked.

the Scott of Selkirkshire, who eventually changed himself, by repeated intermarriage with other races, into something very different from the pure-blooded Scot, whom at last he came to repudiate altogether as a "common thief" or "Egyptian:" and lastly, the Scot of Scotland, who may be the descendant of any one of the numerous races that have settled in Scotland since ever it rose out of the sea. The precise date at which a *Scot* became a *Scott* must differ greatly in the various branches of that clan. It is pretty clear, however, that when the chiefs of the Selkirkshire families began to wear their ancestral crescents as feudal coats-of-arms, the hour had struck for their acceptance of Norman ideas, and Norman blood. David I., it is stated by the very eminent historian already quoted, introduced feudal ideas and new blood into Scotland, and with very little alteration these ideas and men of that blood ruled the country for many centuries. Therefore, when an ante-feudal Scot accepted a coat-of-arms authorized by a Norman-Scottish Lyon King he showed his acquiescence in the new state of things, and his support of the new dynasty. And doing this he naturally allied himself with the gentry of the new *régime:* thereby casting off to a great extent the associations of his Scoto-Pictish ancestry. As a matter of fact, the present titular representative of the traditional "Galloway John" is as much a Norman as anything else. But it is not necessary to select individual examples in order to see that the leaders of that, or of any other tribe in a conquered country (that is, conquered *socially* and *racially*, whether by force of arms or not), must of necessity become the soonest blended with other races. The higher the position of the chief, the more likely was this to happen; for his birth and power gave him a political importance which brought him into contact with the leading men of other races; and, in the case of Scotland, the races that ruled the country, in and after the twelfth century, were not of Early-Scottish descent. On the other hand, the humbler followers of such a chief, living in their hereditary fashion, and associating only with those of kindred blood, remained the purest representatives of the ancestral stock. Had the Great Magician been descended from *none* but the moss-troopers he loved so much to write about, and had such of them as really were his ancestors belonged to the moiety that refused to "assimilate their manners to those of their countrymen" (not "*kins*men") his "magic" would have been nothing greater than that of the dusky fortune-tellers, jugglers, and mountebanks, who were his twentieth cousins. But, since his Early-Scottish forefathers one day realized the fact that if they wished to hand down their possessions and influence to future generations they must become *civilised*, and live according to the new ideas brought in (or resuscitated) about the twelfth century; since they recognized this, and acted accordingly, their greatest descendant became what he was. Of those among the lower ranks of the Scots, to whom this choice of "Be civilized, or perish" presented itself, their very obscurity prevents one from tracing them. But the "black butcher on Ti'otside," in the story of "Simple John,"—referred to previously—may be taken as a sample of those who made the wiser choice; while the traditional Black Morrow of Galloway as clearly represents the intractable and savage marauder, who died a marauder's death. There still, it is true, remained a party of compromise,—those who, deprived by statute of their arms and horses, still clung to their vagrant ways as comparatively harmless *gipsies*. But it was only so long as they behaved themselves quietly that they were permitted to exist thus.

It would be tedious to quote many cases in which the more ferocious of these border clans were subjected to a relentless persecution. Scott tells us of one tribe (the Winters) that, only eighty or ninety years ago, finding their own side of the border (the English side) too hot for them, crossed into Scotland, and from thence were driven back into their native country. "The dalesmen of Reedwater showed great reluctance to receive these returned emigrants. After the Sunday service at a little chapel near Otterbourne one of the squires rose, and addressing the congregation, told them they would be accounted no longer Reedsdale men, but Reedsdale women, if they permitted this marked and atrocious family to enter their district. The people answered that they would not permit them to come that way; and the proscribed family, hearing of the unanimous resolution to oppose their passage, went more southernly, by the heads of the Tyne, and I never heard more of them (adds Scott), but I have little doubt they are all hanged."* Again, we are told that "immediately after the accession of James VI. (of Scotland) to the English crown (a period two hundred years earlier than that to which Scott refers) he issued the following Proclamation, dated December 4, 1603 :—'Divers Borderers, especially the Grahams, having perpetrated sundry outrages; but the Grahams are now at our mercy confessing themselves to be no meet persons to live in those countries, and therefore have humbly besought us that they might be removed to some other parts, where, with our gracious favor they hope to live to become new men and to deserve our mercy. We have rather inclined to this course as more agreeable to our nature than taking so much blood. This for the present proceedeth from no alteration of our detestation of such crimes, but from the lack of means to provide for the transplantation of the Grahams, to the intent that their lands be inhabited by others of good and honest conversation. For the ease of the prisons we dismiss the vulgar sort of them, retaining their heads and principals for pledges that they shall be forthcoming, and for their good behaviour in the meantime.' The Cumbrians, sympathizing with their sovereign's laudable anxiety to free the country of such pests, entered into a subscription, which amounting to £400, they were enabled to freight three vessels from Workington, in which were shipped a number of the Grahams, who were transported to Ireland."† A few years later two "limmers" of the same neighbourhood—"Fergus Graham in Plomp, and Scallet Davie Johnstone"—are accused of murdering the Provost of Dumfries, uncle to the sixth Lord Herries.‡

That all these Borderers were of the same description is evident. The Winters were "gipsies," the Grahams were "limmers," and both were accordingly *græmes, grimes*,‡

---

* Quoted by Mr. Simson at page 97 of his "History of the Gipsies."

† "Transactions of the Dumfriesshire and Galloway Antiquarian Society," Session 1865-66, pp. 34-5.

‡ There seems to have been a period at which the pronunciation of this word was indifferently *grame* and *grime*. At the time when the ballad of *Hughie* the *Græme* was composed, the latter was clearly the commonest accent. In that ballad (as it is given in Scott's "Minstrelsy") "græme" is twice made to rhyme

moors, dubh-glasses, &c. And, like the "Moors" of twelfth-century Moray, or those of nineteenth-century America, they were killed, transplanted, or placed upon reservations, to make room for people who, if not fully entitled to be styled "peaceful," were at least not persistently combative.

But the "gypsy" tribe which ought to be the most emphatically pointed to in this chapter is that one which was particularly distinguished by the descriptive name of Dubh-glas. While all black-swarthy people were, properly speaking, *dubh-glasses*, it seems clear that this title gradually settled down upon one special sept—whose least hybrid descendants were, later on, specified as Black-Douglases. These, again, may have branched off into separate families bearing other names. The posterity of Archibald the Grim may have become Græmes or Grimes: others may have been the founders of clans known by various surnames of various origin—other than "Douglas." But, even after the complete overthrow of the Black-Douglas league, in the latter half of the fifteenth century, there must have survived straggling bands of Douglases who were still "Moors" in complexion, like him of the Bombie tradition. Or, to put it conversely, it is probable that while many of those *dubh-glasses* would, in course of time, be known by other surnames (such as Black, Brown, Moore, Murray, Faw, Young, Gordon, &c.), the original name would long adhere to a portion of the original stock. And this was so. The Black-Douglases, so-called, seem to have lingered on among the fastnesses of Liddesdale, that border upon the scene of their great defeat at Langholm (Arkinholme) in the year 1455—for many generations after that event. And their descendants, whether wild or tame, pure-blooded or half-caste, were still there when Scott began his famous "raids into Liddesdale" nearly a hundred years ago. He went there "to pick up some of the ancient *riding ballads* said to be still preserved among the descendants of

---

with "time," and once with "fine," while the nearest approach to the *grame* sound is in the first verse, where "gane" and "græme" occur at the end of alternate—though not necessarily rhyming—lines. The date of this ballad is uncertain, but we get an exact date for this pronunciation in the inscription upon the Martyrs' stone in Wigtown churchyard, where "grahame" is distinctly made to rhyme with "crime." The year in which the "martyrdom" took place was 1685, so that this accentuation is certainly not two centuries old.

the moss-troopers, who had followed the banner of the Douglasses"; and these "riding ballads," we are told by Mr. Simson, were for ever in the mouths of those Border minstrels and moss-troopers whom he styles "gipsies." To what extent those Liddesdale folk of last century were inheritors of the early Black-Douglas blood is uncertain. But if we travel a little farther along the Border-line, in a north-easterly direction, we come to a district which has been among the last to yield up its ancient character, and in which the Black-Douglases still remained—as a strongly marked type—during the earlier portion of the present century. At that date the Black-Douglases formed one of the most important divisions of the Yetholm "gypsies," and the comparative purity of their descent is seen from the fact that they were, even then, " generally dark-complexioned, with black hair."* They do not seem, at so recent a period, to have been popularly known as *Black* Douglases (though they were so). If specially described, it was probably as "Tinkler-" or "Gypsy-" Douglases. But in those swarthy Douglases of Yetholm, who—like others of their kind—were wild and daring marauders at an astonishingly modern date, we have distinct representatives of the Black-Douglas clans that, in far greater numbers and of far higher importance, terrorised the southern districts of Scotland three or four centuries before. Such Douglases, indeed, must be taken as the only proper representatives of that earlier race. For no other nineteenth-century people, bearing that surname, existed under the same conditions. Douglases there were, and no doubt are, whose lineage might be traced back to the caste that sank below the surface in the fifteenth century. Such people may be descended from, let us say, *Archibald the Grim*, as truly as many living Virginians are descended from Pocahontas (though in a less degree, being more remote). But such Virginians are not typical Red-Indians: it takes more than a few drops of a certain blood to produce resemblance to the type from which it comes. With the Black-Douglases of the Debatable Land around Yetholm, in this present century, the case was different. Here were people inheriting not only an ancient name, but all the peculiarities

* Oliver's "Rambles in Northumberland," &c.: London, 1835, p. 270.

attaching to it, having the same swarthy colour, the same archaic ideas, and living the same wild lives (or nearly so) as all their Black-Douglas progenitors in Scottish history. These people were not merely an aggregation of individuals bearing the surname of "Douglas" (who might have been of all complexions and of the most differing types and pedigrees): they were the latest remnant of a *race*, a *nationality* ;—distinguished from other men by the possession of certain racial characteristics, shared by all of them alike, as members of that nationality ; holding themselves aloof from the farmers and farmer-squires that intruded into their territory ; resenting, as long as they could, the invasion and partition of what they rightly deemed their own country ;* and defying, as long as they could, the laws and usages of those who must be regarded as their conquerors.† Other men, here and there, may possess a partial claim to the blood of the Black-Douglases ; but that clan is not seen anywhere, *as a clan*, during the present century, except in the persons of the "gypsy" Douglases of Yetholm.

. . . . .

Leaving the consideration of particular tribes of *Scots*, let us regard these people from a greater distance.

It was said, on a previous page, that, under other conditions, the "magic" of Scott would have been nothing higher than that of the wandering gipsy. Such a hypothetical "Scott" would not, of course, have been Walter Scott at all ; in lineage or in anything else. But that is what he would have been, had he been, by descent, a pure moss-trooping Scot. This is apparent, not only because *Scot, Moss-trooper,*

---

* See the description (given by Hoyland, p. 107) of the attempted settlement of the Debatable Land during the eighteenth century, and the consequent action on the part of the "gypsy" clans of Yetholm.

† Gipsies, formerly if not now, are described as inveterate law-breakers—smugglers, poachers, "common thieves, commonly called Egyptians." Even yet the policeman (the *gav-mush* or "city-man") is their natural enemy. Mr. Leland evidently is thinking of these traits when he speaks of the "peculiar *morale*" of those whom he looks upon as "Gypsies" of one kind or another. But this *morale*, if peculiar, is only peculiar at the present day. It is nothing else than the old rule of force and robbery—the belief that "might makes right, and the weakest goes to the wall"—which was *law* in these islands once upon a time. At which time the tables were turned ; and the believer in abstract justice, apart from "might," was then the possesssor of a "peculiar *morale*."

and *Gipsy* are interchangeable terms, and therefore equivalent to *Juggler;* but also from a description of the moss-troopers, under that name. "And to convince me (says an old writer, quoted by Scott) . . . . . that they are not utter strangers to the black art of their forefathers, I met with a gentleman in the neighbourhood, who showed me a book of spells and magical receipts, taken, two or three days before, in the pockets of one of our moss-troopers; wherein, among many other conjuring feats, was prescribed a certain remedy for an ague, by applying a few barbarous characters to the body of the party distempered. These, methought, were very near akin to Wormius's Ram Runer, which, he says, differed wholly in figure and in shape from the common runæ." It is, unfortunately, too probable that those "barbarous" characters have been lost for ever; but it ought to be remembered that not only were the Early-Scots traditionally supposed to have come from Egypt, but they also made use of hieroglyphic writing. "Boece tells us, in the 'The New Mannieres and Auld of Scottis,' that 'In all their secret besiness they usit not to write with common letteris usit among other peplis, but erer with sifars, and figures of beistis maid in maner of letteris; sic as thair epitaphis and superscription above thair sepulturis schew; noch-the-less this crafty maner of writing, be quhat slenth I can not say, is perist, and yet thay have certaine letteris propir amang themself, quilkis war some time vulgar and common.'"* Thus the genuine *Scots* of history stand connected with the Egyptians of antiquity as well as with their modern British namesakes, and form the bridge (or one of the bridges) that spans the immense chasm which divides the Great Egypt of history from the much discredited Little Egypt† of to-day.

---

* "Sculptured Stones of Eastern Scotland," R. C. Ellison, 1877, p. 26.

† It is almost superfluous to remind the reader that Little Egypt is a favourite term for a territory occupied by those Egyptians. Simson mentions several inscriptions on Continental tombs to this effect:—An epitaph "in a convent at Steinbach . , . . records that on St. Sebastian's eve, 1445, 'died the Lord Pannel, Duke of Little Egypt, and Baron of Hirschhorn.'" Another, "at Bautmer, records the death of the 'Noble Earl Peter, of Lesser Egypt, in 1453'; and a third, at Pferz, as late as 1498, announces the death of the 'high-born Lord John, Earl of Little Egypt';" while, in 1540, James V. of Scotland entered into a treaty with "John Faw, Lord and Earl of Little Egypt," "to assist him in execution of justice upon his company and folk, conform to the laws of Egypt." ("History," pp. 79 and 101.)

Jugglery proper is one of those vocations that have—though not very long ago—passed away from the gipsies of the camps. It was pointed out, some chapters back, that—just as the genuine prize-fighter shows a hint of his pedigree in the gipsy side-locks of his (almost or altogether invariably) black, straight hair—so the street mountebank suggested a like descent by his fantastic attire, his silver ear-rings, and the gay-coloured handkerchief with which he confines his black and oily locks: and the same *professional* lineage was also discerned in the grotesque, parti-coloured dresses of the clowns of our circuses and theatres; as well as in their painted faces, shaven or bewigged heads, and in the semi-salaam of the circus fraternity, whether clowns or mountebanks. All these things are originally the property of the swarthy races. In the mediæval story of John of Rampayne, the black minstrels were mountebanks, or jugglers, as well. Indeed, *jongleur* and *juggler* are only two different pronunciations of the same word, though in course of time a separate intonation gave a separate meaning. And the Gaelic dictionaries, as we have seen, tell us that such feats of legerdemain are "black tricks," just as magic is "black art." Consequently, it was not wrong in any sense to apply the term "juggler" to the border moss-troopers—to whom "books of spells" and "magical receipts" peculiarly belonged. It is probable, of course, that the fighting-men did not profess "jugglery" themselves, leaving it to a particular division of their kinsmen. One distinct example of this profession is seen in a border Scot of the seventeenth century. (He did not bear the name of Scot, being known as "Reid, the mountebank;"—but since Reid is only a variation of Ruadh, it is likely that the first of his line received that name in its sense of "tawny.") Scott quotes the following, regarding him, from Lord Fountainhall's *Decisions*:—"January 17th, 1687.—Reid the mountebank is received into the Popish Church, and one of his blackamores was persuaded to accept of baptism from the Popish priests, and to turn Christian papist; which was a great trophy: he was called James, after the king and chancellor, and the Apostle James."* That the Borderers were *jongleurs* as well as *jugglers* is a fact that

---

* Appendix to "The Lady of the Lake," note 3 V.

asserts itself without the faintest fear of opposition: it is a fact that can never be overlooked, or forgotten, until we have ceased to remember the existence of all the plaintive ballads and battle-breathing lays that make up "the minstrelsy of the Scottish Border."

But Scott himself has led us dreadfully astray. He was truly a magician, for the magic of his romances so charmed his readers that *all* of his antiquarian portraiture was accepted as truth. Whereas it was only partially true. This, of course, was recognized at the time by his fellow-antiquaries, who were not slow to point out his errors. But of all those who have read his poems and romances how many have read the contemporary criticisms?

Thus, his Border moss-trooper, *Christie o' the Clint-hill*, may be accounted as life-like, so far as his fierce and reckless nature is shown; and such accessories as the long lance, the rusty spurs and skull-cap, and the generally dilapidated state of his accoutrements,—are no doubt most exact representations. But instead of making this wild marauder speak better English than the Mistress of Glendearg, he ought to have put in his mouth the language of all Scottish *mossers* from the time of Severus to that of Scott himself—the language of the gipsies. And instead of making no reference whatever to his complexion, he ought to have emphasized its swarthy hue; while, in the battle-scene where Christie is killed, it should have been specially stated that his face—and the faces of all his dusky comrades—were ruddled like that of Marshall, the Galloway Pict; or painted "of various colours," according to the custom of the Faws from immemorial times up to the present century. As for his chief, Julian Avenel, his savage character, and such details as his adherence to the polygamous and Picto-Scottish custom of "handfasting," would entitle him to be classed among such inferior nobility as might have looked up to "Black Lord Archibald" of "the Old Douglas' day." But, from the lateness of his era, and the comparative importance of his rank, his black hair may be admitted as the only evidence of his Egyptian descent. There would, however, have been no violation of facts had he been made as swarthy as any of his followers.

So, again, with his Last Minstrel. Just as the mother-tongue of the Welsh harper is Gipsy;—just as the harp, still emblematically remembered, was the favourite instrument of the minstrels of Ancient Scotia, whence the swarthy Scot-Egyptians came; so ought this last of the Border Minstrels to have been emphatically a gipsy. On the contrary, he has nothing peculiarly gipsy about him,—unless we except the cheerful alacrity with which he drained the "goblet crown'd with mighty wine," so thoughtfully handed to him by "the observant page." Scott is much nearer the mark in his more prosaic "Wandering Willie," of *Redgauntlet*. He, indeed, is not styled a *gipsy*,—but the description given of him is that of a gipsy. Or, more properly a *gaberlunzie*, or blue-gown; which, I take it, is almost identical with *gipsy*. The "silk handkerchief well knotted about his throat,"—the "long loose-bodied great-coat," or "wrap-rascal," "secured around him by a large old-fashioned belt, with brass studs, in which hung a dirk, with a knife and fork, its usual accompaniments,"—are all distinctly characteristic of the last-century gipsy. His consort, whose attire consisted of a plaid, "a man's hat, a blue coat, which seemed also to have been an article of male apparel, and a red petticoat,"—and who "wore a large amber necklace, and silver ear-rings, and had her plaid fastened across her breast with a brooch of the same metal,"—is as clearly a gipsy woman. The most exact description of a female gipsy, in Mr. Simson's book, seems to be that of a Tweed-dale *raunie* (*ranee* or queen), Mary Yorkston by name. Discounting a few fineries—allowable in one of her exalted rank—her picture closely resembles that of "Wandering Willie's" wife. "She wore a large black beaver-hat, tied down over her ears with a handkerchief, knotted below her chin, in the gipsy fashion. Her upper garment was a dark-blue short cloak, somewhat after the Spanish fashion . . . . The greater part of her other apparel was made of dark-blue camlet cloth, with petticoats so short that they scarcely reached to the calves of her well-set legs . . . . Her stockings were of dark-blue worsted, flowered and ornamented at the ankles with scarlet thread; and in her shoes she displayed large, massy, silver buckles . . . . (She was sometimes dressed in a green gown, trimmed with red ribbons.) Her outer petticoat was folded up round her haunches, for a lap, with a large pocket dangling at each side ; and below her cloak she carried, between her shoulders, a small flat pack, or pad, which contained her most valuable articles. About her person she generally kept a large clasp-knife, with a long, broad blade, resembling a dagger or carving-knife ; and carried in her hand a long pole or pike-staff, that reached about a foot above her head."*

I am particular in describing this "Wandering Willie," and his fellow-wanderer, because he is as *real* as Christopher Sly ; which can scarcely be said of the slightly-"stagey" Minstrel of the *Lay*. It is true that, although a minstrel of the Scottish Border, he was not a harper, but a simple fiddler. But this objection is a very trifling one. What I wish to point out is the great probability that all the *jongleurs* of the Borders (to go no farther at present), from whom we have derived those pathetic and impassioned ballads, belonged to that intensely musical people, whom we vaguely know as "gipsies." A glance at Border story, as recounted by a Borderer, quite strengthens this belief. For example, a traditional tale of a wedding in the family of Polwarth, during the fifteenth century, states that the music to which the marriage-party danced, "proceeded from the pipes of King Johnny Faa, who, with half a dozen of his people, sat each with a pair of union pipes beneath his arm." Another tale of the Borders speaks of "Jamie Allan, the gipsy and Northumberland piper," and of "awd piper Allan—Jamie's faither," (an instance of hereditary bardship.) While an imaginary episode in the life of James V. of Scotland (founded on his well known Bohemian habits) makes him assume the character of "Wat Wilson, the king o' the beggars," or gaberlunzies, "with his pipes and his wallets,"—in which disguise he sets a company of rustic revellers dancing to such airs as " ' Gillquhisker, ' ' Brum on tul, ' ' Tortee Solee Lemendow,' and other good old tunes, now forgotten."† (The names of which airs, by the way, suggest—like the *Shelta Thari*, or Tinklers' Speech—a union between Gaelic and gipsy, or Pictish.) Moreover, Simson

---

* "History," p. 209.
† See Wilson's "Tales of the Borders": "Polwarth on the Green," "The Faa's Revenge," and "The Maiden Feast."

(at page 226 of his "History of the Gipsies") informs us that "many practised music; and the violin and bag-pipes were the instruments they commonly used. This musical talent of the gipsies delighted the country people .... and contributed much to procure the wanderers a night's quarters. Many of the families of the farmers looked forward to the expected visits of the merry gipsies with pleasure, and regretted their departure." And Leyden points to the same characteristic when he says:—

> *On Yeta's banks the vagrant gypsies place*
> *Their turf-built cots; a sun-burnt swarthy race!*
> . . . . .
> *But, in the lonely barn, from towns remote,*
> *The pipe and blauder opes its screaking throat,*
> *To aid the revels of the noisy rout,*
> *Who wanton dance, or push the cups about.*

Of which picture Wordsworth has made a companion sketch. For, when his *Female Vagrant* joined a band of "wild, houseless wanderers," who "with their pannier'd asses semblance made of potters wandering on from door to door," one of the allurements of the gipsy life held out to her was—

> *The bagpipe dinning on the midnight moor*
> *In barn uplighted, and companions boon*
> *Well met from far.*

The favourite airs played at such gatherings, there can be little doubt, were those "good old tunes, now forgotten," which Wilson refers to. And the songs that those wandering minstrels were never tired of singing were (says Mr. Simson) those that recorded the exploits of the Border Thieves; how "Hobbie Noble" helped to rescue "Jock o' the Side" from Newcastle Jail, and was himself hanged at Carlisle for that and other misdeeds—how "Hughie the Græme" stole the bishop of Carlisle's mare, and was afterwards hanged for it —or, how "Archie o' Ca'field's" kinsmen rode into Dumfries one dark night, broke into the jail where he was confined, and carried him off with them in triumph (a feat which "Jock Johnstone's" tribe intended to emulate in the beginning of last century, and at Dumfries also, had not the vigilance of the police been more than a match for them). These were some of the favourite melodies of those Border gipsies: and Scott has preserved them in his "Minstrelsy." But the oldest and most interesting of all their repertory must now be hopelessly lost: because these (says Mr Simson) were in their own language; and, as everything appertaining to them and to their language has been almost effaced by the legislation of the last four centuries, there can be very little of the genuine "Minstrelsy of the Scottish Border" surviving at the present day.

Therefore, whether the bards of Wales—whose mother-tongue is gipsy—are descendants of those Egyptian Scots that overran that territory in the fourth century, and who used such coracles as those still used there,—whether the Welsh bards have this particular ancestry or not, the bards of the Scottish Border, wherever we see them distinctly, are gipsies. They may, in this or that instance, show more of the characteristics of one particular sect or division of this race,—one being more particularly a *gaberlunzie*, or "sturdy rogue," another a beggar, another a thief, or a bard, or a mosser,—a *jongleur*, or a *juggler*,—but they are all united by racial ties. The laws of the Norman Stewarts, directed against this ultra-Scottish section of the Scots, reveal this circumstance as clearly as the links of dress and custom which unite the several varieties of this wandering people. "In the reign of James II., alluded to, we find 'away putting of *sorners* (forcible obtruders), fancied fools, vagabonds, out-liers, masterful beggars, *bairds* (strolling rhymers), and such like runners about' is more than once enforced by act of parliament." And again, it is enacted "That such as make themselves fools and are *bairds*, . . . or other such like runners about, being apprehended, . . . their ears [shall] be nailed to the tron or other tree, and cut off, and (themselves) banished the country; and if thereafter they be found again, . . ." they shall be executed. And again, other statutes are made "for the better trial of common *sorners*, vagabonds, and masterful beggars, fancied fools, and counterfeit Egyptians, to the effect that they may be still preserved till they be compelled to settle at some certain dwelling, or be expelled forth of the country:" others are ordained so that "strong beggars, vagabonds, and Egyptians should be punished:" and, through the non-enforcement of such statutes, it is stated in a later Act, that "strong and idle beggars, being for the most part thieves, *bairds*, and counterfeit *limmers*, living most insolently and ungodly, without marriage or baptism, are suffered to *vaig* and wander throughout the whole country." And, in the more imperative ordinance of 1603, "the Privy Council were induced to venture on the more effectual expedient, ... of at once ordering the whole *race* to leave the kingdom by a certain day, and never to return under the pain of death." In this last statute,* it is plainly intimated that the common bond uniting those diverse characters was one of race: the race of the *Græmes*, or swarthy people. And as the Border traditions, just quoted, show the gaberlunzie, or blue-gown, to be a piper, and a King of the Beggars, and at the same time show that "piper" is really a synonym for "gipsy;" so those acts relating to that race regard as one the *jongleur*, the *juggler*, or clown, and the *thief*, or sturdy beggar. The changes on these names might be rung endlessly, or, at any rate, for a greater length of time than can be spared here. For the "fancied fool," or "counterfeit Egyptian," was a counterfeit "*limmer*," by reason of his being an Egyptian, a Faw, and a Pict. So recently as last century, we have seen that it was said of them that "to colour their impostures they artificially discolour their faces; and (without accepting the correctness of the motive assigned to them) it was evident to us that this custom constituted them Faws, or Picts." So that the "counterfeit *limmer*" was a "counterfeit *limner*" (whether these words are identical or not†). It is difficult to decide whether the word "counterfeit" was used with reference to their jugglery, or to their custom of "artificially discolouring" their faces; but in either acceptation it is very suitably

---

* Quoted, with the others, from Chapter III. of Mr. Simson's "History."

† Whether this *limner-limmer* comparison can only be regarded as a play upon the words, or whether the words are really identical, the latter eventuality would accord with the disreputable character attached to other designations of the black races. For *limmer* subsequently acquired a solely feminine application, akin to the Gaelic *dubh-choitchionn*.

It is noteworthy that Mr. F. W. Fairholt, in a note to one of Barclay's "Eclogues," renders *limnier* as a "rascal," which is precisely the meaning formerly attached to *limmer*.

applied. What, however, is more to the point, at present, is, that the *bairds* (a form of the Gaelic *bard*) are everywhere identified with the *Egyptians;* whether the instrument upon which they play is the harp, the violin, or the bagpipes. Therefore the representative Border minstrel, or *jongleur*, ought to have been clearly depicted as the kinsman of *jugglers* such as " Reid, the mountebank," and his "blackamores."

It is not too much to say that, if the "Author of Waverley" had never lived, the Border "gypsies" would always have been popularly regarded as the unconverted descendants of the earlier Border "moss-troopers." And Mr. Simson would not have required to explain that "the gipsies, in general, appear to have located themselves upon grounds of a flattish character, between the cultivated and uncultivated districts; having, on one side, a fertile and populous country, and, on the other, a heathy, boggy, and barren waste, into which they could retire in times of danger." Because Fuller had long ago stated that such people were " called *moss-troopers*, because dwelling in the mosses, and riding in troops together."

Indeed, the following sentences, published while yet " The Lay of the Last Minstrel" was only three years old—the Waverley Novels unwritten—and before society in general had accustomed itself to look at Border history through the spectacles of Sir Walter Scott,—these sentences show quite plainly that the identity of Border Moss-trooper and Border Gypsy was then regarded as a simple fact:—

" Great Britain is now, perhaps, more free from banditti than any of her neighbours. . . . . But formerly she was as much harassed as most of the nations on the continent. Among these the Border-banditti stood eminently forward.

"The marches between England and Scotland, or the Borders, as they were called, were particularly favourable for the existence of these vermin. . . . . The *Debateable Land*, a tract of country situated between the Esk and the Sarke, was so called because it was claimed by both countries [or, more properly, by the *Borderers* of the South and of the North]; and the inhabitants were inclined to consider themselves as belonging to neither, and to obey neither, though very much disposed to plunder from both. . . . The English borderers were, therefore, ever ready to make a foray, so they called a plundering excursion, into Scotland ; and the Scottish borderers, on the other hand, were as ready to return a raid, as they called a plundering incursion into England, for the foray.

"Some rich and noble families on the borders are said to owe the origin of their wealth and nobility to this species of robbery. And the mottoes of some of the border families to this day attest the fact. . . . .

"These borderers seemed to have considered all this as honourable, or, at least, not disgraceful. . . . . The following distinction of the poet [Scott of Satchells] seems to us now a distinction without a difference :—

> *It's most clear a freebooter doth live in hazard's train,*
> *A freebooter's a cavalier that ventures life for gain :*
> *But, since King James the Sixth to England went,*
>   *Ther has been no cause of grief;*
> *And he that hath transgress'd since then,*
>   *Is no* Freebooter, *but a* Thief.

[And Mr. Simson has told us that when Johnstone, the *Gypsy* chief, was to be hanged at Dumfries, it was rumoured that the *Thieves* of Annandale were mustering to the rescue.]

"The following charges, though the loss on each side will, no doubt, be rather exaggerated than diminished by the complainants, will give us some idea of the depredations committed by the borderers, in their raids and forays, even so late as Queen Elizabeth's reign. . . . . ."

Then, after giving various particulars regarding those earlier Borderers, this writer[*] adds—

"*On the Borders there still exist some remains of these banditti. They travel the country in the character of tinkers, horners or spoonmakers, and occasionally steal sheep and plunder houses. One Tom Gordon, who was condemned to be hanged for sheep-stealing about fifteen years ago, was a noted ringleader of them.*"

This last paragraph (which, of course, is not italicised in the original) brings down the Border moss-troopers into the

---

[*] The author of an article on "Banditti" in Pyne's "Microcosm."

nineteenth century. It expresses the unquestioned opinion of a man who belonged to a generation as yet uninfluenced by the genius of Walter Scott: and it also expresses what will become the opinion of all who take the trouble to examine the characteristics of the Border moss-troopers, and who are thereby made to realise that Scott, however admirable in other respects, was anything but an infallible exponent of Border history.

. . . .

It will be remembered that Lord Fountainhall (with a needless display of the narrow intolerance that characterized a certain division of his contemporaries) refers to the baptism of one of "Reid the Mountebank's" "blackamores" by a Christian priest. And one of the statutes, cited above, describes such blackamores as "living most insolently and ungodly, without marriage or baptism." While another writer of that period, to whom we turned for information (Dr. Fuller), has also said — speaking of those moss-troopers,—"They come to church as seldom as the 29th of February comes into the kalendar." From all of which it is apparent that this irreconcilable remnant of the early Scots and Picts had never accepted, even in form, the Christian religion,—as the greater part of their kindred had now done. Their nearest approach to marriage was the concubinage and polygamy openly practised, within the last century, by such gipsy chiefs as the Fifeshire Drummond, and Marshall of Galloway; openly practised in the sixteenth century (according to Scott) by such of them as Julian Avenel represents; and openly practised, with even slighter lines of demarcation, by certain tribes of early Picts and Scots, described by such classical writers as Solinus and Strabo. That such men should never attend a Christian church is, therefore, not astonishing; for, in fact, Christianity was to them a wholly alien creed. *Their* religion was represented by the "books of spells, and magical receipts," that they carried about with them; whose hieroglyphic characters may connect them with Egypt itself, or else with the shamanism of Ancient Persia, which Pliny thought so closely resembled the mystic religion of Druidism. To say that they lived *without* marriage or baptism was incorrect: they lived according to their own laws, religious and social; though these laws were vastly different from those favoured by Christianity,—to whose followers such practices were only a part of "the black art of their (the gipsies') forefathers." Not being Christians themselves, they did not feel bound in any way to obey the laws of Christianity: but they had their own religious ceremonies, nevertheless. What these were may be learned from several learned writers upon the "Gipsies;" and others who have described the customs of various races of ante-Norman Britons. And they may also be traced in many observances not yet extinct among ourselves.

It is of great importance to bear in mind this "religious" phase of the question. One can never hope to understand, however slightly, the movements of past centuries, unless one sees that they were the struggles between wholly antagonistic sets of ideas, as well as between wholly different races of men. All those laws of the Stewarts, framed against Egyptians, thieves, and jugglers, aimed at the complete stamping out of certain modes of life, and ways of thought, that were utterly opposed to the ideas brought in at the Norman Conquest, and existent, though not paramount, before that date. What those laws, in effect, said, was this: "Become civilized according to our ideas—the ideas of the law-makers; profess our religion, and live as we do: refuse to do this, and we (being stronger) will expatriate you, will enslave you,* will kill you 'at sight;' your women shall be burned as witches; and the unreclaimed portion of your race shall be outlawed everywhere."

The question as to whether one race of men has the right to treat another as a nation of criminals, simply because the latter refuses to accept the laws and ideas of the former—is subsidiary to the present theme. But this—the radical belief of most Modern Europeans, and their offshoots, (although

---

* Mr. James Simson (at page 111 of the "History") remarks in a foot-note: "By the above and subsequent statutes in the reign of James VI. 'coal and salt-masters might apprehend and put to labour all vagabonds and sturdy beggars.' The truth is, these kidnapped individuals and their children were made slaves of to these masters. The colliers were emancipated only within these fifty years." This fact, and the degraded existence of such colliers and "salters," is familiar to every reader of Hugh Miller's "My Schools and Schoolmasters."

not plainly formulated by them)—was held, as a matter above dispute, by our predecessors of the seventeenth century. We learned this from the statement made by Dr Fuller, in his description of the Border mossers of that period. "After that they are outlawed (he says, quoting the deliverance of a celebrated lawyer) . . . . . they lawfully may be destroyed, without any judicial inquisition, as who carry their own condemnation about them, and deservedly die without law, because they refused to live according to law. But for what were they outlawed? Not for the taking away of life (or not by any means *invariably* so), but for practising the "black art of their forefathers"—for being *sorcerers* and *magicians* and polygamists—for being "such as make themselves fools and are bairds, or other such like runners about: in other words, for following the non-Christian, idle, and vagabond habits of their ancestors. For doing this they were punished; and if they would not see the error of their ways, they were executed. The principle thus laid down by the conquering race was very simple. It was this: when one race refuses "to live according to law," as law is understood by another, that other is quite justified in treating members of the first race as escaped criminals: *it being always understood that the race of amateur judges is vastly more powerful than that of the assumed law-breakers*. The argument is plausible, and the action it inculcates makes a ready way out of a troublesome question; but its morality is a little dubious.

Perhaps the fairest way to regard the question is this:— Those mossers, marsh-dwellers, Egyptians, minstrels, jugglers, "fancied fools," and what not, were the lineal descendants of various piratical nations that, at one time or another, had molested the peace-loving sections of the population of Early Britain. They had overrun the whole country at various epochs, and under various historical names. Those divisions of them that we have more particularly regarded—the Scots, Picts Proper, and Black Danes, that devastated the northern portion of the main island—had, apparently, been the sovereigns of that territory during many of the earlier centuries of the Christian era. No exact date can be fixed upon as the time of their overthrow, but we know that, by the tenth century, the "black divisions" of Scotland had dwindled down to three; and that, by the twelfth century, the "Moors," or "Morays," had been broken up into detached clans. By the end of the fifteenth century one of the most powerful (and perhaps the latest) of such "black" confederacies had been hurled from all political position down to the level of persecuting and persecuted banditti, diminishing in numbers and importance with each successive generation. It is immaterial whether the successful race ought to be called Romanized-Celtic, or Anglo-Norman, or Dutch: it is enough that these races resembled each other in ideas, as they probably did in feature. They believed in Christianity, and the results that flow from its practice—while the ways of the savage "Scythians" were always abhorrent to them; from the time of Gildas onward, if not from an earlier date. Therefore, since warfare against them was legitimate in the days of their ascendancy, and of their later rivalry, it did not at once cease to be lawful after their power was broken. Not, at any rate, so long as they retained those fierce and hateful qualities that made them originally regarded with aversion by the nobler-living races by whom they were conquered. That large numbers of them became gradually *converted*, and incorporated into the main body of the composite British nation (bringing with them an added vigour and certain new attributes) is stated by Sir Walter Scott, in the passages just quoted;—is stated also by the historian of the Scottish "gipsies;"—and is confirmed by the pedigree which an eminent living ethnologist assigns to the mixed type which he styles *Melanochroi:* which type, being that of an alleged majority of the present British people, argues a very important minority of swarthy ancestors. These, gradually falling in with the ideas prevalent since the Norman Conquest (and steadily gaining ground for many centuries before), became members of the civilized British nation; and, in their turn, became the opponents of their own distant kinsfolk, the "Irreconcilable" section of the Scythian races. Those "Irreconcilables"—the "bigoted Tories"* of their race—

---

* A little reflection makes it apparent that this name was transferred from the marauding *tories* to a political party, *because* the marauders were "habit and repute" Orientalists, and utterly averse to the adoption of new ideas—whether

maintained, as long as they were permitted to do so, the fiercest and most objectionable characteristics of their ancestry; and refused most absolutely to conform to the laws and customs that were now those of the nation. Had they been left to themselves they would have retarded the progress of peace and culture by a thousand years. Consequently, the severe and imperious measures taken by the Stewart kings formed the only practicable solution of the difficulty. For the sake of the rest of the community it was imperative that these savages should cease to be savage, or —cease to be.

Besides, it is apparent (or it will be increasingly apparent, the more the matter is investigated), that those proscribed vagabonds were mostly of an extremely low type of humanity. This is seen, in one instance, by looking at those gipsies that were enslaved in the reign of James VI., and sent down to work in the coal-pits of the Lothians. (They and theirs were absolute slaves, and it is one of the strangest facts in history that they remained so, in a nominally free country, until the latter part of last century.*) The appearance of

social or religious. Taking "Tory" to signify—as it once did, and perhaps still does—a man who objects to any kind of innovation, it is plain that those ferocious moss-troopers, clinging to "the black art of their forefathers," living "without [Christian] marriage or baptism," refusing to recognize either the religion or the laws that eventually prevailed in Britain, were "Tories," pure and simple. This sense — that of *Orientalist* or, *Anti-Progressionist* — has only been borne by "Tory" for about two hundred years (as Mr. Skeat informs us, in his Etymological Dictionary). Before that time it was simply an equivalent of *mosser*, *moss-trooper*, *marsh-dweller*, *bog-trotter*, and *marauder*. It could not have been applied to a political party on account of any of these meanings: and the conventional reason given, namely, that it was because the *tories* of Ireland were "in arms for the royal cause" during the Civil War is not wholly satisfactory. But it might easily have been applied contemptuously—by their opponents—"to those who sought to maintain the extreme prerogatives of the Crown," when the tenacious Toryism of the marauding *tories* was a well-known, every-day fact.

* "Curious as the fact may seem (says Hugh Miller, speaking of his experiences of the year 1824), all the older men of that village, though situated little more than four miles from Edinburgh, had been born slaves. Nay, eighteen years later .... there was a collier still living that had never been twenty miles from the Scottish capital, who could state .... that both his father and grandfather had been slaves—that he himself had been born a slave—and that he had wrought for years in a pit in the neighbourhood of Musselburgh ere the colliers got their freedom. Father and grandfather .... were cotemporary with Chatham and Cowper, and Burke and Fox; and at a time when Granville Sharpe could have stepped forward and effectually protected the runaway negro

the descendants of those "vagabonds and sturdy beggars" of the sixteenth century is described by Hugh Miller, from the evidence of his own eyesight, not "sixty years since." "The collier women of this village—poor over-toiled creatures, who carried up all the coal from underground on their backs, by a long turnpike stair inserted in one of the shafts*—continued to bear more of the marks of serfdom still about them than even the men. How these poor women did labour, and how thoroughly, even at this time, were they characterized by the slave nature! . . . . . They were marked by a peculiar type of mouth, by which I learned to distinguish them from all the other females of the country. It was wide open, thick-lipped, projecting equally above and below, and exactly resembled that which we find in the prints given of savages in their lowest and most degraded state, in such narratives of our modern voyagers, as for instance, the 'Narrative of Captain Fitzroy's Second Voyage of the *Beagle*.' . . . . . It was accompanied by traits of almost infantile weakness. I have seen these collier women crying like children, when toiling under their load along the upper rounds of the wooden stair that traversed the shaft; and then returning, scarce a minute after, with the empty creel, singing with glee." This, then, was the mouth of the sixteenth century vagabond;—the identical mouth that heraldry has registered as the mouth of the British "Moor";—the "very wide mouth" and "thick lips" of the mulatto-hued Gitanoes of the Pyrenees;—the "blubber-lips" of the naked *ciuthach* of the Hebridean caves; and the very mouth that, by a happy chance, our circus clowns have preserved to us as that of the "fancied fools" of the past. And not only have these last preserved to us a semblance of the features,—a probably exact picture of the style of painting the face, of dressing the hair, and of wearing the clothes,—characterizing those former "fancied fools," once the *clowns* of the country; but they have also retained

---

who had taken refuge from the tyranny of his master in a British port, no man could have protected *them* from the Inveresk laird, their proprietor. . . . ." ('My Schools and Schoolmasters," Chapter XIV.)

* "It has been estimated by a man who knew them well—Mr. Robert Bald — that one of their ordinary day's work was equal to the carrying of a hundred-weight from the level o: the sea to the top of Ben Lomond (3,192 feet high]." (*Ibid.*)

for us an exact representation of their brain-power; which was almost *nil.* So that both the actual posterity of those "counterfeit Egyptians," and the guise in which one branch of their *professional* descendants appear before us to-day, agree in representing the painted "Moors" of the sixteenth century (or rather, one division of them, and that the lowest, in all probability), as alike hideous in aspect and feeble in intellect. Add to this, that one quality inseparable from the buffoon of other days is typified by the "jest obscene," referred to by Garth, as quoted by Dr. Johnson, and it will be seen that, had the civilized portion of the Scotch people, during the sixteenth century, accorded to such a race the full rights and liberties of "the lieges," they would have been something more than quixotic. Those vagabonds and "fancied fools" may, indeed, have had the excuse that their ways and their religion (such as it was) were their inheritance; but these ways and that religion were so foul and degraded that toleration would have been pushed to the extreme of foolishness, had the dominant power acted otherwise than it did. Therefore, all those acts against Egyptians, witches, sorners, and suchlike, were, in reality, so many manifestations of that world-old tendency, whose operation we call Evolution: the working of which is manifested at the present day every time a criminal is executed, or a lunatic sequestered.

It is somewhat premature, however, to moralize upon the rights and wrongs of the action taken by the civilized Scotch (using that word in its widest sense) two or three centuries ago, and previously, in dealing with the dregs of certain races that once existed in these islands. We have been trying to ascertain the chief characteristics of this vagabond refuse, and what we seem to have discovered is, that the nearest living representatives of that class are the people whom we know as gipsies: that if the modern gipsies are, as they often are, handsome in body and mind, it is because they have mingled with other and higher races, and have also imbibed higher ideas than those held by the purely "Egyptian" branch of their ancestry, who are everywhere seen to have been "black and hideous" outwardly; and inwardly anything but fair and lovely. We have also seen that the robber-tribes, whose nick-name has become affixed to the country and people of Scotland, were Egyptians by tradition, by the use of hieroglyphics, by complexion, and perhaps by other characteristics. This was seen both by regarding them as so many "black herds" of fourth century pirates, and by looking at them in separate clans of Black-Douglases, Scots, and other moss-troopers. In all these instances we discerned the lineaments and customs of the greatly-mixed people known as gipsies. But since the district selected for examination was limited to the southern portion of Scotland, it is necessary that we should glance at other parts of that country, to see if the same identification can be made elsewhere than in the south.

NOTE 1.—It is evident that the opinions just enunciated, regarding the Early Scots, or Scots Proper, are quite inconsistent with the belief that the Early Scots and the Gaels were one and the same people. Politically they may, at one period or another, have become one. Or, racially, they may have become blended into a mixed race that believed itself to be "Gaelic." This, indeed, is what has apparently happened. But, originally, they must have been wholly distinct. Because, if the Gaels were a Celtic people, they belonged to a race that was, "almost beyond question," fair-skinned, blue-eyed, and yellow-haired: whereas those marauding Scots have been handed down to us as composing the chief element in a "hideous swarm" of swarthy pirates: and this by a South-Briton of their own era. And the correctness of Gildas' description has been borne out in every instance cited in this chapter. That the Gaels Proper were white men is inferred from the translation given by Captain Burt, in 1726, of the word *Gaelic*,—"the language of the white men." And it is *in Gaelic* that the word *scuit*—believed to be a variation of Scot—bears the meaning of "a vagabond." Moreover, in "the language of the white men," "the conversation of the mob" (*gràisg-chomradh*) is synonymous with "black speech" (*dubh-chainnt*); and "a girl of the lowest order of peasantry" is "a black wench" (*dubh-chaile*).

Therefore, if North Britain contained nothing but Picts and Scots at the time of the Roman invasion, it is pretty certain that it contained no white men at that date: and the first "fair whites" that entered Scotland must have been the Batavian soldiers of the Roman army; or the Celts of Southern Britain; or the Norsemen, or "Gentiles of pure colour." If, on the other hand, Mr. Grant Allen's supposition that a body of Celtic, or early Belgian invaders had crossed into Britain "before the dawn of history," and (though numerically few) had established themselves in that island as a ruling military caste,—if this supposition be held to extend to North Britain also,—then it is probable that, while the majority of the North British were certainly painted *Mauri*, yet the aristocracy of that territory, like the aristocracy of the south, was composed of white men. Again, if this numerically weak invading caste of white men had established themselves in North Britain at a period very much earlier than Cæsar's arrival, it is likely that, by that latter date, they had lost the purity of their blood to a very great extent, by commingling with the subordinate races. Some hint of this is perceptible in the mention (in Gaelic records) of a race called "the *fair Gael;*" and also in the sub-division of the Caledonii, or Caledones, into Caledones Proper and Deu-Caledones, or Dii-Caledonii ;—the latter division being possibly Dubh, or Black Caledonians. Indeed, the word that has been latinized into Caledones may itself be nothing else than *Gaidheldonn,* or "brown Gaels." If this were so, we should have pre-Roman Scotland occupied by black, brown, and fair Gaels, just as pre-Roman England is believed to have been occupied by black, brown, and fair South-British. Thus, the North-British of ante-Roman times, though almost entirely painted Moors, may still have been Gaels by nationality, and to some extent in speech : though the super-imposed white, or pure Gaelic element, may have almost disappeared out of sight ; swallowed up, ethnologically, by the swarthy Moorish population.

However that may be, of this we may be certain, that the "black herds of Scots and Picts," that ravaged the southern districts of early Britain, were very far removed, physically, as well as morally, from the civilized races of the south : if these latter were *actually,* "beyond question," fair-skinned, blue-eyed *Xanthochroi.*

NOTE 2.—In Nicholson's collection of Historical and Traditional Tales of the South of Scotland, another version is given of the "Blackamore" story. This atrocious *dubh-glass* is here styled "Black Murray," and is described as "swarthy and grim." "Tradition affirms (it is stated) that the outlaw above alluded to was a foreigner—a runaway from some vessel which had put in at the Manxman's Lake ; that he used to cross the Dee, in a small boat, to the opposite coast of Borgue, where he committed many depredations. . . . . Murray's, or, as it is more commonly called, the Blackamoor's Well, is situated in the Blackmorrow wood, lying to the south of Kircudbright, and distant only a few yards from the public road leading to the Manxman's Lake." The same account describes the *grogging* of the well, much as Mactaggart does. It also states that "Maclellan, younger of Bombie," was the hero of the incident : and, further, it speaks of Black Murray as the *Captain.* Here, then, is a mingling of the other versions. This one contradicts itself, to a certain extent. For the term of *Captain* is quite unsuitable to a solitary "Moor," though the common designation of a leader of black "gipsies." One or two of its particulars are interesting. It states that he was a foreigner ; that is to say, a *dubh gall;* and if the vessel he came in put in at the Manxman's Lake, it is probable that the foreign country was no farther off than the Isle of Man,—so long the country of the *dubh galls,* whose memory is still preserved in the name of its chief town. In all these versions young Maclellan is introduced, which seems to hint that, however they may vary in detail, these stories are all the confused remembrance of one particular event. On the other hand, such incidents as this one must have been of every-day occurrence, during the indefinite period preceding the time when the people of Galloway—of whatever lineage—quietly settled down into a civilized life. And, therefore, the swarthy marauder of the Blackamoor's Well district, and his gang (for he was *Captain*), may have been quite separate, in time, rank, and place, from the savage chief who murdered the Tutor of Bombie.

CHAPTER XIV.

THE Scots of ancient Scotia (now Ireland) having spread themselves over the greater part of that province of our country which has become known by their name; and the earlier *Mauri* of Scotland having been seated in that territory for a longer period than their swarthy comrades of the south-west; and a later flood of *nigræ gentes, dubh galls*, or "black foreigners," having invaded, and ruled over, a large portion of Northern and Western Scotland; it is clear that the inhabitants of various districts of North Britain ought to show their connection with the still-existent *tory* clans of our country, generally,—whom we conventionally style "Gipsies."

These, as we have seen, were, till quite recently, *Picts*. And, to some extent, they are still Moors, like their forefathers. Therefore we need not—and indeed cannot—distinguish between an Early Scot and an Early Pict, since, although "somewhat different in manners," they resembled each other closely enough in complexion and temperament to be equally the ancestors of certain divisions of the modern gipsy race. (As equally, also, they may be regarded as ancestors of certain among the civilized *Melanochroi* of the British islands; but these, having long ago given up their distinctive habits, do not now differ from any other portion of the civilized population, and are therefore out of court.) The famous league of the Black-Douglases, for example, may either be regarded as Wild *Scots* of Galloway, or as Galloway *Picts*. So, also, those untamable Græmes who were expelled the country may have belonged to either of the same two divisions. Or, in these and other instances, where the first record of a black race cannot be traced beyond the date of the Danish invasion, that race may have sprung from

Black-Danish or other kindred stock. The tenth-century Kenneth, king of Alban, who was known as Dubh, Niger, or The Black, seems, however, to have been a Scot;—and accordingly his swarthy complexion was quite in keeping with his supposed descent. From him, it may be assumed, those Maormors of Fife who came to bear the name of Mac Duff are also descended. They, at any rate, do not appear in history until shortly after the death of Dubh: and as there does not seem to have been any other Dubh or Black—distinguished by that epithet—at that time; and as the Macduffs come on to the stage as men of high rank, it is reasonable to assume that the "Black," whose "sons" they were, was the celebrated Kenneth, or Niger, of the tenth century. "Sibbald, in his History of Fife, says, 'that as Niger and Rufus were names of families amongst the Romans, from the colour and complexion of men, so it seems Duff was, from the swarthy and black colour of those of the tribe,' or clan of Macduff."* Thus, in this swarthy tribe, we may detect the originals of these Fifeshire gipsies, whose ancestral habits of plundering and morris-dancing, as well as the equally ancient practice of polygamy, are all particularized by Mr. Simson. (The Fifeshire *gipsies*, of course, represent the "Irreconcilables" of the race,—who only partially united their blood with that of the whites, and who were so averse to the newer faith and more sober habits that prevailed in late times, that they are not, even yet, properly within the pale of civilization. As already insisted upon, such *tories* have only been "conservative" of their ancestral habits—in a *limited* degree. The higher qualities of the race, or races, they represent, have long ago become the property of the heterogeneous modern British nation, which has received some of its most powerful impulses from this origin.) Of those veritable Macduffs—the sons of *the Black*—we see a specimen so recently as the reign of Queen Mary, in the person of "blak Mr. John Spens, wha was principal deviser of the murder"† of Darnley; and whose family point to the lion rampant in their arms as proving their descent from the semi-royal Mac Dubh. Like the Black-Douglases and other Scoto-Pictish

---

* Anderson's "Scottish Nation," Vol. II. p. 71.
† Anderson's "Scottish Nation," Vol. I. p. 450.

tribes, those Macduffs who desired to retain the political power of their ancestors, gradually identified themselves with the winning races (Normans and others), until, as in similar cases, the nominal heads of such families are, at the darkest, *Melanochroi*, and often *Xanthochroi;* their claim to Pictish blood being no stronger than that of certain Virginian families to the blood of Pocahontas, whose descendants they certainly are. Perhaps this "blak Mr. John Spens" may be taken as one of the latest examples of the genuine Moor, or Pict, who still retained a great deal of his ancestral rank. By last century, the aristocratic descent of the purest-blooded "sons of the Black," still remaining in the province over which their great ancestor ruled, is displayed in the attitude held by the "Lochgellie band" of "gipsies," who looked upon such a chief as George Drummond (himself a chief of importance among his own people) as "quite inferior" to themselves, and nothing better than a "beggar Tinkler."

Of those Macduffs that became gradually less and less "Moorish" in blood and habits, we need not speak here. It is questionable how far Shaw Macduff, second son of a twelfth-century Thane of Fife, was a Moor in blood. At any rate, he comes on to the stage of history as an *aide de camp* of King Malcolm, in his wars against the rebellious Moors of the district of Moravia, or Moray. This does not argue that those Moors were *not* his distant kinsmen, for history shows us a thousand instances of tribes and nations of dissimilar type, uniting for political reasons against an enemy composed of equally heterogeneous ingredients. But it is likely that this Shaw, or Seach, was to some extent a Moor ; though, like "the good Sir James" Douglas, a Moor that was on the side of modern civilization, and the spread of Christian ideas. Whatever his own exact lineage, his wife was apparently a Norman, being a "daughter of Hugh of Montgomery, one of his brother captains in the expedition against the Moraymen." To what extent the chiefs and aristocracy of North-Eastern Scotland were, by this time, Norman, it is difficult and even impossible to decide. But, at any rate, from this Shaw Macduff and his wife Giles of Montgomery, descends one of the most important sections of the previously-existing confederacy of Clan Chattan. For this Macduff and his posterity came to bear the surname of Mackintosh, which, it is believed, signifies *Mac-an-Toiseach*, the son of the chief, or leader: (one of that large class of names latterly associated with Ireland and certain parts of Scotland, but which may have originated among Dutchmen as likely as among any other of the many races to whom the prefix *Mac, Mag*, or *Maga* belongs.) Eventually, in the person of Angus, his sixth successor, the actual Captainship of this powerful tribe became vested in the Mackintosh line; this Angus having married, in the year 1291, Eva, the only child of Dougal Dall, the last chief of the ancient Clan Chattan.*

The lineage and probable origin of the ante-Mackintosh Captains of Clan Chattan has been a source of much discussion; and many conflicting theories have been broached on this subject. The name of its last chief, Dubhgal (*Dall*, or "Blind"), would lead one to believe that, by the thirteenth century, and perhaps long before, it had contained a certain amount of the blood of the piratical Black Danes;—although the name of Dougal had probably become "fossilized" some time previous to its possession by the father-in-law of Angus Mackintosh. Whatever the origin of the Clan Cattan, or Chattan (for the *ch* receives a guttural pronunciation), it is indubitably ancient; and tribes bearing the mountain-cat for crest are visible a long way back, and in various parts of the British Islands. We saw such a tribe included under the "Sons to the King of Rualay," of whom a very old Gaelic poem (given in *The Dean of Lismore's Book*) states that one battalion was "cat-headed." And that the same bearing was known in Wales is evident from the allusion that Hotspur makes in his petulant tirade against Glendower,†—and no doubt the correctness of the allusion is borne out by actual

---

* "The Mackintoshes and Clan Chattan," Alexander Mackintosh Shaw, 1880.
† In the First Part of *King Henry IV.*:

>   . . .   sometime he angers me
> With telling me of the moldwarp and the ant,
> Of the dreamer Merlin and his prophecies,
> And of a dragon and a finless fish,
> A clip-wing'd griffin and a moulten raven,
> A couching lion and a ramping cat,
> And such a deal of skimble-skamble stuff
> As puts me from my faith.

facts. The Clan Cattan was therefore a very early intra-British race; whether it ought to be regarded as originally Black-Danish, or Early-Scottish, or Pictish. The last designation, in its widest sense, is too wide to lead us to any conclusion; but in its restricted sense it signifies the Moorish inhabitants of Scotland at the time of the Roman invasion, and subsequently. Such " Picts," the early Cattanachs, or members of Clan Chattan, were popularly believed to be, some centuries ago. The ballad of *Hardyknute*, as it is given in Allan Ramsay's *Ever Green* (" a collection of Scots Poems, wrote by the Ingenious before 1600"), contains the following lines—

> "Syne he has gane far hynd attowre,
> Lord *Chattans* Land sae wyde,
> That Lord a worthy Wicht was ay,
> Quhen Faes his Courage seyd [tried]:
> Of *Pictish* Race by Mothers Syde,
> Quhen *Picts* ruld *Caledon*,
> Lord *Chattan* claimd the princely Maid
> Quhen he saift *Pictish* Crown."

Who this particular Captain of the Clan Cattan was, the ballad does not make sure. If this Hardyknute was the Danish king (and the lines

> "Then reid, reid grow his *dark-brown* Cheiks,
> Sae did his *dark-brown* Brow ——"

argue a mixture of some such dark blood as that of the Danes),—then the " Lord Chattan " of the ballad was a chief of the eleventh century. He cannot, indeed, have belonged to a later period, for then there was no " Pictish crown " to save. So that, whether "the princely Maid" referred to was merely an heiress of the Cattan line, or, higher than that, the daughter of the reigning Pictish house, it is evident that, many generations before the chiefship of Blind Dougal, the blood of the Cattan chiefs was only semi-Pictish. But that, *originally*, the Cattan tribe was purely Pictish, is, I think, indicated by the etymology of the name: which, however, is a point for after consideration.

Although the lands which King Malcolm granted to the first Mackintosh were in " the north-east corner of Inverness-shire;" and although his descendant, Angus, who married the heiress of Clan Chattan, acquired (by this marriage) the sovereignty of the lands in Lochaber which formed the home of his adopted tribe, yet this Angus was as much a Hebridean in blood as a Norman. For his mother was the daughter of "Angus Mor of Isla";* and his maternal uncle married a daughter of Mac Dubhgal of Lorn,—the head of a very powerful section of the race of "black strangers." And his father had apparently been the associate of other island tribes; since it is stated that his death was the outcome of a quarrel arising during a game of draughts, chess or "tables" —with one of the Islanders.† Therefore, this descendant of "Kenneth *vel* Dubh," of "the three black divisions," had inherited the blood of Hebridean or Danish "Moors;" as well as that of the mainland Picts, although both these streams were apparently neutralised by currents of whiter blood. It is to the Hebridean section, however, that we ought to turn, if we wish to ascertain whether, as on the mainland in some remote districts, the un-modernized ways of the people resemble those of our modern "gipsies." Because, from its isolated position, this archipelago ought to have been one of the latest territories to conform to modern ways and fashions.

The inhabitants, generally, of the Hebrides are described by Dr. Skene as composed of ingredients closely akin to those that made up the mixed race of Gallowaymen, or *Gallgaidhel*—that is, they were a compound of Gaels and Galls. "The wars between the Gaidhel and the Gaill" have been many and of long duration, and they have been closely studied by one eminent scholar in particular. At whatsoever date they began, the Hebridean archipelago appears to have been known as Inchegall, Innse-Gaill, or the "Islands of the Foreigners," from an early time. These islands are regarded as the immemorial home of the Picts, and it is probably for this reason that the Gaelic term for an islander, *innseanach*, is also a synonym for "an Indian." Otherwise, the natives of this archipelago are styled Deucaledones, and the ocean all around them, "the Deucaledonian Sea." A later race of Galls, or Foreigners, than the Picts, however, was that of the

---

* Mr. Shaw's "History of the Mackintoshes."
† "History of the Mackintoshes," Vol. I. p. 31. For references to the game of "tables," see Note appended to this chapter.

Northmen, or Finn Galls, who were "Gentiles of pure colour," or white men. With them, in point of time, came the opposing type of Galls, known to the Gaels as "black heathen," and to history as Danes. These, then, with Picts, Gaels, and subsequent Normans and others, make up a great jumble of races within the Hebridean area. But we can at least ascertain something about certain sections of those islanders. And, of course, in searching for gipsy-like people, our attention must be chiefly directed to those of black complexion. The traditionary inhabitants of some of these islands, it will be remembered, are actually known as gipsies; for they are styled *ciuthachs* and *ciofachs* (described as "naked wild men living in caves," and with plaited locks), and *ciofach*, or *giobag* —for the transition is one of the easiest possible, in Gaelic —is rendered "a gipsy" by the dictionaries. Let us look, then, at the gipsy-like portions of the Hebridean people, whether these are of Black-Danish or of Scoto-Pictish origin.

In a previous chapter the physical characteristics of some of these islanders have already been glanced at. It was seen that Martin, writing more than a century ago, stated that the people of the island of Skye were "for the most part black;" those of Jura were "generally black of complexion;" and the Arran islanders were "generally brown, and some of a black complexion." At least *one* native of the Isle of Raasay was "black by nature" as well as by name; and the clan of McRaa, though not at the time of Boswell's visit inhabiting the island which had taken their name, contained among its members some who were "as black and wild in their appearance as any American savages whatever." Of the islesmen that rowed the doctor and himself among the islands, Boswell (it was also noticed) remarked that they "seemed so like wild Indians, that a very little imagination was necessary to give one an impression of being upon an American river." One of them he particularized as "a robust, black-haired fellow, half-naked, and bareheaded, something between a wild Indian and an English tar."*

* The appearance of an "English tar" of last century was, in many ways, very different from that of a modern man-of-war's man. It is probable that his body was more completely tattooed than nowadays: it is certain that he wore a long pigtail of natural hair, of which (if the author of "Poor Jack" is to be credited) he was as proud as a nineteenth-century Chinaman: it is also certain

It was also noticed that, half a century back, the people of Harris were thus described: —"In general the natives are of small stature. . . . . [Their] cheek-bones are rather prominent, and the nose is invariably short, the space between it and the chin being disproportionately long. The complexion is of all tints. Many individuals are as dark as mulattoes. . . . ." While a later writer still, Mr. J. F. Campbell, has spoken of the "short, dark natives of Barra;" and has described a girl whom he saw among them (but not of them) in these terms:—" Her hair was as black as night, and her clear dark eyes glittered through the peat smoke. Her complexion was dark, and her features so unlike those who sat about her, that I asked if she were a native of the island, and learned that she was a Highland girl." Her face, generally, reminded the observer "of the Nineveh sculptures, and of faces seen in St. Sebastian." In all these cases, we can find every reason for understanding why the Tales of the West Highlands should abound with encounters (friendly and inimical) with black people.

In such a rough and general survey as this, taking in the descendants of so many different races, there must necessarily arise several apparent inconsistencies. At one point, the black races are seen to be of short stature (confirming the opinion of Professor Huxley); at another—as in Harris, they are taller than the whites. It has been maintained, or insinuated, that the reason why "black" is a synomym for everything atrocious, is because the black races of Scotland—and elsewhere— were fierce, cruel, and lustful. And that in the

that he stripped himself to the waist when he went into action. If—as is possible —there were still sailors in Boswell's time who adhered to the naval costume that preceded the loose, flapping knee-breeches of the eighteenth century, then such old-fashioned seamen wore no head-gear whatever : their dress consisted of a shirt, falling down to the knee as a kilt, and above this shirt was worn a waistcoat, striped horizontally (with, I believe, blue and white stripes). This comprised the whole body-clothing of an ordinary seaman, as portrayed by Benjamin West in his picture of Penn's "Treaty with the Indians"—an event of the closing quarter of the seventeenth century. On shore, no doubt, shoes and stockings were worn; but on board ship, it is pretty certain that a common sailor went about his work bare-legged and bare-footed. The appearance of such men—especially when of swarthy hue—must have very closely resembled that of a crew of Malays. And this black-haired, half naked, bareheaded descendant of the black prince of Man may have been "something between a wild Indian and an English tar," without being very different from either.

Hebrides—as elsewhere—certain races were absolute savages there can be no doubt. But, on the other hand, some of the writers quoted (such as the one who describes the Harris "mulattoes") ascribe to the dark-hued natives the possession of intellectual and moral attributes of the highest kind: attributes which rendered the Harrisian "mulattoes" the superiors of the Harrisian whites—in the opinion of their visitor. And the same testimony is afforded by the seventeenth-century writer (formerly quoted) who pictured to us the male inhabitants of Mull in the year 1688, as wearing a sporran, or purse, very similar to that worn by some Hottentot races; and for the same purpose. Yet, in spite of their scanty dress, he does not fail to state most emphatically that the men of this race were brave and handsome, and the women characterized by "a natural beauty and a graceful modesty." But such inconsistencies must be overlooked in a hasty sketch, that takes in all races and all periods. A detailed examination of the various types (if this be yet possible) would explain away such superficial contradictions to a certainty. It is enough, at present, to assume that all varieties of humanity were at one time low and brutal; and that a race, black or white, that in one century was essentially savage, can be accurately described as refined and gentle in a later century, if, in the interval, it has been subjected to such an ennobling influence as Christianity.

Those *ciuthachs*, or gipsies of the Hebrides, then, were actual black savages—although, like all "savages," they possessed a civilization and a polity of their own. They bear different race-names, and historians have told us much about them and their fierce nature: how they plundered and ravaged the early homes of learning and religion in Ireland, in the Isles, and throughout the larger of the main British Islands. Chiefly, they are remembered as Danes, or "black heathen." One of these was previously cited in the person of a fifteenth-century pirate, known as Allan Mac Ruari; figured in an ancient Gaelic poem as "the one demon of the Gael," "Inche Gall's great curse," "the bald-head, heavy worthless boar" (an allusion, it was supposed, to his boar-crested helmet), the "fierce ravager of Church and Cross," who "ravaged I[ona] and Relig Oran," and several other such titles. From what period those swarthy, piratical races began to make their savage depredations it is impossible to say. But they did not cease with "bald-headed Allan" and his following of "devils." A century after his death this Dyak element still existed. Buchanan, in his description of the Hebrides, informs us that the island of "Uist has numerous caves covered with heath, the lurking places of robbers;" and that "opposite Loch Broom is situate the island Eu [? *Eilean Dhubh*, the Island of the Blacks], almost wholly covered with wood, and of service only to the robbers, who lurk there to surprise travellers;" while "more to the north lies Gruinort, also darkened with wood, and infested with robbers." And Pennant, writing at Dunvegan last century, and referring to a period antecedent to his own, tells us that, "Each chieftain [of the civilized races] had his armour-bearer, who preceded his master in time of war, and, by my author's account, in time of peace; for they went armed even to church, in the manner the North Americans do at present in the frontier settlement, and for the same reason, the dread of savages."*

But those savages were only the "Irreconcilables" of their race. As on the Borders we saw that, although it took three generations to do it, and although many lives were sacrificed in the struggle, the once savage moss-troopers became—to a great extent—peaceful, law-abiding members of the commonwealth; so, in the Hebrides, a glance at the seventeenth-century measures adopted by the governing

---

* This state of things is shewn by certain statutes and ordinances given in the *Collectanea de Rebus Albanicis*, pp. 111, 115, 120, and 121, in which the Islanders are styled "wild savageis voide of Godis feare and our [the King's] obedience," "rude barbarous and uncivill people," &c., &c. It is also there stated that the "Ylanders comes in troupes and compameis out of the Yles where they dwell to the Yles and Loches where the fishes ar tane and there violentlie spoyles his Majesteis subjects of their fisches and sometimes of their victualls and other furniture, and persewes thame of their lyffes." The distinction here between "the lieges" and certain island tribes is as marked as that between the contemporary mosstroopers of the Borders and the King's subjects. Those sea-pirates of Danish and Norse descent are also remembered in the Orkneys and Shetland by living people, as will be shortly pointed out. It is a difficult thing to fix a point at which Scotland can be said to have been wholly under the sway of one central government. The above extracts show that it was not in the seventeenth century.

powers reveals to us that the process of civilization, and the preaching of Christianity (for the second time) was steadily going on. Therefore, since the converted Islesmen were of the same blood as the marauding pirates, these Islesmen ought to have retained something of their former manners, even after they had begun to adopt those that now prevailed throughout the greater part of Britain.

Let us first glance at some of their habitations. The simplest of all these was of wholly inartificial character, and it is still in use. We talk of "cave-dwellers" as though they are separated from us by a great stretch of time: (the cave-dwellers of Europe, that is to say). But it is a simple fact that, even at this day, there are many of our fellow-countrymen who are cave-dwellers. This has been pointed out more than once by Dr. Arthur Mitchell; and quite recently, in a paper on the "Antiquities of the Islands of Colonsay and Oransay."* Nowadays, the caves in these islands do not appear to be inhabited from year's end to year's end; but only for some months at a time.† But in Martin's time the caves of Jura were apparently regularly inhabited. The

---

* Published in the "Proceedings of the Society of Antiquaries of Scotland," 1880-81, pp. 140, 141.

† Or, perhaps, even less than that. The authority just quoted has, in another place, fully described one cave (in the neighbourhood of Wick) which is regularly inhabited. But the people whose home it is are of the lowest description, being apparently gipsified vagrants, though not of actual "gipsy" blood. On the other hand, those who still occasionally use the caves of the western islands are intelligent and respectable people—fishermen and others. Dr. Mitchell himself has repeatedly pointed out the error of judging a people by their dwellings; and if, in these pages, it is necessary to emphasize the poverty of the homes of certain races, and their utterly primitive formation, it is by no means intended that the dwellers themselves are *thereby* proved to be of a low type. An able archæologist has said on this subject: "In the Highlands I have myself seen men living in hovels, dark and inexpressibly low in material civilization, whilst the inmates had really as much good feeling and general wisdom in their speech as many men who gave much better dwellings to their cows, and incomparably better to their horses. . . . . The dwelling does not show the civilization of the occupant correctly, neither does the food. . . . . We have dwellings from London to Caithness and Kerry in abundance as uncomfortable as those of many savages, but out of some of the worst some of our best minds have emerged." ("Loch Etive and the Sons of Uisnach," p. 234.) This emphatic truth cannot be asserted too strongly at a time when comfortable and rich surroundings are so often regarded as evidences of the civilization of their owner, who may easily be of the lowest possible type himself.

summer habitations of these Jura islanders are particularly described by Pennant, and they closely resemble the dwellings of the natives of Lochaber, as pictured by that traveller. Lochaber, which lies some distance to the north-east of Jura (though within easy reach of it by water), was stated to be the country of the "Moorish," or semi-Pictish, tribe of the Cattanachs, or Clan Chattan. Of their dwellings, at the time of his first visit to the Highlands, Pennant says: "The houses of the peasants in Lochaber are the most wretched that can be imagined; framed of upright poles, which are wattled; the roof is formed of boughs like a wigwam, and the whole is covered with sods." In his second tour he describes the summer dwellings of the Jura islanders in similar terms: "These formed a grotesque groupe; some were oblong, many conic, and so low that entrance is forbidden without creeping through the little opening, which has no other door than a faggot of birch twigs placed there occasionally. They are constructed of branches of trees, covered with sods; the furniture a bed of heath, placed on a bank of sod; two blankets and a rug; some dairy vessels, and above, certain pendant shelves, made of basket-work, to hold the cheese, the produce of the summer." The annexed woodcut is copied from the illustrations in Pennant's travels.

Wigwams of the natives of the Island of Jura, in the year 1772. (Copied from "Pennant's Second Tour.")

Now, this is distinctly an encampment of gipsies, or of Lapps, or Northern Asiatics, or North Americans. It is the turf-covered *gamme*, or *cota** of the Lapps, and its architecture is visibly the same as that of a Red Indian camp (although I am not aware that the *material*, turf, is employed by any American tribe). As to its being *gipsy* there is as little doubt. " In cold countries they find shelter in caves, or build huts sunk in the earth, and cover them with sods laid on poles."† And Leyden says of the Yetholm gipsies:

> " On Yeta's banks the vagrant gypsies place
> Their turf-built cots—a sun-burnt swarthy race ; "

while the same description is given of the dwellings of the Border *Scots* during the early part of the fifteenth century.

"When Æneas Sylvius, afterwards Pius II., made an adventurous visit into Scotland, ... he found that most of the houses [on the Scottish borders] were not even huts, as they were generally a small breast-work composed of mud, or such materials as were at hand, and raised to a sufficient height by three or four poles meeting a-top, and covered with straw or turf; while those of the villages were little better, and had no door but a cow's hide suspended at the entrance."‡ In short, these turf-built wigwams are the dwellings of the Scoto-Picts, or Egyptian Moors, whether we look at these people in their latest individual form, or as they appeared in the Hebrides last century, or at an earlier date than that—when they formed an important political entity in the British Islands (which their civilized and hybrid descendants still do). And their dwellings form one of the very numerous links that unite the painted "Moors" of Scotland with certain kindred races in Europe, Asia, and America.

The turf-built cots, or wigwams, which Æneas Silvius

---

* Compare English *cot*, *cote*, and *cottage:* also Gaelic *cot*, *cota*, a cottage ; *cota*, a coat, a petticoat. The radical meaning of this word would seem to be "something that covers or encloses." In its Gaelic sense of a covering for the body, it is found among the " Moors " of North America, as, for example, in the matche-*cota* or principal female garment (referred to by Longfellow in a note to " Hiawatha "), which word seems as if it had once been used with petti-coat— " the principal garment " and " the under garment." (There are other so-called " Indian " words, which are still to be found in English dictionaries, and where the resemblance increases to absolute identity.)

† "Encyclopædia Britannica," 8th edition, article "Gypsy."

‡ "The Comprehensive History of England," Vol. 1. p. 705.

pictures as the common habitation of the Border Scots, Moors, or Picts,—during the early part of the fifteenth century (at that period still one of the most powerful sections of the population of Scotland: the chief of those *dubh-glasses* even threatening the supremacy of the Norman faction; himself a man of the greatest power, and living in a stone-built castle)—those wigwams of the Scottish Borders were to be seen quite recently "on Yeta's banks;" and others of the same description formed the summer habitations of the Jura islanders in the year 1772. But this sod-covered wigwam can hardly be said to be the common form of "gipsy" dwelling, at the present day. Indeed, it seems to have been given up by the Yetholm "gipsies" since Leyden wrote. At any rate, the usual dwelling of the modern gipsy is the canvas tent, of oval or oblong shape. This structure is clearly that of the most nomadic of "gipsies," and liable to be taken down at any moment. And, just as the sod-covered wigwam is a survival of the common habitation of historical fifteenth century *Scots*, so is this tent nothing more than a relic of the movable dwellings of the poorer *Scots*. "Patten gives a curious description of that [mode of encampment] which he saw after the battle of Pinkey, in 1547:—'Here now, to say somewhat of the manner of their camp. As they had no pavilions, or round houses, of any commendable compass, so wear there few other tentes with posts, as the used manner of making is; and of these few also, none of above twenty foot length, but most far under ..... These white ridges, as I call them, that, as we stood on Fauxsyde Bray, did make so great muster toward us, which I did take then to be a number of tentes, when we came, we found it a linen drapery, of the coarser cambryk in dede, for it was all of canvas sheets, and wear the tenticles, or rather cabyns and couches of their soldiers; the which (*much after the common building of their country beside*) had they framed of four sticks, about an ell long a piece, whearof two fastened together at one end aloft, and the two endes beneath stuck in the ground, an ell asunder, standing in fashion like the bowes of a sowes yoke; over two such bowes (one, as it were, at their head, the other at their feet) they stretched a sheet down on both sides, whereby their cabin became roofed like a ridge, but skant shut at both ends, and not very close beneath on the sides, unless their sticks were the shorter, or their wives the more liberal to lend them larger napery; howbeit, when they had lined them, and stuff'd them so thick with straw, with the weather as it was not very cold, when they wear ones couched, they were as warm as they had been wrapt in horses dung.'" (Patten's *Account of Somerset's Expedition;* quoted in the Appendix to *Marmion,* Note 3 F.) In this description we see plainly the ordinary tent of the modern nomadic "gipsy:" which style of dwelling was once—so far as the Egyptian-Scots are concerned—"the common building of their country."

It is not likely that British "gipsies," in recent times, have made use of the hides of animals as coverings for their tents, or wigwams, for the obvious reason that, in a civilized country, these could not well be obtained except by purchase. Sir Thomas Dick Lauder, however, in his story of *Glengarry's Revenge,* seems to indicate the use of skin-covered tents, when he speaks of "the little group of black bothies, that at such times formed his [the chief's] temporary place of encampment." A Highland *bothy* or *buth*—the same as *booth, boutique, buddika,* and other forms—is, radically, *a dwelling* (more strictly, "a place to be in," according to Mr. Skeat); and in this instance it is of a temporary kind. In a hunting expedition, such as that alluded to, the readiest-made *buth* would be one of skins stretched over a framework of branches; and probably this was the kind in use in such instances.

The people whom we are accustomed to regard as "gipsies" are not everywhere identical in dress and customs. Nor is this to be wondered at, since "gipsies" are merely the residuum of various epochs and various nationalities. With regard to the Early Scoto-Egyptians, or Scoto-Picts, dress, for example, seems to have been regarded as a superfluity. This has already been noticed. Captain Burt, in those "Letters" which Scott has frequently quoted, says (in an appendix to Letter XXII.): "In Ireland [ancient Scotia], a few centuries ago, the *lower class* seldom encumbered themselves with dress of any kind within doors; and there is every reason to suppose that this was also the case among their brethren in Scotland." The extracts made in a previous chapter, concerning the "naked rebels" of Elizabeth's and earlier reigns, quite corroborated this. Spenser also, "in describing a class of Irishmen called Carrows, whose sole occupation was gambling,* tells us, 'They wander up and down, living upon cards and dice; the which, though they have little or nothing of their own, yet they will play for much money, which, if they win, they waste most lightly, and if they lose they pay as slenderly.' Campion is more particular when he informs us of these Carrows—'They play away mantle and all, to the bare skin, and then truss themselves in straw or in leaves.'" The same interesting history† also states: "The style of living among these native Irish chiefs [a dreadfully loose designation, since the race of these "Irishmen" is not indicated by it] was characteristic of a people whose barbarism had only been indurated and confirmed by conquest . . . . . [The attendants of the "Great O'Neil," Earl of Tyrone] 'for the most part were beardless boys without shirts, who, in the frost, wade as familiarly through rivers as water spaniels' . . . . . As a match to the home life of O'Neil was that of O'Kane, a great chieftain of Ulster, according to the description of a Bohemian nobleman, given by Fynes Moryson, who, on visiting him, tells us 'he was met at the door with sixteen women, all naked, except their loose mantles, whereof eight or ten were very fair, and two seemed very nymphs; with which strange sight his (the nobleman's) eyes being dazzled, they led him into the house, and there sitting down by the fire, with crossed legs like tailors, and so low as could not but offend chaste eyes, desired him to sit down with them. Soon after, O'Kane, the lord of the country, came in, all naked, excepting a loose mantle and shoes, which he put off as soon as he came in, and entertaining the baron after his best manner in the Latin tongue, desired him to put off his apparel, which he thought to be a burden to him, and to sit naked by the fire with this

---

* The passion for gambling is a pronounced Red-Indian feature, and is equally a characteristic of the heroes of the "West Highland Tales." The modern gipsies are notorious for thimble-rigging and kindred games of chance. "Thimble-rigging (says Mr. Simson, junior, p. 325, note), according to Sir J. Gardner Wilkinson, was practised in ancient Egypt."

† "The Comprehensive History of England," Vol. II. pp. 282-3.

naked company.' It is surely unnecessary to add that the astounded Bohemian excused himself from complying."*

These and the former extracts all show that the Pictish contempt for clothing was held by certain tribes of Ancient Scotia during many centuries. And the extract just made is only one of many, asserting the same thing. Dr. Jamieson, in his remarks upon the word *Sorner* or *Sornar*, makes an additional quotation from Fynes Moryson, to the same effect as the one just given. Those Sorners, it will be remembered, were particularly named—along with "sturdy beggars," "fancied fools," and others—in the acts of the Stewart kings, which statutes were enacted with the express aim of putting down "sorning," and similar customs, that were totally opposed to modern civilization, though quite lawful in the society to which they belonged. Dr. Jamieson, like the Scotch historian of the "gipsies," clearly identifies *Sorners* with Tinklers, or Cairds, Bards, "sturdy beggars," "spae-wives" (fortune-tellers), and "horse-coupers;"† and it will be seen, from an examination of their characteristics, that Sorners were undoubtedly Egyptians, or Scots. Mr. Simson correctly defines Sorners as "forcible obtruders," and Dr. Jamieson derives the word from *Sorehon* or *Sorohen*, a tribute exacted by certain chiefs in Ireland from their dependants.

---

* The Bohemian's decision in this very perplexing dilemma was not so much a foregone conclusion as the above writer seems to think. At any rate, a very recent traveller in "the land of the midnight sun," when placed in similar circumstances, arrived at a conclusion quite the reverse of the Bohemian's. The puzzling question as to how far one ought to go in doing as Rome does, while in Rome, could hardly assume a more delicate phase than this.

† The above category, to be correct, ought to be made fuller (which, however, the present occasion does not demand). Mr. Leland, whose experience of gipsy life cannot be surpassed, says that "it is worth noting that among all these show-men and show-women, acrobats, exhibitors of giants, purse-droppers, ginger-bread-wheel gamblers, shilling knife-throwers, pitch-in-his-mouths, Punches, cheap Jacks, thimble-rigs, and patterers of every kind, there is always a leaven and a suspicion of gypsiness. If there be not descent, there is affinity by marriage, familiarity, knowledge of words and ways, sweethearting and trafficking, so that they know the children of the Rom as the house-world does not know them, and they in some sort belong together." (p. 140.) As to the "horse-coupers," Mr. Leland states that he once thought, with Mr. Borrow, that the word "jockey" was derived from the gipsy *chückni,* "a heavy-handled whip." Mr. Leland changed his mind subsequently, for the reason that "there were 'jockeys' in England before gypsies." But that is, of course, no objection to any one holding the opinions expressed in this book.

This *Sorohen* seems to be only another name for the custom which he describes as styled *Coshering* (or, perhaps, the former word denotes the tribute exacted, and the latter the manner of exacting it). "Besides the *Sorohen*, the Irish lords, at least in the time of Elizabeth, subjected their tenants to a pretty severe visitation, which they called *Coshering*. Fynes Moryson gives a strange account of their manners in a passage in which he mentions this custom.

"They sleepe," he says, "vnder the canopy of heauen, or in a poore house of clay, or in a cabbin made of the boughs of trees, and couered with turffe [a Hebridean wigwam, in short], for such are the dwellings of the very Lords among them. And in such places, they make a fier in the middest of the roume, and round about it they sleepe vpon the ground, without straw or other thing vnder them, lying all in a circle about the fier, with their feete towards it. And their bodies being naked, they couer their heads and vpper parts with their mantels, which they first make very wet, steeping them in water of purpose, for they finde that when their bodies haue once warmed the wet mantels, the smoake of them keepes their bodies in temperate heate all the night following. And this manner of lodging not onely the meere Irish Lords and their followers vse, but euen some of the English Irish Lords and their followers, when after the old but tyranicall and prohibited manner vulgarly called *Coshering*, they goe (as it were) on progresse, to liue vpon their tenants, til they have consumed al the victuals that the poore men haue or can get.' Itinerary, P. III. p. 164."

This, then, is *sorning* ; and it is plain that the custom was one that could not be endured in a properly-civilized society. It was once as common in Scotland as in Ireland, as the various statutes of the Jameses show. And, indeed, the descendants of the Sorners,—now as low in the social scale as they were once high—have not yet forgotten that era. They still tell their children "of the 'good old times'—the 'golden age' of the gipsies—when they could wander hither and thither, with little molestation, and live, in a measure, at free-quarters, wherever they went."*

The foregoing extracts have all endorsed Captain Burt's

* Simson's "History," p. 368, note.

statement, that "in Ireland, a few centuries ago, the *lower class* seldom encumbered themselves with dress of any kind within doors;" and they have also made it evident that the upper classes—at any rate, in some districts,—held equally broad views. It is astonishing how long such notions lingered on. A visitor to the territory and islands known as The Rosses of Donegal, in the north-west corner of Ireland, gives us a picture of the manners of the natives at the time of his visit—the years 1753 and 1754—very much like those sketches of Fynes Moryson. "Their houses were but mere huts, consisting chiefly of one room, with the fire in the middle of it: but what surprised Mr. N—— most, was their extraordinary mode of accommodation for the night's repose. All the family lay together in one bed; and, if any visitors came in the evening, they too slept with them; for they set no bounds to their hospitality. To provide lodging for the whole company, the youngest men were sent out for heath or bent bushes: which they spread across the floor, to a length sufficient for the number present, and in breadth about six feet: over this litter the mistress of the house laid part of a long plaid or blanket, on which the others, having stripped off their clothes, lay down as fast as they could; men and women together all naked: then the mistress having drawn the rest of the blanket over them, lay down last herself, naked also. This they call a thorough-bed, and Mr. N—— was perhaps the only person who had ever before worn a shirt in it. Yet this hospitable people, so friendly and generous to those they knew, appeared at first to strangers to be wild and fierce; but, after a little acquaintance, proved gentle and humane, especially to those they were in awe of; for, in all their simplicity, there was a strong mixture of cunning." Thus, about the time of Pennant's visit to the Hebrides, a section of a race akin to some Hebrideans, lived in wigwams such as those of the Islanders and other "Gipsies," in Britain or out of it; and possessed ideas of propriety quite different from those now in vogue, though identical with those possessed by their ancestors, and by the Lapps of to-day (as pictured by Mr. Du Chaillu); the ideas, in short, of all "gipsies," past and present.

After his statement as to the primitive ideas of some of

the people of Ireland, a few centuries ago, Captain Burt adds—"and there is every reason to suppose that this was also the case among their brethren in Scotland." The fact that their dwellings were one-roomed wigwams is, of itself, almost a sufficient proof of the correctness of this supposition. But it is also confirmed by the writer of the above last-century article: "In conversation with an elderly gentleman, who had above forty years ago made the tour of North Britain, when I communicated what I had learned concerning the Rosses, he assured me that my description of these islanders is an exact picture of what he had seen in the Scotch Highlands and the Orkney Islands."*

The description given of the dwellings of certain gipsies, who "find shelter in caves, or build huts sunk in the earth and cover them with sods laid on poles," is therefore a description of the dwellings of the Jura Islanders, in past times. So that the traditional definition of *ciuthachs*, as "naked wild men living in caves," is a very correct one. Those Jura Islanders were *ciuthachs*, *ciofachs*, *giobags*, or gipsies; they lived in caves; and there is good reason to suppose that at one period they, like their brethren in Ireland, went naked. That they, at one stage of their existence, or in certain particular instances, were "wild," is equally clear. *Uamh*, which in Gaelic means "a cave,"—is also (according to

---

* This account is taken from "The New Annual Register" for the year 1788, and it bears to be an extract from "Mr. Walker's Historical Essay on the Dress of the Ancient and Modern Irish." The remarks recently made, to the effect that the dwelling and the dress is a very indifferent gauge of the *potentialities* of the dweller, come in very appositely here. The same writer says that "these same islanders, so irreconcileable then to the modes of their civilized countrymen, in less than forty years became quite another kind of people, totally altered in their carriage and conduct, their habiliments and habitations, their occupations and manner of living." To quote again the author of "Loch Etive and the Sons of Uisnach": "According to Scott, many of the Highlanders of last century were savage, but a sudden peace brought an almost instant civilization. The talent for rising was there; where was it prepared?" The *standards* of civilization and propriety had altered, but the people were the same. Mr. Du Chaillu's Lapps, who went to Chicago, did not thereby become more virtuous and intelligent than their kinsmen in Northern Europe, although it is certain they would relinquish some of their own simple habits. The customs that so staggered "Mr. N——" in Donegal last century were terribly primitive; but they were the customs of a people that, in the main, are the most virtuous in the United Kingdom.

McAlpine) "a chief of savages," "a terrible fellow;" and, of course, is literally "a cave-dweller." And all history tells us that, whether under historical names, or more recently as "pirates" and "robbers," certain fierce and savage tribes harassed the peaceable inhabitants of the Hebrides up till a very recent date. When, and to what extent, the non-piratical Hebrideans were "peaceable" people, may be a matter of dispute. The terms "savage" and "barbarous" are applied most indiscriminately by such writers as those already referred to (the reference being the *Collectanea de Rebus Albanicis*): so lately as the year 1615, the Bishop of Argyle complains to King James that "the pairtis of your Majesteis Kingdome committit to my spirituall ouersicht" are "so barbarous that without sever animadversione thay can nocht be cohibite from thair wonted savage behaviour." Therefore, while it is unsafe to generalize from particular instances, there is much reason for believing that the peaceable natives of the Hebrides attained that condition of peace by a process very similar to that by which their kinsmen on the Borders became civilized. It is true that peaceful and savage tribes, of kindred stock, may be found living in close proximity to each other: (as, for example, the quiet, orderly Zuñi Indians of Arizona, and their neighbours, the intractable and marauding Apaches). It is also true that men are, to a great extent, hostile or friendly, in proportion to the amount of friendliness shown by those who come in contact with them. But still, making allowances for all these things, it seems very probable that the orderly Hebrideans who dwelt in caves and wigwams were the civilized descendants of the "naked *wild* men." That those wild men were the far-down descendants of a civilization as old as Egypt is beside the question. That they knew how to carve chessmen from the ivory of the walrus, and how to play the game when they had carved them, is a simple fact. And they had inherited a vast deal more than that. But it is a curious, and indisputable truth, that a high civilization and very savage habits may be found in unison; of which the cannibal feasts of the civilized races of Ancient Mexico offer an example. Therefore, it is no error of diction to say that those fierce, marauding pirates of the Hebrides—and elsewhere—were *savages:*

whatever remnants they may have retained of a remote civilization.*

To return from the uncertain region of theory to the firmer ground of fact, let us continue to search for any additional reasons for the conviction that the early historic nations of Ancient Scotia and Scotland were nothing else than nations of "gipsies." And, in the meantime, let us chiefly regard the Hebrideans.

As already remarked, "gipsies" are composed of so many various nations, arriving in these islands at various dates, that we cannot expect to find among them an unvarying sameness in dress, manners, and speech. (Nor, indeed, do we find this among their straggling representatives at the present day.) Those that we have looked at just now took after the earliest " Moors " of Scotland, in their disregard for clothing. But the Hebridean archipelago was tenanted by many races, and it is probable that scarcely two out of its many islands are identical in the race-mixture of their natives, or received those various races in the same proportion and the same order of time. We find, therefore, that the fashions of the people of Skye and the islands near it, as these fashions existed at a period anterior to Martin's visit, are not identical with those of such islands as Jura and Mull.

He describes the dress (almost out of vogue by his time) of these islanders in the following terms :—

> The first habit wore by persons of distinction in the islands was the *leni-croich*, from the Irish word *leni*, which signifies a shirt, and *croich*, saffron, because their shirt was dyed with that herb : the ordinary number of ells used to make this robe was twenty-four ; it was the upper garb, reaching below the knees, and was tied with a belt round the middle : but the islanders have laid it aside about a hundred years ago . . . . . .
> The shoes anciently wore were a piece of the hide of a deer, cow, or

---

* Besides, whether the knowledge of certain arts, sciences, and religions, which they brought with them to Britain, were of Egyptian, Persian, or Assyrian origin (or of all these), it is not necessary to assume that those Eastern adventurers belonged to the higher ranks of the country or countries, under whose laws they were bred. The Messrs. Simson's remarks, in the Editor's Preface and elsewhere, are well worthy of consideration in this connection, both with regard to the "mixed multitude" theory, and also the evidences of various customs and ceremonies.

horse, with the hair on, being tied behind and before with a point of leather . . . . . .

The ancient dress wore by the women, and which is yet wore by some of the vulgar, called *arisad*, is a white plad, having a few small stripes of black, blue, and red ; it reached from the neck to the heels, and was tied before on the breast with a buckle of silver or brass, according to the quality of the person. I have seen some of the former of an hundred marks value ; it was broad as an ordinary pewter plate, the whole curiously engraven with various animals, &c. There was a lesser buckle, which was wore in the middle of the larger, and above two ounces weight ; it had in the centre a large piece of chrystal, or some finer stone, and this was set all round with several finer stones of a lesser size.

The plad being plaited all round, was tied with a belt below the breast ; the belt was of leather, and several pieces of silver intermixed with the leather like a chain. The lower end of the belt has a piece of plate about eight inches long, and three in breadth, curiously engraven ; the end of which was adorned with fine stones, or pieces of red coral. They wore sleeves of scarlet cloth, closed at the end as men's vests, with gold lace round them, having plate buttons set with fine stones. The head dress was a fine kerchief of linen strait about the head, hanging down the back taper-wise ; a large lock of hair hangs down their cheeks above their breast, the lower end tied with a knot of ribbands.

To complete the picture, be it remembered that the descendants of these people were, at the date of Martin's visit, "for the most part black."

In his *Voyage to St. Kilda* he uses similar terms in portraying the appearance of the natives of that island, which shows that the ancient fashions were still retained there at the date of his visit. For the inhabitants of St. Kilda, then as now, were descended from people of Skye and others of the Hebrides.* It is noticeable, however, that the majority of the St. Kildians were " of a fair complexion," the others being somewhat vaguely described as " not fair." His picture of the dress of their women, though partly a repetition of that just quoted, is nevertheless worth extracting.

The women wear upon their heads a linen dress, strait before, and drawing to a small point behind below the shoulders, a foot and a half in length, and a lock of about sixty hairs hanging down each cheek, to their breasts, the lower end tied with a knot ; their plaid, which is

* It is most unfortunate, from an antiquarian and ethnological point of view, that the aborigines of St. Kilda became wholly extinct about two centuries ago.

the upper garment, is fastened upon their breasts with a large round buckle of brass in form of a circle; the buckles anciently worn by the stewards' wives were of silver, but the present steward's wife makes no use of either this dress or buckle. The women inhabiting this isle wear no shoes nor stockings in the summer time: their ordinary and only shoes are made of the necks of Solan geese, which they cut above the eyes, the crown of the head serves for the heel, the whole skin being cut close at the breast, which end being sowed, the foot enters into it as into a piece of narrow stocking; this shoe does not last above five days, and if the downy side be next the ground, then not above three or four; however, there are plenty of them, some thousands being catched, or, as they term it, stolen every March.

Now, what manner of people are these? Certainly not the conventional "Highlanders" of the modern artists. Here we have a swarthy race, whose men wear long tunics of saffron colour, and whose women are clothed in a most picturesque and "foreign" fashion. Round their tawny foreheads they wear "a fine kerchief of linen . . . . hanging down the back taper-wise," their long black hair hangs down on either breast in [plaited?] locks, "the lower end tied with a knot of ribbands," their flowing white garment, "having a few small stripes of black, blue, and red," falls "from the neck to the heels," and is gathered in front with a broad plate of silver or brass "curiously engraven with various animals, &c," and having in the middle of it a lesser buckle set round with precious stones.* Their sleeves are of scarlet cloth, embroidered with gold lace, and "having plate buttons set with fine stones." The white robe is belted in below the breast with a leather belt, having "several pieces of silver intermixed with the leather like a chain," and at its lower end there is "a piece of plate about eight inches long, and three in breadth, curiously engraven; the end of which is adorned with fine stones, or pieces of red coral."†

* Some of these brooches are now in the possession of the Scottish Antiquarian Society.

† The coral, like the people, was indigenous. In his description of the island of Lewis, Martin says—" The bays and coasts of this island afford great quantity of small coral, not exceeding six inches in length, and about the bigness of a goose's quill. This abounds most in Loch-sea-fort, and there is coraline likewise on this coast." As a complement to this statement, let me quote from Pennant's diary during his second tour (1772). "Am informed of a basking shark that had been harpooned some days before . . . . there have been instances of their being from thirty-six to forty-eight feet in length. This [caught on the Arran

Of the dress of *gipsies* (regarded as such) I have seen no picture at such an early date as this. But the remarks made upon this point, in the *Encyclopædia* article, indicate a fashion closely resembling that of Martin's Islanders. "Gipsies formerly had a distinctive costume, consisting of a turban-like headdress of many colours, together with a large cloak, worn after the fashion of a toga, over a long loose under-skirt ... The English gipsy woman may be known by her bright silk handkerchief, her curiously-plaited hair, her massy rings, her coral or bead necklace, and by the *monging-guno*, a tablecloth arranged bagwise over her back. ... On the other hand, the dress of the children upon the Continent is simple, not to say scanty." This last feature attracted the attention of Dr. Johnson, during his Hebridean tour, and it has already been particularly dwelt upon here. Burt (Letter XXII.) remarks the same thing: "The young children of the ordinary Islanders are miserable objects indeed .... I have often seen them come out from the huts early in a cold morning stark naked." His descriptions relate more closely to the mainland, but the race-mixtures of Northern and North-Western Scotland resemble those of the Isles, in certain districts, to a considerable extent. Another statement of his (in the same letter) is this: "The ordinary girls wear nothing upon their heads until they are married or have a child, except sometimes a fillet of red or blue coarse cloth,* of which they are very proud; but often their hair hangs down over the forehead

coast] was twenty-seven feet four inches long. . . . . These fish are called in the Erse Cairban, the Scotch sail fish, from the appearance of the dorsal fins above water. They inhabit most parts of the western coasts of the northern seas: Linnæus says within the arctic circle; they are found lower, on the coast of Norway, about the Orkney Isles, the Hebrides, and on the coast of Ireland in the bay of Balishannon, and on the Welsh coasts about Anglesea."

The western coasts of Scotland are known to possess a climate as mild as that of any portion of the British Isles. The Secretary of the Scottish Meteorological Society reported not long ago that during a period of five or six years the average winter temperature of the island of St. Kilda was as high as that of Penzance, and the temperature at Cape Wrath as high as that of the Isle of Wight. But surely it cannot be said that in any of these places coral and basking sharks may be included in the list of "common objects by the sea-shore" in the year 1883! It would appear that, owing to some such cause as a slight deflection of the Gulf Stream, the climate of our western coasts was much warmer a hundred and ten years ago than now.

* In his Appendix to the same letter, he also states that "in the days of our grandfathers [say, the end of the seventeenth century] the lower class of High-

like that of a wild colt. If they wear stockings, which is very rare, they lay them in plaits one above another, from the ancle up to the calf, to make their legs appear as near as they can in the form of a cylinder; but I think I have seen something like this among the poor German refugee women and the Moorish men in London." This allusion to "Moorish men" is very appropriate, when describing a custom of a race that was probably descended from the *Mauri* of Scotland: but, at first sight, the "German refugee women" seem a little out of place. But what kind of *Germans* were expelled from Germany when Burt wrote? "So late as the time of the celebrated Baron Trenck [a contemporary of Burt], it would

landers were, by their Lowland neighbours (in the north-east Lowlands, at least), denominated *humblies*, from their wearing no covering on their head but their hair, which, at a more early period, they probably matted and felted, for horror and defence, as the Irish did in Queen Elizabeth's time." Even many years after Burt wrote, there remained at least one instance of a survival of this or a kindred fashion. In a remote corner of the *Black Mount* district of Argyleshire there lived in 1781 a solitary individual who is styled a "savage" by the minister of the parish, who says of him: "His hair, which is naturally curled and very thick, is always tied with a silken or variegated cord at the root, and being loose towards the crop, it curls, and forms a great bunch, in size and figure resembling a large bunch of heath. This he esteems as one of his brightest ornaments." Now, this is exactly the fillet and head-gear of the heraldic Moor (whether that worn by the girls, described by Burt, has the same origin or not). This man, who lived in shealings or wigwams; who kept almost wholly aloof from the people of Glenorchay (although, excepting the head-gear, his attire seems to have been like theirs); whose "notions of religion" the parish minister "apprehended" to be "faint and obscure"—since he never attended church—this man was evidently the representative of an ancient race. The article is too long to quote here, but the whole character of the man—intensely proud and exclusive—and his mode of living, point him out as one of a different (and, in his opinion, a better) race than that of the other dwellers in the district. He was known as Angus Roy (Ruadh) Fletcher, and it is likely that he was one of the Fletchers, or arrow-makers of Glenlyon, in Perthshire, the head of which glen almost meets Glenorchay. Mr. Nicol (in his "Remarks" on Dr. Johnson's "Journey" p. 362), while stating that certain crafts were hereditary in certain tribes (a very Oriental and "gipsy" trait), cites, as one of these, the Glenlyon Fletchers. The word, as every one knows, signifies "Arrow-maker"; but it is perhaps not so well known that it is found in Gaelic (*fleisdear*) as well as in French (*flêchier*), and, therefore, it is probably a word of great antiquity. These Glenlyon Fletchers "were the most famous arrow-makers of their time so long as that weapon continued to be used;" and there is every reason to suppose that from his character, his insulated position and habits, and from the 'Moorish" fillet and his shock of curling hair (equally a feature of the heraldic Moor), that "Tawny Angus" was one of this ancient tribe. [He is described in the "Annual Register" for the year 1781.]

appear that Germany was still infested with prodigiously large bands of gipsies."* And Grellman, who—although his book was not published till nearly thirty years after Burt's—may easily have referred to the period of which Burt speaks, says: "Some years ago there were such numbers of them in the Duchy of Wurtemburg that they were seen lying about everywhere; but the Government ordered departments [? detachments] of soldiers to drive them from their holes and lurking-places throughout the country, and then transported the congregated swarm."* Therefore, the most likely refugees from Germany in the middle of last century were the German *gipsies*.

Whatever the precise pedigree of those swarthy natives of Skye and the neighbouring isles, it is not improbable that their blood was chiefly that of the Black Danes. The Hebridean women were dressed in white robes with sleeves of scarlet cloth, embroidered with gold lace. It is said of a tribe of ninth century Danes† who landed in Fife, that they wore, over their armour, " white shirts, stitch with red silk :" and the famous eleventh-century chief, Thorfinn, who was " one of the largest men in point of stature, ugly of aspect, black haired, sharp featured, and somewhat tawny," was enveloped in a white mantle on the day when, with his two war-ships "of twenty benches," he rowed into the harbour of Seley (off the Norway coast), and stepped on to the quarter-deck of Harald Sigurdson's galley. And as a counterpart to the gold lace, the broad plates of silver, and the buckles set round with precious stones, which formed part of the attire of the Hebridean women, we have the gilt helmet of the same Thorfinn, and the dress of Kara, the son of Solmund, who was a powerful chief in these Inner Hebrides, many centuries before the days that Martin writes about. We are told that when Kara was returning, with his fleet of ten galleys, after receiving tribute from the Islanders (on behalf of Earl Sigurd),

---

* Simson's "History," pp. 75 and 86.

† " They came out of their trenches in confusion, their fierce countenance and the bulk of their bodies, being big men, the different arms they used, and the accoutrement they had, wearing white shirts, stitch with red silk, upon their armour, made them terrible to the Scots at their first approaching to them; but after they had viewed each other a while, the Scots fell in upon them with a loud shout." (*Sir Robert Sibbald's Account of Fife and Kinross.*)

he interrupted a sea-fight between the sons of Nial (Grim and Helgi) with other Icelanders,—and thirteen galley-loads of pirates, or Vickings; the scene of the engagement being apparently among the Outer Hebrides. Kara, the son of Solmund, is thus described: ... "On that vessel which went foremost a man stood at the mast: He was in a silken jacket, and had a golden helmet, but the hair was both long and fair: This man had a gold-studded spear in his hand." Farther a twelfth-century Earl of the Orkneys is stated to have met his death by putting on a linen garment, newly made and white as snow," "embroidered with gold;"— (which garment had apparently been contaminated by some poisonous preparation).*

These silks, and jewels, and ornamentations of gold and silver, were probably inherited by Martin's Hebrideans from this source. To a considerable extent, at any rate. For although our Scottish antiquaries have collected gold brooches of exquisite workmanship, that belong to a period far older than the date of the Danish invasions; and although the Scoto-Egyptians and Pictish-Moors have bequeathed many other orientalisms to their descendants everywhere; yet it is likely that, since the Danish was the latest *Eastern* element in the Hebrides, many of the seventeenth-century Hebridean fashions were Danish.† But speculations upon this point are, at this juncture, somewhat out of place.

There is still in Ireland one colony (at least) of a people that has preserved wonderfully its ancient habits, and that suggests—in its fashions—a kinship with Martin's natives of Skye, and—in its physical characteristics—a descent from the

---

* See Dr. Joseph Anderson's edition of the "Orkneyinga Saga," pages 40 and 72; and *Collectanea de Rebus Albanicis*, pages 335, 341, and 344.

† Of the two or three examples just given, the ninth-century Fifeshire Danes alone can be taken as pure specimens of their race. Thorfinn, who was only "*somewhat* tawny," was plainly a half-breed; while Kara, the son of Solmund (in spite of his "black" name), must have been of the blood of the Norsemen or the Celts, for his hair was "both long and *fair*." But, by the era of "the son of Solmund," even the latest infusion of black blood had in many cases been mingled with that of previous races, as the recorded genealogies of the Islesmen and their own physiognomies clearly show. By that era also (it ought to be remarked) the return of some of the Northmen from the Holy Land might account for the presence of certain Oriental fashions and garments. But it is not *necessary* to take this into account.

dark-skinned race that peopled a portion of the Island of Lewis and other small islands,—that territory, in short, that is included in the modern parish of Harris. It will be remembered that of the Harrisians, generally, it was said (in the earlier part of this century) that their distinctive features were these—"the cheek bones rather prominent, the nose invariably short, the space between it and the chin disproportionately long, the complexion of all tints."* Many of these Harrisians were "as dark as mulattoes;" and these were "superior in stature and strength" to their fair-skinned brethren. The Skye people at Martin's time were "for the most part black," and their earlier fashions have just been described. The Irish colony, now to be glanced at, occupies a small territory known as the *Claddagh*,† at the inner end of Galway Bay, and just outside of Galway Harbour. The Claddagh (says a recent writer) "is entirely inhabited by the fishermen and their families. These form quite a clan, and are exceedingly clannish in their sentiments, not allowing a stranger to set foot in their village or meddle with their fishing. Such a one would find it as much as his life was worth to fish anywhere within the 'Claddagh' district. These people live quite apart in a world of their own, subsisting almost entirely on the produce of their fishing, and they talk Irish with an accent peculiar to themselves."

"Every market day the women may be seen in the market with fish for sale. They wear red petticoats, over which gay cotton dresses are looped up, and bright kerchiefs cover their abundant tresses of jet black hair. These are allowed to fall in a peak on the neck. The women are of a peculiar type,

* Quoted in Dawson's "Statistical History of Scotland," p. 550.
† "Claddagh" appears to be simply "the shore." The neighbouring nomenclature is suggestive. *Galway*, of course (like *Galloway*, *Innse Gaill*, *Gallibh* or Caithness, and *Wales*), points to the former ownership of *Galls*. And at the mouth of Galway Bay are the *Aran* Islands. They are situated close to a colony of distinctly dark-skinned people, and perhaps their own inhabitants are dark also. The natives of the Island of *Arran* in the Firth of Clyde were "generally brown, and some of a black complexion," in Martin's time. The chief island of "the Rosses" of Donegal, whose naked inhabitants were lately described, is *Aran* Island, and there is a fourth example (in Scotland, and to be specified afterwards) of an *Aran* which is distinctly connected with one of the early races. Whatever it means, *Aran* is evidently in some way identified with those "Moorish" people.

as are also their husbands; tall, dark, muscular, and with shapely limbs, though on a large scale. A finer race could hardly be seen thirty years ago than the 'Claddagh' people. At that time they could boast of no less than one thousand strong, able-bodied men, thoroughly acquainted with the sea, such as would be a credit to our navy; but since the famine the race has degenerated sadly. . . . . These people have a king of their own (or had a few years ago), who is chosen from among the oldest and most renowned of the 'Claddagh' families, and is arbitrator of all the disputes that may rise among his subjects, so that they scarcely ever appear before a court of justice."*

The physiognomy of these Claddagh people is not described, but it is not improbable that it will be found to correspond with that of the tall, dark Harrisians, whom they resemble in stature and strength: while the head-dress of their women reminds one of the "fine kerchief of linen strait about the head, hanging down the back taper-wise," that was once worn by the dusky women of the Inner Hebrides. And these, again—the "bright kerchief" of Claddagh, and that of Skye,—are, as already seen, simply varieties of the "bright silk handkerchief" that used to constitute the head-dress of "the English gipsy woman." For all these people are virtually gipsies, sea-gipsies, Algerines, Malays, or whatever they may best be compared to. The Claddagh people are, no doubt, harmless, well-meaning, and virtuous, when suitably dealt with; but let any one attempt to encroach upon the fishings of which they believe themselves the absolute owners, and it is "as much as his life is worth." This is precisely the state of things in the Hebrides in 1635. "Forasmekle as the . . . . Ylanders comes in troupes and companeis out of the Yles where they dwell to the Yles and Loches where the fishes ar tane and there violentlie spoyles his Majesteis subjects of their fisches, and sometimes of thair victualls and other furniture and persewes thame of their lyffes."† In either case the *casus belli* is the same. An "irreconcilable" section refuses to acknowledge the ascen-

---

* "A Market Day in an Irish County Town," contributed by "E.B.M." to *The Leisure Hour*, 1880.
† *Coll. de Reb. Alb.*, p. 111.

dancy of a newer power that has become—by the almost unanimous consent of the nation—the arbiter of the nation's destiny. This "irreconcilable" section, whether in the Hebrides, on the Galway coast, on the Scoto-English border, or among the scattered tribes of modern "gipsies," by virtue of its intense conservatism refuses to recognise that the old order has yielded place to new; adheres to its ancient laws and customs; and, consequently, finds that these occasionally lead to a direct conflict with those ideas accepted by the nation generally. How far this is the cause of certain local disturbances at the present day need not be discussed here; but it is certain that if such moderns as the Claddagh folk, and the "gipsies," were to obey the commands of their own self-chosen kings, in opposition to those of the national government, they would—in certain events—place themselves in direct antagonism to what we understand as law. And the only remedy for such an evil would be that adopted by the national government of Scotland in their dealings with the Scots Proper, or *Tories* of the Borders, two or three centuries ago: a patient toleration of their differences as far as that was consistent with peace and the progress of civilization; and, in inveterate cases, a distinct assertion of governmental power. But, nowadays, the ancestral customs still retained by "gipsies" are inoffensive. Their fiercest ancestors—whether as Hebridean pirates, or as border mossers, or in whatsoever form—were either killed off as intractable marauders, or else became orderly and civilized people; and their offspring now constitute a large proportion of the British nation.

It is more to the purpose, however, to reflect that those Galway coast people are plainly "gipsies"—in their attire—in their adherence to ancestral customs, and their obedience to a king who is, in their eyes, of ancient royal descent,—as also in their swarthy complexion; and (probably) in their language.*

---

* It is extremely likely that the "accent peculiar to themselves" renders their speech something very like the Gaelic-Pictish dialect of Mr. Leland's Irish tinker. (It is enough to use the word "accent," for accent is really the dividing line between one "language" and another of the same stock.) This question of language, however, can only be dealt with by linguists, who, unfortunately, are pre-

Other points of resemblance between the Pictish races of history and that portion of our population that has longest adhered to Pictish fashions are these:—

It is remarked, more than once,* in the History of the Gipsies of Scotland, that it was the custom of gipsy chiefs (if not of their followers) to openly practise polygamy. This, it was noticed, was also a custom of the border thieves, mossers, or Scots, to whom this practice (or something very like it) was known as "hand-fasting." The relations between the sexes was even less formal than this, in the Western Islands, as Dr. Skene informs us, and such usages were not put down by law until the beginning of the seventeenth century.†

But it is everywhere apparent that "gipsies" are only the remnants of the wilder races of the country. Mr. Simson has virtually recognized this when he says that they seem to have been "classed with our own native vagabonds, moss-troopers, border and Highland thieves, broken clans and masterless men." In his eyes, of course, "gipsies" were not "our own native vagabonds," but foreigners (which, *at one time*, they certainly were). But he sees, what one cannot help seeing, that the acts directed against them (as "gipsies") were one with those directed against Highland and Border banditti. The statutes quoted by Captain Burt, with regard to the *Sorners*, &c., of the Highlands, are word for word the same as those quoted by Mr. Simson in relation to *Gipsies*; and virtually the same as those that Scott cites when he describes the suppression of the border *mossers, Scots*, or *thieves*. The acts in Burt's *Appendix*, which *he* holds as relating to "Highlanders" and "Islesmen" (as distinct from other natives of the British Islands) are specially aimed at "sorners;" "sturdy beggars;" "idle bellies;" "thieves and intolerable oppressors;" "limmers," "delyting in no thing els bot in cruell and detestable murthouris, fyre-raisings, sorceryis," &c.; "bards" and "profest pleisants" (*i.e.*,

---

vented by circumstances from associating with the very classes that are the likeliest to retain archaic forms of speech.

* At p. 200, note, for instance.

† This is stated, among other things, in the edicts quoted by Burt in his "Appendix."

"fancied fools" or "clowns") "pretending liberty to bard and flatter;"* "vagabonds, bards, juglers, and such like:" the "entertainment and bearing with" whom, was accounted "amongst the remanent abuses which, without reformation, has defiled the whole Isles." All the qualities of these particular Highlanders and Islesmen were, at one time, embraced within the appellation "Egyptian," and the nicknames "Scot" (vagabond†) and "Pict" (painted or tattooed); whether these names be held as applying to the earlier "Moors" and "Egyptians" of early Britain, or to the somewhat later invasions of such races of "Picts" and "Scots" as were known to the christianized Britons by the titles of "Saracens" and "black heathen." And, as on the Borders, so in the Highlands and Isles, the time when such people were most vigorously suppressed was the reign of James VI. (of Scotland—I. of Great Britain); at which time Andrew, Lord Steuart, was able to report on his return from the Hebrides, that he had "brokin and distroyit the haill (whole) gallayis, lumfaddis (*long war-barges*), and birlingis that he could find in

---

* This is a gipsy feature which might have been indicated when speaking of the *Scots* or *Egyptians* of the Borders. In the quotation from Camden's "Britannia," which is given in the introduction to the "Minstrelsy," it is stated that those "mossers," when captured, "have so much persuasive eloquence, and so many smooth insinuating words at command, that if they do not move their judges . . . . to have mercy, yet they incite them to admiration and compassion." This gipsy trait of "wheedling" has been remarked upon by Mr. Simson, junior (at p. 115, note), who pertinently observes that the Spanish name for "gipsy," *gitano*, is a synonym for "flatterer"—that *gitanear* is "to flatter, entice," and that *gitaneria* signifies "wheedling, flattery." It is important also to notice that the Gaelic word *bladair* (from which has been evolved *blarney* in one part of the country, and *flattery*, *viâ bh*ladair, in another) is derived from *blad*, a foul or abusive mouth; which, with its derivative *bladach*, wide-mouthed, suggests (like *black-mouthed* and *dubh-fhocal*) some of the worst moral and physical aspects of the "blubber-lipped foreigners."

† For when applied by non-"Egyptians" to "Egyptians," the name of *Scot* very naturally bore this meaning, although when used by the Scot-Egyptians themselves it had as naturally quite a different significance, being, indeed, derived (according to one tradition) from *Scota*, the daughter of [a] Pharaoh. There are many Gaelic words apparently traceable to this source, *e.g.*, *Scuite* or *Sguite*, a wanderer; *Sgùd*, a scout (which latter is only the modern intonation of the word); *Scuide* (pronounced *skoodgie*), a drudge; *Sguidseach*, a prostitute, &c. The last two examples, like other "black" names, mark the degraded condition of one section of the Scots Proper; while one is tempted to assume that the "Scout" (*Sgùd*, scout or caterer; *Scuide*, drudge) of Oxford, and the "Gyp" of Cambridge, are also descended (etymologically) from the Scoto-Egyptians.

ony pairt of the yllis he resortit vnto." "The drift of all this indiscriminate destruction of vessels [adds Captain Burt] of every description (except as much as might be necessary for conveying his majesty's rents), was to encourage the 'trade of fischeing, whiche the peaceable subjects of the incuntrey wald interteny in the saidis yllis, to the honnour and benefeit of the haill kingdome.'" Those war-galleys were the vessels of the people who have been already spoken of as "pirates," "savages," "naked wild men living in caves," "*ciuthachs*," or gipsies; the people who lurked in every creek and wooded island of the Hebrides, as depicted by the scholarly tutor of that first king of United Britain, in whose reign so many laws were passed against those idlers and marauders. Buchanan's description of the Hebrides has already been extracted from: "Opposite loch Broom is situate the island Eu,* almost wholly covered with wood, and of service only to the robbers, who lurk there to surprise travellers. More to the north lies Gruinort, also darkened with wood, and infested with robbers." "Half a mile from Raarsa [Raasay, or Raa's Isle] is Rona, covered with wood and heath. In a deep bay it has a harbour, dangerous for voyagers, as it affords a covert for pirates, whence to surprise the passengers." And, lying off the site of what is now Broadford, in Skye, was "Paba, infamous for robberies, where the thieves, from their lurking places in the

---

* Assumed to be *Eilean Dhubh* (which is pronounced *Yew*), "the Island of the Blacks." The map accompanying "The County Directory of Scotland" (though pretty minute), does not show an island so named "opposite Loch Broom." But a little to the south of Loch Brown is "Loch Ewe," containing "Ewe Island." This, as formerly pointed out, is certainly Loch *Dhubh*, and its island is very likely Buchanan's *Eilean Dhubh*. The small River *Dhubh* (to adopt this spelling) runs into it from Loch Maree; which long sheet of water was, as Hugh Miller points out, at one period simply the inner portion of Loch Dhubh, for at its inmost end is Kinlochewe, *i.e.*, Ceann-loch-Dhubh, "the head of the Loch of the Blacks." *Poolewe*, *Letterewe*, and *Inverewe* are places adjoining this loch or lochs; and at the western extremity of its entrance there is a small stream, called the "Black Burn." A hill overlooking "the loch of the Blacks" is Beinn Brenc, "the Tattooed Mountain"; and a near promontory is Carr (*Ciar*, or swarthy) point: which last, however, may *possibly* have a superficial and physical meaning. There are other important names in this vicinity identifying it with the "blackamoors" or "painted people," but these will be afterwards referred to.

woods, with which it is covered,* intercept the unwary travellers."

Those Hebridean Malays, Algerines, or what not, were thus the "savages" of whom Pennant speaks: whose depredations were so frequent and so much to be dreaded, several centuries ago, that the chiefs of the civilized inhabitants of Skye were accustomed to go armed to church, as did the Puritan settlers in New England,—"and for the same reason, the dread of savages." They are better known in modern history under their general designation of Vickings, or Creek-men; and were plainly the same as those pirates that we lately saw attacking the Icelandic vessels that carried the Sons of Nial and the Icelandic merchants. From the time they were first seen in history, or tradition, down to the days of Buchanan (to which period Pennant reverts), they must have altered greatly in *breed*. For that embraces a great stretch of time, during which the Deucaledonian Archipelago was the scene of unceasing strife, the actors in which were of every variety of "British" stock; which is almost equivalent to saying—every variety of mankind. But it seems likely that the Creek-men, or Pirates, were chiefly of the races of Cimbri, or Black-Danes, and *Mauri*, or blackamoors, of an earlier date, known vaguely as *Picti*, or "painted people," and *Scots*, or "vagabonds." And there is much reason for believing that the ante-British home of one section of those "Scots," was Egypt: that the Ost-men, or Men of the East, known as Cimbri, Dani, black heathen, and *latrones*, were—to some extent—a wave of the Black-Hun flood that had previously deluged Southern Europe: while the earliest "blackamoors," whom we regard *separately* as "Picts" (though without reason, since the nick-name applies to all of these races), may also be faintly seen to have migrated westward from Asia. But these points of pedigree, and the question as to how far those savage races are repre-

* It will be noticed that three centuries ago many of the islands of this archipelago were covered with dense forests. It is curious to reflect how entirely the place is changed from the time when its woods were infested with swarthy savages; when sharks swarmed in its waters; when coral abounded on its shores; and when the wigwams reared in more civilized districts were tenanted by a race of dusky, richly-clad "gipsies" or "Indians."

sented by the Modern-British people,* are matters which there is no room to discuss here.

There is nothing inappropriate in styling those piratical Creek-men "Malays,"—so far as character and habits go. And the term is not very faulty otherwise. The swarthy skins and prominent cheek-bones of certain Hebrideans connect them very distinctly with the Vickings of the Eastern Archipelago. Martin points out some characteristics of a plainly Mongoloid nature, when he describes the men of St. Kilda. They "have generally but very thin beards, and those, too, do not appear till they arrive at the age of thirty, and in some not till after thirty-five; they have all but a few hairs upon the upper lip, and point of the chin." And he recalls the Swedish explorer's recent account of a North-Ugrian people, the Siberian Chukches, when he says—" Both sexes [of the St. Kildians] have a lisp, but more especially the women, neither of them pronouncing the letters d, g, or r."†

But we are more particularly concerned with the "gipsy" parallel at present. When Martin said of these same St. Kildians, that "they marry very young, the women about thirteen or fourteen,"—he was only stating in advance what the "Encyclopædia" contributor has told us of "gipsies:" they "marry very early: boys of fourteen and girls of twelve are often man and wife." And an equally forcible illustration is afforded by a comparison between the culinary customs of the "gipsies," and those of other sections of the population of Scotland—not popularly regarded as "gipsies." Mr. Simson tells us that "the ancient method of cooking practised among the Scottish gipsies is very curious, and extremely primitive, and appears to be of the highest antiquity." "The gipsies, on such occasions, make use of

* It is, of course, only a question of degree. *All* Modern Britons represent savage ancestors: only some divisions have been a little longer civilized than others.

† He says also that the St. Kildians "speak the Irish tongue only; they express themselves slowly but pertinently, and have the same language with those of Harries and other isles, who retain the Irish in its purity." But this again raises the question—" What *was* ' the Irish in its purity?'" We have already seen that Dr. McLauchlan regards the "Irish" of only a few centuries back as " very different from that written and read now"; and when Shaw brought out his Dictionary last century, there was an effort made by his rivals to get the book suppressed, for the reason that the words it contained *were not Gaelic*.

neither pot, pan, spit, nor oven, in cooking fowls. They twist a strong rope of straw, which they wind very tightly around the fowl, just as it is killed, with the whole of its feathers on, and its entrails untouched. It is then covered with hot peat ashes, and a slow fire is kept up around and about the ashes, till the fowl is sufficiently done. When taken out from beneath the fire, it is stripped of its hull, or shell, of half-burned straw-rope and feathers, and presents a very fine appearance." "It is said, likewise (says Burt, speaking of 'the meaner sort of people' in the Hebrides), that they roast a fowl in the embers, with the guts and feathers; and when they think it done enough, they strip off the skin, and then think it fit for the table." Again,—Captain Burt states that these Islanders "still retain the custom of boiling their beef in the hide;" and Mr. Simson caps this by remarking that "these singular people," the "Gipsies" of Scotland, "also boiled the flesh of sheep in the skins of the animals,"—adding, with unintentional aptness,—"like the Scottish soldiers in their wars with the English nation, when their camp-kettles were nothing but the hides of the oxen, suspended from poles, driven into the ground."*

At page 350 of his book, Mr. Simson informs us that the most conservative of all divisions of the Scottish gipsies is that division whose men are "tinkers," and whose women are engaged in the sale of articles made from horn. This particular tribe is known, he says, to other quasi-gipsies, as "gipsies;" and he adds that this horn-making is so essentially a gipsy craft that an ordinary potter, or "mugger," becomes alarmed if one asks him whether he ever *makes*

* Simson, pp. 232-3; Burt, Letter xxv. Both of these descriptions deserve a fuller attention. The Hebridean custom of boiling meat in a wooden vessel, by means of red-hot stones dropped into the water (which Burt speaks of); and the "gipsy" method of cooking flesh by encasing it in an envelope of rags and clay, and then heaping hot ashes over and around it—described by Mr. Simson—and also the comparison he draws between this fashion and others of a kindred nature, practised by *kindred* tribes, throughout the world; these facts are of considerable importance, and, in proper hands, may form a link of the chain of reasoning by which we ascertain the pedigrees of nations.

(Buchanan, in his "History of Scotland," Book I. chap. I. § xxxiii., confirms the statements made by others as to the custom of boiling meat in skins and paunches; and he further states that "sometimes they eat the flesh raw, merely squeezing out the blood.")

horn spoons. For this is virtually asking him if he is a *gipsy:* a fact, as Mr. Simson and Mr. Leland agree in saying, that every gipsy tries, if possible, to conceal. (For it must be remembered, that to be by "habit and repute" an "Egyptian," was to be under the ban of the law, and in danger of one's life,—not many generations ago: and it is not to be wondered at if the feeling still survives.) And this essentially gipsy custom, the making and, inferentially, the using horn spoons, is as old a custom of the *Scots** as are the cooking fashions just described; or as any other of the traits which have lately been pointed out as the common property of *Egyptians* of popular speech and the *Scots* of history.

In looking at the Scots, Egyptians, or Picts of the south of Scotland, it was noticed that they were *jongleurs* as much as *jugglers* or anything else: that they were, in short, the "Minstrels of the Scottish Border." Examples of these were seen in "Jamie Allan, the Gypsy and Northumberland Piper," "Awd piper Allan—Jamie's faither," Johnnie Faa and six of his people, "each with a pair of union pipes beneath his arm;" —and, in the story of James V., when disguised as a gaberlunzie, or sturdy beggar, he is described as equipped "with his pipes and his wallets," without which he would not have been in character. In the ballad of the abduction of the Countess of Cassilis by Johnny Faw,—

> The Gipsies came to my Lord Cassilis' yett,
> And oh! but they sang bonnie;

and (to take an example out of a more southern "land of the Galls," in which the Scoto-Egyptians were found so early as the fourth century) the best speaker of "gipsy," at the present day, is a harper. As before observed, it is not necessary to confine our regards to one particular musical instrument: it is enough that the "gipsy" races were peculiarly musical: they were jongleurs, minstrels, bards. But their favourite instruments seem clearly to have been the harp, the violin, and the bagpipes.

Speaking of the Hebrideans of three hundred years ago, Buchanan says:—†"Instead of a trumpet, they use a bagpipe.

---

* See note at end of Letter iv. of Burt's "Letters."
† "History of Scotland," Book I. Chap. I. § xxxiii.

They are exceedingly fond of music, and employ harps of a peculiar kind, some of which are strung with brass, and some with catgut. In playing they strike the wires either with a quill, or with their nails, suffered to grow long for the purpose; but their grand ambition is to adorn their harps with great quantities of silver and gems, those who are too poor to afford jewels substituting crystals in their stead. Their songs are not inelegant, and, in general, celebrate the praises of brave men; their bards seldom choosing any other subject.[*] They speak the ancient Gaelic language a little altered." Pennant, referring to the "Highlanders" generally,[†] tells us that "in former times the harp was the favourite instrument, covered with leather, and hung with wire, but at present is quite lost. Bagpipes are supposed to have been introduced by the Danes; this is very doubtful, ... the oldest are played with the mouth, the loudest and most ear-piercing of any wind music; the others, played with the fingers only, are of Irish origin: .... The trum, or Jew's harp, would not merit the mention among the Highland instruments of music, if it was not to prove its origin and antiquity. ... Vocal music was much in vogue amongst them, and their songs were chiefly in praise of their antient heroes. I was told that they still have fragments of the story of Fingal and others, which they carrol as they go along: ...."

A few specimens of these harps, jewelled, and decorated with dragonesque- and scroll-work of the most delicate workmanship, are yet extant; and two of them (for example) are particularly described in the Proceedings of the Society of Antiquaries of Scotland, 1880-81.[‡] But the use of them, in the Scottish Highlands and Isles, by wandering or resident Bards, has, apparently, quite died out. One still does see, in Scotland, the larger and more angular harp played by occasional wandering street-minstrels; to investigate whose antecedents might perhaps prove very interesting. But, as compared with the bagpipes, the harp in Scotland is

---

[*] Whence, as just noticed, "to bard" and "to flatter" were synonymous expressions.

[†] Pinkerton's "Voyages," Vol. III. p. 95.

[‡] By Charles D. Bell, Esq., F.S.A., Scot.

nowhere. The bagpipes, of course, still keep their ground there, to a considerable extent; and people who have never taken the trouble to examine the history of this instrument are, in very many cases, impressed with the idea that it belongs exclusively to Scotland: even in the face of the fact that a similar instrument (though with less to recommend it) drones and shrieks through our thoroughfares every day, played upon by swarthy *pifferarii* whose birthplace is certainly not Scotland. But any one who has paid any attention to the subject knows that the bagpipes are not of spontaneous Scottish growth : and, indeed, Pennant has just told us that they are believed to have been brought into Scotland by the "black heathen,"—the Danes. If so, this would at once account for their use in Southern Europe, in which there is such a strong infusion of the swarthy Hun blood. And it would account, also, for the presence of the same instrument in England,—without requiring to look farther back than the Danish inroads and Conquest. For it unquestionably belongs to South- as well as to North-Britain. Shakespeare knew this when he spoke of "the drone of a Lincolnshire bagpipe:" and Chaucer, too, when he said of his Pilgrim-Miller

" A baggepipe cowde he blowe and sowne."

And this Miller is of other importance, in this respect. Because there is much reason to believe that he was typical of a certain race. The physical peculiarities that lead one to believe this may be glanced at afterwards; but it is a striking thing that, possessing the "gipsy" qualification of bag-piper, he was also "a jangler, and a golyardeys,"—that is, a *jongleur* and a buffoon,—regarding both of which callings something has already been said.

Shakespeare seems to have regarded the bagpipe as identified with Lincolnshire, and probably it was an instrument quite alien to the people of Warwickshire; whatever may be the races from which these two populations were chiefly descended. There is a record of some English pipers who played before James the Fourth of Scotland at Edinburgh, in the year 1489, but there is no clue as to the locality from which they came. We are told that "in 1489, ... a band of English pipers came to Edinburgh, and they played at the Castle gate, where his Majesty heard them, and rewarded them with twelve *demyes*. In 1491, three English pipers were heard by the king at Linlithgow, and paid seven unicorns." * Of course, the word "piper" need not necessarily signify a *bag*-piper, although it does so in Scotland to-day. But it seems very probable that the terms "pipes" and "pipers" have generally been used to denote this particular instrument and the players on it. In a song of the year 1591—*The Hunting of Cupid*, by George Peele—the words "when swains' sweet pipes are *puffed*" seems to hint at the bagpipe. If "swains" be held to mean "rustics," then more than one passage in Barclay's *Eclogues* (written eighty years or so before *The Hunting of Cupid*) shows very clearly that the bagpipe was the "swain's" dearest instrument. *Amyntas*, in one of these "Eclogues," speaking of the rustics of England and the way in which they spend their Sundays, says that

> *if they ones here a bagpype or a drone,*
> *Anone to the elme or oke be they gone!*
> *There use they to daunce, to gambaud, and to rage,*
> *Suche is the custome and use of the vyllage.*

And *Faustus*, a "shepherd," is made to admit—

> *As soone as we here a bagpype or a drowne,*
> *Than leve we labour, there is our monaye gone.*

If any difference ever existed between a "bagpipe" and a "drone," it must have been infinitesimal. And neither of these names appear to have been inapplicable to those "swains' sweet pipes" which are referred to in *The Hunting of Cupid*. Two of these "swains" or "shepherds" figure in another of Barclay's *Eclogues*, and one of them says of the other—

> *With us was thou wont to sing full merily,*
> *And to lye piping oftetime among the floures,*
> *What time thy beastes were feding among ours:*

and although this "swain" was now a tattered outcast, "yet coulde he pipe and finger well a drone." Here it seems evi-

---

* Mr. James Paterson's "Life and Poems of William Dunbar" (Edinburgh, 1860), p. 108. "Demyes" and "unicorns" were gold coins of different values.

dent that this swain's "sweet pipe" was a drone or bagpipe, and nothing else. Again, in Butler's account of the custom known as "the riding of the Stang," the procession was headed by men playing upon

> *bagpipes of the loudest drones,*
> *With snuffling broken-winded tones:*

and it may be questioned whether the "whifflers" in the same procession were not also bag-pipers. Halliwell says that whifflers " were generally pipers and horn-blowers who headed a procession, and cleared the way for it : " and Wright adds, "particularly in the corporation of Norwich." And Shakespeare, in the return of Henry the Fifth from France, speaks of

> *the deep-mouthed sea,*
> *Which like a mighty whiffler 'fore the king*
> *Seems to prepare his way:*

which is suggestive rather of the bagpipe than of anything else. However, "whiffler" must have been a somewhat comprehensive term, if it included all kinds of "pipers" and also horn-blowers.

A writer upon this subject makes these remarks: "The bagpipe was apparently in common use some centuries ago both in England and Scotland . . . . in the old Scottish poem of 'Peebles to the Play,' the bagpipe is the pipe among the merry May-day folks :—

> ' Hop, Calyé, and Cardrone,*
> Gadert them out thick fald ;
> The bagpipe blew, and they out threw
> Out of the touns untald.'

But the bagpipe appears to have begun to retire [about the time of the Reformation ; an event of that or a somewhat later period proving that] by this time the bagpipe must have retired to the hills."†

At whatever date it "retired to the hills" in Scotland, the references already made to the Northumbrian gipsy-pipers,

---

* Localities in Peeblesshire ; here, of course, used to denote their inhabitants.

† "Transactions, &c., of the Dumfriesshire and Galloway Antiquarian Society," Session 1865-66, pp. 58, 59.

Allan, *père et fils*, (the younger of whom, at any rate, seems to have lived into this century) would apparently denote that the bagpipe died a harder death in the chiefly-lowland county of Northumberland: a district which was once a stronghold of the Black Danes. Indeed, it is evident that when Wordsworth and Leyden—men of the same generation—described as common features of North-English and South-Scottish life

> *The bagpipe dinning on the midnight moor*
> *In barn uplighted;*

and when their contemporary, Mr. Walter Simson, refers to the same feature in exactly the same way (if in less poetical terms), it is evident that in various Border localities the bagpipe was an everyday sight so lately as the earlier years of the present century. How long it continued to be so must be known to men acquainted with the manners of the counties lying immediately north and south of the Borders; but, that the Northumbrian pipes were still played upon by wandering minstrels as recently as 1861, is seen from a passage in one of the Border guide-books.* And it is probable that the caste is even yet not quite extinct, in that neighbourhood. The bard of 1861 is not specified as a gypsy, but it is almost certain he was one, since Wordsworth, Leyden, and Simson are unanimous in identifying the instrument with those people.

Thus the bagpipe,—like the harp, or the dirk,† or the oath on the dirk,—is not in any way the peculiar property of the Scottish Highlands. These things are all distinctly "gipsy" or "Scythian" attributes: although, naturally, like other archaisms, they have lingered longest in remote districts; or among a class of people who are the *toriest* Tories in the country.

That the bagpipe is an instrument identified with England,

---

* Mason's "Guide to Gilsland," p. 33. Like Wilson, this writer speaks of several "good old tunes" as (presumably) peculiar to the Borders and Border pipers.

† To this might be added the *sgian dubh*, or "black knife," which is not, in appearance, any "blacker" than a dirk. But I see no direct proof that it was, like the dirk, a "gipsy" weapon. Its name alone leads one to think that it was.

Ireland, and other parts of Europe, as well as with Scotland, is a fact that has often been pointed out; although there is still—even among educated people—a good deal of ignorance existing, in this respect. But how much more incorrect are our notions regarding the manners and customs of the Hebrideans of three centuries ago! It may be questioned whether half a dozen people have ever tried to realize the conditions of Hebridean life at that period; but if we have any hazy ideas on the subject, they are surely very far removed from the truth. "The truth" is a thing that can never be ascertained by people living three hundred years later: but if there are any popular beliefs existent as to the life of that time and place, they are surely quite out of keeping with such facts as these quoted in the previous pages. Particular islands of the Hebrides—particular sections, even, of some of them—may have differed from others, in the appearance of their inhabitants, as much as night from day. The presence of, at least, two wholly different races, at the same time, and in the same districts, was clearly indicated by Pennant's reference to the former condition of Skye; when the civilized inhabitants "went armed even to church, in the manner the North Americans do at present in the frontier settlement, and for the same reason, the dread of savages." Whether the Skye-men of to-day are the unmixed descendants of the civilized Skye-men of three hundred years ago (the "savages" having been killed off, like the Tasmanians or the Red-Indians); or whether they share the blood of both races; is a question which need not be entered into. It is enough that this state of things formerly existed in the Island of Skye. The kind of people who have been sought out in this chapter may have constituted a majority among the earlier Hebrideans—or they may not. But they were there. And we know as a fact, therefore, that that Archipelago—even down to the time of James VI. of Scotland—swarmed with tawny pirates, possessing all the characteristics of "gipsies," and known to their civilized contemporaries as "Egyptians." And that this section of the Hebrideans possessed the long war-canoes mentioned by Andrew, Lord Stewart (in the account of his expedition undertaken for their suppression), is a conclusion which one has every reason to draw. In the acts for their suppression, these people were described, as we have seen, as *sorners, thieves and intolerable oppressors, limmers, delighting in nothing else but in cruel and detestable murders, fire-raisings, and sorceries;* whose existence, about three hundred years ago, was "among the remanent abuses which, without reformation, had defiled the whole Isles." These people were distinctly *gipsies*. When not so called, they receive names which, at the time they were used, signified the same thing. Fletcher of Salton, writing in 1680, states that there were then a hundred thousand people in Scotland leading the life of "gypsies, jockies, or cairds"; and that the Highlands of Scotland "was an inexhaustible source of beggars,"* that is of *gipsies*,—for *gipsy* and *beggar* were then synonymous terms. But "beggar," it must be remembered, did not mean an insignificant outcast at that date; a "beggar" was then a "bandit," a powerful and ferocious marauder, an "intolerable oppressor,"—such a man, in short, as we get a glimpse of in such early accounts of the Scotch *gipsies* as that brought out by a Dr. Pennecuick, in the year 1715. These gipsies, then, constituted one of those abuses that "defiled the whole Isles," in the reign of James the Sixth of Scotland. And, whether lurking in the caves of Uist; or in the islands of Gruinort, Rona, Paba, and *Eilean Dhubh;* from which hiding-places they darted out upon "unwary travellers"; they are presented to us as piratical Vickings or Creek-men, fit descendants of those "black heathen" that murdered, robbed, and burned, all along our shores, as far back as the ninth century.

Coming under the ban of the governing powers of that day, and apparently forming a part of the same system—so abhorrent to the peaceably-disposed community in general—were the *sorcerers, bards, jugglers, players at "fast-and-loose," fortune-tellers, fancied fools* or *professed pleasants*, and suchlike: the kind of people, in short, whose representatives in this country at the present day are described by a student of gipsiology as being impregnated throughout with what he calls "gipsiness." Indeed, it is an inaccuracy to speak of them as "forming *a part* of the same system" as that which em-

* These exact phrases may not be Fletcher's: they are quoted from Mr. Simson's "History."

braced the "masterful beggars," "intolerable oppressors," and "murderers," spoken of above. For one cannot separate the one from the other. The statutes quoted by Mr. Simson (in his third chapter) show that the robbers and jugglers were one and the same people. The act that makes reference to "the thieves and limmers" who "unite themselves in infamous companies and societies, under commanders," "committing open and avowed robberies in all parts, murders, common theft, and pickery," states also that the same marauders " do shamefully and mischievously abuse the simple and ignorant people, by telling fortunes, and using charms, and a number of juggling tricks and falseties, unworthy to be heard of in a country subject to religion, law and justice." But, that the "counterfeit limmer" and the "counterfeit Egyptian," the "sturdy beggar" and the "gipsy," the "bard" or minstrel, and the "caird" or tinker, were only so many varieties of the same species, is a fact that has been already recorded. And the reason for introducing these characteristics at this point is simply to observe that if the dusky skins, the long side-locks with their knotted ribbons, the gipsy kerchief (*couvre-chef*), the flowing white dress, the scarlet gold-embroidered sleeves, the ornaments of gold, silver, coral, and precious stones, that formed the most salient features of certain archaic Hebridean communities,—and the Indian-like wigwams that were the dwellings of such people —if these most important particulars have quite been omitted in any pictures of ancient West-Highland manners,—so also have such other traits as jugglery, dice-throwing, thimble-rigging, and the buffoonery of the circus-clown,—all of which were once equally characteristic of West-Highland life. For these "professed pleasants" and "fancied fools" were nothing else than harlequins and clowns: the bard and the mountebank,—the *jongleur* and the *juggler*,—were one. A poet like Scott was at liberty, if he chose, to imagine a minstrel as a venerable patriarch of a dignified presence; but the few facts we know seem to say that he was a glib-tongued flatterer and a mountebank. Indeed, this minstrel-mountebank had not completely disappeared from the Hebrides several generations after those severe statutes were enacted against him. We get a picture of a harper "who made himself a buffoon for his bread," wearing a long fool's-cap, bifurcated, with bells attached, who wandered through the islands of Barray and Skye, at a period subsequent to those statutes by fully a hundred years.* And, whether or not he was the last of his kind, his dress indicates very fairly the appearance of the earlier *bards* and *professed pleasants* who were among "the remanent abuses that had defiled the whole Isles." There must almost certainly be much information still afloat among Gaelic-speaking people with regard to all this class of Hebrideans. For Gaelic, however it may have altered from time to time—owing to various causes—and whatever may have been its first shape, and at whatever date it may have been first spoken in the British Islands,—Gaelic has been the language of the civilized element in the Scottish Highlands (as "civilization" is now understood). And it is *not* the language of those "gipsies." It is not the language native to Highland tinkers and tinker-fiddlers at the present day: it is in Gaelic that we hear of the vulgar tongue as "black speech." Nor is the language of the Welsh minstrel of to-day that variety of speech known as "Welsh." On the contrary, it is "black speech," or "gipsy." Neither did the earlier harpers and pipers of the sister island employ that language —Gaelic—which was so pre-eminently the speech of Ireland. Whatever their tongue, it was not Gaelic. "On the revival of Literature in the 11th century (says Mr. Walker, in his *Historical Memoirs of the Irish Bards*), ... the order of the bards was .... divided into two classes, viz, *Ollamh Re Seanachas* and *Ollamh Re Dan* [*Doctors*, or *learned-men of genealogy*, and of *poetry* or *song*]. The *Ollamhain Re Seana-chaidhe* were Historians and Antiquaries. Their office was confined to certain families; and they held their properties by hereditary right .... The *Ollamhain Re Dan* .... were Panegyrists or Rhapsodists, in whom the characters of the Troubadour and Jongleur of Provence seem to have been united." And the same writer quotes this from Stanihurst's *Description of Ireland* ("compiled from several authors of this period")—"the toong [*i.e.* tongue, or language—of these minstrels] is sharpe and sententious, and offereth great occa-

* Martin, I believe, gives this in his "Description of the Western Isles," but it is here quoted (as Martin's) from De Foe's "Duncan Campbell."

sion to quicke apophthegms and proper allusions. Wherefore their common jesters and rimers, whom they terme Bards, are said to delight passinglie these that conceive the grace and propertie of the toong. *But the true Irish indeed differeth so much from that they commonlie speake, that scarce one in five hundred can either read, write, or understand it.*" Thus the "common jesters and rhymers" of Early Ireland, whose business it was to "bard and flatter" certain Gaelic-speaking families,— these *jongleur-juggler*s possessed a language that not one in five hundred [of the Gaelic people] could read, write, or understand. These men were identical with the black-skinned minstrel-jugglers of the John-of-Rampayne story, and with the "bards and profest-pleisants" of the Scottish Highlands, in their most striking characteristics: and, in at least two of these instances, the language of such people was "black-speech."

Since, therefore, there are particular accounts of those non-Gaelic classes, recorded by the Gaelic-speaking families of Ireland—if not of Scotland—it may be taken as probable that a great deal of information regarding their outward appearance is yet existing in ancient Irish books and manuscripts. And it can hardly be believed that such information will contradict the scanty items that have been gathered in these pages.

. . . .

Whether regarded as "gipsies" or as members of various "Pictish" races, those Islemen whom we have just been looking at must have been *Faws* or *Painted Men*. So great was the race-mixture in that archipelago, that there must have been every variety of painted and tattooed men among them: ruddled, like the Galloway chief, woad-stained, like the archaic Green-Man, tattooed, like the famous Donald *Breac*, and other "iron-graved" Moors; or painted "of various colours," like the *Faws* Proper. Probably an investigation of ancient chronicles (with this object in view) would result in discovering numberless instances of this. The fact that one division of *Dubh Galls* became known as the seed of Ruaidhri, Rothri, Roderick, Ruari, or Rory, whose name signified, alternatively, "The Chief of the Tawny, or Red People," and "The Tawny or Red Chief," renders it likely that this tribe of swarthy "devils" (as the Gaelic poem politely calls them), used to smear themselves over with iron ore, as in the historical cases already cited. And, indeed, the fact that *ruadh* signifies "tawny" as well as "red," may also be held to support this belief.* That others were woad-stained "green-men," like the "savages" of the popular memory and of history, is shown by the prevalence of the title "Gorm," after the names of Islanders. This word, it has been noticed, is translated either "blue" or "green," just as the Romans styled certain Ancient Britons "Cærulei" and "Virides," indifferently; for the reason that the colour of woad, or *gorman*, may be described by either adjective. As an agnomen, "Gorm" must at one time or another have become fossilized, perhaps at different dates in different families. It is usually translated "Blue" or "Green"—in such connections—without any attempt to explain the meaning of the appellation. The many agnomens that denote the colours *black, brown, tawny, grey, red, yellow, white*, are usually rendered black, &c., -*haired*, as formerly observed. And no doubt this translation is sometimes correct. But it was evident to any translator that *blue* and *green* could never relate to the hair, and so the many Donalds and Duncans bearing this title have been abruptly introduced to us as Blue Donald, or Blue Duncan, without any attempted explanation of so odd a nickname. In one instance† I have seen it rendered "blue-*eyed*," but against this there is the twofold objection that it might as well have been translated "*green*-eyed," and also that such a free acceptation of one colour-nickname would entitle one to render the others as black-, red-, or yellow-*eyed*, with as much reason as black-, red-, or yellow-*haired*. The real solution of the difficulty seems undoubtedly to be that, *certainly* in the case of "Gorm," and probably in a large number of other cases, no direct reference is made either to hair or to eyes.

The date at which "Gorm" lost its original significance,

---

* *Ruadh*, however, may have become equivalent to "tawny" for two other reasons. The one is, that the Irish *Cruithnigh*, or Picts, or Agathyrsi, are said to have come from Thrace; and the people of Thrace are stated to have been *Red-skins*. The other reason will come in at another place.

† I think somewhere in the *Collectanea de Rebus Albanicis*.

and became a mere hereditary name, as meaningless as the surnames White, Black, and Brown now are, cannot be decided. As just suggested, it probably became "fossilized" at various dates in various races. "Gorm the Old," the fierce old pagan Dane, who died in the year 935, and who was ancestor of Sven and Knud of England, was likely suitably named, being presumably *Gorm*, "*the* woad-coloured man," just as his contemporary, "*Dubh* vel *Niger*," of Scotland, was "*the* black man." There is a traditionary story, of uncertain age, which comes in in Mr. Campbell's "West Highland Tales," and which very clearly relates to the staining, or perhaps to the tattooing, of a chief's daughter, by the magicians, or Druids. And although in his English version of the incident he does not give the words that refer to its most important point (important, at any rate, for the present purpose), it is certain that the word *gorm* must have been used by the narrator. "The king of the Ailp (the story goes) quarrelled with the Druids, and was killed, leaving a single daughter and a son. She was educated by the Druids till she was able to do many of their tricks, *but they coloured her skin as green as grass*."* This last phrase is exactly what one definition of "gorm" implies: *gorm*, "blue of whatever shade; also green, as grass." That the Druids—whose name, in several forms, came gradually to mean gipsies, fortune-tellers, sorcerers, &c.—had tattooed or stained this girl's skin, is as clear as can be. Another instance of a somewhat similar kind is seen, and at a far later date, in a well-authenticated family sketch, also given by Mr. Campbell. Although the traditional account of the affair is very much garbled, it is impossible to avoid the conviction that in it we have a distinct example of the epithet "gorm" applied to an individual in its original sense. The incident belongs to the period of the barbarous act that gave the "Lady's Rock" (at the inner entrance of the Sound of Mull) its title; and which is familiar to every one who has visited Oban, or read William Black's novels, or indeed any collection of West Highland traditions. The savage chief of the MacLeans had sent his wife to a cruel death (as he thought) on this tidal "Lady's Rock;" and after they had

---

* "West Highland Tales," Vol. IV. p. 292.

carried out their barbarous orders, "these very men (says Mr. Campbell) . . . . . returned to Duart Castle, where John Gorm, the first of the family of Lochnell, a boy of three or four years of age, was (dwelling) with his aunt, the Lady MacLean, whom they had left upon the naked rock." (She, as is known, was rescued; but with her we are not concerned here.) "And as soon as they had entered the castle of Duart, they kindled a great fire on the middle of the hall floor, and formed themselves into a circle around the fire, and caused strip the boy John Gorm naked, and placed him between them and the fire, when the boy, by reason of the heat, was forced to run round the fire, while each of them, as he passed within the circle, rubbed his naked skin with an hot roasted apple, which occasioned blue spots on the boy's skin ever after, *for which he was called John Gorm, or Blue John.*"*

As it stands, the story is manifestly absurd. The effect of repeated "dabs" with roasted apples could never result in this, if ever the *bizarre* experiment was tried. It is probable that the confusion has arisen in this way: The Gaelic *ubhal*, "an apple," is plainly a near relation of the adjective *ubhail*, "elliptical." Now, the tale in which this *ubhal* figures is three or four centuries old. It relates to a time when a practice, which existed in the time of Grose, the antiquary, and even yet, must have been much more widely practised. To make these punctured figures, "iron-graved," there must have been an instrument (*breacair*). As likely as not, it was elliptical in shape: it was *ubhail*. If so, it would as likely have an alternative name denoting its shape, some noun very like *ubhal*, if not identical with it. This is probable, since *ubhal* (pronounced *ooval*) is virtually *oval*, or egg-shaped, from Latin *ovum*, Gaelic *ubh*† (*oov*), an egg. So that *ubhal*, the noun, would thus originally indicate "anything oval," or approaching that figure (in fact, *an oval*).

But, when the custom of tattooing became obsolete in the Hebrides, and in consequence the tattooing instrument also, this meaning of the noun *ubhal* would also become obsolete.

---

* "West Highland Tales," Vol. IV. pp. 64, 65.
† Another (and an earlier?) form of this word is *ob*, "round."

So that the modern narrator* of the story, knowing no such nouns, except *ubh,* "an egg," and *ubhal,* "an apple," would take for granted that the *ubhal* of Blue John's experience was the only *ubhal* she knew by this name.

The incident is also interesting in this way, that it indicates that the *Virides, Cærulei,* or "green-men," did not *paint* their skins with woad-dye, but pricked it in after the fashion of the existing Tatâren, or "gipsies" of Egypt,—the Dyaks of Borneo, and the official descendants of the Frisians, our own sailors, who produce the blue colour by means of gunpowder and of Indian ink. If woad, therefore, was invariably applied in this way, *gorm* would be included in the larger term, *breac.*

This "Blue John," then, was clearly not nicknamed after the colour of his eyes, or of his hair, but of his skin. The story does not warrant us in believing that tattooing was a custom of his paternal tribe, the Campbells (for he was a son of Colin Campbell, third earl of Argyle). On the contrary, the usage was apparently familiar to the followers of MacLean, who perpetrated the act. The origin of the Campbells has been much disputed, and probably their pedigree is as mixed as that of most British people. One of them was certainly a "Black Colin of Rome," and the West Highland traditions speak of "swarthy men from Lorn," and the "Black Knights of Lochawe." But, probably, as in every tribe and nation that has endured for many centuries, the ruling dynasty had changed over and over again. At that period, the MacLeans and the Campbells seemed to have been ranged on different sides, although "Blue John's" aunt, his father's sister, had married the savage MacLean chief. This, however, might have been, racially, an alliance of a Rolfe-Pocahontas nature. Altogether, without fuller information, it is not easy to decide as to the side on which the "green-man" preponderated: nor is such knowledge needful at this juncture.

Alexander Smith† tells us a story of a Macdonald of

---

* The narrator was an old woman, who was "very old" in 1861, who spoke "hardly any English," and who, "like many of her class," uttered "oracular predictions now and then": in short, a Druidess, a fortune-teller, a gipsy-wife.

† In "A Summer in Skye," "Orbost and Dunvegan."

Sleat—"Donald Gorm, or Blue Donald, as he was called"—who is another example of this usage. Sir Walter Scott, also, in *The History of Donald the Hammerer*,* introduces a similar specimen, in the person of "the celebrated *Cailen Uaine*, or Green Colin." This personal application of the adjective *uan*, or *uaine*, "green," is seemingly very rare; and it is also very instructive. For it again brings to memory that the "black man" of Scottish-Gaelic (*duine dubh*) is the "green man" (*duine gorm*) of the Gaelic of Ireland. It does so in this way. The same word that is here translated "green," *uaine* or *uan*, is in another place† rendered "dark-coloured." The spelling, in this instance, corresponds with that now in use in what we call (with very little reason) the English language. It is spelled *wan*. It is a question whether, in the days of Harry the Minstrel, the "dark-coloured" sense of the word was expressed by the quickened intonation, or whether he and his contemporaries still gave it the dissyllabic utterance that its "green" signification still possesses in the more archaic speech.‡ But, at any rate, this twin-meaning of *uan*, corresponding as it does with the identity between *duine dubh* and *duine gorm*, makes one long to learn more precisely the exact ethnological position of those southern tribes, of whom this *gorm* custom was a

---

* Prefixed to the fifth edition of Burt's "Letters."

† Dr. Jamieson's Glossary annexed to Blind Harry's "Wallace." The word is also translated by him "gloomy," which phase has counterparts in such "black" expressions as *grim, morose, dubh-ghruaim* (according to McLeod and Dewar, "a dark frown," and apparently a tautological compound of *dubh* and *græme*), and also in the more modern "black looks," "to look black," &c.

‡ Some very important fact seems to underlie the introduction of the letter *w*. Either a quicker-speaking race was asserting itself at that period (the twelfth century is the date of birth of the *w* according to one authority), or else the speech of the higher classes generally—in certain districts of the country—was, by a movement of evolution, becoming more direct and crisp. (Other examples of the same tendency are seen in the monosyllables—if they may be called so—*i* and *u*, which are only quickened enunciations of the dissyllables *ah-ee* and *ee-oo*.) The letter *w*, at any rate, though erroneously called "double-*yew*," represents very plainly the sound "double *oo*." And if, in investigating the etymology of a word in which the letter *w* occurs, the student were to substitute the sign *oo* in its place—as *oo-an* for *wan*—he would find it a considerable help in the attainment of the proper analysis.

characteristic, at the time of Cæsar's landing. This, however, is a side question.*

The precise date at which tattooing, or painting, ceased to be a Hebridean custom, cannot easily be fixed. Although Boswell does not mention it, it is quite within the bounds of possibility that the black-haired, half-naked MacLeod (true descendant of the "black Prince of Man,") who pulled an oar in the doctor's boat, and who was something between "a wild Indian" and "an English tar," resembled either of these in the possession of this peculiarity. The comparatively recent date of Johnson's Journey offers no obstacle whatever to such an assumption: for that was the era of Grose, when "gypsies" were still accustomed to "artificially discolour their faces,"—the era of the Galloway Pict, Marshall, and the era when "English tars" had not yet forsaken the Mongolian pigtail, and most certainly had not forsaken the custom of tattooing their bodies.

In none of these cases, *Blue John*, *Blue Donald*, and *Green Colin*, is there direct evidence that the "green man" was a "black man"; and, in the first example, the probability is quite the other way. For the rule of the "black knights" over that clan had probably, by that time, yielded to the supremacy of a fairer race; either by the overthrow of a dynasty (as in the case of the Black-Douglas nobles, half a century earlier); or by repeated intermarrying of swarthy chiefs, generation after generation, with members of the fair-skinned races,—Gaels, Norsemen, Normans, and others. This revolution, gradual or sudden, must have taken place some time or another,—perhaps before the time of John Gorm, perhaps after,—for the eminent chieftain of that race who has given the tradition to the public, remarks elsewhere that his clansmen regard light, yellow hair as one of the belongings of a Campbell. Also, the fact that the tattooing of

---

* Grose, in his "Classical Dictionary of the Vulgar Tongue," gives the noun *Blue-skin*, and defines it characteristically thus: "A person begotten on a black woman by a white man. One of the blue squadron; any one having a cross of the black breed. . . . ." Now, every one knows that the skin of a mulatto is not *blue*. There seems little doubt that this again points to the identity of *gorm* with *dubh*. Grose knew that gipsies of his day used to "artificially discolour their faces," and when he speaks of "the blue squadron" and "the black breed," he almost certainly has these in view.

John Gorm was performed by his enemies, and strongly resented by his friends, apparently indicates that it was not a custom of his race: while it undoubtedly was a "black" usage.

The conclusion which one naturally reaches, after regarding the foregoing evidence on this question—fragmentary though it be—is, therefore, that "the black breed," and "the blue squadron," as Grose puts it, were identical; and that the members of this "squadron," in whatever part of our islands they existed, even so lately as Grose's time, represented the least civilized portion of our population; as "civilization" is now understood. That, in fact, the archaic term of "green-man" is fitly rendered "savage." And, although the straggling examples we have taken of Deucaledonian "green-men," do not distinctly say so, yet the presumption is that such Blue Duncans and Green Donalds are to be identified with the "savages" who molested peaceable church-goers in the Hebrides some centuries ago; and with the "pirates," "robbers," "Creek-men," "Sorners," and "vagabonds," generally, who plundered travellers by land and sea; and whose homes and lurking-places were appropriately named when they received such titles as *Eilean Dhubh*, on the North-Western, and "the Black Isle" on the North-Eastern coast of Scotland. To what extent such marauders shared the usual fate of law-breakers, or how many of them are represented in the great army of Modern Britons, is another matter altogether.

But, what is more to the point is, that in this—as in every other feature to which attention has been drawn—the particular section of the heterogeneous "Scotch" people whom we have been regarding, are plainly nothing else than "gipsies." The people whom we now know by this name have so dwindled down, in numbers and importance; have become so much less formidable in character; their appellation bears now such a restricted meaning; that it requires something of an effort to realize everything that is meant by this term. Even so lately as the time of Grose, the "blue squadron" was composed of thieves and marauders: a notorious member of the Dick Turpin brotherhood being handed down to posterity as *Blueskin*. And that even such recent "Blueskins" were, in some degree or another of the "black breed" is likely, for more reasons than one. "Black" is a very usual prefix to the names of highwaymen and robbers everywhere: *Black Ralph* in England, *Black Peter* in Holland, and many others. Not to stray, however, from Scotland—the author of Waverley has given us, whether by design or not, several instances of this. One of his most famous freebooters was Roderick *Dubh;* another, of minor importance, was *Black* Donacha,* in "The Heart of Mid-Lothian." And the very frequent occurrence of the descriptive epithet *Dubh,* in the names of Highland and Island chiefs, as well as the equally frequent occurrence of various names denoting varying degrees of "blackness," points most distinctly to the complexion of such leaders.

The historical races, then, whose ways and attributes have been—after a too imperfect and desultory fashion—examined within the last few chapters, are plainly represented more exactly by the Scottish "gypsies" of to-day, than by any other section of the population of Scotland: descended though that population is, in great measure, from the same ancestral stock. One particular instance of this identity could not, we saw, be ignored even by the Scotch-gypsy historian himself, when describing the culinary operations of "this singular people" (to use his own most ill-timed expression). Nor could Sir Walter Scott omit to make a similar observation. In a note to "Guy Mannering" (*Note F*), on the subject of "gipsy superstitions,"—as these are detailed by a writer in *Blackwood's Magazine,*—he makes this remark:

---

* His appearance is thus described at the moment of Lady Staunton's (Effie Deans) encounter with him: "In this moment of terror and perplexity, a human face, black, and having grizzled hair hanging down over the forehead and cheeks, and mixing with moustaches and a beard of the same colour, and as much matted and tangled, looked down on them from a broken part of the rock above." His adopted son (who is erroneously figured as "equally swart and begrimed") is very appropriately described as wearing his hair "twisted and matted like the *glibbe* of the ancient wild Irish, and, like theirs, forming a natural thicket, stout enough to bear off the cut of a sword" "Appropriately described," because—although Effie's own child—his upbringing was that of a young *ciuthach* or "Black Irishman." Scott rightly makes this Black Donacha a gipsy; and accepting him as a representative Highland bandit, and the Laird of Knockdunder as a representative (excluding his oddities) of the "Highlanders" who were *not* banditti, we have the whole question in a nutshell.

"These notions are not peculiar to the gipsies, but having been once generally entertained among the Scottish common people, are now only found among those who are the most rude in their habits, and most devoid of instruction." And this so exactly hits the mark: and it was said by a man who was such a zealous antiquary: and who *must* have known that gypsies were *Picts:* and who certainly knew that they were marauding moss-troopers, even in his own day: that it is a perpetual wonder how Scott did not *see* that the wandering "Egyptians"* were only the residuum of the historical "Scots."

* This name and its abbreviation "gypsy" is used here and elsewhere in a very loose fashion. For it only refers properly to one section of the " dreadfully mixed" race, which, for the sake of convenience, we denominate "gypsy." They have a dozen other names, all of which, no doubt, describe correctly the separate lines of their genealogy. "Gypsy," in reality, is as comprehensive a term as "Asiatic," "Oriental," or "Polynesian."

Scott again touches the truth, in his *Advertisement* to "The Antiquary," when remarking upon the class of men to which Edie Ochiltree is supposed to belong. It would seem that the more "gypsy" characteristics of this class were not strongly marked at so recent a date as that of "The Antiquary"; but there can be no doubt that the "Blue-gowns" formed merely a variety of the class, or classes, coming under the designations of Bards, Sorners, Sturdy Beggars, Minstrels, Jugglers, Egyptians, and so on. Indeed, Scott distinctly states that "Martin, author of the *Reliquiæ Divi Sancti Andreæ*, written in 1683," "conceives them to be descended from the ancient bards." This writer says of them: "They are called by others and by themselves Jockies [which very name links them with the "horse-coupers," who are identified with "gypsies" by Jamieson, Simson, and Leland], who go about begging, and use still to recite the Sloggorne (gathering-words or war-cries) of most of the true ancient surnames of Scotland, from old experience and observation. Some of them I have discoursed, and found to have reason and discretion. One of them told me there were not now above twelve of them in the whole isle; but he remembered when they abounded, so as at one time he was one of five that met usually at St. Andrews." Monkbarns, again, says of Edie, that he had been " soldier, balladsinger, travelling tinker," and, lastly, a beggar; that he was " one of the last specimens of the old-fashioned Scottish mendicant, who kept his rounds within a particular space, and was the news-carrier, the minstrel, and sometimes the historian of the district;" and that he knew "more old ballads and traditions than any other man in this and the four next parishes." In short, his character and his "havings" unite in making him a counterpart of such a minstrel-vagrant as "Piper Allan," the celebrated Northumbrian gipsy, formerly referred to. It was noticed that at least *two* scions of this Allan stock are locally remembered by the title of "Piper Allan" (the pipe upon which they played being the bagpipe). Dr. John Brown, in speaking of his dog *Crab*, "the Mugger's dog," "come of the pure Piper Allan's breed," places one of this family as far back as two centuries ago. "This Piper Allan, you must know, lived some two hundred years

The case is put pretty correctly by Robert Jamieson, in his introduction to Burt's *Letters*. He refers, of course, solely to the Highlands and Isles of Scotland. "From the accounts to be found in various parts of this work, particularly in the Gartmore MS. it will be seen that, from the manner in which the lands, the superiority of which belonged to the chief of a clan, were portioned out by division and sub-division, according to proximity of blood, to the cadets of great families [invading families], the aboriginal inhabitants of the country must in the end have been actually shouldered out of existence, because no means were left for their support, ... These men, attached by habit, language, and prejudice, to their native country, upon which they had little claim but for benevolence, became *sorners* and sturdy beggars, and were tolerated and supported, as the *Lazzaroni* were in Naples, and as *Abraham-men*, and sturdy beggars of all sorts were in England, after the suppression of the monasteries and before there was any regular parochial provision for the poor." It is of such people that Burt speaks, when he says (in his Twenty-fourth Letter): "Besides these ill-minded people among the clans, there are some stragglers in the Hills, who, like our gypsies, have no certain habitation, only they do not stroll about in numbers like them. These go singly, and, though perfectly unknown, do not beg at the door, but without invitation or formal leave, go into a hut, and sit themselves down by the fire expecting to be supplied with oatmeal for their present food."* To what extent these were "aborigines" and "native men," one can only guess. To the Norman and Dutch settlers, who, after the Norman Conquest, became the rulers of a great part (if not all) of Great

ago in Cocquet Water, piping like Homer from place to place, and famous not less for his dog than for his music, his news and his songs." "Mugger," or potter, we have seen is only a variety of "gypsy"; and those swarthy minstrels of Scotland and of England, who are the repositories of the oldest traditions and usages of their environment, point back to the dusky *jongleurs* of mediæval story; and, farther back still, to "the ancient bards," from whom they are "conceived to be descended."

* These last are, of course, *sorners* or "forcible obtruders," and their going singly may be explained by the fact that they were once *Sorohen*, or nobles, accustomed (as described by Dr. Jamieson) to live thus upon their dependents. Once dispossessed by the victorious invaders, they had either to serve them, or else live, after a decayed fashion, in their old way.

Britain, the descendants of ninth-century Danes were "native men." The Moors of the District of Moravia, ousted by incoming Flemings and Normans, need not have been descended from the *Mauri* of Claudian, and may have been only "natives" of three centuries' standing: their ancestors being the Danes, or "black heathen." But, to the newcomers they would be "aborigines," as much as the Tasmanians of to-day (who are all of European stock) would be "aborigines" to a possible race of successful invaders in the year 2150. Or, again, such Moors may have been a mixture of earlier Mauri and later Danes. But these are matters of pure speculation.

The Gartmore MS., which was made public by Scott, describes the Highlanders of 1747 thus: "the commonalty are of a smaller size than the people of the low country; and, as they are not accustomed to any hard labour, and are in the constant use of hunting, fowling, and following their cattle through the mountains, they are of wonderful agility of body, and capable to travel with ease at a great rate." "The tacksmen, or good-men, as well as the gentry are generally larger bodied men than the inferior sort."* "The people are extremely prolific, and therefore so numerous that there is not business in that country, according to its present order and economy, for above the one half of them." "The other half, then, must be idle, and beggars, while in the country; that is there are in the Highlands no fewer than 115,000 poor people, and of these, there are 28,750 able-bodied men between the ages of 18 and 56 fitt to bear arms." Of the 115,000 a large number, says the manuscript, work honestly as herders, harvesters, &c., "in the Low-countrys;" "but then the rest of these people must be supported in the Highlands, where they constantly reside, as they gain nothing. These we cannot suppose under one half of the whole num-

---

* These statements bear out Professor Huxley's remarks as to the average stature of "dark whites." On the other hand, the superior height and strength of the dark-skinned Harrisians and the people of Claddagh show that the *Melanochroi* are, in certain cases, taller than the whites. Mr. James Simson (in a foot-note, p. 139) says that "with gipsies of mixed blood the individual, if he takes after the gipsy, is apt to be short and thick-set." It is worth remarking also that in Wales, or a part of Wales, the word for "the nobility" is *uckelwyr* (so spelled by Scott in "The Betrothed"), literally "tall men."

ber, so that there are in that country 57,500 souls who live, so many of them upon charity, and who are vagrant beggars through the Highlands and the borders of it. Many of them live an idle sauntering life among their acquaintance and relations, and are supported by their bounty; others get a livelihood by *blackmail* contracts, by which they receive certain sums of money from people of substance in the country, to abstain from stealing their cattle; and the last class of them gain their expence by stealing, robbing, and committing depredations." "Every place is full of idle people, accustomed to arms, and lazy in everything but rapines and depredations." "A person who had the greatest correspondence with the thieves was agreed with to preserve the lands contracted for from thefts, for certain sums to be paid yearly out of these lands. Upon this fund he employed one half of the thieves to recover stolen cattle, and the other half of them to steal, in order to make this agreement and blackmail contract necessary. . . . . He calls himself the *Captain* of the *Watch*, and his banditti go by that name.* And as this gives them a kind of authority to traverse the country, so it makes them capable of doing much mischief." "There is paid in *blackmail* or *watch-money*, openly and privately, 5,000*l.*; and there is a yearly loss by understocking the grounds, by reason of thefts, of at least 15,000*l.*; which is altogether a loss to landlords and farmers, in the Highlands, of 37,000*l.* sterling a year."

One cannot draw a hard and fast line between the two classes into which the population of the Scotch Highlands was at that time thus divided. That is to say, from an *ethnological* point of view. It would be contrary to all the teaching of history and of ethnology to suppose that this could be done. Assuming that, after the Norman Conquest, the aristocracy of the Highlands was composed chiefly of an element introduced subsequently to that Conquest (as history seems to indicate, and as a great number of Highland gene-

---

* "Sir George Staunton's enquiries ran chiefly on the subject of the Highland banditti who had infested that country since the year 1745. Butler informed him that many of them were not native Highlanders, but gipsies, tinkers, and other men of desperate fortunes." ("The Heart of Mid-Lothian.") Mr. Simson mentions that *Captain* is a favourite title for a "gypsy" leader. A *Watch* composed of such materials was, of course, a *Black Watch*.

alogies assert);—it is certain that, about six hundred years after the arrival of the intruders, the two castes would not be found existing side by side, unaffected by the blood of either. No such thing has ever happened, or can ever happen. A race of half-breeds, and ultimately a jumble of both races, in every variety of degree, would assuredly be the result of the invasion. The MacRaas, for example, of Johnson's time, were, in some cases, "as black and wild as any American savages whatever," while others were "as comely as Sappho."* The pedigrees of other clans show a similar mixture; the result of which is seen in the greatly-blended races of the Hebrides, and of the Highlands, whose complexions have been remarked upon by various travellers. And one curious outcome of this is, that many of the West Highland tales, related of "black fishermen," "black thieves," "dusky young men," and women, are told by people whose physical features are more allied to the swarthy than to the white-skinned side of their ancestry; although the stories in which such phrases occur must plainly have originated in the latter of these branches.

Therefore, although *Black Duncan*, the Gypsy-Cateran of "The Heart of Mid-Lothian," was accepted as typical of the robber caste; and the resident Laird—presumably a white man—as the representative of the law-abiding and reputable Highlanders (whose existence is apparent in all the allusions of travellers, and in all the statutes against *sorners* and thieves, which have been quoted); yet, in *each* of these two main divisions, there must have been a large number of hybrids. Again, owing to political differences, national and tribal, many who were born in the one caste must have passed into the other. This is actually stated in the Gartmore MS.: "Fewds and differences among familys in that country do not a little contribute to promote this mischief [thieving]; stealing and robbing by means of villains kept thus in dependance, and under absolute command, being the

---

* The amalgamating of most opposite races had really been going on for centuries before the Norman Conquest—White Gaels and Northmen marrying with Moors and Black Danes—but in this instance the white blood is traditionally assigned to the Norman widows of the chiefs; and probably it is only one instance out of many.

common way of resenting quarrels against one another." In the earlier part of last century, "thefts, robberys, rapines, and depredations became so common, that they began to be looked upon as neither shameful nor dishonourable; and people of a station somewhat above the vulgar, did sometimes countenance, encourage, nay head gangs of banditts in those detestable villanys." This latter feature was aptly typified in the person of MacDonell of Barisdale, of whom our author says, "that this gentleman, descended of the Glengary family, by the indolence and negligence of the head of that tribe, procured to himself such advantages and such interest with that branch of the clan, that he was able to force an extensive Highland neighbourhood, where are people of no small interest, to contribute to him a very considerable sum yearly for their protection"* But Barisdale, and others like him, belonged to a period subsequent, by many generations, to the days of Buchanan, when the creeks and forests of the Deucaledonian Islands were infested with vickings and robbers. And as the differences of race and custom were more strongly marked at that and earlier dates, it is better for our purpose that we should regard these times more particularly than those that are nearer our own day.

The *genuine* banditti of the Highlands and Islands, therefore, were of kindred race (to speak broadly): and that kinship ante-dated the Norman Conquest. In the words of Bailie Macwheeble,—" from the maist ancient times of record, the lawless thieves, limmers, and broken men of the Highlands, had been in fellowship together by reason of their surnames, for the committing of divers thefts, reifs, and herships upon the honest men of the Low Country.† . . . . All which was directly prohibited in divers parts of the

---

* It is stated by Scott, in a note to "Waverley," that this Barisdale, who was "one of the very last Highland gentlemen who carried on the plundering system to any great extent, was a scholar and a well-bred gentleman. He engraved on his broadswords the well-known lines—

' Hæ tibi erunt artes—pacisque imponere morem,
Parcere subjectis, et debellare superbos.' "

† And of the Highlands also. The words that describe such men, from the days when they were formidable *Galls* down to the last century, when they were simply *Caterans*, are words that belong to the speech of the Highlands—not of the Low Country alone.

Characteristics of the Highland Banditti. 327

Statute Book, both by the act one thousand five hundred and sixty-seven, and various others; the whilk statutes . . . . were shamefully broken and vilipended by the said sorners, limmers, and broken men, associated into fellowships, for the aforesaid purposes of theft, stouthreef, fire-raising, murther, *raptus mulierum*, or forcible abduction of women, and such like as aforesaid."

The other terms used in the laws that were passed for the suppression of such marauders were, it will be remembered, such as these—*sorcerers, bards, profest pleisants* (clowns), *sturdy beggars, thieves, idle bellies*, and *intolerable oppressors:* all of which, it was noticed, applied equally to the Scots, mossers, or bog-trotters,* and thieves, of the Borders, as well as to their later representatives, the Egyptians, or "gipsies." And the same likeness that was discernible between the historical *Scots* and *Picts* of Southern Scotland, and the scattered wanderers just spoken of, is visible as clearly in the Northern and Western portions of that country. Certain sections of the population of Scotland, not hitherto regarded as "gipsies," have distinctly their ancient ways and customs more fully represented by that lightly-esteemed caste, than by any other division of our fellow-countrymen, at the present day.† This identity was evident wherever we looked at particular sections of the Scottish people of the North-West :—in the fashion of their dwellings, whether turf-built wigwam, or skin- or canvas-

---

* This alternative epithet is used in a contemptuous fashion by the modern writers, though it ought to have held the same rank as "moss-trooper"; for it is precisely what is meant by "moss-trooper" and "mosser." Scott's Border predilections prevented him from making use of it in describing the "bog-trotters" of his own fatherland; though I think he employs it in describing the same race of people in Ireland—the wild, glibbed *ciuthachs*, or Black Irishmen. It is probably as applicable to the *ciuthachs* of the North-West. One of the last-century travellers (Pennant or Martin) somewhere makes reference to a band of sixty mounted natives, whom he saw disappearing over the crest of a hill (bent on the harmless errand of gathering shell-fish). He does not mention if the breed was in any way peculiar; but it is not unlikely that it resembled the small "Galloway nag" or "Irish hobby," on which the various divisions of those bog-trotters rode.

† "More fully" represented—especially in blood—but not wholly. Their *Pictish* peculiarity is now preserved only by the official descendants of those "fancied fools" and "profest pleisants," and, in a modified way, by our sailors. Others of their customs have also forsaken the gipsies proper, and are found in the mixed classes (referred to by Mr. Leland as, in some fashion or another, of gipsy kin), whose members are acrobats, cheap-jacks, prize-fighters, &c.

covered tent ; in the appearance of the people—in their dusky complexion, plaited hair, bright-coloured garments, the kerchiefs of the women, their ornaments of coral, silver, and, in some cases, jewels ; in their painted and tattooed skins ; in their avowed polygamy ; in their primitive culinary customs ; in such things as the manufacture of horn utensils, and of pottery ;* in the oath taken upon the dirk ; in the dirk itself ; in their favourite instruments of music, the harp, the violin, and the bagpipe, and in their love of song and minstrelsy ; in their practice of the arts of the seer, the "magician," and the mountebank ; and, lastly, in the habits which made them known as *sorners*, idlers, intolerable oppressors, depredators of the fiercest kind,—" murderers."

And those last characteristics, unamiable though they be, are by no means the least important. For they point back to the time when the *sorners* were *sorohen*, or chiefs, ruling over a territory, which was ultimately taken from them by strangers ; and over a tribe whose members, by degrees, acknowledged another allegiance ;—as, finally, they were obliged to do themselves, however reluctantly. Although, at the Claddagh, and among the scattered and wasted tribes of gypsies, there still exists a shadowy kingship,—a feeble *imperium in imperio* ; yet those tribal kings have a very limited sway ; and if, by any chance, their laws and those of the nation should jar against each other, there is no question as to which must be obeyed. But the existence of these relations is a fact of the deepest meaning.

NOTE.—It is recorded that Ferquhard, chief of the Mackintoshes, while playing at the game of "tables" in The Islands of the Foreigners (better known nowadays as The Hebrides), became involved in a quarrel which cost him his life. This was in the year 1274. Martin, again, referring probably to a time comparatively near our own, speaks of a "Sir Norman Macleod, and some others, playing at tables, at a game called in Irish, Falmermore, wherein there are three of a side, and each of them throw the dice by turns"; in the course of which game "there happened to be one difficult point in the disposing of one of the tablemen." The game of "tables" is stated in one account ("The Comprehensive His-

* This was not particularized ; but the manufacture of pottery is still carried on in the Hebrides, after a primitive manner ; a description of which has been given by Dr. Arthur Mitchell, Vice-President of the Scottish Antiquarian Society.

tory of England," Vol. II., p. 264) to have been draughts, and to have been a popular game in Scotland during the fifteenth century. But it is clear that "Falmermore" was not draughts. It is a game which depends upon the casting of dice ; and into which, therefore, the element of chance enters. Spenser, as we have seen, says of the "Carrows" of Ireland—" They wander up and down, living upon cards and dice ; the which, though they have little or nothing of their own, yet they will play for much money, which, if they win, they waste most lightly, and if they lose they pay as slenderly." And those "Carrows" were pretty clearly *ciuthachs* and naked men (for their only garment was the mantle, and that—says Spenser—they very often gambled away). The traditional *ciuthach*, who figures so prominently in the story of Diarmaid and Grainne, is also described as playing with Diarmaid at a game which Mr. Campbell spells, alternatively, *dinnsirean* and *disnean*—suggesting, as the translation, either "wedges" or "dice" The passion for gambling and games of chance asserts itself strongly throughout the West Highland Tales ; and these were among the things put down by law, two or three hundred years ago, as being "amongst the remanent abuses which, without reformation, defiled the whole Isles." In the traditions of Wales, also, it was noticed that the "bald, swarthy youths," whom Peredur discovered sitting at the hall-door of the "Black Oppressor," were engaged playing at chess. If the "tablemen" in the Hebridean and Irish game of "Falmermore" were really chessmen, then it would seem that this was a variety of that game unknown to us.

There is no doubt that chess, and one or many games of chance (perhaps inclusive of cards), must be placed very far back as "British" games. The discovery of one notable set of chessmen, during this century, is recounted by Dr. Wilson ("Old Edinburgh," Vol. I. p. 29) in these words :—" In 1831, a peasant in the parish of Uig, Isle of Lewis, on looking into a rude stone-built structure recently exposed by the waves, was affrighted at the sight of an assembly of elves or gnomes, and fled in dismay to his home ; but, urged by the curiosity of his wife, the superstitious Highlander was induced to return, and so became the possessor of the famous Lewis chessmen, subsequently described and illustrated in the 'Archæologia' by Sir Frederick Madden. They included in all fifty-eight pieces, ingeniously and elaborately carved from the walrus tooth. Ultimately the larger number of them were secured for the British Museum, where they now are." Other examples of this kind of chessman, "exactly similar, as well in style as in material," were found " in a bog in the county of Meath," in the early part of this century ; and one of them is represented in Mr. O'Donovan's edition of "The Book of Rights." And in that book (in the Introduction, pp. lxi-lxiv) the editor furnishes several important instances of Early-Irish chess-playing. That is to say, if it be right to regard "tables" as "chess." The word which Mr. O'Donovan regards as equivalent to chess, namely *fithcheall*, is not that which is given in Connellan's Irish Dictionary (in which *branamh* is stated to be "chess"). But, with regard to *fithcheall*, Mr. O'Donovan says : "The word *fithcheall* is translated 'tabulæ lusoriæ' by O'Flaherty, where he notices the bequests of Cathaeir Mor, monarch of Ireland, *Ogygia*, p. 311. In Cormac's Glossary, the *fithcheall* is described as quadrangular, having straight spots of black and white. It is referred to in the oldest Irish stories and historical tales extant, as in the very old one called Tochmarc Etaine, preserved in Leabhar na h-Uidhri, a manuscript of the twelfth century," in which one belonging to a certain queen is described as "a board of silver and pure gold, and every angle was illuminated with precious stones, and a man-bag of woven brass wire." In this instance the players play for stakes ("fifty dark grey steeds"); as it is pretty evident the "carrows" and "ciuthachs" of the Hebrides and of Ireland were accustomed to do. And in the special instance just referred to one of the players "arranges the *fithcheall*" before the game is begun. The chessmen themselves were not always of so inferior a quality as those found in county Meath and at Uig; for it is stated that of those belonging to "the chess-board of Crimthann Nia-nair," the one-half were made of gold and the other half of *findruine* (which is said to have been "brass, with silver hammered on it"). The value of one of these pieces is reckoned at "six *cumhals*"; or equivalent to eighteen cows. And these pieces must have been of considerable size, since it is stated that "The Hound of Cullin," while playing at this game on one occasion, with his own charioteer, hurled one of the figures at a messenger who had roused his anger by the nature of his message—piercing to the centre of his brain.

The "tabulæ lusoriæ," or "tables," may have included other games beside *fithcheall*. Shaw defines *beart* as "a game at tables," and Connellan says that *beartrach* is "backgammon"; and, while *taileasg, taimhleasg*, or *taibhleas*, is applied indifferently to chess, backgammon, and draughts, by Armstrong, McAlpine, and McLeod and Dewar, *chess* is distinguished as *branamh* by Connellan, and as *fedirn* by Shaw. There is thus considerable confusion of nomenclature. But when Martin speaks of "playing at tables, at a game called in Irish, Falmermore, wherein there are three of a side, and each of them throw the dice by turns," it is not only clear that the game described does not correspond to any of that kind now practised, but it is also evident that the term "tables" was so comprehensive that the name of the particular game, "Falmermore," required to be added.

These games appear to have been identified originally with certain races. They were "popular" in Scotland in the fifteenth century, the period in which such gypsy clans as the Black Douglases and the Gordons were the rulers of large districts of North Britain, and the "common dwelling" of South-Scotland was the wigwam of the gypsy. And the enactments against such games, and the people who played them, were first made by the king who overthrew the gypsy confederation of the fifteenth century—James the Second of Scotland. The glibbed "carrows" of Ireland—Wild or Black Irishmen—who were naked *ciuthachs, giofags*, or gypsies, were also dice-players and gamblers of the most inveterate sort: and it is with the gypsy classes that dice-players, players at fast-and-loose, thimble-riggers, and such-like are even yet identified by modern gypsiologists. There is one distinct Scotch example of this identity in the person of the gypsy Gemmell (whom Scott had in view when he painted Edie Ochiltree). This man seems to have traversed the greater part of southern Scotland—in the character of sorner, minstrel, jester, and newsmonger. He was styled the "King of the Beggars" —at a time when a *beggar* had little fear of a refusal to his demands— and possessed a harem of gypsy-queans "who ran the country and begged for him." Among his accomplishments was that of being a keen and skilful player of draughts; and he was also "ready and willing to play at cards or dice with any one who desired such amusement,"—playing sometimes for considerable stakes. (For we must learn to understand that the *beggar* of former days neither was, nor pretended to be, an object of compassion: he *demanded* a tribute rather than craved an alms.) These latter characteristics, it may be regarded as almost certain, had descended to him from the same source as that from which he derived his knowledge of genealogies, of old ballads and stories, his nomadic, polygamous habits, and all the accessories that made him a "gypsy."

In this, as in other instances, we have glimpses (fleeting and imperfect though they be) of a remote civilization which was yet hand-in-hand with what we now call barbarism. Those Irish "carrows," who would "play away mantle and all, to the bare skin, and then truss themselves in straw or in leaves," were certainly not "civilized." And many other features appertaining to them and to other tribes of Great Britain, which have been already pointed out, were equally of "savage" description. And yet those "savages" seem clearly to be the latest remnants of what, in some aspects, were highly civilized races; practising astrology and other sciences, or pseudo-sciences, and possessed of harps, chess-boards, chessmen, and personal ornaments, all of the most exquisite workmanship, and made of the costliest metals,—together with jewels and precious stones, which, like all the other attributes of those people, seem to point most distinctly to the East.

(A sketch of Gemmell will be seen in the Gallovidian Encyclopedia, under the name "An'ro Gemmle"; and he is also described by Scott, in his " Advertisement to The Antiquary." Some of the particulars with regard to "tables" are given by Dr. Skene, in his "Celtic Scotland," Vol. II. p. 507.)

BOOK II.

BOOK II.

CHAPTER I.

IN any attempt to realize the position of the "gypsy" races of Britain, as these existed before the Railway Era (a period effecting a complete revolution in "gypsydom,") it is essential that the following facts be kept in view. These all tend to confirm certain statements made, or theories advanced, in the foregoing chapters: in one or other of which they would have found a place, had they come under notice at an earlier date.

The various aspects of the question shade into each other so imperceptibly that it is not easy to separate one from another. But some attempt at classification may be made; and those many-sided people regarded, as far as possible, from different points. It may be as well, then, to consider "gypsies":—

I. As Pugilists and Prizefighters.

A perusal of Mr. Borrow's writings plainly reveals that, as recently as the earlier part of this century, pugilism and prize-fighting formed a striking characteristic of gypsy life. His purest gypsies, as well as those whose position is not so clearly definable, show this trait unmistakably. Jasper Petulengro, the leading gypsy of *Lavengro* and *The Romany Rye*, is a master of pugilism, and a professional fighter as well. "'I have been in the Big City, too,' said Mr. Petulengro; [*Lavengro*, vol. II. ch. 26] . . . 'I have fought in the ring—I have fifty pounds in my pocket . . .' '. . . as I said before, I have fifty pounds, all lawfully earnt money, got by fighting in the ring.'" Again [vol. II. ch. 22], "Lavengro" says to the Armenian, "fighting is a rough trade, and I am by no means certain that you are calculated for the scratch. It is not every one who has been brought up in the school of Mr. Petulengro and Tawno Chikno." At the end of Chapter 25 [of the first volume], Jasper says to his adopted brother—"We'll now go to the tents and put on the gloves; and I'll try to make you feel what a sweet thing it is to be alive, brother." Later on, these two have a more serious encounter (to appease the shade of the deceased Mrs. Herne), and after half an hour's fighting—with little advantage to the hero—Jasper declares that enough has been done to satisfy the feelings of his family; adding, that he finds his antagonist, as he expected, "less apt with the naked mauleys than the stuffed gloves." "Lavengro," also, in recalling various prize-fighting notables, says of "Black Richmond," "I knew him well; he was the most dangerous of blacks, even with a broken thigh." And "Big Ben" (Brain)—of whom he elsewhere says that he, with Johnson, was the last of the "old school" of prize-fighters—is thus pictured to us —"when he bared his mighty chest and back for combat . . . his skin was brown and dusky as that of a toad." [*Lavengro*, Chapters 26 and 27, of the first volume.] It is true that these two, Black Richmond and Ben Brain, are not proved by these extracts to have been *gypsies;* but, when other circumstances are remembered, it seems almost certain that they were so. In the famous battle, also, between "Lavengro" and "Black Jack," *The Flaming Tinman*, it is plain that the tinker is a thorough pugilist. He is, at the same time, a gypsy. He is sometimes called *Bosville*, sometimes *Anselo*,—both of which names Mr. Leland regards as peculiarly "gypsy." The place at which the fight takes place, is regarded by the neighbourhood—and by himself— as exclusively his own; and its name is *Mumpers'* or *Gypsies' Dingle*. Black Jack is perhaps more of what is called a "half-and-half" than a regular gypsy;* which variety is ex-

---

* The expression "a regular gypsy" will not stand analysis. "Gypsies" are admitted by those who know them, to show signs of the most opposite origins, being possessed of physical traits of the most varied kind. But there is a conventional gypsy; and there is a conventional prize-fighter. The former is dark-skinned, black-eyed, black-haired; the latter is never darker than *sallowness*, he

plained by Ursula Petulengro to be a mixture of genuine "Romanies" and "gorgios [*whites*], trampers, and basket-makers who live in caravans." Such a man would probably be best represented by the kind of prize fighter typified in the "Putney Pet" of *Verdant Green*, the genuine "bruiser,"—whose gypsy blood shows itself chiefly in the darkness of the hair, and in the stunted gypsy locks that hang down in front of each ear.* That prize-fighters, generally, were once identified with a certain *race*, seems also to be indicated by a reference that Thackeray makes in *The Virginians*. In describing the appearance of Sutton and Figg, two celebrated fighters of last century, he states that "their heads were shaven clean;" and he bases this statement on a description of the combat given in Dodsley's *Collection*. Now, this shaving of the head—whatever may have been the reason for it, was and is a favourite practice of various Mongoloid peoples: and I believe the professional acrobats and mountebanks of Tartary still follow this custom, as do also certain Mongoloid tribes of North America. The resemblances of physique and of customs, between British gypsies, and such nations in Asia and in America, has often been noticed. And if such bruisers as "Black Richmond" and "Big Ben" had their heads "shaven clean," like Sutton and Figg, of the eighteenth century—which was almost certainly the case, since they represented the "old school" of prize-fighters—then, in the persons of "Black Richmond" and "Big Ben" we have quite modern counterparts of the "bald, swarthy youths" who figure in the traditions of Wales and of the Western Highlands. For it is quite evident that "bald," when applied in a wholesale manner to young men and young women (as it is done in these legends) cannot refer to the natural baldness that comes from age. Indeed, the Gaelic word that expresses this quality (*maol*) is sometimes translated "cropped," by Mr. J. F. Campbell. Thus, the "bald, swarthy" people who swarm throughout those traditions were only

---

may have black eyes, he is usually black-haired. The former is not necessarily either ugly or handsome; the latter is usually ugly—of the "bull-dog" type. The former confesses himself a mixture of many races (says Mr. Simson); the latter seems to be a fresh crossing—between the already-hybrid gypsy and the lowest grade of white.

the prototypes of such dusky "bruisers" as Richmond and Brain. And it is likely that the Hebridean pirate of the fifteenth century, the "bald-headed, black-skinned" Allan MacRuari, belonged to the same aggressive, pugnacious stock.

Mr. C. G. Leland, also, in sketching the characteristics of our modern English gypsies,* pictures them as "living in the open air, taking much exercise, constantly practising boxing, rough riding, and other manly sports"; and he, further, makes allusion to the "old-fashioned gypsy bruiser" as a type that was once common, if it is not so now. Of modern "gypsy bruisers" he gives us a glimpse, when he speaks of "Single-Stick Dick," who "got his leg broken fightin' Lancaster Sam"; and another of these is Sam Smith, or Petulengro, who was always known on the roads as "Fighting Sam." Mr. Simson, when speaking of the Scotch gypsies, does not seem to emphasize (if he specifies at all) the particular branch of pugilism known as "prize-fighting"; though he very frequently indicates that those people were intensely combative. But when he states that "they were constantly exercising themselves in leaping, cudgel-playing," and other phases of athleticism; and that their great ambition was to "beat every one they met with, at these exercises"; it is not unlikely he includes pugilism among such exercises, whether the encounters were dependent upon prizes or not. The celebrated Will Faw of Yetholm, who died in 1847, at the age of ninety-five, is described as "a noted athlete in his day"; and this most likely includes the art of the pugilist. And Mactaggart says of the Galloway chief, Will Marshall, that he was "a good boxer," as well as "famous at the quarter-staff."

In nearly all these cases, then, we see how the gypsies have been identified with pugilism and prize-fighting; whether or not these attributes have been exclusively their property. We shall now regard them in another character.

* The only one of Mr. Leland's books that has been examined by the present writer is "The Gypsies"—his latest work. No doubt his other writings furnish additional proofs of the various features to which attention is drawn in these pages.

II. The Gypsies as Horse-dealers, Horsemen, and Jockeys.

How much was comprehended under the term "gypsy" only fifty years ago, it is difficult to realize now. So many characteristics have slipped away from "gypsydom" during the last generation or two; and have been appropriated by people of mixed and uncertain lineage. When Mr. Borrow, as a young man, was mingling with these people, they were pugilists. They were also famous horsemen.

In Scotland (Dr. Jamieson tells us, in his Dictionary) a *Caird*, or *gypsy*, was also known as a *jockie*. Mr. Borrow shows us that if that word be spelled *jockey* it is no misnomer. His first meeting with the tribe that he most associated with discloses this. In *Lavengro* (vol. I. chap. 16), his account of one scene at the horse-fair runs thus:—" Two or three men on horseback are hurrying through the crowd; they are widely different in their appearance from the other people of the fair; not so much in dress, for they are clad something after the fashion of rustic jockeys [*old-fashioned* jockeys], but in their look. No light brown hair have they, no ruddy cheeks, no blue quiet glances belong to them; their features are dark, their locks long, black, and shining, and there eyes are wild; they are admirable horsemen, but they do not sit the saddle in the manner of common jockeys, they seem to float or hover upon it, like gulls upon the waves; two of them are mere striplings, but the third [who is "Tawno Chikno"] is a very tall man with a countenance heroically beautiful, but wild, wild, wild."

When "Lavengro" associates with these people afterwards, he sees that they are masters of riding, and perfect judges of horseflesh (as he finds to his advantage, in the transaction recorded in *The Romany Rye*). They habitually attend horse-fairs for the purpose of buying and selling, and their leaders always travel on horseback. At the time when these books were written jockeys—as we now understand them—had already been evolved as a separate professional class, of no particular lineage. But the tie between the gypsy and the jockey had not been wholly broken even then. For example,

"Lavengro's" jockey friend at Horncastle speaks of "the gypsies as though they were of quite a different race from his own, with a different language, and different manners; but when he tells his history you learn that his father and grandfather both belonged to the classes which are inseparably connected with "gypsies," though perhaps not identical with them. And that he himself was brought up by a travelling basket-maker (who, apparently, was *not* of dark complexion, though of semi-gypsy habits). So far as regards his own colour, he is "a bit of a black myself." He is described as "a thin, wiry-made individual, with wiry curling brown hair; his face was dark, ... he might be about forty, wore a green jockey coat, and held in his hand a black riding-whip, with a knob of silver wire." This "green jockey coat" might, of itself, be held to hint at a connection with gypsies, who are described usually as wearing either green or scarlet. Green "is their favourite colour," says Mr. Simson. Besides, when this jockey at length discovers that he is conversing with "The Romany Rye" he displays an amount of interest that is unaccountable if he be not regarded as some kind of a "gypsy" himself: and forthwith he sacrifices two bottles of champagne "to the sweet master," "to the Romany Rye." The book, of course, is "fiction," but Borrow's "fiction" is generally accepted as very thinly-veiled fact. What kind of jockey-coat was worn as an ordinary garment for daily use can no doubt be learned from contemporary prints: but it is noticeable that Borrow's prize-fighters—though not spoken of as "gypsies"—are usually clothed in "jockey-coats;" sometimes in "Newmarket coats," which may be only another name for the same thing. Several of the gypsies pictured in Pyne's "Microcosm" (which takes us back seventy or eighty years) are clad in long Newmarket coats; and in the *Encyclopædia* article, which has frequently been referred to, it is stated that the English gypsy of (probably) an old-fashioned kind, "decks his Newmarket coat with spade-guineas or crown-pieces." And it is not going out of the way to observe that one of Mr. Leland's gypsy-friends, Anselo, "a determined and vigorous specimen of an old-fashioned English gypsy," whose coat had "a cutaway, sporting look" about it, carried in his hand "a regular Romany *tchupni* or *chŭckni*, which Mr. Borrow thinks gave rise to the word 'jockey.'"

Mr. Simson confirms these statements by many remarks in his *History*. Speaking of the Linlithgowshire bands, he says, "Many of the males dealt in horses, with which they frequented fairs—that great resort of the gipsies ; and these wanderers, in general, were considered excellent judges of horses." Two of the most celebrated leaders of this particular confederacy, "Captain" Alexander Macdonald, and his brother-in-law, "Captain" James Jamieson, "often dealt in horses, and were themselves frequently mounted upon the best of animals. The Arabians and Tartars (he adds) are scarcely more partial to horses than the gipsies." Another of his "gypsies,"—surely the most notable of all—"Captain "* William Baillie, "generally rode one of the best horses the kingdom could produce ; " and all of that chief's immediate kindred are figured as cavaliers. Of a Stirlingshire chief, of superior rank (among his kind), Charles Wilson by name, Mr. Simson says:—" He was a pretty extensive horse-dealer, having at times in his possession numbers of the best bred horses in the country. He most commonly bought and sold hunters, and such as were suitable for cavalry; and for some of his horses he received upwards of a hundred guineas apiece. . . . . Wilson himself was almost always mounted on a blood-horse of the highest mettle." These statements —and others could be cited if it were necessary—clearly show that a certain section of the Scottish gypsies are, or were, horse-dealers and horsemen, like their English kindred. None of these quotations prove that the "gypsy" of recent times was a "jockey" in the special race-course sense that that word now bears, though the *Lavengro* scene very nearly

* This title of "captain" is said to be very commonly applied to "gypsy" chiefs; and it also appears to have been hereditary, the son of a chief assuming it after his father's death, but not till then. This is stated at page 129 of Simson's "History," and Borrow says the same thing in effect, when—on meeting the gypsy Bosville in "Wild Wales"—he assumes that he is now "captain," as his father has died since they last met. It may be remembered that the leader of the Highland gypsy-leagues of a hundred and fifty years ago were always known as "Captain of the (Black) Watch." One—probably the only—instance of this custom yet remaining among the modernized classes is found in the title of "Captain" of the Cattan Clan—a hereditary title, about which there was once a celebrated dispute.

does this. But there is enough evidence to support the belief that the jockey *special* is merely a ramification from the general jockey or gypsy stock; the date of departure being not very much earlier than the time of which Mr. Borrow writes. As modern jockeys are of no special complexion—and perhaps mostly "fair whites," it may either be that that occupation fell eventually into the hands of men of a different race (much as the game of *lacrosse* is becoming monopolized by people of modern European blood, though borrowed from another people); or it may be that, even yet, the majority of the jockies of the present day consists of the descendants of white-skinned "gypsies," such as the Baillie and Wilson just spoken of. However this may be explained, it is at any rate clear that when Dr. Jamieson (in his Scottish Dictionary) identifies *Jockies* with *Cairds* (or gypsies), and with *Horse-Coupers* (or Horse-dealers), he has every reason to do so. In the North of England and the South of Scotland, at the present day, there are many memories of the marauding "Border-Coupers" of former times; whose habits were simply those of "moss-troopers," "mossers," or "gypsies."*

In speaking of that desolate moorland country, of which the Waste of Bewcastle forms an important section, a local guide-book states that "at one time the place was much inhabited by dealers in horses and cattle, called 'Border Coupers.' They were generally men full of a rude and ready kind of wit, continual talkers, hard drinkers, and often quarrelsome companions." This is really nothing else than a modified description (possibly referring to a more recent and quieter era) of the inhabitants of the same neighbourhood as they are described by the same writer, in other words. "The country around was in former times of bad repute, being the abode of the worst specimens of robbers and freebooters;

* Two examples in Border nomenclature seem to indicate this gypsy-jockey connection: *Jockeys' Shields*, a secluded retreat in the Geltsdale district of Cumberland; and *Black Shields*, an equally remote nook in Spadeadam Waste, once so dreaded as the haunt of "mosstroopers" and "freebooters," both places being in the one neighbourhood. ("*Shields*" is here used in the sense of *shield* or *shelter*, that is, *dwelling*; of which other examples may be seen in *Shields*, *Pollockshields*—a suburb of Glasgow—*Galashiels*, and *Blackshiels*—in Mid-Lothian.)

and the evil fame of the district had spread so wide that there was a by-law of the Corporation of Newcastle prohibiting any freeman of that city to take for apprentice a native of certain of these dales." These "robbers and freebooters" were plainly the people whom Scott at one time glorifies as "moss-troopers," and at another denounces as "gypsies."* And these are the people to whom he refers in the story he appends to *Guy Mannering* (as the foundation of Dandie Dinmont's adventure among the Cheviots). The little inn at which the betrayed farmer put up was known as *Mumps' Hall*, and it "had a bad reputation for harbouring the banditti who committed such depredations." Scott renders *Mumps' Hall* as *Beggars' Hotel;* and "beggar" was at one time a synonym for "gypsy."† The word *mumper* also signified *gypsy* (*e.g. Mumpers' Dingle* and *Gypsies' Dingle* are used alternately by the author of *The Romany Rye*). Grose, indeed, signifies that this title—which he writes "*Mumpers' Hall*"—is, or was, a common term for "an alehouse where beggars are harboured." So that this *Mumpers' Hall* at Gilsland was what in Scotland was styled a *Tinkler Howff*, or *Gypsies' Public-house*. And the landlady's nickname of *Meg Mumps* signified *Gypsy Meg:* her real name having been, it is stated, Margaret Carrick. And the "banditti" from whom the place got its name were therefore *mumpers* or *gypsies*. At a time when none of their kind dreamt of *paying* for anything they could take by force or by craft, these borderers were horse-thieves: later on, they were obliged to become horse-

---

* In his romances, at any rate, he unduly exalts these cut-throats and robbers. In his prose descriptions he is more just; for example, in the picture of Border life, which he gives us in the Introduction to the "Minstrelsy."

(In that description compare his statement that borderers "were not legally entitled to inhabit" the districts of Fife and Lothian during the sixteenth century with the similar law made by the citizens of Newcastle.)

When, as Sheriff of Selkirkshire, he answered Mr. Hoyland's queries as to the "gypsies" of his neighbourhood, he was very practical. He did not use such semi-romantic expressions as "moss-troopers," "freebooters," or "borderers" then. "They were thorough desperadoes, of the worst class of vagabonds. . . . Formerly, I believe ["I believe"—from the author of "The Monastery" and "The Lay of the Last Minstrel!"], they were much more desperate in their conduct than at present. But some of the most atrocious families have been extirpated."

† This may be taken for granted here: there are many proofs of the statement.

dealers. As one writer says of the Scotch gypsy-Baillies, they called themselves horse-*dealers*, but they were really horse-*stealers*,—whenever the opportunity offered. Even the respectable modern Stirlingshire gypsy, Wilson, to whom reference has been already made, did not scruple to steal a horse when he could. "It is said his people stole horses in Ireland, and sent them to him, to dispose of in Scotland. On one occasion his gang stole and sold in Edinburgh, Stirling and Dumbarton, a grey stallion three different times in one week." In course of time, therefore, and by the force of circumstances, the thieving marauders of the Borders became partly disciplined into paying for what they took: the horse-*stealers* became horse-*dealers*, or "coupers," to use the local word. But "moss-trooper" or "horse-couper," they were virtually the same people; those whom we loosely style "gypsies."

At the present day you will find that the principal horse-fairs of the Borders are largely attended by "gypsy" families, who are often extensive horse-dealers, and people of substance—though continuing to live the nomadic life, by preference. And Mr. Simson states, also, that apart from these unconverted gypsies, the horse-dealing fraternity in Scotland is largely made up of men of "gypsy" blood—though of modern, civilized habits—and that the gypsy dialects, or many words belonging to them, are heard all around you at a Scotch horse-market. Mr. Leland, also, bears similar testimony (in his latest book on the subject). The commonest offence for which his gypsies are "wanted" by the police is that of horse-stealing. "Horse-stealing (we are told) is not a crime, but only 'rough gambling' on the roads." This does not, of course, prove that modern gypsies are horse-*dealers:* though there is food for reflection in the Philadelphia gypsy's dictum that "horse-dealin' is horse-stealin', in a way, among real gentlemen." But the horse-*dealing* side of the gypsy is seen again and again throughout the book we are speaking of; and, indeed, to those men who have studied gypsy life it must appear an absurdly superfluous thing to regard the point as one that requires proof. And the authority we are quoting plainly announces that the other meaning of "jockey"—that of horseman—has not yet ceased to describe one characteristic of that caste. The "old-fashioned English gypsy" who paid him a visit in London, carrying in his hand "a heavy-handled whip, a regular Romany *tchupni* or *chŭckni*," came *on horseback:* and the typical English gypsy of the present day is represented as "living in the open air, taking much exercise, constantly practising boxing, *rough riding*, and other manly sports."

III. *Gypsies as Mountebanks and Jugglers.*

When Mr. Leland compares George Borrow—at one moment of his life—to "an old-fashioned gypsy bruiser, full of craft and merry tricks," he may mean much by the latter clause, or he may mean—not so much. I do not think the bull-dog-visaged pugilist, who is not inaptly represented by *The Putney Pet*, is popularly believed to be a man "full of craft and merry tricks." His expression is not emphatically "merry," whatever it may hint of "craft." And yet a man who has studied closely the ways of such as he could not have used such a phrase in a meaningless, and even perverse fashion. If the allusion is not explained by any other of this writer's statements, he, at any rate, must fully appreciate its value.

Certain characteristics of the gypsies who figure in *Lavengro* and *The Romany Rye* go far to make one understand this connection between the "old-fashioned gypsy bruiser," and "tricks" of one kind or another. So, indeed, do the remarks of Mr. Borrow's American successor. Both of these authors (and their Scotch congeners as well) indicate to us very plainly " that among all these show-men and show-women, acrobats, exhibitors of giants, purse-droppers, ginger-bread-wheel-gamblers, shilling knife-throwers, pitch-in-his-mouths, punches, cheap-jacks, thimble-rigs, and patterers of every kind, there is always a leaven and a suspicion of gypsiness." And it is not a very uncharitable thing to say that most of these people may be described as "full of craft," and tricks (whose "merry" nature is perhaps more clearly seen by the successful trickster than by his dupe). Out of the catalogue of professions just given, that of the acrobat approaches most nearly to the phase of gypsydom to be considered just now; though "acrobat" has now, like "jockey" and "prize-fighter"—acquired a special and restricted meaning.

At the horse-fair, in *Lavengro*, where "Tawno Chikno" and his comrades are first seen, and their wild appearance and splendid horsemanship described, they are pictured as going through certain performances that are now usually dissociated from gypsies, jockeys, pugilists, and horse-dealers. "As they rush along, the crowd give way on all sides, and now a kind of ring or circus is formed, within which the strange men exhibit their horsemanship, rushing past each other, in and out, after the manner of a reel, the tall man occasionally balancing himself upon the saddle, and standing erect on one foot." Mr. Simson's Linlithgowshire chief, "Captain" M'Donald, was a counterpart to these. "He took great pains in training and learning some of his horses various evolutions and tricks. He had, at one time, a piebald horse so efficiently trained, and so completely under his management, that it, in some respects, assisted him in his depredations. By certain signals and motions, he could, when he found it necessary, make it clap close to the ground, like a hare in its furrow. It would crouch down in a hollow piece of ground, in a ditch, or at the side of a hedge, so as to hide itself, when M'Donald's situation was like to expose him to detection." Now, in these instances, which are not of an exceptional nature, we have distinctly the characteristics of circus-riders and mountebanks. Such a horse as M'Donald's piebald would be the delight of any "hippodrome"; and you may see any number of Tawno-Chiknoes all over the kingdom,—"balancing themselves upon the saddle and standing erect on one foot." Moreover, we must remember that, although Mr. Borrow was of too late a generation to bear testimony to the practice, it was the prevailing custom of those gypsy-mountebanks—a few years before "Lavengro's" day—to "artificially discolour their countenances": for which reason, they were known in some parts of the country as *faws*, or painted men. They were also known as *blueskins*, and *green-men* (Gaelic, *daoine-guirm*) : and, at an earlier period still,* when they used to "travel about the country in compani.s of nearly a hundred persons each," they "*usually dressed themselves in a fantastic costume.*" Those of them who were "old-fashioned gypsy bruisers" were accustomed, as Thackeray reminds us, to shave their heads. Now, try to figure such a man before you, and what have you but a painted circus-clown?

It was taken for granted, at an earlier stage, that the harlequins and mountebanks of our circuses and pantomimes were called *clowns*, because they were once *aborigines*; in the eyes of a race of conquerors, who made them perform for their delectation (a proceeding paralleled in conquered countries, at the present day). And the fact that among the earliest-known races of this country were those "nimble blackamoors" whose painted faces confronted the Roman legions in many a fierce encounter, was held as in itself a good reason for giving this pedigree to the modern Clown-Pict of the circus. It was assumed that this clown-pedigree must have ceased to be *racial* at a very early date, and to have been *professional* only, for many generations. (That is, the practice of circus or pantomimic drollery doing as little to prove the lineage of the performer, as the ability to play the game of *lacrosse* proves the player to be descended from the Red Indians who have taught it to Modern-Americans.) But, after considering the statements just made, the period at which the *Clown* and *Pict* was also *Moor*, does not seem so very remote. Those nomadic *faws* who "usually dressed themselves in a fantastic costume," appear to have been describable by *all* of the terms just employed: the word "clown" being, indeed, used in both of its significations. For such people are not understood to have lived in cities. Now, all civilization has proceeded—and must proceed— from cities. When one looks back at early England, one sees that what we call "civilization" has resulted from the spread of *city*† ideas: the influence of the towns gradually

---

* Further reference to these points will be made a few pages hence.

† The enforcer of modern law is known to our *tory* classes (who detest him and the civilization he represents)—as a *gav-moosh*, *i.e.*, "city-man" (literally, "*polis*-man").

spreading out and out into the wilder districts, and becoming paramount. So that these nomadic mountebanks may have been "clowns" (as opposed to "citizens") not very many centuries ago.

Mr. Borrow's handsome gypsy is only partially a representative of the mountebank. He has nothing grotesque about him: his face is not painted: his dress is more that of a jockey: and the ugly features of the early "Moor"—mimicked on the painted face of the modern Clown—have not been inherited by him. Neither is he a good specimen of the conventional horse-dealer, or the conventional jockey. But he offers a sample of the "gypsy" at a time when all these qualities or attributes met in the members of a certain caste. And, at the same time, he and his comrades, while representing the various phases of gypsy life already dwelt upon, are distinctly nomadic circus-riders, mountebanks and acrobats, as they are seen riding round and round the open space at the horse-fair. The *clown*, pure and simple, does not appear in this picture of Borrow's; but it does not follow that none of the gypsies present took that part. Those wandering, open-air circuses are fast becoming obsolete; and the members of such troupes are not obviously *gypsies* now-a-days; but when you do stumble upon a performance of this sort, in some remote common, do you not always find a "Mr. Merryman" there, to crack his stale jokes? And if among people of this description, in nineteenth-century England, "there is always a leaven and a suspicion of gypsiness," there seems more than a suspicion of it in Germany of the eighteenth century. The rope-dancers in *Wilhelm Meister* are pretty clearly gypsies: at any rate, it is evident that Goethe was thinking of a gypsy girl when he drew *Mignon*, who was a little painted mountebank. "Her brownish complexion could scarcely be discerned through the paint." After her purchase—"She was frequently observed going to a basin of water, and washing her face with such diligence and violence, that she almost wore the skin from her cheeks; till Laertes, by dint of questions and reproofs, learned that she was striving by all means to get the paint from her skin; . . . . after which, having come again to her natural state, she exhibited a fine brown com-

plexion, beautiful, though sparingly intermingled with red."*
When she saluted Wilhelm, she "laid her right hand on her breast, the left on her brow, and bowed deeply: . . . she gave her answers in a kind of broken German, and with a strangely solemn manner, every time laying her hands on her breast and brow, and bowing deeply." From which it may be gathered, that the eighteenth-century German mountebanks used to "artificially discolour" their skins, like the *faws, blueskins,* and *green-men* of the British Islands: their complexion may be assumed to have been brown: and they saluted with the semi-*salaam* of our modern circus acrobats and painted clowns. If the German refugees whose fashions are compared by Captain Burt to those of "Moorish" people, and of certain castes in the Scotch Highlands, were refugees of the *gypsy* kind (and it was precisely at this period that Germany was expelling and hanging its gypsies), then it is easy to understand that comparison. The fact that such German gypsies took refuge in this country last century may account for certain details of "gypsydom," such as the presence of words that appear to be of purely Modern-German nature, in the Slang vocabulary; Slang and the various gypsy dialects being closely related to each other.†

But it is not necessary to turn to Germany to account for the fact that "the great residuum" in our islands (to borrow the very apt phrase of a writer upon this subject) is *largely* made up of what are called "gypsies,"—more or less pure in blood. And it is not necessary to suppose that the street acrobat, with his tawdry, tinselled garments, his black eyes, black hair and sallow face, or the mixed population of thimble-riggers, acrobats, and tricksters of all kinds

---

* Afterwards—when she is dead—her skin is described as *white*. But Mignon is a fictitious personage; and when Goethe wrote of her, later on, he had plainly half-forgotten the little gypsy he had first introduced. *She* was no doubt taken from the every-day life that passed before his eyes.

(The quotations are, of course, taken from Carlyle's Translation.)

† For example: *kinchin*, for child. This is simply *kindchen*, and not an earlier form of Dutch origin (such as *mannikin, napkin, Wilkin, Tomkin, Jenkin,* &c.). Other examples may be seen in a Scotch "gypsy" word for "ass,"—*aizel*, which is likely nothing but the German *esel*, written phonetically by Mr. Simson; and also *vrouw*, which is included among the "cant" terms for "a wife," and which may be either Modern German or Modern-Dutch. The transition from German *aber* (but) to "gypsy" *awer*, is also very slight.

that one sees at country-fairs and race-courses, are merely descended from a recent immigration of such people as the eighteenth-century mountebanks of Germany. There ought to be abundance of evidence obtainable—there certainly is *some*—which will go to prove that there has been a population of this sort existent in these islands for a length of time that cannot be defined, but that *certainly* goes back a thousand years, and probably as far again—and farther. Such people—presumably swarthy—will shortly be glanced at as Faws, Green-men and Blueskins. In the meantime, it is enough to observe that the salient features of this kind of people were apparently characteristic of British "gypsies," less than a century ago: those of that caste, as represented under fictitious (?) names by a thorough student of their habits, having been as much mountebanks and circus-riders as they were prize-fighters, jockeys and gypsies. So that, when "an old-fashioned gypsy bruiser" is referred to as "full of craft and merry tricks," there is no contradiction whatever in the combination of terms.

There are other features of "gypsydom," to which only a passing reference need be made here. We have seen that "show-men" are included among those who are, in some way, connected with this caste, or these castes, in England. The same thing is indicated as existing in Germany, at the period of *Wilhelm Meister*. Those rope-dancers from whom Mignon was bought were very plainly gypsies (of perhaps an uncertain degree of intensity). They were also a kind of actors, or strolling-players: and, indeed, the line that divides them from Wilhelm's theatrical associates is not very strongly defined. If one is to accept *literally* a certain passage in that book, those strolling actors who were his companions were nothing else than "gypsies." At a later period of the story (in the third chapter of Book VII., Carlyle's Translation), Jarno asks Wilhelm—" How is it with your ancient maggot of producing something beautiful and good in the society of *gypsies?*" The word may only have been used contemptuously without any precise meaning; but perhaps it was appropriate enough. But if strolling players, generally, during the eighteenth and preceding centuries, are to be regarded as chiefly belonging to a certain *race*, then a field of conjecture opens out before us which is too extensive to enter upon at present.

What is more to the purpose is the fact, that all the sketches of British gypsies, by men who are best entitled to describe them, reveal them to us as intimately associated with our "old English pastimes." Mr. Leland's typical English gypsy is represented to us as "living in the open air, taking much exercise, constantly practising boxing, rough riding, and other manly sports" (and, at the same time, strongly attached to the "old English pastime" of drinking beer). The same testimony is given by Mr. Borrow, whose gypsies have all the national love of horse-racing and horse-dealing; who are capital riders; and who are equally first-rate boxers, whether "with the naked mauleys or the stuffed gloves." So with Mr. Simson: his gypsies "were constantly exercising themselves in leaping, cudgel-playing, throwing the hammer, casting the putting-stone, playing at golf, quoits, and other games; .... they were extremely fond of the athletic amusement of 'o'erending the tree'"—a feat of strength very much like that known in the Highlands as "tossing the caber." The most eminent of the Galloway gypsies of last century was celebrated both for his skill at fisticuffs and with the quarter-staff. When Mr. Hughes pictures an old English fair in the Vale of White Horse, he puts in a gypsy as one of the champions in "the noble old game of backsword"; which "is sadly gone out of late"—like the gypsies. When Washington Irving delineated the oldest-fashioned neighbourhood that was possible in the England of his day, and the oldest-fashioned squire, he had to say of "Starlight Tom," the chief of the local gypsies: "It is said that the squire winks hard at his misdeeds, having an indulgent feeling towards the vagabond, because of his being very expert at all kinds of games, a great shot with the crossbow, and the best morris dancer in the country." The crossbow has been laid aside long ago; and the morris dance—unless in very modified forms—is no longer danced (which is not to be regretted, if it resembled the mænad-reel that Mr. Simson pictures). But this "blackamoors' dance,"* and the use of

* The term was given by white people to one dance at least. But the name

the crossbow, are two of our most ancient usages, the former having been regarded by Continental people of last century as peculiarly *British*. Again, other such old practices as cock-fighting, badger-baiting, rat-catching, and the other pleasures of the cock-pit, are understood to be specially "Old English" amusements. Mr. Emerson remarks upon such customs, and the people who practise them, as being markedly English. "Dear to the English heart is a fair stand-up fight. The brutality of the manners in the lower class appears in the boxing, bear-baiting, cock-fighting, love of executions, and in the readiness for a set-to in the streets, delightful to the English of all classes. The costermongers of London streets hold cowardice in loathing: 'we must work our fists well; we are all handy with our fists.'" "Cromwell, Blake, Marlborough, Chatham, Nelson, and Wellington are not to be trifled with, and the brutal strength which lies at the bottom of society, the animal ferocity of the quays and cockpits, the bullies of the costermongers of Shoreditch, Seven Dials, and Spitalfields, they know how to wake up." That is to say, Emerson regarded this bullying, cock-fighting disposition as forming the foundation of English strength—as the backbone of British nationality: its worst features being refined away in the more cultivated classes.

Now, the very people in whom this bullying, cock-fighting element bulks most largely are those semi-gypsy "bruisers,' whose bull-dog features are exemplified by *The Putney Pet*. When Borrow visited the cock-pit at Westminster, the proprietor ("dressed in a brown jockey coat, and top boots") was a typical man of this sort, believing in nothing but dog-fighting, rat-catching, badger-baiting, and bull-baiting (not then given up). And he, though not spoken of as a "gypsy," has certainly "a leaven and a suspicion of gypsiness." Cock-fighting, indeed, is a practice that in Scotland seems to

---

is one of a general nature, and the "Moors" themselves had probably a great variety of dances. What was afterwards remembered as "Kemp's Morris," seems to have differed somewhat from the commonest kind of "Moors' Dance." This man—himself, no doubt, a "gypsy"—is said to have "danced a morris from London to Norwich in nine days, of which he printed the account, A.D. 1600, entitled 'Kemp's Nine Days' Wonder.'" (Referred to by Grose.)

have been almost identified* with "gypsies"; and if their English kindred had been as closely described, it is probable the same statement could have been made regarding them. As for the brutal, bullying nature which Emerson found to underlie English society, that—if we are to believe our artists—goes along with a particular *type* of face and figure, that of the prize-fighter and burglar: a type whose chief points are—a strong, thick-set frame, a large, ugly mouth, a short nose, black hair (trained in a lock before each ear), and a "bullet" head. The physique, in short, of a certain *race*, and that, apparently, the mixed caste known on the roads as half-and-halfs, or mumpers.

When Mr. Emerson recognized that "brutal strength which lies at the bottom of society, the animal ferocity of the quays and cock-pits," as the basis upon which much that is peculiarly English has been reared, he was in accordance with many other observers of "English Traits." But his *ethnological* statements—on this subject—are so confused and contradictory as to be practically worthless.† He takes one

---

* "The gipsies in Fife followed the same occupations, in all respects, as those in other parts of Scotland, and were also dexterous at all athletic exercises. They were exceedingly fond of cock-fighting, and, when the season came round for that amusement, many a good cock was missing from the farm-yards." (Simson's "History," p. 182.)

† For example, in his chapter on "Race," he remarks thus—"Again, as if to intensate the influences that are not of race, what we think of when we talk of English traits really narrows itself to a small district. It excludes Ireland, and Scotland, and Wales, and reduces itself at last to London, that is, to those who come and go thither. The portraits that hang on the walls in the Academy Exhibition at London, the figures in *Punch's* drawings of the public men, or of the club-houses, the prints in the shop-windows, are distinctive English, and not American, no, nor Scotch, nor Irish; but 'tis a very restricted nationality." It is not easy to understand what is here meant by "the influences that are not of race." But there have been portraits upon the Academy walls within recent years, with regard to the originals of two of which it may be observed—that one was described by a contemporary as "very like a gypsy," and "almost Indian-looking," while the other's cast of countenance has been successfully likened to that of a Red Indian. These were men of purely insular lineage, and specimens of our very best kind of Englishmen. Both belonged to that "restricted nationality," which Mr. Emerson says "we think of when we talk of English traits." And Mr. Emerson's representative "Englishman" is a *fair*-white.

Again, while restricting the typical Englishman to these narrow limits, he tells us—in the same chapter—that, as soon as he landed at *Liverpool*, he found himself among the orthodox "Englishmen." And when he speaks of English sportsmen, he says—"These men have written the game-books of all countries, as

particular type, and dubs it "English," without giving any reason for doing so. And the one type which he chooses to call "English" is precisely the opposite of that which is identified with all our oldest observances. "On the English face (says he) are combined decision and nerve, with the fair complexion, blue eyes, and open and florid aspect." "The old men are as red as roses, and still handsome. A clear skin, a peach-bloom complexion, and good teeth are found all over the island." This, no doubt, is a true picture of certain kinds of Englishmen. But it does not describe even one-half of the mixed people whom we call "English." According to our modern ethnologists, a great proportion—the majority, some say—of our population is made up of *dark* whites (*melanochroi*), the hypothetical descendants (on one side) of purely *black* men. And it is exactly this class of Englishman that comes most prominently into view when we try to investigate the typical "Old English" customs. Not the men of "clear skins, and peach-bloom complexions" at all: at any rate, not such people *conspicuously*.

That there are people who are thoroughly "English," and who are yet as unlike Mr. Emerson's rosy, white-skinned Englishmen as they can well be, is a fact that more than one of Mr. Emerson's fellow-countrymen have recorded. Here is one transatlantic sketch of an ordinary Englishwoman, not supposed to represent any special lineage, and certainly not understood to be in any degree of foreign extraction:—" Lady Verifier was spare, angular, and sallow, with large black eyes and coarse black hair, like a squaw's; a sort of woman less

Hawker, Scrope, *Murray*, Herbert, *Maxwell*, *Cumming*, and a host of travellers." That is, fifty per cent. of his South South-Britons are Scotchmen.

But it is unnecessary to make farther extracts. Whatever Mr. Emerson understood by "the influences that are not of race," he must have meant the above remarks to apply to racial differences; or they were very much out of place in a chapter that is headed "Race." The fact is, that while the observations of educated visitors to our country must always be interesting (doubly interesting when these hail from America), and often instructive, yet the opinions of a mere *visitor* are of little value in deciding questions affecting the ethnology of Modern Britons. Mr. Emerson (in this chapter) appears for the moment in exactly the same light as those European travellers who, after a hasty scamper through the States, from Maine to Texas, believe themselves fitted to give an opinion on the racial position of the Americans. A question of this kind can only be decided by statistical inquiry; though the remarks of men who have studied certain divisions of humanity for many years have certainly a recognizable value.

uncommon in England than she is supposed to be."* Such a woman, if found dwelling in a caravan or a tent, would be popularly regarded as at least a quadroon "gypsy," if not a half-blood. But when seen in cultivated society, and possessed of education and the current manners, she does not attract the least attention: because her physical attributes are similar to those of half the people she meets. And if, as we may suppose, her ancestors for five, ten, or even fifteen generations, are known to history—and veritably her ancestors—no one thinks of saying that she is of "gypsy" descent. But a man cannot look like a gypsy, nor a woman like an Indian squaw, without having inherited blood of a kindred strain.

Thus, one who has observed our characteristics as closely as Emerson, has stated that the "squaw" type of Englishwoman is not uncommon. Another American—and one whose long residence in England, and whose study of the residuum of both countries, enables him to speak with some authority for either side of the Atlantic—has made the discovery "that our entire nomadic population, excepting tramps, is not, as we thought in our childhood, composed of English people like ourselves. It is leavened with direct Indian blood. . . . It was old before the Saxon heptarchy." Again, he says, "I was much impressed at this fair (Cobham Fair) with the extensive and unsuspected amount of Romany existent in our rural population." And that this element is not confined to rustics and nomads he shows us in his Canterbury sketch, wherein we see that not only the knife-grinding tinker with whom he conversed, and the gypsy woman with the hand-cart, who passed along the street,—not only these two were quite conversant with the "Romany" speech, but a "fat, little, elderly" tradesman, standing near, was quite as much at home in that dialect as either of the peripatetic tinkers, or the "Romany Rye" himself!

The fair held at Cobham, at which Mr. Leland was "much impressed with the extensive and unsuspected amount of Romany existent in our rural population," is characterized by him as "an old-fashioned rural fair," "pleasant and *purely*

* From a recent skit by Mr. R. G. White in *The Atlantic Monthly* of July, 1883.

English," and, regretfully commenting upon the decay of such gatherings, he says, "In a few years the last of them will have been closed, and *the last gypsy will be there to look on.*" That is, at a "purely English" fair, the gypsy element was everywhere so apparent as to greatly impress an observant student of men: and, step by step with the departure of such distinctively "Old English" gatherings, goes the fast-vanishing "gypsy" type.

But this—however much at variance with the generally received theories of the "gypsy" pedigree—is all of a piece with the facts that the foregoing pages have spoken of. All these things tell us one consistent story of their own—ignoring altogether any modern "theory." They show us that these supposititiously-alien people have proved themselves the very life of our old-world fairs and such-like gatherings. When the general population of the country (whether by reason of blood, or merely of "evolution") has shown its indifference to our oldest sports and pastimes—shooting with the crossbow, morris-dancing, "the noble old game of back-sword," quarter-staff play, minstrelsy (of the ancient order), and a score of quaint and antique customs, now half-forgotten, and only partly represented by circus-performers, mountebanks, and travelling showmen; while the general population has either been indifferent to these things, or has taken an occasional and forced interest in them, those intensely-conservative people known as "gypsies" have clung to them as the most important things in the world.

As Mr. Leland writes from what may be called the conventional standing-point, some of his phrases must be accepted (in these pages) in a different sense from his own. There is no reason why we should not recognize this "Old English" element as "old before the Saxon heptarchy"— in some degree. Nor why we should say that the blood of our population is *not* "leavened with Indian blood." But what are "English people like ourselves"? Some of these —a minority, it is believed,—have the "fair complexion, blue eyes, and open and florid aspect," that Mr. Emerson noticed (to the exclusion of all other types). Some of these fair-whites *are* "ourselves": when not "ourselves," they are our brothers and sisters. But what of the dark-whites that are found everywhere—in the Peerage, the learned professions, in all ranks of our population, from the Duke to the Costermonger? Whence did they come? Or, whence did *we* come —for the dark-whites are "ourselves" too: whence did "we" come? From a blending of fair-whites and pure *blacks*, says Professor Huxley. The blood of all the educated British *Melanochroi*, like that of the uneducated classes of which Mr. Leland writes, is "leavened with Indian blood." Our nomadic population, after all, *is* "composed of English people like ourselves."

It is not so very long ago that the conventional "gypsy" was of almost black complexion. The followers of John the Faw, in the old ballad, are spoken of as "the *black* crew," and as "*black*, but very bonny." The rhyme with which Scotch mothers used to awe their children spoke of "the *black* Tinkler." And in 1681, the Indians of New England, or "Moors" as they were also styled by the settlers, were pronounced by William Penn to be "as black as gypsies."* Now, at that period, or not much earlier, those British gypsies used to "travel about the country in companies of nearly a hundred persons each." (At earlier dates, in companies of thousands, but we need not look so far back at present.) These companies have dwindled down to tens and fives and units. What has become of the people?

Jasper Petulengro's answer to Mr. Borrow is, in some sense an answer to this question. When he is asked whether his people will always keep their individuality, he replies:— "Can't say, brother; nothing lasts for ever. Romany chies (women) are Romany chies still, though not exactly what they were sixty years ago. . . . I tell you what, brother, if ever gypsyism breaks up, it will be owing to our chies having been bitten by that mad puppy they call gentility." For

---

* See Mr. Eggleston's article in *The Century Magazine* of May, 1883. This statement of Penn's may even mean that the British gypsies of 1681 were *quite* black: indeed, it is very likely, for various reasons, that they were so. Penn says the Indians were as black as gypsies, "*but by design*"; and it seems that other travellers held a like opinion at that date. Various dark-skinned races of the Pacific are accustomed to make their brown skins *black* by artificial means; so that, if Penn's Indians did so, they did nothing extraordinary. To say, then, that those Indians made themselves "as black as gypsies" may signify that the gypsies of 1681 were distinctly "blackamoors."

"gentility," substitute "pseudo-Christian civilization," and Jasper's answer is good enough. Borrow's most inveterate gypsies announce their preference for doing things "Romanly" rather than "Christianly;" and one woman contemptuously advises another, who has shown some modern tendency, to "take a fan and a sacrament." The "peculiar *morale*" of our gypsy classes is nothing more than the early heathenism of our islands; modified in many ways. And the reason why gypsyism has broken up—for its reign in the British Islands* is nearly over—and why the gypsy bands have dwindled down from hundreds to tens, is this—that Christianity (or what passes for Christianity) and modern civilization have been gradually getting the better of Paganism and the earliest kind of Toryism. That, as the historian of the Scotch gypsies continually impresses upon his readers, *gypsies* have, for many generations, been giving up the ancestral way of living, and identifying themselves with the general population of the country. On this account, therefore, the proverbially *black* gypsies that used to range the country in bands of a hundred or so, are now represented by small families that are merely *tawny* in complexion. The black men have only disappeared *as* black men. Their blood is only more widely diffused to-day, and they live again as *Melanochroi*. This means that, during an uncertain period of the past, the increase of "fair whites" has been checked, and the existence of purely black Britons put an end to, by the amalgamation of the former with the latter. Because, of course, for every Black that has disappeared by the union of the opposite races, a White has disappeared also. And the extinction of the "Moors," with the consequent diminution of the Fair Whites, has caused a steady increase of the Dark White class, or *Melanochroi*.

---

* In the United States, as Mr. Leland points out, gypsyism is in a more flourishing condition than in this country, and is likely to survive for an indefinite period. The day when all the "commons" in the United States will be private property is so remote that it can scarcely be realized. And not till then can "gypsies" be as fettered as in these islands. Till which period they will not feel themselves compelled to relinquish their ancient habits.

The same may be said of those gypsies who have been transported, and emigrated voluntarily, to Australia. In that country they also abound, and there—as in the States—they will have every opportunity for continuing their archaic habits for many generations.

But the *Melanochroi*,—the bulk of the Modern-Britons,—have made a new people. These are not identified, by blood, with the traditions of either stock from which they descend. What the usages and traditions of the various White-British races have been, it is not our purpose to consider here. The facts that have been touched upon in this chapter seem to say very strongly that very many of those practices which we are accustomed to regard as immemorially attached to British ground, have been bound up with the existence of the swarthiest sections of the community. These ancient usages have nearly all left us: and their latest guardians have been the dusky people whom we call gypsies. It was at one of the most primitive gatherings yet to be seen in this country—" an old-fashioned rural fair," " pleasant and purely English "—that an experienced student of British types was " very much impressed . . . with the extensive and unsuspected amount of Romany existent in our rural population." The gypsy, as a separate individual type, has almost vanished, and these ancient usages, with which he is identified, have almost vanished too. "Old-fashioned rural fairs," like this—so deeply impregnated with gypsyism—are almost done. "In a few years the last of them will have been closed, *and the last gypsy will be there to look on.*"

. . . .

"It is worth noting that among all these show-men and show-women, acrobats, exhibitors of giants, purse-droppers, ginger-bread-wheel gamblers, shilling knife-throwers, pitch-in-his-mouths, punches, cheap jacks, thimble-rigs and patterers of every kind there is always a leaven and a suspicion of gypsiness." This announcement, made by one who has made himself intimately acquainted with the life of such people, is—as we have seen—quite in accordance with the glimpses given us in certain statutes, enacted against the Scotch gypsies of about three hundred years ago. These, it was noticed, were players at fast-and-loose, fortune-tellers, glib-tongued minstrels (accustomed to "bard and flatter"), mountebacks ("fancied fools," "professed pleasants," or clowns), and "sorcerers"—given over to "the black art of their forefathers" which they studied in "books of spells" that no moss-trooping Border Gypsy ever travelled without.

These people, whether looked at in the northern or the southern portions of Great Britain, during the fifteenth, sixteenth, and seventeenth centuries, were described as traversing the country in powerful bands: "masterful beggars," "insolent oppressors," "sorners."

But a community of this description seems to have existed also in London, from a very early period. At the time of the Great Plague the municipal government of London had to take stringent measures against "the multitude of rogues and wandering beggars that swarm about in every place about the city." At that period, or earlier, we read of "such places as Smithfield, with its world of cut-purses, drolls ['fancied fools'], and 'motions' [Punch-and-Judy Shows],"* and "Moorfields, where ballad-mongers and cudgel-players abounded." That these last were utter ruffians we learn from, at least, one instance. For Lord Rochester, in return for a satirical allusion attributed to Dryden, hired a gang of these cudgel-fighters to waylay the poet one night, as he passed up a retired alley on his way home. The leader of this gang was known as *Black Will,* and it is likely he and his crew were all of the same "bludgeon tribe" (to use one of Mactaggart's synonyms for "gypsies") as those cudgel-fighting gypsies of Galloway, or as the "swarthy and barbarous looking" English mugger, seen by Mr. Simson at St. Boswell's Fair, twirling his cudgel "in the gipsy manner." Indeed, a reference in the Prologue to one of Dryden's own plays† seems to say that the lowest classes frequenting the London theatres of his time consisted largely of black people. And it is not at all unlikely that *Black Will,* and his ruffianly bravoes, belonged *by the ties of blood,* as well as by a common character, to the caste that became known to a later generation as "the Mohocks." Because the Mohocks were *black-skinned* men. The *Spectator* tells us this:—" My friend [Sir Roger de Coverley] asked me in the next place, if there would not be some danger in coming home late [from a

* Ben Jonson (Epigram xcvii.) speaks of one of these "motions," or puppet-shows, as a "fa-ding"; and the context shows that "ding" is simply an older form of "thing," both of these forms being used in the same passage to denote the same "thing." The transition from *Fa-Thing* to *Faw-Thing* (*i.e.,* gypsy-show) is, therefore, not only easy, but quite warrantable.

† *Cleomenes; or, The Spartan Hero.*

proposed visit to the theatre], in case the Mohocks should be abroad. 'I assure you,' says he, 'I thought I had fallen into their hands last night; for I observed two or three lusty black men that followed me half way up Fleet Street, and wended their pace behind me, in proportion as I put on to get away from them. You must know,' continued the knight with a smile, 'I fancied they had a mind to hunt me;' .... Sir Roger added, that 'if these gentlemen had any such intention, they did not succeed very well in it; for I threw them out,' says he, 'at the end of Norfolk-street, where I doubled the corner, and got shelter in my lodgings before they could imagine what was become of me.'" And we have been lately informed that, during the early part of the fourteenth century—a period that ante-dates even *Black Will* by three hundred and fifty years—"the city [London] was perambulated by bands of marauders, 'the ancestors of the Mohawks of Queen Anne's days.'" Moreover (and this is a piece of evidence which one must accept without any hesitation), a sixteenth-century writer plainly states that certain districts of London were then the particular dwellings of gypsies. He calls them Tinkers: and Shakespeare also uses this term to describe gypsies. Harman, then, recounting the theft, from him, of a large copper cauldron, goes on to say—"I then immediately the next day sent one of my men to London, and there gave warning in Sothwarke, kent strete, and Barmesey streete, to all the Tynckars there dwelling,—that if any such caudron came thether to be sold, the bringar thereof should be stayed, and promised twenty shyllings for a reward." And, as he tells us that "these droncken Tynckers, called also Prygges, be beastly people," who "with picking and stealing, mingled with a lytle worke for a coulour, passe their time," it is clear that his "tinkers" were "gypsies."* Therefore, when our artists, in portraying our London roughs, prize-

---

* He does not specify those *London* Tinkers as belonging to the class of "droncken Tynckers, called also Prygges"; but the cauldron incident seems to show that he did not make much distinction between them and their brethren of the country.

The above extracts will be found in No. 335 of *The Spectator*; in Mr. W. J. Loftie's "History of London," Vol. I. p. 203; and in "The Rogues and Vagabonds of Shakspere's Youth," compiled by Messrs. Viles and Furnivall for the Early English Text Society, pages 35 and 59 of the reprint of 1880.

fighters, and burglars, "called also prygges," give to them a certain physiognomy—and that strongly suggestive of the gypsy or semi-gypsy caste, once known as "mumpers,"— they rather bear out than contradict the facts of history. And a significant detail of those semi-gypsy roughs is the fur-cap which seems to characterize them, and which also characterized those gypsies who are portrayed in earlier engravings. Thus Bill Sykes is the legitimate descendant of Black Will; and the Mohocks are still represented by the midnight roughs of the Thames Embankment.*

The Moorfields of three hundred years ago swarmed with ballad-mongers, or minstrels, as well as with "Mohock" cudgel-fighters; and "a world" of thieves, mountebanks, jugglers and showmen, thronged the adjoining district of Smithfield. How such people, from the time of the mediæval juggler-minstrels of the John-of-Rampayne adventure down to the present day, have either been "gypsies," pure and simple, or have been leavened to some extent with "gypsiness," has been remarked often enough already. "Banks the juggler," who lived in the sixteenth century, was as famous a horsetrainer as any "gypsy" of our grandfathers' day; and, like all such people, he was supposed to possess "magical" powers. And again, in the person of "Skogan the jester," the attributes of *jongleur, juggler* and *professed pleasant*, were all combined.

At the time when De Foe wrote—the era of *The Spectator* and *Sir Roger de Coverley*—Moorfields bore the same character. De Foe talks of "Moorfields, Lincoln-inn-fields, &c., where idle fellows resort," and which abound with gamblers and thimble-riggers. And these he describes under

---

* Since men of the *Black Will* stamp—thorough-paced ruffians and murderers—have been systematically hanged during the past few centuries, the tribe must have decreased in numbers with every generation. It is rather a matter of wonder that any traces of their blood whatsoever should be traceable in the *Black Wills* of this era.

In regarding our "bruisers" and "roughs" as nineteenth-century Mohocks, it must be remembered that those of the seventeenth and eighteenth centuries possessed various higher qualities as well. "Black George Barnes" of Clement's Inn was both a "Mohock" and a "gentleman"; like those "lusty black men" that followed Sir Roger de Coverley. But whatever the better qualities of some —or many—of those people, they were also unmistakable ruffians; a perpetual annoyance and danger to the best part of the community.

their guise of "japanners," in these terms:—"The next great abuse among us is that, under the notion of cleaning our shoes, above ten thousand wicked, idle, pilfering vagrants are permitted to patrol about our city and suburbs. These are called the black-guard, who black your honour's shoes, and incorporate themselves under the title of the Worshipful Company of Japanners; . . . . oaths and impudence are their only flowers of rhetoric; gaming and thieving are the principal parts of their profession: japanning but the pretence; . . . . yet are they permitted, to the shame of all our good laws, and the scandal of our most excellent government, to lurk about our streets, to debauch our servants and apprentices, and support an infinite number of scandalous, shameless trulls, yet more wicked than themselves, for not a Jack among them but must have his Gill. By whom such indecencies are daily acted, even in our open streets, as are very offensive to the eyes and ears of all sober persons, and even abominable in a Christian country; . . . . modest women are every day insulted by them and their strumpets . . . [and it is their "daily practice" to] knock down gentlemen in drink, or lead others out of the way into dark remote places, where they either put out their lights, and rob them themselves, or run away and leave them to be pillaged by others."*

So that it seems quite probable that the name of *Moorfields* was only a variety of *Black Heath*;† and that these places, and Smithfield, were so designated because they were almost or quite exclusively inhabited by *petulengres* and *gypsies*. Indeed, when we examine the peculiarities of particular districts, this probability becomes strengthened into something very like certainty. Harman, in the sixteenth century, regarded Southwark as a locality that was largely, if not exclusively, inhabited by "Tinkers, called also Prigs." And, in the year 1773, Southwark was still a peculiarly "gypsy" neighbourhood. In the *Annual Register* for that year (page 142), it is stated that "the clothes of the late

---

* De Foe's "Everybody's Business Is Nobody's Business."

† Previous to the year 1612 (and probably after it) Blackheath was a celebrated rendezvous of the "Egyptians" of England: "Retbroak at Blackheath" is the precise quarter. (Hoyland.)

Diana Boswell, Queen of the Gipsies, value £50, were burnt in the Mint, *Southwark*, by her principal courtiers, according to ancient custom."* Moreover, the nomenclature of the precise localities referred to by Harman speaks of the presence of those gypsies even at the present day. "Southwark, Kent Street, and Barmesey (Bermondsey) Street" are the places he names; and, while Diana Boswell and her "courtiers" betoken a gypsy occupation of that neighbourhood so recently as 1773, there is confirmatory proof of that fact in such existing names—in the same vicinity—as "Blackman Street" and "The Green Man" (the sign of a neighbouring tavern): which latter combination reminds us that, in Gaelic, "a black man" and "a green man" are synonymous terms, and that those Britons whom Pliny characterized as *Æthiopes* were styled *Virides* by Caesar. Thus, this special district bears many traces of its occupants; and as Moorfields and Smithfield are contiguous to each other, and were once pictured as containing populations possessing the same characteristics, the "blackamoor"-tinker connection is equally visible on either side of the river. Again, we are told that Norwood was also particularly identified with these people. 'In May, 1797 (says the author of *The Yetholm History of the Gypsies*), the Gypsy settlement at Norwood, from which Gypsy Hill takes its name, was broken up, and they were treated as vagrants." Now, in the face of what has been written in the preceding pages, it seems absurd to regard as a mere *coincidence* such statements as these that follow—extracted from a journal of the year 1883:—"At Lambeth, the other day, two men were charged with being drunk and disorderly in the Norwood Road, and two other men with attempting to rescue the prisoners. It seems that the neighbourhood has long been infested with ruffians of this description, who nightly insult and assault respectable persons who pass by. They are armed with sticks, spikes, and pieces of chain, 'which they are in the habit of flourishing about in a threatening manner.' They are known as the

---

* "Encyc. Brit." 9th edition, article "Gipsies." This "ancient custom," it has already been remarked, is associated with one or more of the tribes that became "British" at periods ante-dating the Norman Conquest by five, ten, or fifteen centuries.

'Norwood gang of roughs,' of which Miller, one of the prisoners, is 'king.' Last Saturday night three hundred of these people assembled in the Norwood road to enjoy their usual recreation, when the police intervened and arrested, not without great difficulty, two of the ringleaders and two others who tried to rescue them. Miller, the 'king,' was sentenced, we regret to see, to only one month's hard labour, and before the end of October will doubtless resume his regal functions in Norwood or elsewhere."* That these modern "Mohocks" who "are permitted, to the shame of all our good laws, and the scandal of our most excellent government, to lurk about our streets" and "to patrol about our city and suburbs;" and of whom it may be said that "oaths and impudence are their only flowers of rhetoric; gaming and thieving are the principal parts of their profession;" that these Norwood *Roughs*, who live under a king of their own, are in a great measure the direct descendants of the Norwood *Gypsies* of 1797—seems manifestly a conclusion which would be ratified by an examination of their customs and forms of speech. And thus it would appear that British Civilization, in opposing itself to the objectionable characteristics of these people, is dealing a final blow to an immemorial Heathenism.

* *Saturday Review*, September 22, 1883.

CHAPTER II.

It may be urged that the reason why "gypsies," instead of traversing England "in companies of nearly a hundred persons each," are reduced to groups of ten or twelve, is this, that, owing to the fierce and desperate nature of these castes, up till quite modern times, great numbers of them suffered violent deaths, or were transported. People who are perpetually fighting each other, and as persistently breaking the laws of the country, cannot be expected to live long themselves, and consequently cannot leave many representatives behind them. And where they have been transported to the "plantations," as many were, their connection with this country has equally come to an end (though their descendants are found in great numbers in these same "plantations," at the present day; coming under the heading of "American and Australian gypsies"). There can be no doubt that such people have been *greatly* diminished in number from these causes. But it is not probable that this accounts completely for the reduction of those large companies to small groups and pairs and units. It is not probable that eighty or ninety per cent. of the "gypsy" population has been exterminated or transported during the last two or three centuries. Violent deaths (at each others' hands, or by the public executioner) and banishment for life, have certainly made an immense difference in the numerical strength of such people; but other causes have worked to bring about this result. Intermarriage with other castes, and the adoption of modern ideas.

Still, it can reasonably be objected that the number of "gypsies" who have become civilized, or modernized, since the time when their gangs comprised "nearly a hundred persons each," is so small, comparatively, that such amalgamation could not produce any important effect on the other parts of the community. That the *black* ancestry of the *Melanochroi* is not explained, satisfactorily, by the miscegenation of the past few centuries. This can readily be admitted, if necessary. Indeed, the race-mixture of the last few centuries does *not* explain the history of the dark whites, except in a partial degree. In looking back a few centuries we are only surveying the later acts of the drama—a drama that has not yet closed. To understand fully—or as nearly as we may—the ancestry of the dark-whites, we must not confine our gaze to the periods when the dark races, retaining something of their individuality, moved about in gangs of ten, or twenty, or a hundred. We must go back to the time when their companies were thousands—when a "gang" was an army—when such black races were known as *Dani* and *Mauri*, "not wrongly named 'the painted folk.'"

These remarks have been made in order to correct any misapprehension as to the meaning of the previous chapter. It is not intended, in the present chapter, to touch upon the Black Danes, or the earlier Moors, or any other races that may not have been specified—that have invaded Britain in remote times. But rather to continue to seek for the traces of such warlike and nomadic tribes at periods that are nearer our own; and without much speculation as to the probable names by which they are known in history.

We have looked for "gypsies" in Scotland, and have seen that, in the Islands of the Foreigners, and throughout various parts of the North-British mainland, the dwellings of the people—or of certain tribes—have been exactly like those of the last century gypsies "on Yeta's banks." And that the customs and superstitions of these Scotch people have been identical with those of "gypsies." That, in short, the "gypsies" of Scotland are nothing but the untamed remnants of the early races of Scotland: or, at least, of some of them.

In England the same state of things ought to be discoverable. For history tells us that the heathen invaders of Britain overran the larger portion of the island, as well as its smaller northern province. And a few glances at early England reveal much the same state of things as was visible in early Scotland. Archaic Englishmen, or certain varieties of

Englishmen, lived very much like those early Scots, and later gypsies. So far as dwellings go, those inhabited by the common people of Norfolk in the thirteenth century appear to have been exactly like the turf-built cots of the last-century gypsies of Yetholm, or the dwellers in the Isles of the Strangers. An authority on this matter informs us that, six hundred years ago, "the poorer houses [in Norfolk] were dirty hovels, run up 'anyhow,' sometimes covered with turf, sometimes with thatch. None of them had chimneys. . . . . The labourer's dwelling had no windows; the hole in the roof which let out the smoke rendered windows unnecessary [or, at least, the inhabitants of these wigwams had no more thought of windows than a North American Indian in a similar dwelling]. . . . . The labourer's fire was in the middle of his house; he and his wife and children huddled round it, sometimes grovelling in the ashes; and going to bed meant flinging themselves down upon the straw which served them as mattress and feather bed, exactly as it does to the present day in the gipsy's tent in our byways. The labourer's only light by night was the smouldering fire."* It is likely that these people, if all "labourers," were not labourers from choice; but rather the bondsmen of an alien aristocracy. The races who dwell in such wigwams at the present day are, by nature, averse to the constant strain of agricultural toil: they are usually hunters and fishers. It is, I think, in this corner of England that some ethnologists see a markedly *Eskimo* type of face: and it seems probable that this district was settled by one of the invading Mongoloid tribes, whose historical names may be guessed at in another place. But, at any rate, these thirteenth-century dwellers in Norfolk—so far as their manner of living enables us to judge—were thorough-paced "gypsies."

As a very early example of the turf wigwam that was the almost invariable dwelling in the Southern Scotland of two or three centuries later (as we have been assured), and that was probably as common in that part of Scotland in the thirteenth century also, this glimpse of the kind of habitation used by a certain tribe in Norfolk, six hundred years ago, is so far in-

---

* "Village Life in Norfolk Six Hundred Years Ago," Rev. Dr. Jessop, *Nineteenth Century*, February, 1883.

teresting. But while revealing that those people inhabited gypsy wigwams, it does nothing more. Norfolk may perhaps supply further proofs that its thirteenth-century natives—living in gypsy huts—were "moors" in complexion, and "faws" by practice; but if so, the evidence does not seem to be lying ready to hand. Of those people who were specially styled *faws* there is much more known, though of later date than the thirteenth century.

It has already been noticed that "Francis Heron, king of the Faws," was buried at Jarrow, County Durham, on the 13th of January, 1756: and his burial is duly recorded in the parish register. This man's designation, of itself, is enough to show that, although this word *Faw, Faa, Fall*, and *Fah*, became eventually used as a surname by certain families (and apparently even *before* the year 1756), yet it was first used to denote a particular race, or nation, and not a family. Proof of this is further seen in the statement that, in Northumberland, "the whole tribe of travelling tinkers and muggers. . . . are much more frequently called Faas than gipsies:" a statement which—made by a modern tourist in that district—is corroborated by the author of the *Tales of the Borders*, who informs us "that the name *Faa* not only was given to individuals whose surname might be *Fall*, but to the *Winters* and *Clarkes—id genus omne*—gipsy families well known on the Borders." And Wright, in his Provincial Dictionary, defines a *faw* as "an itinerant tinker, potter, &c;" while Halliwell gives *faw-gang* as a Cumberland term, explaining it to mean "a gang of faws." The town of Falkirk, in Stirlingshire, which is still pronounced *Faw*kirk by many Scotchmen, and which is spoken of as "*the* Fawkyrk" in Henry the Minstrel's *Wallace*, was further assumed to have derived its name from the Faws: and a like derivation may be assigned to such names as *Fawdoun, Fawside*, and (perhaps) *Fala* and *Falmouth*. It is certain that the obsolete adjective *fah* signified "parti-coloured;" and, when we find this term applied to a certain race, or nation, of swarthy complexion, in a country that we know was previously inhabited by a painted, black-skinned people, we may justifiably assume that the *Faws* were so named because they were *Picts*. Whether the Northumbrian Faws of the last few centuries were the descendants of the earlier Picts of the same neighbourhood; or whether they were altogether, or partly, descended from painted races that entered the island after the fifth century, these are points which need not be discussed here.

The Faw-Kirk in Stirlingshire was known in Gaelic as *Eaglais Bhreac:* which may either be *The Tattooed* (or *Flecked*) *Ecclesia*, or *The Ecclesia of the Tattooed* (or *Flecked*) *People*. There may have been something in the appearance of the church to warrant the former translation,* though its situation in a Pictish district makes the latter rendering the more likely to be correct. This is unimportant. But the Gaelic form of *Faw*,—*Breac*,—is worth considering. It has already been observed that the author of *Celtic Scotland* refers to this as a nickname very commonly given by Gaelic-speaking people to Pictish celebrities; and an examination of its radical meaning seemed to show that its best modern translation is "tattooed." To give the right sound to modern ears, the word should be spelled *breck;* and, when aspirated, *vreck* (in Gaelic, *bhreac*). But this adjective, *vreck*, might easily pass into *vleck*, in many parts of this country.† It evidently has done so. For we find a word in "Middle English" which Mr. Skeat, in his Etymological Dictionary, tells us is the same as that which, in Dutch, is spelled *vlek*. This is *flek*. Halliwell states that "it occurs in Chaucer, Piers Ploughman, &c;" and he adds—somewhat needlessly, —that it is "still in use in Lincolnshire." "Needlessly," because it is still in use wherever the "English" language is spoken; being now written *fleck*. Halliwell's definition of *flecked*—"marked; spotted; streaked;" is a very good rendering of the word that in Gaelic books is written *bhreac*, pronounced *vreck*. Consequently, *breac* or *bhreac*, and *fleck*, are equivalents of *faw*. And when we read that many of the

---

* The Latin form used was *Varia Capella*. This either means that the church itself was "of many colours," or else that those who put the name into Latin did not fully understand why the name *Eaglais Bhreac* had been given.

† The natives of St Kilda, for instance, at the date of Martin's visit could not pronounce the letter *r*: neither can a Chinaman. A certain Forfarshire accent transforms *Kirriemuir* into *Kellymuir*. People with such an accent—a St. Kildian of last century, or a Chinaman of this—in trying to pronounce the word *vreck*, would say *vleck*.

Yetholm gypsies were known, at one time, by the names of *Faw* and *Fleckie*, we see the same parallel before us again.*

However widely "faw" may have been once used, it seems latterly to have become restricted to a certain district —the northern counties of England, and the South-East of Scotland. In these places it was applied to "the whole tribe of travelling tinkers and muggers" that used to range that territory; and a horde of such people was there denominated a "faw-gang." "Horde" is not too large a word to use in this connection, because not only has the word "gang" shrunk in dimensions (and become degraded, socially,) in the course of time, but we know that "a gang of faws" consisted of about a hundred persons, at a period not very remote: and that, in earlier times, "a gang of *Faws*" was "an army of *Picts*." The appearance of "a gang of faws," about the year 1620, is described by Dekker the dramatist—in his *Lanthorne and Candle-light*. They are there† referred to as "moon-men;" a term that Grose simply translates, "gypsies;" and that Wright, in his Provincial Dictionary, explains, was used to denote "Beggars, generally of the gipsy tribe, who travelled about the country in companies of nearly a hundred persons each. They were great thieves, and usually dressed themselves in a fantastic costume." The reason of their being styled "moon-men" has already been casually discussed. The name may have arisen from their midnight habits, as described by Sir Walter Scott in his remarks upon the thieving "mossers" of the Borders; whose Normanized chieftains very commonly bore crescents and stars in their coats-of-arms. Or the origin of the name—and the armorial bearings—may be vastly older than the Norman Conquest; and of mythical derivation (as suggested by Mr. Leland in his discussion of their name of *Zingani*). At any rate, an Englishman, of presumably Dutch blood, tells us that, two or three centuries ago, they traversed England in bands of a hundred or so, "dressed in a fantastic costume." Wright says these *moon-men* were "beggars, generally of the gipsy

---

* The name of *Fleckie* does not seem a common one among gypsies; but it is one of those given by Mr. Smith, of Kelso, in his account of the Yetholm people.

† This is only stated at second-hand. Wright mentions that "Dekker gives a graphic account of them in his Lanthorne and Candle-light, 1620."

tribe:" but the word "beggar" has been used so often interchangeably with "gypsy," that to call them "beggars" was tantamount once to saying that they were "gypsies." These two words were synonyms quite recently. We noticed that Grose and Scott have both explained *Mumps'* or *Mumpers' Hall* to mean Beggars' Ale-house; while, on the other hand, Borrow and Leland regard *mumper* as equivalent to *gypsy*—the latter in a partial degree, at any rate.* Wordsworth's beggar-woman, whose face "was of Egyptian brown," was plainly a gypsy: and so were the two young brats whose countenances were "like that woman's face as gold is like to gold." But he only calls them "Beggars." Similarly, Butler speaks of

"the privileges
That beggars challenge under hedges,
Who, when they're grieved, can make dead horses
Their spiritual judges of divorces;

and this ceremony of divorce, performed over the body of a slaughtered horse, is described by Mr. Simson as a peculiarly *gypsy* ceremony. Grose, too, defines the *patricoes*, or *pattercoves*, as "strolling priests that marry people under a hedge without gospel or common prayer-book: the couple, standing on each side of a dead beast, are bid to live together till death does them part: so, shaking hands, the wedding is ended." It is likely enough that Grose's account is very garbled (for the 'dead beast' does not figure in the *marriage* ritual as described by Mr. Simson, though a necessary adjunct in that of *divorce*); but his "strolling priests," or "patricoes," form a part of the *gypsy* fraternity. He includes them under his *beggars;* or "canting crew," that is, those who talk "cant"—a word which still means "speech" in Gaelic,† but which, in English slang, is understood to denote the speech of semi-gypsies, if not of out-and-out gypsies as

---

* Mr. Leland regards the *mumpers* as only half "gypsies"; what he terms half-bloods or *diddikai*.

† The speech of the riff-raff is not *cant* in Gaelic precisely, but rather *dubh-chainnt* or "black speech," *i.e.*, "gypsies' speech." The Latin *cantare* is, of course, another form. It is, perhaps, worth noting that in Latin this word has the meaning of *divination* or *fortune-telling;* of incan*ta*tion or enchan*t*ment; that these are "gypsy" qualities; and that one, at least, of Mr. J. F. Campbell's West Highland reciters—many of whom were "gypsies"—did not *speak* his story in the modern fashion, but *intoned* or *chanted* it.

well. Grose, indeed, means little else than "gypsies" by his "canting crew," or "crew." He defines *dimber-damber* as "a top man, or prince, among the canting crew;" and, in his sketch of the *gypsies*, the "dimber-damber" is "the principal man of the gang." Under the term, *upright man*,—a synonym for *dimber-damber*—he gives a representation of the habits of a "crew" which is nothing else than the picture of a troop of "gypsies." Indeed, in his description of the gypsies (under that word), he talks of them as "canters." And an instance (almost contemporary with these of Grose's) of the same usage is visible in the name of a ballad* published in 1737, which is called *The Canters' Holiday*, and is supposed to have been "sung on the electing of a new *Dimber Damber*, or *King of the gypsies*." Thus, *canters* are *gypsies*, and—which is more to the point—*beggars* are *gypsies*. The same identity of *gypsy* with *beggar* is seen in the following quotation from one of Oldham's Satires (and, like that taken from *Hudibras*, it proves that the usage was common in the seventeenth century) :—

> " Tis so, 'twas ever so, since heretofore
> The blind old bard, with dog and bell before,
> Was fain to sing for bread from door to door :
> The needy muses all turned *gipsies* then,
> And of the *begging* trade e'er since have been."

And a South-Scottish gypsy-chief of last century, Andrew Gemmell by name, was known to the yeomanry of that quarter as a "King of the *Beggars*."

But previous chapters, in referring more especially to the Scotch gypsies, have shown that these were no other than the *sorners*, or *masterful beggars*, that so long oppressed the peaceably-inclined sections of the North British population. This identity is very clearly placed before us by Sir John Sinclair, in his Statistical Account of Scotland; where, "in describing the village of Eaglesham, he remarks: 'There is no magistrate nearer than four miles, and the place is oppressed with gangs of gypsies, *commonly called Tinklers, or sturdy beggars.*'"†

* Included in "A Pedlar's Pack of Ballads and Songs," by W. H. Logan, Edinburgh, 1869.
† Hoyland's "Historical Survey of the Gypsies," York, 1816, p. 112.

Consequently, those *moon-men*, "who travelled about the country in companies of nearly a hundred persons each," dressed in "fantastic costumes," during the early part of the seventeenth century, were distinctly *gypsies* : not only because Grose tells us that "moon-man" is a synomyn for "gypsy," but also because he and many others show us that "gypsies" and "beggars" were formerly one and the same people.

Grose is a writer of too recent a date—though he is not of this century—to give us much help in forming a dim idea of the appearance of a gang of faws, or moon-men, about the year 1620. Except for the allusion to the practice that rendered them "not wrongly named 'the painted people'" (regarding which practice he displays a total absence of curiosity, and a dense non-appreciation of its meaning) —except for this, Grose's picture of the eighteenth-century gypsies gives us no additional hints as to their outward appearance. He tells us that they are "A set of vagrants, who, to the great disgrace of our police, are suffered to wander about the country. They pretend that they derive their origin from the ancient Egyptians, who were famous for their knowledge in astronomy and other sciences; and, under the pretence of fortune-telling, find means to rob or defraud the ignorant and superstitious. To colour their impostures they artificially discolour their faces, and speak a kind of gibberish peculiar to themselves. They rove up and down the country in large companies, to the great terror of the farmers, from whose geese, turkeys, and fowls, they take very considerable contributions."

Still, this does show these people to us in a stronger light than that in which they are placed by nineteenth-century writers. This tells us that England was over-run last century by "*large* companies" of marauders ; who *sorned* upon the agricultural castes of England, much as they did in Ireland and Scotland ; "to the great terror" of these agriculturists. And these "oppressors" were "*black* oppressors" (like those of the Welsh *Mabinogion*). The Englishmen who had colonised the western shores of the Atlantic, not more than a generation or two before Grose, spoke of the Indians there as being "as black as gypsies." In 1676 the native races of New England were spoken of indifferently as "Indians" and "Moors;"* and our British "Indians" are also remembered as "Moors." Therefore, Grose is virtually telling us that "large companies" of *Moors*, or black people, roamed up and down the country, rather more than a hundred years ago, taking "very considerable contributions" from the farming classes and others; besides being possessed of many fierce and aggressive qualities. And these *Moors*, at that quite recent period, had not relinquished the custom that distinguished those black people against whom Cæsar fought —those eighteenth-century *Moors* were also *painted people.*

The distinguishing war-paint of the eighteenth-century Moors of Galloway was, we have seen, of a blood-red colour; derived from the hæmatite, or ruddle, that is found throughout Western Europe. It is almost certain that such *keeled* clans were found in other parts of the British Islands a hundred years ago, and farther back; but, so far, there is no direct evidence of this. The word *keel*, it was noticed, is only the modernized, phonetic spelling of the word that in Gaelic is spelled† *cil, cille,* and *gille;* and this word, whether we pronounce it, unwarrantably, *gilly,* or as Sir Walter Scott and his schoolboy companions used correctly to pronounce it, *keelie* (a pronunciation by no means obsolete in Scotland at the present day), in either of these cases the word denotes "one of a humble class." The history of such a meaning, it has been assumed, is this, that certain *ruddled* tribes, or *keelies*, were overcome by certain non-painted races, and sank into the inferior position of a conquered people: the actual word surviving, as a memory of this period, ages after conqueror and conquered had become so blended that the name of *keelie* had long ceased to signify anything racial whatever. But, in certain localities, the word would not have been wrongly used if applied to various clans that had not reached this lower level, even so lately as last century. It does not appear that the Galloway gypsies were known as *keelies,* though it is quite certain that they painted their faces with

---

* "News from New-England," 1676; reprinted at Albany, N.Y., 1865.

† The Gaelic spelling is also phonetical, according to the principles of Gaelic pronunciation. Indeed, according to the principles of most languages. It is curious how far we English-speaking people are separated in this century from most nations, and from our own forefathers, by our modern pronunciation of the vowels *i* and *e*.

keel. In Fife, however, it is only the other day that the local gypsies "were all known .... by the name of 'Gillie Wheesels,' or ' Killie Wheesh ;' "* and it is not unlikely that the first of these words was often used by itself to denote these people. That, in short, the villagers at North Queensferry, when they spoke of "the gypsies," called them, as often as not, "the keelies." At any rate, the fact of their using this word, in a district where Gaelic was long spoken, to denote the "Moors" of that neighbourhood, would seem to signify that these "Moors" were united to those of Galloway by a kindred custom ; and, if so, were probably united to them by the ties of blood. That the "black heathen" who landed in Galloway, using ruddle, or *keel*, as their favourite (and perhaps only) war-paint, were of the same nation as those who landed in Fife, and whose descendants were styled by a name that indicates the use of the same pigment.

Other conjectural instances were adduced, in former pages, of the presence, in other districts, of ruddled people. The Lake of the Red Women, on Coom Ruadh (the Red Combe), in the south of Ireland, is a combination, clearly showing that the *colour*, in this case, had no reference to any geological feature. In Wales, again, the common occurrence of the adjective *coch*, or *goch* (red), in the names of people and of places suggests that a ruddled tribe had effected landings in that province also. Mr. Borrow was struck with the reiteration of this adjective *coch* (*goch*), in his rambles through "Wild Wales." At *Traeth Coch* ("The Red Stratum"), he asks "Why is this sand called the red sand ?" From which question, it is obvious to those who have not visited the place that the beach there has nothing remarkably red about it. All the answer he gets is "I cannot tell you." The village near is called *Llan Peder Goch*, "Red Peter's *Land*."†

---

* Mr. Simson renders this—"the lads that take the purses." *Wheesels* or *wheesh* must be a corruption of some Gaelic word, or words, which no doubt a scholar could analyze successfully.

† Mr. Borrow (who gives these things in his " Wild Wales," Vol. I. pp. 386, 387, and 394) translates this—if one can talk of *translation* where the difference is only one of accent—as "The Church of Red Saint Peter." But there is no word for *saint*. And *llan*, though it has come to mean *church*—perhaps (in Wales) to the exclusion of all other meanings—is apparently the word that, in

Going on to Llanfair, he finds that the poet Gronwy's house is known as *Tafarn Goch*, "The Red Tavern:" and he cries in perplexity, "The Red Tavern? ... How is it that so many of your places are called Goch? there is Pentraeth Goch, there is Saint Pedair Goch, and here at Llanfair is Tafarn Goch." But he receives no enlightenment from the natives.

Again, it was noticed that the adjective *ruadh*,—or as we now pronounce it in "English," *ruddy* and *red*—signifies both *black*, or *tawny*, and *red*, or *ruddy*, in the Western Highlands; being translated both ways by Mr. J. F. Campbell, in his *Tales*. Also that *dearg*, which is understood to mean *red* in "Gaelic," has become *dark** in "English." Traces of these words were seen in the surname *Darg*, which goes back to the days of the traditional "Dargo the *druid*," or soothsayer; and in such names as Rory and Roderick, which are best translatable in their Gaelic form of *Ruaidh-ri*, or "the Ri (chief) of the Tawny, or Red People." What removes such derivations from the domain of mere guess-work is the known fact that a tribe which is said to have inhabited Galloway "time out of mind," was composed of swarthy *gypsies* or *Moors*, who, up till last century made use of this ruddle as their tribal war-paint; and the equally-solid fact that Britain was invaded fully twelve hundred years before

---

eighteenth-century "English" and earlier, was spelt *laund*, and is nowadays represented by *land* and *lawn*. (See Mr. Skeat's remarks on these words in his Dictionary.) Its earliest meaning seems to have been "enclosed—but untilled—ground." It has even yet an application akin to this among farmers and plough-men, who mark off unploughed ground into *lands*, or divisions, before ploughing (with the view of rendering the work easier). As for the favourite Welsh rendering of this word, it is easy to see how *llan* could acquire the meaning of *church*, if we remember that the earliest churches in these islands—so far as we can guess—were simply circular *enclosures*.

* In Carleton's "Traits and Stories of the Irish Peasantry," *fardoroughah* is translated "the dark man." *Far* is that word which, in Scotch-Gaelic, is spelt *fear*; in Anglo-Saxon, *wer*; in Latin, *vir*; being the same word—variously pronounced (or, at least, variously *spelt*)—and signifying "man." *Doroughah* is usually given as *dorca* and *dorcha* by Gaelic writers; and always as *dark* in Modern-English dictionaries, though stated to have once been written *dearc*. The connection between the Gaelic *dorca* and *dargo*, or *dearg*, is a degree less apparent to the eye; but it seems very clear that all these words—whatever proper name we may ticket them with—are so many varieties from the one common stock; acquiring, in course of time, a different intonation, in order to express the particular shade of meaning that attached to each.

the era of Will Marshall of Galloway, by sections of a confederacy whose members—on the authority of a sixth-century Bishop of Ravenna, named Jornandes,—are stated to have followed the same practice. We can say with certainty that the Galloway gypsies of last century were *dark* and *ruadh* (in its sense of *tawny*) when in their natural state; and *darg* and *ruddy* when they had painted their faces with keel: though we can only *assume* that the earlier invaders who followed the same custom were the ancestors of these, and consequently of dark complexion. But the simple fact that the British Islands were invaded by various races of *dubh galls, nigrae gentes,* or black foreigners, during an indefinable but most extensive period; and the fact that some of these, at any rate, followed this practice; quite entitles one to assume (in the absence of contrary evidence) that *red* and *black* place-names, of the kind indicated, bore reference to them, and that *red* and *black* were expressed by a single word for the same reason.

Whether many *faw-gangs* or tribes of *moon-men*, during the seventeenth century, were distinguished by the use of this particular pigment, does not appear. Of all the colours, the most common seems always to have been that which was commonest when Cæsar came: that colour whose varying shades caused those painted natives to be styled by their Latin conquerors—sometimes *Virides*, or Green-men—and sometimes *Cærulei*, or Blue-skins. Here again, the same superficial contradiction is noticeable: just as *black* and *red* could be fitly applied to the complexion, real or assumed, of Will Marshall's gypsy-gang in Galloway, so the colour of the people whom Cæsar styled *green-men* and *blue-skins*, is described by Pliny as *æthiopium* (as black as a "blackamoor's"). The same parallel is seen in the Gaelic names for a "blackamoor:" what is *duine-dubh*, "a black man," in one part of the country, is *duine-gorm*, "a blue-green man," in another. And as the Gaelic word for "a wild Irishman" signifies literally "a Black-Irishman," and as it is in Ireland that "a black man" is "a blue-green man," it may be assumed that most—or all—of the wild tribes of Ireland were *blue-skins* or *green-men*, also during an undefinable period. Whether the blue-green dye derived from woad, or *gorman*, was ever

painted over the surface of the skin, or whether it was invariably punctured in, or tattooed, cannot be decided. But the Latin records seem to indicate that the latter custom prevailed: since they speak of the *stigmata* of these British *Blueskins*, on whose dying bodies the Latin soldiers " saw the rude figures, *iron-graved.*" Also in the traditional story which was quoted in previous references to this practice—that in which the daughter of a Highland kinglet is stated to have been educated by the Magi (Druidhean), who, among other things, " coloured her skin as green as grass "—in this tradition it is pretty evident that the girl was *tattooed*, not painted. Paint is not indelible: tattooing is. And it was when this girl had completed her education, and had been returned to her own people by her instructors, the *Magi*, that this peculiarity was remarked by her friends. From which it is to be inferred, that her own kindred did *not* follow such a custom, that the *Magi* were of a different race from them, and that the colour had been punctured into her skin after the fashion still followed by the Tatâren (gypsies) of Egypt.*
The case of *Ian gorm*, " Blue-green (or Woad-coloured) John," is distinctly one of *permanent* colouring; that is, tattooing. It will be remembered that the account which is given by his descendant in his collection of West Highland tales, states that his enemies—the MacLeans—stripped him naked and marked his skin all over with a heated *oval*, " which occasioned blue spots on the boy's skin *ever after*, for which he was called John Gorm, or blue John." This story was received from an ancient Hebridean gypsy-crone, who was " very old," in the year 1861 ; and it was assumed that even one whose youth was so far back as hers, was still of too modern a day to have ever seen a tattooing-instrument, or *breacair*. This belief may be correct as regards that particular locality. But it appears, from Carleton's *Traits and Stories of the Irish Peasantry*, that those *breacaircan*, or graving-tools, were used for this purpose, in the Ireland of our grandfathers —if not yet. One of the chief actors in Mr. Carleton's

* This last inference is only drawn from the impression received in reading the account ; for one might suppose that a merely ephemeral colouring would not have been thought deserving of record. Based upon so slight a foundation, this theory need not necessarily be deemed worthy of acceptance.

sketch of *The Midnight Mass*—in which tale a half-smothered paganism is every now and then making itself apparent—is "Darby More," who can be best described as "a gypsy priest," although he is not so called. He belonged to "that description of mendicants which differs so strikingly from the common crowd of beggars as to constitute a distinct species." His characteristics, as delineated by Mr. Carleton, are precisely those of the same kind of people in Scotland, whom "Martin, author of the *Reliquiæ Divi Sancti Andreæ*, written in 1683, . . . conceives to be descended from the ancient Bards; "and regarding whom he says; "They are called by others, and by themselves, Jockies [*Gypsies, Cairds*], who go about begging; and use still to recite the Sloggorne (gathering-words or war-cries) of most of the true ancient surnames of Scotland, from old experience and observation." These are the same people as those "bards and profest pleisants [mountebanks]," "pretending liberty to bard and flatter," that were regarded as among the pests of the Hebridean islands by the Sixth James of Scotland. And an old writer (previously quoted), in speaking of the speech of the Irish section of this gypsy-caste, remarks thus: "The tongue is sharp and sententious, and offereth great occasion to quick apophthegms and proper allusions. Wherefore their common jesters and rhymers, whom they term Bards, are said to delight passingly those that conceive the grace and property of the tongue. But the true Irish [the Gaelic] indeed differeth so much from that they commonly speak, that scarce one in five hundred can either read, write, or understand it." They spoke the *dubh-chainnt*, or black speech of the gypsies; just as the oldest living bard in Wales does at the present day: and they united, in their own caste, all the complex features that have formerly distinguished the gypsy races—the characteristics of *Minstrel*, *Juggler* (which is an offshoot of *Jongleur*), *Genealogist*, *Jockey*, *Mountebank* and *Priest*.*

---

* To prove, in detail, that these were all the same description of people would lead us into too long a digression. But there can be no doubt that they *were* the same; and the points indicated in this and previous pages will, I think, prove generally convincing. (See Walker's "Irish Bards," Carleton's "Traits," and Scott's Advertisement to "The Antiquary."

It is in this last character that Darby More is introduced here. Like those of his order, his accomplishments were many ; but he is said to have " made most money by a knack which he possessed of tattooing into the naked breast the representation of Christ upon the Cross. This was a secret of considerable value, for many of the superstitious people believed that by having this stained in upon them they would escape unnatural deaths, and be almost sure of heaven." He says himself—" this sacred thing, that I put the crass upon people's breasts wid, saves people from hangin' an' unnatural deaths." And this " sacred thing " is spoken of by another in these words:—" ' Darby,' said he, ' I want you to come up to our house in the mornin', an' bring along wid you the things that you stamp the crass upon the skin wid.' " Whether this instrument—or instruments—resembled in shape the *ubhal* that branded young John Campbell as *Ian Gorm*, or Blue John, at an earlier day, is not told us by Mr. Carleton. We can only call it *breacair*, a graving-tool ; not *ubhal*, an oval. But since the custom was apparently quite common in the latter part of last century, among the Irish peasantry, it is very likely that some of these " sacred things " may yet be seen—in Irish museums, if nowhere else. In this instance, the tattooing-instrument had a half-Christian character ; for, although the cross itself has been a sacred emblem among heathen races, it is not likely that any pagan cross ever bore the representation of a dying man upon it. But the *idea* of the thing—the idea that a particular emblem, punctured into the skin by a medicine-man, could save a man from a violent death and make him " almost sure of heaven " —is a wholly pagan idea. And although the instrument, like the class of men who were qualified to use it, may have been transmuted into a *quasi*-Christian form, yet the instrument, and the man, must be regarded as survivals of heathenism. And heathenism of a very old date. For this tattooing custom is one of the most ancient in Britain. And the Irish mendicants, who still retained it up to the close of last century, belonged to a caste which is not only described as old in the Ireland of the eleventh century,* but which shows itself, by many inherent traits, to be descended from those

* See Walker's " Historical Memoirs of the Irish Bards," London, 1786.

castes which were regarded as the most *aboriginal* at the time of Cæsar's landing in Britain.*

We are not enlightened as to the colour used by this wandering gypsy-priest; but it was probably blue-green—or red. Red was the representative colour of one section (at least) of the Irish gypsies, during the seventeenth century,† as it was among their contemporary "Galloways." But *gorm* or woad-colour, whether in its aspect of blue or of green,‡ seems to have been the favourite dye throughout the British Islands. Nineteen centuries ago our British Picts were notably *Virides* or *Cærulei;* among Gaelic-speaking people, a *black man* was so often a *blue-green* man that the terms became interchangeable; in the two instances taken from Scotch tradition, the colour punctured in was *gorm;* and epithets signifying *blue* or *green* are attached to the names of several West Highland celebrities. It is likely that many Hebridean examples of this nick-name could be dug up here and there; but the only ones that offered themselves, in looking at that particular locality, were those of the Blue John (Campbell), who has just been spoken of again,—of Blue Donald (Macdonald of Slate),—and of the celebrated pirate, *Cailean Uaine*, or Green Colin. Without going so far north as *Innse-Gaill*, either, we find a comparatively modern specimen in the person of Joseph Blake (a comrade of Jack Sheppard), who was hanged at Tyburn on the 11th November 1724, and who was commonly known by his nick-name of *Blueskin*.

While this last form is a free translation of the Latin nick-

---

* Grose's picture of gypsydom—especially as regards the intercourse of the sexes—is simply a copy of that represented by the early writers, as these are quoted to us in the first volume of "Celtic Scotland" (p. 33); Strabo's account of the native customs of "Ierne" particularly. And the privileges which Grose assigns to the "Dimber-Damber," "Upright Man," or king of a gypsy tribe, are precisely those which Dr. Johnson remarks upon as having been long retained by the chiefs of the Macquarries of Ulva.

† A quotation, lately given in *Notes and Queries* from "'Oliver Heywood's Diaries,' &c., 1630-1702, vol. ii. p. 285 (edited by J. Horsfall Turner, 1881)," shows that the Irish *tory* colour of 1681 was Red. And the modern name for *tory* is *gypsy*.

‡ *Distinctly* green and *distinctly* blue shades have been evolved from the original *gorm;* but that adjective—though not Modern English—expresses the blue-green or woad-colour as no other word can do.

name, *Cœruleus*, it had become identified—like the Irish *duinegorm*—with dark-complexioned people, rather than with any artificial peculiarity belonging to them, at the period when Captain Grose made up his Dictionary of the Vulgar Tongue. Whatever he may have known of the matter, he defines a *blueskin* as simply—" a person begotten on a black woman by a white man: one of the blue squadron; any one having a cross of the black breed." In effect, the eighteenth-century *blueskins* were nothing else than Mr. Leland's half-blood gypsies, *diddikais*, or *mumpers*. Therefore Joseph Blake, the highwayman, was more or less of a "gypsy." On the other hand, those Scotch "gypsies" of the eighteenth century, whose habits have been so carefully recorded by Mr. Simson, were highwaymen. Such gypsies as Captain Baillie, Captain McDonald, and Captain Jamieson,—men of fine presence and brave attire; mounted on horses of the very best breeds (and as thorough *outlaws* as their masters); easing some corpulent Scotch bailie of his superfluous coin, and giving away a considerable portion of it to the poor; such mounted "gypsies" were perfect models of the Dick Turpin kind of man. We cannot say that all the seventeenth—and eighteenth—century knights of the road were *gypsies:* but it is clear that all the mounted gypsies were *highwaymen*, of this order. When such highwaymen were "Galloways," they painted their skins with ruddle, before setting out on an expedition: when they belonged to the country that stretched to a considerable distance north and south of the Border-land, they were *faws*, " of various colours:" when their habitat was placed in certain other districts, they were *blueskins*. Although Joseph Blake may be the only producible specimen of the eighteenth-century *blueskin*, under that name, yet the way in which Grose speaks of such people shows that Blake had any number of comrades bearing that title; who were half-blood " Moors," and members of " the blue squadron."

But, while the *cœruleus* of Cæsar was represented down to the eighteenth-century, so also were his *virides*, or " greenmen." Halliwell's definition of "a green-man" is exactly that which any one of Cæsar's officers might have given—"a savage." It is possible—and probable—that, although *green-men* and *blueskins* were once the same people, the title of *green-man* had become archaic at a much earlier date than *blueskin;* and that, having thus become fossilized so early, it remained for all time the expression of a much cruder heathenism than that of the *blueskins.* What Halliwell tells one, in his Dictionary, seems to hint this. After defining a *green-man* as "a savage," he continues : "Strutt describes the green-men of the old shows as 'whimsically attired, and disguised with droll masks, having large staves or clubs headed with cases of crackers.'" This description does certainly not coincide wholly with that of the *blueskin* highwaymen pictured above. Rather does it suggest the *mountebank* aspect of these wandering *faws;* whose "staves or clubs headed with cases of crackers" have not yet disappeared from our circuses. Nor, indeed, is the wearing of "droll masks" a completely forgotten custom, though only practised on rare occasions nowadays. (And it is worth remarking that one of the equivalents for "a black man"—namely *græme, grim,* or *grime,* yet applied to the Blacks' Dyke between the Forth and Clyde—is associated also with the wearing of a "false face :" for Mr. Skeat gives this as one of the meanings attaching to the word *grima,*—which is rendered "a cowl worn for disguise, a mask.") But, although these *green-men* are not precisely identical with such *blueskins* as the highwaymen of last century, yet they cannot be dissociated from the society to which these belonged. If the eighteenth-century *green-man* was not the brother of his contemporaneous *blueskin,* he was his cousin. The sketch of him and his kindred, given by Strutt, suggests at once the *moon-men,* or *gypsies* of the same period. If the *green-men* were "savages," they were no fiercer than the Scottish "gypsies" of a hundred and fifty years ago : if they were "whimsically attired" they did not differ—on that account—from the gangs of gypsy *moon-men* who "usually dressed themselves in a fantastic costume."* Indeed, if a divergence between the significations of these cognate terms ever took place, it cannot have been at so very remote a period after all. Between the "savage," "whimsically attired" *green-*

---

* Probably this "fantastic costume," this "whimsical attire," is what Gloucestershire people used to know as *Gally-traps,* defined by Halliwell as "any frightful ornaments, head-dresses, hoods, &c." Compare *Gall,* "a foreigner," and *Gally-halfpenny* –"an inferior foreign coin prohibited by Henry VIII."

man, and the ferocious *moon-man, gypsy*, or *blueskin*, the difference is so slight as to be almost inappreciable. Let us suppose that the *green-man* most fully preserves the *mountebank* or *Merry-Andrew* qualities of the gypsy tribes, while the *blueskin* is less of a clown and more of a *jockey* and *marauder*,—and we shall probably be making as strong a distinction between the two varieties as we possibly can. Originally, of course, they were one: woad-coloured men, blueskins and green-men, *Cærulei* and *Virides*.

Up to what date this latter term remained in currency can never be made sure. But an allusion of Butler's to "our green-men" (*Hudibras*, Part III. Canto I.), seems to show that the name was perfectly familiar to seventeenth-century readers; and also that it included the *Virides*, generally, of either sex. A reference to Strutt's *Sports and Pastimes* would, no doubt, throw a good deal of light upon this matter. Though it is difficult to arrive, even approximately, at the exact date at which a certain usage, or a certain term, went out of vogue. The very commonest features of every-day life are often those of which the people who are familiar with them have the least to say, because they *are* so common. Mr. Henry James has said something to this effect, not long ago, in remarking upon *Punch's* sketches of London life. We are told something like this, by this writer, that an untravelled American will gain a much better notion of the customs and appearance of English people, by studying a volume of *Punch*, than by reading all the books that were ever written, descriptive of English manners. Because the pictures are faithful delineations of every-day life, chiefly as it goes on in London. In these drawings, details are given of which the importance (to an outsider) is probably not realized by the artist himself. The appearance of a sweep or a costermonger, a butcher boy's board, a rustic's smock frock, the general effect of a London street, or the Row of an afternoon, all these are points which the artist puts in, because he has the talent to reproduce life as it goes on around him. But the very touches that reveal to a stranger certain fashions and ways of living that are to him picturesque, or interesting, or odd, but always unsuspected, these very touches do not excite the least surprise or interest in the people who have the privilege of seeing them first; because the things they represent are (to them) unimportant and commonplace. Yet some of these every-day customs and fashions are the first to catch the eye of a stranger; and, in his opinion, are among the most striking features of English life—although, often no hint of their existence is given by English writers, and not invariably by those of other countries. And the appropriateness of these remarks lies in this—that people who have not been born or bred in this country, wherever their fatherland may be, are (in some respects) as much strangers to Modern-British life as we, and they, are strangers to the British life of two hundred years ago. Stay-at-home foreigners (what *we* call foreigners) read about this country; and hear more or less about it; but how imperfect an idea of our every-day life such people would form if they had only books to guide them! They have a great deal more. They have the descriptions given by their own friends, and they have the delightful and instructive pages of *Punch*. But we moderns, who, rooted for life in the country of the Present, try to realize what has gone on from day to day in that foreign country of the Past, how poorly off are we! The oldest man alive knows as little (by virtue of his date) of the ways of the seventeenth century as does the child of five years old. No visitor has ever come from those remote shores to tell us how the natives lived, and how they looked. Nor can we turn for answer to volume upon volume of faithful delineation, each picture a story, the one supplementing the other, photographs from a camera that is turned, now to this side, now to that, but always in the face of real life, always photographing for posterity the figures of real people. We have a few old prints, but how many before Hogarth? And even he, who illustrated one of the books that have just been quoted from, *Hudibras*, even Hogarth did not portray the England of Butler. For Hogarth drew when the last volume of *Hudibras* was nearly half a century old: Hogarth himself was of the generation of Butler's great-grandsons. But even though the artist had been the contemporary of the satirist, and though every one of his pictures were preserved in the National Gallery, even then we should have a mere glimpse of the characteristics of his time. What we should thus know would only be the slightest fraction of the truth: the impressions of one man, and the record of a few phases of life. The immense advantage of such a collection as the drawings of *Punch* consists in this, that it is the work of many men; each man representing the society of his day in whatever aspects it presents itself to him, as an individual. (That the incidents in these pictures are mostly humorous, and the figures often caricatures, does not really detract from their historical value. The grotesque element could easily be discounted by any intelligent man of a future age.) Thus we have innumerable sketches of modern British life, taken from many points of view, and seen through spectacles of every shade.

But the value of this unequalled collection is, after all, relative. There are British traits that utterly repel the humourist; and scenes that he would not care to sketch. The squalor, the misery, the crime, these are things that he dare not touch. And yet their existence is most undeniable. Other features of our life there are, too, that of necessity escape the etcher's stylus. Perhaps because they do not catch the eye; perhaps because they do not affect the artistic sense: in many cases, because their meaning could not properly be conveyed by the draughtsman.

Thus it is that the people of the twenty-first century, wishing to find out as much as possible of our ways of living, might miss altogether some of our customs that would surprise them most. Some of those things which we do, almost unconsciously, may seem the oddest freaks to the people of two hundred years hence, if they ever hear of them. How many customs, words, fashions, must wholly disappear in the course of seven generations! Which are likeliest to live, and which are soon to die, of all those now in vogue—it would take a prophet to tell. But it is, at least, certain that when a usage has quite lost its original significance, it has reached its grand climacteric, though death may be a long way off. Inherited customs have a vitality that is amazing: nevertheless, when these have become wholly meaningless, they cannot for ever be practised by races of civilized men. And many of our customs have now reached this stage. Every day we are dropping traditional habits, though with reluctance. And those of them that do not outlive this century, will appear indescribably strange to our posterity of the sixth or seventh descent, should these ever hear anything about them.

And thus it is that habits, fashions,—even races—that were conspicuous in seventeenth-century England, may have completely disappeared from sight; while others, scarcely referred to in the most casual way by writers of that period because they seemed so unimportant, appear as strange to us as if they belonged to a foreign country. When Butler spoke of "our green-men;" when Grose referred to "the blue squadron," "the blueskins"—those having a "cross of the black breed;" when Mactaggart described his Galloway gypsies as "painting their faces with *keel*"; these writers were as little aware of the significance of their remarks, in our eyes, as we are aware of the significance which many of our existing customs will assume in the estimation of posterity. For it is beyond a doubt that no extinct phase of British life can affect the imagination of this age more strongly than that which is indicated, however slightly, by the allusions and statements of these writers. The Past must always be a "foreign country" to the Present, but nothing it contains is stranger than this—that, in the British Islands of a period almost touching our own, an important part of the population was made up of castes and tribes whose manners and physical attributes connect them more closely with the "Indians" of Fenimore Cooper than with any* section of Modern Britons.

* The British *tories* of this present year are not overlooked. But these are much more modern than archaic. The tents of even the most conservative gypsies contain such modern superfluities as looking-glasses and brushes and boots, and cutlery and carpets from Birmingham. After the tawny druidess has cast your horoscope on the same conditions as those imposed by her British predecessors in the time of Patricius, she pays the proceeds into her bank account, or—as prosaically—transmits it by Post Office Order. When it suits them, "gypsies" can travel by train or steamboat like anybody else. Of the war-paint, the bloodshed, the robberies, the "fantastic" and "droll" attire that formerly distinguished them, there is no trace remaining. And the *kaulo rat*—the "black blood"—is growing "whiter," by intermarriage, every day.

CHAPTER III.

THE following particulars, which have been encountered subsequent to the writing of the preceding chapters, will serve to emphasize the identity between British "gypsies" and one or more sections of the British people.

Of the superstitions with regard to which Scott has said that "these notions are not peculiar to the gypsies; but having been once generally entertained among the Scottish common people, are now only found among those who are the most rude in their habits, and most devoid of instruction;" of these superstitions enough might be written to fill a volume. But it is sufficient to say that such of them as have come under the observation of the present writer do not tend, in the least degree, to prove that the British "gypsies" own a different origin from the general population of the British islands. (Or, it may be more correct to say that the existence of many beliefs and customs that are common to British "gypsies" and to British nondescripts, render it almost a matter of certainty that by one line of its ancestry the Modern-British nation is of "gypsy" lineage.) Mr. C. G. Leland, for example, refers to such practices as the nailing-up of a horse-shoe, or the tying of a red thread round one's finger, as gypsy observances for warding off all evil or "unlucky" influences. Students of such matters can best say how many localities will father such beliefs; but the efficacy of a red thread or ribbon as a charm is believed in by the superstitious classes of Provence, of Lapland, and of Scotland,—and, doubtless, of many other parts of Europe; while the mystic power of the horse-shoe is acknowledged in many countries. The custom of sitting-up all night in the presence of the dead, mingling tears and lamentations with the liberal consumption of intoxicating drinks, is popularly styled "the Irish wake;" but it was as much a characteristic of the Yetholm gypsies in the beginning of the present century. To spit upon a coin before pocketing it may appear ungracious in the recipient of the gift, and it is certainly a disagreeable practice; but it is done both by gypsies and by other sections of our population; and it is done by all of them "for luck." A certain primitive fashion of cooking fowls, it has been noticed, was once common to "the meaner sort of people" in the Hebrides and to the whole of the "gypsies" in Scotland. It is quite as much a fashion of the "tory" classes in England; and is described by Borrow (*Romano Lavo-Lil*, p. 137) in terms similar to those of Burt and Simson, already quoted. The gypsiologists, again, refer to the *patteran, patrin*, or "trail," as something that renders our modern nomads "a peculiar people." (Reference is made to it in Borrow's *Lavo-Lil*, p. 133; in Mr. Groome's *In Gipsy Tents*, Chap. X.; at pp. 24-5 of Mr. Leland's *English Gipsies*; and again in the adventures of *The Romany Rye*.) "*Patrin* is the name of the signs by which the gypsies who go before show the road they have taken to those who follow behind. We flings handfuls of grass down at the head of the road we takes, or we makes with the finger a cross-mark on the ground, or we sticks up branches of trees by the side of the hedge." With some trifling variations, all the accounts agree; and Mr. Borrow makes us understand that so much individuality could be put into a "patteran" that the tracker knew whether the trail he was following was that of a friend. Scott describes the same usage in these words: "For smaller predatory expeditions, the borderers had signals, and places of rendezvous, peculiar to each tribe. If the party set forward before all the members had joined, a mark, cut in the turf, or on the back of a tree, pointed out to the stragglers the direction the main body had pursued" (Introduction to *Minstrelsy*). Of course, since Scott's "Borderers" are manifestly the ancestors of Simson's Border "gypsies," it may be said this extract only shows that the "patteran" was as well known to them as to many others of their kind. But the "Borderers"—on either side of the line—are also the ancestors of vast numbers of civilized Britons, whose families have relinquished that nomadic life many generations ago, and whose manners have been (in Scott's words) "assimilated to those of their countrymen" for a very long period. So that the use of the "patteran" was familiar to a great many of the forefathers of the composite Modern-British people.

The custom of holding a "wake" over the dead was no more peculiar to any part of Ireland than to the Border district of Yetholm, in the beginning of this century. But the whole burial ceremonies of our British "gypsies" are those of some of the most important of the early races of Britain. Our archæologists are busy at the present day in examining the oldest entombments that are discoverable. And they learn from these that those early Britons used, in some cases, to practise cremation; and in other cases (perhaps in these also), to bury the valuables of the dead along with the corpse, burning such things as were of perishable nature, and slaughtering the favourite horse of the deceased. If any fragment of such races had adhered to the ancestral customs, such would still be its practice. And these customs are precisely the customs of our gypsies, or our "tories," as they used to be called. Most of such customs—all of them, even,—may have been relinquished by this year 1884; but if so, their abandonment is of quite recent date. It seems to be some time ago since English gypsies (so-called) were accustomed to burn their dead; but that they did so is recorded by, at least, one writer. The slaughter of the deceased's animals; the destruction—by fire and otherwise—of his least valuable effects; and the burial, beside his corpse, of his money and jewels; these are practices that many writers ascribe to the British gypsies of the present century. (For instances of which, see Mr. Groome's "In Gipsy Tents," pp. 116, 117 and 120-123; Mr. Leland's "English Gipsies," pp. 58, 59; and page 128 (*note*) of Mr. Simson's "History of the Gipsies.")

But the ancestral connection of the gypsies with these islands and with Europe is nowhere more clearly seen than in the fact that *their* traditions are *ours*. More than that, they are the preservers of "our" traditions. And it is worth mentioning that the authority for this statement is one whose acquaintance with the life of our tented fellow-Britons has been intimate, and whose knowledge of their ways is unsurpassed. There is a scene "In Gipsy Tents" which enables one to form something of a sound conception of gypsy life, as it existed in its prime; although it is to be feared (or hoped—according to individual choice) that such scenes cannot be witnessed in these islands for many years longer. The picture is of an evening camp in a Welsh meadow; and by the fire are gathered several gypsies, of various ages and of either sex. And one of them is a celebrated harper. The whole evening is devoted to story-telling, to laughter, and to song; and both songs and stories are of the kind that we—the house-dwellers—would know little of were it not for books. The stories told might, as their recorder hints, have come out of any collection of European folk-tales. And the songs are old ballads of England, and Wales, and Scotland; such as one finds in Scott's "Minstrelsy" and kindred books. But those gypsies had never learnt them from books! And that is what makes such people so genuinely the representatives of our minstrels. One hears those ballads sung in drawing-rooms and concert-halls—and beautifully sung,— but it is a revival. Our gypsies know them, and sing them, by inherited custom. They are the ancient ditties that their forefathers knew, and "were never tired of singing" (as Simson says). And these were the kind of songs that were sung at this gypsy-camp in Wales. Of which some of them were— *Cold blows the wind over my true love, A brisk young sailor came courting me, The Leather Bottél, Down in merry merry Scotland* (a version of *Hugh of Lincoln*), *The Bells of Aberdovey*, and a north-country ballad of "three sisters," through which there ripples an "owercome" of

>*All in a lea and alony, oh!*
>* * * *
>*Down by the bonny banks of Airdrie, oh!*

Such are the songs of our nomads, Mr. Groome tells us, and his account tallies with that of the Scotch historian; who has said that *Hughie the Græme*, and all the other ballads of Scott's "Minstrelsy," were chanted with unabating fervour round the camp-fires of the northern Borderers, in the early part of the present century. More than that, there are still extant, among those wandering minstrels, songs and music that have not yet been committed to paper. One of the ballads referred to above is "printed in no known collection"; and presumably was never printed at all before the date of "In Gipsy Tents." And yet it is a fine old ballad, and sung to "a lovely old air" (also unknown to the music-sellers). The first verse of it goes—

> *Cold blows the wind over my true love,*
> *Cold blows the drops of rain;*
> *I never, never had but one sweetheart,*
> *In the green wood he was slain.*

That such a fine specimen of the pathetic old love-lament should never have been known to literature until the other day, while pages of the most stupid doggerel have been in print for generations, is a most exasperating fact. It is hardly less vexing than the knowledge that had Scott only associated as a friend with the "Borderers" of his own generation, he would have secured a vast number of ancient Border lays that must have perished with the people who were identified with them.

That version of *Hugh of Lincoln*, which begins with the words "Down in merry merry Scotland," is, says Mr. Groome, "familiar to most London gipsies." And he also remarks that the story of *The Master Thief*—which seems to be known in all European countries—is both a "gypsy" and a "Gaelic" legend,—being included among Mr. Campbell's West Highland Tales. "Herodotus' story of Rhampsinitus (says Mr. Groome) has often been called their prototype [the prototype of the various versions], and it is curious that the gipsy and Gaelic versions resemble it far more closely than do the Italian, German, and Scandinavian." But this is just what should be. Mr. Campbell collected his stories in the Western Highlands, and it was only last century that "the meaner sort of people" in that district used to do their cooking in what the gypsiologists would call the "Romany" fashion; and—in many other respects—they were gypsies. Therefore their version of "The Master Thief" *ought* to resemble that of their more southern kindred "far more closely" than those of any foreign country (whatever may be the explanation of their mutual resemblance to the story given by Herodotus). The *British* character of other British gypsy stories would, no doubt, become evident by comparison with those of various parts of the country. *Jack and his Golden Snuffbox*, for example, which is related in "In Gipsy Tents," is of exactly the same nature as Carleton's *Three Tasks;* and either of these would fit quite naturally into Mr. Campbell's collection (which very likely does supply a counterpart to them).

There is thus nothing in the traditions and songs of our tent-dwelling compatriots to indicate that their origin is different from "ours"; and, on the contrary, the argument leads quite the other way. It was a "gypsy" who told Mr. Groome that Mary, Queen of Scots, "was so passing fair that the wine could be seen as it ran down her throat;" and it was a "gypsy" that ascribed the same peculiarity to Fair Rosamond. Many other legends, of mediæval date and of quasi-religious nature, are also recorded as being still existent among the same kind of people.

This evening in the Welsh camp was almost superlatively representative of archaic British life. While their elders were otherwise engaged, "the children fell to asking riddles, not modern conundrums, but good old-fashioned 'sense-riddles';" of a kind that must be familiar to very many British people who have never slept out-of-doors in their lives, but who, in childhood, have been influenced by a mother or a nurse of comparatively-primitive upbringing. Some of the riddles given by these little gypsies, on the occasion referred to, were these:—" In the hedge, and out of the hedge, and if you touch it, it will bite you?" ("A nettle.") " Under water, and over water, and never touches water?" ("A woman crossing a bridge with a pail of water on her head.") "It plays in the wood, and sings in the wood, and gets its master many a penny?" ("A fiddle.") "As I was a-going along the road one day, I met a man coming through the hedge with a lot of pins and needles on his back?" ("A hedgehog.") And "'a cherry' was less obviously suggested by—

'Riddle me, riddle me, red coat,
A stick in his hand, a stone in his throat;
Riddle me, riddle me, roti tot.'"

In all these riddles, and in all riddles of this *kind*, there is nothing that is not British; nothing that is not familiar to the children of England, Ireland, Wales and Scotland. Or if the present race of children—or some of the past races of children—have never heard such riddles, it is simply because the "old-fashioned" element has never surrounded their childhood, or even casually touched it.

"Representative of archaic British life": that is what that scene in the Welsh camp most distinctly was. It was, of course, an anachronism—pathetically such; a remnant of an old-time system lingering on in this modern age. To many men it is a delightful thought that such a thing could happen in these days of railways, telegraphs, and electric light: that a scholar, a minstrel, and a group of un-modernized Britons could "foregather" by a camp-fire on a summer night, and could fill the flying hours with old-world legends, and the songs of long ago—sung by real lovers of music, and the melody strengthened by the vibrant voices of the harp. No lower roof above them than the sky—no music-room narrower than the world—no restrictions of time or fee—and, instead of gas or electricity, the wavering firelight, and the faint reflection of the stars. It was a wild anachronism. There is no place for such things in Modern Britain. Society looks coldly on such people, and calls them "vagrants"; and the policeman is empowered to direct them to "move on."

. . . .

In the mediæval anecdote that Scott appends to *Ivanhoe*, it was remarked that when a man (a native of this country) wished to simulate a *jongleur*, he had to transform himself, temporarily, into an Ethiopian. And it was suggested that when Alfred entered the Danish camp in the disguise of a "harper," he had followed this plan (because it is to be supposed that his face, in its natural condition, would be too well known to his enemies to allow of his mingling with them except in such a way as this). It is possible there are many other recorded examples of such a procedure. Something of this kind seems to be indicated in the account of a foray made in the Isle of Man by the "heroes of the red branch," in some remote period. For it is said of those raiders that they were "disguised like jugglers." There is also a traditional story regarding an Irish chief who lived about three hundred years ago, which is to this effect:—This chief, Carroll O'Daly, one day found himself in the position of young Lochinvar, and many other ardent lovers; rejected, that is to say, by the father, though not by the daughter. On the day on which she was to be married to the successful suitor, it is told that, "Disguising himself as a *Jugleur* or *Glee-man*, he [O'Daly] hastened to her father's house, which he found filled with guests, who were invited to the wedding. Having amused the company a while with some tricks of legerdemain, he took up his harp, and played and sang the song of *Eibhlin a Ruin* [*O Evelyn, my love*], which he had composed for the occasion. This, and a private sign, discovered him to his mistress." Now, this latter story (which is quoted by Walker in his "History of the Irish Bards"—Appendix, p. 60) indicates very strongly that this "disguise" was of the same nature as John of Rampayne's. It is most unlikely that a mere change of dress could so conceal the identity of a man placed in the conspicuous position of a performing juggler-and-minstrel that none of the company should recognize his features, with which the most of them must have been familiar; and that even his own lady-love (still fondly attached to him) should require the introduction of her own name into the song, and "a private sign" into the bargain, before she understood that the man whom all present were regarding was no other than her lover.

The Morris Dance of Ireland, which, under the name of "Rinkey" or *Rinceadh-fada* (? "the long dance"), is described by Walker, in his "Memoirs of the Irish Bards," was plainly a Minstrels' Dance; and clearly it was substantially the Moors' Dance that was once common to Western Europe. Now, although it eventually came to be danced by men of white complexion, this dance (as already pointed out) was originally "the dance of the Blacks." In "a short description of the *uncorrupted morris dance*, as practised in France about the beginning of the sixteenth century," it is stated that—about that period—"it was the custom in good societies for a boy to come into the hall, when supper was finished, with his face blackened, his forehead bound with white or yellow taffeta, and bells tied to his legs. He then proceeded to dance the *Morisco*, the whole length of the hall, backwards and forwards, to the great amusement of the company." There are other French examples of Morris-dancing, of earlier date than that; one so early as 1440, and another of 1458—on which latter occasion the dancers were "attired like savages." We are told that in Spain "the morris dancers usually blackened their faces with soot, that they might the better pass for Moors." During the early part of the sixteenth century, it was the common custom for the citizens of Edinburgh to conclude an evening's amusement by "bringing in the Moors, or Morris;" and it is on record that, at that period "the Egyptians" "danced before the king at Holyroodhouse" on at least one occasion. Whatever, therefore, may have been the natural complexion of those Dancers and Minstrels who are stated by Walker to have welcomed James II. with the *Rinceadh-fada* when he landed at Kinsale two centuries ago, it seems most probable that their faces were, at least, temporarily blackened; if not "Moors" by descent, they were probably "Moors" in appearance—like all the earlier dancers of the Moors' Dance.*

It does not appear that this fashion of blackening the face, in memory of the complexion of the earliest *Jongleurs*, is really extinct in modern England. Mr. C. G. Leland (at page 114 of his "English Gipsies") remarks as follows:—
"*Naubat* in the language of the Hindu Nāts signifies 'time, turn, and instruments of music sounding at the gate of a great man, at certain intervals.' 'Nobbet,' which is a Gipsy word well known to all itinerant negro minstrels, means to go about with music to get money. 'To nobbet round the tem, bosherin'.' It also implies time or turn, as I inferred from what I was told on inquiry. 'You can shoon dovo at the wellgooras when yeck rākkers the waver, you jāl and nobbet.' 'You can hear that at the fairs when one says to the other, You go and nobbet,' meaning, 'It is your turn to play now.'"

When Mr. Leland speaks of "itinerant negro minstrels" it is evident he means the kind that one sees at Epsom or

---

* These facts regarding the Morris-dancers will be found in Douce's "Illustrations of Shakspeare;" and also in Walker's "Irish Bards."

Brighton; and these, of course, are not real negroes. The important point is that he ascribes to such men a knowledge of the gypsy language; and, indeed, he almost identifies them with "gypsies," although it is likely they have only "a suspicion of gypsiness" in them. Thus, it would seem that those "itinerant negro minstrels" are not at all a result of the modern "Christy-Minstrel" movement; although they may have adopted some of its peculiarities. It seems impossible to point to a time when there have *not* been "itinerant negro minstrels" in England—though their colour may have become more and more artificial in nature as time has gone on.

.   .   .   .   .

With regard to the use of the Bagpipes in England, it may be pointed out that, whether or not the "Northumbrian Pipes" may still be represented, many of the bagpipers that may yet be seen in England are of Irish birth; and the instrument they play upon is that one which seems always to have been identified with Ireland, and not at all with the larger island. It has no mouthpiece; the bag being supplied from a small pair of bellows, worked by the right elbow, under which it is fastened. This instrument, while having the "chanter" of the one usually identified with the Scotch Highlands, has the addition of keys—after the fashion of other wind-instruments. From one of these pipers (a native of Galway, and a man possessed of so much natural refinement that one rather regards him as representing the earlier bard—in the palmy days of itinerant minstrelsy—than the usual *un*musical "musician" of our streets) the writer learns that Ireland and Scotland are the least likely places to find specimens of this particular kind of piper. There are, unfortunately, too few attractions for them in Ireland at present, and when they cross the channel they find that Scotland is a most indifferent asylum. For it is necessary that the player of the Irish Bagpipe should be in a sitting position, when playing; in order to do justice to himself and the instrument (as any one knows who has seen its complicated nature). Now, it appears that in Scotland the itinerant musician, who is the "bard" of the poorer classes, is not permitted to sit down and play in taverns, as he is in England;

and, consequently, the Irish Bagpiper who has ventured into Scotland must either continue to compromise the matter by playing in the streets, in a most uncomfortable posture, or else gravitate southward. Thus, the likeliest place in which to discover the players on this ancient and interesting variety of bagpipe, is England itself.

In his "Memoirs" (pp. 164-5), Walker gives several "curious notices concerning the Bagpipe:" such as, that two varieties of it were in use in Lapland last century; and that "a learned friend" of his remarks—"The *Wal-Pipe* of the Finns seems to me to be the *Cala-Mala* of the Zingari of Swinburne, and *Mala-Pioba* of the Irish."

.   .   .   .   .

As supplementary to the remarks already made on the subject of British *blueskins* and *green-men*, it may be stated that the practice of tattooing seems to have lingered latest of all among a Cambridgeshire tribe. A writer who is quoted largely in the tenth chapter of "In Gipsy Tents," states, in his description of a Cambridgeshire gypsy girl— "On each side of her little mouth, and in the centre of her soft round chin, was *a small blue tattoo mark*." This corresponds exactly with Mr. Leland's description of the "gypsies" of Egypt: "The women had their under lips coloured dark blue, like female Bedouins, and a few eaten-in points around the mouth of like colour" ("English Gipsies," p. 194). The Cambridgeshire example is now forty or fifty years old, and the woman referred to may not now be alive. Whether or not she was the only illustration of this custom, among her own kindred, we have in her a much later example of the "Pict" than Marshall of Galloway, and a "Blueskin" of a generation far removed from that of Blake, the highwayman.

.   .   .   .   .

The reference made to Wilhelm Meister's companions gave rise to the suggestion that "strolling players" were originally of "Egyptian" stock. Now, it has been stated that James the Fifth of Scotland was entertained by "Egyptian" dancers at Holyrood in 1530, and that—at the same period—"the Moors" (virtually another term for the same people) used to amuse the burghers of Edinburgh on occasions of festivity. When "Moors" (such as "Reid the mountebank and his blackamores," previously referred to ; or the general examples just spoken of) were dancers, and clowns, and jugglers, they approached the profession of the *actor* very closely. But Mr. Groome supplies evidence of a more direct nature. He tells us that "about 1623 Sir William Sinclair 'delivered one Egyptian from the gibbet in the Burrow Moore, ready to be strangled, returning from Edinburgh to Roslin, upon which accoumpt the whole body of gypsies were, of old, accustomed to gather in the stanks of Roslin every year, *where they acted severall plays*, dureing the moneths of May and June. There are two towers which were allowed them for their residence, the one called Robin Hood, the other Little John.'" This—even to the residence in the tower—is quite a counterpart to the picture of Wilhelm's strolling-players, whom Jarno called "gypsies." Actors, it must be remembered, were formerly legislated against in the same terms, and at the same periods, as "gypsies;" and it is difficult to see why any laws should ever have been passed against them, unless for racial reasons. Mr. Groome (at page 296 of "In Gipsy Tents"—the previous extract was from page 106 of the same book) speaks of one or more nineteenth-century strolling players who were also gypsies. And Mr. Leland states that "there are several stage words of manifest gipsy origin" (one or two examples of which he gives at pp. 87, 88, and 94 of his "English Gipsies").

.   .   .   .   .

The remarks relating to Gypsy Pugilism were made in ignorance of the fact that the present "champion of the world" belongs in every respect to "the school of Mr. Petulengro and Tawno Chikno;" being an "English gypsy" by descent—through both parents. There are other members of his paternal clan who are also adepts in this art; and indeed it is their pride that they are born pugilists. It further appears that both of the grandfathers of Sylvester Boswell—who is unanimously pronounced a typical gypsy—were also brought up in the same "school." One of these was a Herne, the other (of course) a Boswell; and their grandson, Sylvester, has recorded of them that—"Both my grandfathers used to fight on stages."* Mr. Groome mentions, in addition, the "famous Gipsy prize-fighters," Cooper, Winter, and Oliver; and, of course, he does not overlook the celebrated "champion" just referred to. All these names, when considered with those previously given—Borrow's "Black Richmond" and "Big Ben," and his fictitious (?) Jasper Petulengro and Tawno Chikno—make out a pretty fair list of celebrated prize-fighters who were distinctly gypsies. It is a most significant fact that so genuine a gypsy as Sylvester Boswell—who is as "precious ointment" in the sight of the gypsiologists—is the grandson, on both sides, of professional fighters. Mr. Leland's "old-fashioned gypsy bruisers," and his modern pugnacious gypsies (one of whom asserts that he would rather fight and get thrashed than not fight at all), these are men of less note. But they possess the same bellicose nature as their better-known kinsmen. All of these considerations, therefore, when taken in connection with the remarks already made † regarding this particular gypsy characteristic, denote with very considerable emphasis that, not only have British gypsies been inextricably associated with British pugilism, but British pugilism seems to have been almost wholly maintained by this special division of the British people.

* Smart and Crofton's "Dialect of the English Gypsies," p. 253.
† In the first chapter of this "Book."

END OF VOL. I.

www.ingramcontent.com/pod-product-compliance
Lightning Source LLC
Chambersburg PA
CBHW060550230426
43670CB00011B/1756